MEDIA LAW

By
Peter Carey
and
Nick Armstrong, Duncan Lamont and
James Quartermaine

SWEET & MAXWELL

 THOMSON REUTERS

First edition 1996
Second edition 1999
Third edition 2004
Fourth edition 2007 by Peter Carey

Published in 2010 by Thomson Reuters (Legal) Limited
(Registered in England & Wales, Company No 1679046.
Registered Office and address for service:
100 Avenue Road, London NW3 3PF)
trading as Sweet & Maxwell

For further information on our products and services, visit
www.sweetandmaxwell.co.uk

Typeset by YHT Ltd, London
Printed in the UK by
CPI William Clowes Beccles NR34 7TL

ISBN 978-0-414-04213-1

No natural forests were destroyed to make this product; only farmed
timber was used and re-planted.

A CIP catalogue record for this book is available from the British Library

ACKNOWLEDGEMENTS

Special thanks to members of the Charles Russell media team, for their invaluable advice and support in the preparation of this edition, in particular Vicky Butterworth who has spent considerable time and effort in writing for this new edition.

The authors also wish to express their continued thanks to those who gave assistance with previous editions: Peter Coles, Jo Sanders, Rory Sullivan, Martin Cruddace, Professor Gerald Wakefield, Paul Hosford, Andrew Ketteringham, Sandra Brannigan, Laura Perito, Caroline Smith, Marie-Anne Denicolo and Harriet Kimbell.

Grateful acknowledgement is made to the following for permission to quote from their works:

The National Union of Journalists has given its permission to reproduce the NUJ Code of Conduct.

The Press Complaints Commission has given its permission to reproduce the PCC Code of Practice.

Ofcom have given its permission to reproduce the Ofcom Broadcasting Code.

Thanks, as always, to the publishing and editorial teams at Sweet & Maxwell for their expertise and patience.

Whilst every care has been taken to establish and acknowledge copyright, and contact the copyright owners, the publishers tender their apologies for any accidental infringement. They would be pleased to come to a suitable arrangement with the rightful owners in each case.

FOREWORD TO THE FOURTH EDITION

"Strange! That a man who has wit enough
to write a satire should have folly enough
to publish it."

Thus wrote Benjamin Franklin some 300 years ago. Clearly his message was that no writer should be so foolish as to expose himself to the risk of humiliation and financial ruin by publishing material that might rouse the libel lawyers to action. Nowadays, one would hope that those in the satire business are more adventurous and combative. After all, Richard Ingrams, when editor of *Private Eye*, was reported to have remarked, "my motto is publish and be sued". If that indicated a view that a satirical piece was not necessarily indefensible, Mr Ingrams was clearly right. Over the years, common law defences to defamation complaints have been extended and expanded, and, with the assistance of statutory reforms and modifications, there has been achieved a more equable balance between the right to attack and criticise and the protection of reputation. This process has been accelerated by the procedures introduced in the Defamation Act 1996 and by the concept of public interest privilege originally expounded by the House of Lords in *Reynolds v Times Newspapers* (1999).

However, there has been, and there is always likely to be, a degree of tension between what the author, publisher and broadcaster regard as their entitlement (namely, unrestricted freedom to communicate, comment and inform) and what the individual considers are his private rights and the State determines are restrictions necessary to protect the public interest. As regards the individual, his rights to reputation and to ownership of creative work (copyright) have always been acknowledged. In more recent times attention has focused on a comparatively new principle in this country, the right to privacy, enshrined in the European Convention on Human Rights, most of which was incorporated into our domestic law with effect from

October 2000. Breach of privacy has rapidly become a frequent complaint levelled against the media especially as it can provide a means of obtaining a "prior restraint" injunction which is rarely granted in a libel claim. As regards the State, it has enacted draconian laws to protect its secrets, and has purported to defend the public interest on a broader basis by prohibiting obscene publications or material which might incite racial hatred; and the courts and the State have combined to bar dissemination of information, or the reporting of cases, which might interfere with the administration of justice.

Where the line is to be drawn between unrestricted freedom to communicate and express opinions and the protection of the rights of individuals and the public interest has not only been difficult to define but is constantly shifting on account of the pressure imposed by public opinion and the changing attitudes of governments, and indeed judges. The situation is now additionally complicated by the revolution in the communications industry resulting from electronic technology which enables global publication to take place almost instantaneously.

It is in this setting that increasing attention is being given to those areas of law which concern the communications industry, and they are becoming the focus of many solicitors' and barristers' practices. There is now recognition that such areas can be justifiably and conveniently assembled and discussed under one description and title, namely, "media law". Media law is complex, relevant, constantly undergoing change, and embraces a wide field. For an in-depth study of all aspects of media law, the practitioner would probably require at least half-a-dozen weighty textbooks.

Peter Carey's invaluable contribution to this topic has been to gather together and set out with lucidity and precision in one relatively slim volume the essential principles and features of all the various branches of media law. Clearly it will be the student or the non-lawyer working in the media, both of whom require for different purposes an accessible and intelligible explanation of the laws applicable to publication and communication, who will most readily profit from reference to this book, particularly as the author assumes that some readers will have no knowledge of the structure of the court system and how procedurally they operate. Journalists and those in broadcasting will additionally obtain assistance from the Appendices in which appear the text of Codes of Practice issued by the regulatory bodies governing these responsibilities, as well as an outline of their procedures and significant decisions. But there will surely be many practitioners—one has in mind those who are not specialists in this field—who will find Mr Carey's concise statements of elemental propositions, and his identification and exposition of the main principles, of great practical benefit.

Previous editions of Media Law have been popularly received. This new edition covers all recent developments, with special attention appropriately being given to the evolution through case law of the right of privacy, and pivotal libel decisions such as *Jameel* receiving in-depth analysis. The chapter dealing with Television has been radically revised to take account of the new Ofcom code, and other subjects updated in separate chapters are copyright, confidential information and the internet. The book should again attract many grateful readers. I warmly recommend it to anyone wishing to obtain a grasp of the fundamentals of the law applying to the communication of information by whatever means.

Patrick Milmo Q.C.
5 Raymond Buildings
Gray's Inn

PREFACE

We are living in fascinating times of great change. The challenge for the law is to keep pace with rapid developments in technology, political aspiration and human development. The way that we think about legal rights and responsibilities in the United Kingdom is evolving at a faster pace than at any time in history. Although traditionally somewhat conservative and slow to change, the legal system, particularly in the form of the decisions of judges in the higher courts, is attempting to anticipate the direction of society and the needs of people and commerce. Nowhere is this more so than in the field of media law. It is the media that informs the public of its news, educates the public on virtually everything, and entertains the public in a manner that can be persuasive of opinion formation.

To take the example of privacy, a decade ago there was no clear right to privacy in English law. That position has changed dramatically, partly as a result of domestic judicial intervention, and partly as a result of decisions made and laws enacted at the European level. We now have firmly established data protection law, which guarantees certain privacy rights regarding the use of "personal data". We also, as a result of various judicial decisions culminating in the *Max Mosley* case, have a privacy law that prevents the publication of personal information in certain circumstances (see Chapter 4). And it won't end there. It is interesting to note that in the new coalition government's May 12, 2010 press conference, the Deputy Prime Minister, Nick Clegg, said that his aspiration was for "a government that hands back your liberties and your privacy." We await developments with eager anticipation.

For this 5th edition of Media Law, I am grateful for the continued support and contribution of Nick Armstrong and Duncan Lamont from the Media Department at London law firm, Charles Russell. Joining them on the front cover for this new edition is their colleague James Quartermaine, also an expert media lawyer. My special thanks go to all three for their valuable contributions and insights.

We continue to receive positive and intelligent feedback from a variety of people working in the media—lawyers, media law students, media studies students and those working in the media industries generally. We are pleased that the book continues to receive a wide audience. We hope that those involved with the media—whether journalists, editors, producers, writers, artists, photographers or lawyers—continue to find much of use and interest in this new edition.

We welcome your feedback, which we will utilise for subsequent editions.

Peter Carey
London, May 2010

CONTENTS

Acknowledgments	v
Foreword to the Fourth Edition	vii
Preface	xi
Table of Cases	xxi
Table of Statutes	xxix
Table of Statutory Instruments	xxxiii
Table of European Legislation	xxxv

1. INTRODUCTION TO THE LAW	1
Sources of Law	1
Parliament	1
Acts of Parliament	2
Delegated Legislation	2
The Sovereignty of Parliament	3
Judges	3
The European Sources	4
The European Union	4
European Convention on Human Rights	6
The Courts	7
Civil Courts	8
Criminal Courts	12
European Courts	16
The Legal Action	17
The civil action	18

The criminal action 20
Mode of trial procedure 22

Lawyers 27
Barristers 27
Solicitors 28
Legal executives 28
Lord Chancellor 28
Crown Prosecution Service (CPS) 29
Director of Public Prosecutions (DPP) 29
Attorney General 29

2. REPUTATION 30

Defamation 31
Definition 33
Trial by judge and jury 34
Libel or slander? 35
Publication 36
Words must be defamatory 39
Innuendo 42
Words must refer to the claimant 43
Defamation of a "class" 44
Defamation of an entity 45
Forum shopping 45
Defences 46
Justification 46
Fair comment 49
Absolute privilege 52
Qualified privilege 55
Duty or interest 57
Malice and qualified privilege 61
Innocent dissemination 62
Offer of amends 63
Consent 66
Remedies 66
Statement in open court 70

Malicious Falsehood 71
Definition 71
Untrue statement about the claimant 71
Malice 72
Special damage 73
Defamation and malicious falsehood compared 73

Press Complaints Commission (PCC) 74

3. COPYRIGHT AND RELATED RIGHTS 76

Copyright 76
The creation of a copyright work 77

Literary, dramatic, musical and artistic works 78
Sound recordings, films and broadcasts 79
Typographical arrangement 81
Qualification 82
Duration, authorship and ownership 82
Dealings and transfers 83
Assignments 83
Licences 84
Infringement of copyright 87
Copying 88
Issuing copies to the public 89
Rental or lending 89
Performing, showing, playing 90
Communicating to the public 90
Adapting 90

Permitted Acts 90
Fair dealing 90
Other defences 99

Moral Rights 99
The right to be identified 100
The right to object to derogatory treatment 101
The false attribution right 102
The privacy right 102

Performers' Rights 102

Artists' Resale Rights 105

Rental Rights 106

4. PRIVACY AND CONFIDENTIAL INFORMATION 107

Human Rights 108
Confidential information 109
Campbell Confidence: Misuse of Private Information 111

Two-Step Test 114

Step one: Article 8—Is the Information Private? 114
Triviality 115
Photographs 116
Pre-existing relationship 120

Step Two: Article 10—The Balancing Exercise 124
Information in the public domain 125
False private information 127

Unauthorised use 127

Disclosure in the Public Interest   128

Remedies   130
    Injunctions   130
    "Super injunctions"   131

Protection from Harassment   131
    Harassment by journalists   133

Further reading   134

5. OBSCENITY AND INDECENCY   135

Definition   136
    Statutory Obscenity—definition   136

The Offences   140

Defences   140
    Public good   140
    Innocent publication or possession   141
    Aversion   142

Common Law Offences   142
    Terrestrial television   144
    Protecting children   145

Ofcom and Adults   145
    Digital multi-channel television   145
    Cinema exhibition   146
    Videotape and DVD recordings   147
    The internet   149
    Children   150

Further reading   151

6. RACIAL AND RELIGIOUS HATRED   153

Inciting Racial or Religious Hatred   153
    Definition   153
    The offences   154
    Defences   156

7. CONTEMPT   158

Strict Liability Contempt   161
    Substantial risk of serious prejudice   161
    Active proceedings   167
    Media defences   168
    Innocent publication or distribution   168

Intentional Contempt   172

Contempt by Publishing Jury Deliberations   175

Injunctions   176

8. REPORTING CURRENT AFFAIRS   178

Reporting the Courts   179
  Access to the courts   179
  Reporting restrictions   180
  Adult criminal courts   185
  General   188
  The courts and television   192

Reporting Parliament   194

Official Secrets   195
  The 1911 Act   195
  The 1989 Act   195
  Defence advisory notices   197

Protection of Journalists' Sources   197
  Contempt of Court Act 1981   198
  The Police and Criminal Evidence Act 1984   201
  The Official Secrets Act 1989   203
  Terrorism   203

9. THE INTERNET   204

The Nature of the Internet   204
  Internet Service Providers (ISPs)   206
  World Wide Web (WWW)   206
  Search engines   207
  Email   207
  Instant messaging and voice calling   207
  Forums and message boards   207
  Blogs   208
  Social networking sites   208

Data Protection   208
  Introduction   208
  The individual's rights   209
  The Data Protection Principles   213
  Exemption for journalism, literature and art   218

Defamation   220
  Internet Service Providers   220
  Online archives   223
  International publication   224
  Abuse of process   226

Combatting anonymity   227
Blogs and newspapers: regulation   229

Pornography   230

Copyright   232
Permitted acts for computer programs   234

Database Right   235

Further reading   237

10. TELEVISION   238

The Provision of Television   239
BBC   239
ITV (Channel 3)   239
Channel 4   240
Five (Channel 5)   240
Satellite television   241
Cable television   242
Digital television   242

The Regulation of Television   242
Ofcom   242

The Legacy Codes   244

The Ofcom Code   244
Section 1—Protecting the under eighteens   245
Section 2—Harm and offence   245
Section 3—Crime   247
Section 4—Religion   247
Section 5—Due impartiality, due accuracy and undue
            prominence of views and opinions   247
Section 6—Elections and referendums   248
Section 7—Fairness   248
Section 8—Privacy   249

Examples of Ofcom decisions   251

GLOSSARY   278

APPENDICES   287
Appendix A—Defamation Act 1952   287
Appendix B—Defamation Act 1996   291
Appendix C—Human Rights Act 1998   309
Appendix D—Electronic Commerce (EC Directive)
            Regulations 2002   332
Appendix E—Editors' Commission Code of Practice   343
Appendix F—Ofcom Broadcasting Code   347

Appendix G—The NUJ Code of Conduct　　　　376
Appendix H—Useful addresses and websites　　378

Index　　　　　　　　　　　　　　381

TABLE OF CASES

A v B Plc; sub nom. B and C v A; A v B (A Firm) [2002] EWCA Civ 337; [2003] Q.B. 195; [2002] 3 W.L.R. 542; [2002] 2 All E.R. 545, CA (Civ Div).......................... 114, 122, 124, 129

A&M Records Inc v Napster Inc, 239 F.3d 1004 (9th Cir., 2001)................................. 233

Addie v Dembreck; sub nom Dumbreck v Robert Addie & Sons (Collieries) Ltd; Dumbreck v Addie & Sons Collieries [1929] A.C. 358; 1929 S.C. (H.L.) 51; 1929 S.L.T. 242, HL.. 12

Aiken v Police Review Publishing Co Ltd, unreported, April 12, 1995, CA (Civ Div) ... 44

Alexander v Arts Council of Wales [2001] EWCA Civ 514; [2001] 1 W.L.R. 1840; [2001] 4 All E.R. 205, CA (Civ Div)... 61

Al-Fagih v HH Saudi Research & Marketing (UK) Ltd [2001] EWCA Civ 1634; [2002] E.M.L.R. 13, CA... 60

Al-Koronky v Time Life Entertainment Group Ltd [2006] EWCA Civ 1123; [2006] C.P. Rep. 47; [2007] 1 Costs L.R. 57, CA... 46

Anacon Corp Ltd v Environmental Research Technology Ltd [1994] F.S.R. 659, Ch D... 79

Angel v Stainton [2006] EWHC 637, QBD.. 66

Applause Store Productions Ltd v Raphael [2008] EWHC 1781 (QB); [2008] Info. T.L.R. 318, QBD 229

Archer v Williams. See Lady Archer v Williams

Argyll v Argyll. See Duchess of Argyll v Duke of Argyll

Armstrong v Times Newspapers Ltd [2006] EWCA Civ 519; [2006] 1 W.L.R. 2462, CA (Civ Div); affirming [2005] EWHC 2816 (QB); [2006] E.M.L.R. 9, QBD 40

Ashdown v Telegraph Group Ltd [2001] EWCA Civ 1142; [2002] Ch. 149; [2001] 3 W.L.R. 1368; [2001] 4 All E.R. 666, CA (Civ Div)... 94, 95, 96, 98

Ashworth Hospital Authority v MGN Ltd; sub nom. Ashworth Security Hospital v MGN Ltd [2002] UKHL 29; [2002] 1 W.L.R. 2033; [2002] 4 All E.R. 193, HL............. 200

Atkins v DPP; Goodland v DPP; sub nom. DPP v Atkins [2000] 1 W.L.R. 1427; [2000] 2 All E.R. 425; [2000] 2 Cr. App. R. 248, DC 150

Att Gen v Associated Newspapers, The Times, February 12, 1983 170

Att Gen v Associated Newspapers Ltd (1992) [1994] 2 A.C. 238; [1994] 2 W.L.R. 277; [1994] 1 All E.R. 556, HL.. 175

Att Gen v (1) British Broadcasting Corp (2) Hat Trick Productions Ltd, unreported, June 12, 1996.. 163

Att Gen v Daily Star. See Att Gen v Express Newspapers

Att Gen v English [1983] 1 A.C. 116; [1982] 3 W.L.R. 278; [1982] 2 All E.R. 903, HL 159, 162, 170, 171

Att Gen v Express Newspapers [2004] EWHC 2859 (Admin); [2005] E.M.L.R. 13; [2005] A.C.D. 41, DC 167

Att Gen v Guardian Newspapers Ltd (No.2); Att Gen v Observer Ltd (No.2); Att Gen v Times Newspapers Ltd (No.2) [1990] 1 A.C. 109; [1988] 3 W.L.R. 776; [1988] 3 All E.R. 545, HL 125, 129

Att Gen v Guardian Newspapers Ltd (No.3) [1992] 1 W.L.R. 874; [1992] 3 All E.R. 38; [1992] C.O.D. 338, QBD 161

Att Gen v Hislop [1991] 1 Q.B. 514; [1991] 2 W.L.R. 219; [1991] 1 All E.R. 911, CA (Civ Div) 174

Att Gen v Independent Television News Ltd [1995] 2 All E.R. 370; [1995] 1 Cr. App. R. 204; [1994] C.O.D. 370, QBD 163

Att Gen v MGN Ltd (Contempt: Appropriate Penalty) [2002] EWHC 907, QBD 164

Att Gen v MGN Ltd; sub nom. Mirror Group Newspapers, Re [1997] 1 All E.R. 456; [1997] E.M.L.R. 284, DC 164

Att Gen v Morgan; Att Gen v News Group Newspapers Ltd [1998] E.M.L.R. 294, Data Protection Tr 163

Att Gen v News Group Newspapers Ltd [1989] Q.B. 110; [1988] 3 W.L.R. 163; [1988] 2 All E.R. 906, QBD 173

Att Gen v News Group Newspapers, unreported, April 16, 1999 164

Att Gen v Newspaper Publishing Plc [1988] Ch. 333; [1987] 3 W.L.R. 942; [1987] 3 All E.R. 276, CA (Civ Div) 158

Att Gen v Random House Group Ltd [2009] EWHC 1727 (QB), QBD 177

Att Gen v Sport Newspapers [1991] 1 W.L.R. 1194; [1992] 1 All E.R. 503; [1992] C.O.D. 9, DC 173

Att Gen v Times Newspapers Ltd, *The Times*, February 12, 1983 162

Att Gen v TVS Television Ltd; Att Gen v HW Southey; *The Times*, July 7, 1989, DC 171

Attorney General's Reference (No.3 of 1977), Re [1978] 1 W.L.R. 1123; [1978] 3 All E.R. 1166; (1978) 67 Cr. App. R. 393, CA (Crim Div) 141

Author of a Blog v Times Newspapers Ltd [2009] EWHC 1358 (QB); [2009] E.M.L.R. 22; (2009) 106(26) L.S.G. 18, QBD 115, 228

B (A Child) (Disclosure), Re. *See* Kent CC v B (A Child)

BBC v British Satellite Broadcasting Ltd [1992] Ch. 141; [1991] 3 W.L.R. 174; [1991] 3 All E.R. 833, Ch D 93

BBC v BskyB 94

BBC v K (A Child); K (A Child), Re [2001] Fam. 59; [2001] 2 W.L.R. 253; [2001] 1 All E.R. 323, Fam Div 181

Baigent v Random House Group Ltd [2007] EWCA Civ 247; [2008] E.M.L.R. 7; [2007] F.S.R. 24, CA 88

Balogh v St Albans Crown Court [1975] Q.B. 73; [1974] 3 W.L.R. 314; [1974] 3 All E.R. 283, CA (Civ Div) 158

Bata v Bata [1948] W.N. 366; (1948) 92 S.J. 574, CA 225

Berkoff v Burchill [1996] 4 All E.R. 1008; [1997] E.M.L.R. 139, CA (Civ Div) 33, 34

Beta Construction Ltd v Channel Four Television Co Ltd [1990] 1 W.L.R. 1042; [1990] 2 All E.R. 1012; (1989) 139 N.L.J. 1561, CA (Civ Div) 35

Bonnard v Perryman [1891] 2 Ch. 269; [1891-94] All E.R. Rep. 965, CA 69, 110, 111

Branson v Bower (No.2) [2002] Q.B. 737; [2002] 2 W.L.R. 452; [2001] E.M.L.R. 33, QBD. 51

British Horseracing Board Ltd v William Hill Organisation Ltd [2005] EWCA Civ 863; [2006] E.C.C. 16; [2005] E.C.D.R. 28, CA (Civ Div) 235

British Railways Board v Herrington; sub nom. Herrington v British Railways Board [1972] A.C. 877; [1972] 2 W.L.R. 537; [1972] 1 All E.R. 749, HL 12

British Steel Corp v Granada Television Ltd [1981] A.C. 1096; [1980] 3 W.L.R. 774; [1981] 1 All E.R. 417, HL 202

British Telecommunications Plc v One in a Million Ltd; Marks & Spencer Plc v One in a Million Ltd; Virgin Enterprises Ltd v One in a Million Ltd; J Sainsbury Plc v One in a Million Ltd; Ladbroke Group Plc v One in a Million Ltd [1999] 1 W.L.R. 903; [1998] 4 All E.R. 476; [1999] E.T.M.R. 61 CA (Civ Div) 206

Browne v Associated Newspapers Ltd [2007] EWCA Civ 295; [2008] Q.B. 103; [2007] 3 W.L.R. 289, CA (Civ Div); reversing in part [2007] EWHC 202 (QB); [2007] E.M.L.R. 19; (2007) 157 N.L.J. 670, QBD 122, 125, 127

Bunt v Tilley [2006] EWHC 407; [2006] 3 All E.R. 336; [2006] E.M.L.R. 18, QBD... 63, 221, 222

Burstein v Times Newspapers Ltd [2001] 1 W.L.R. 579; [2001] E.M.L.R. 14; (2001) 98(8)
L.S.G. 44, CA (Civ Div) 65

CC v AB [2006] EWHC 3083; [2007] E.M.L.R. 11; [2007] 2 F.L.R. 301, QBD 122, 124
Campbell v Mirror Group Newspapers Ltd; sub nom. Campbell v MGN Ltd [2004]
UKHL 22; [2004] 2 A.C. 457; [2004] 2 W.L.R. 1232, HL; reversing [2002] EWCA Civ
1373; [2003] Q.B. 633; [2003] 2 W.L.R. 80; [2003] E.M.L.R. 2, CA 110, 111, 114,
116, 117, 118, 129, 219
Campbell-James v Guardian Media Group Plc [2005] EWHC 893; [2005] E.M.L.R. 24,
QBD 65
Charleston v News Group Newspapers Ltd [1995] 2 A.C. 65; [1995] 2 W.L.R. 450; [1995] 2
All E.R. 313, HL.. 41, 42
Charman v Orion Publishing Group Ltd [2005] EWHC 2187 (QB)............................ 40
Chase v News Group Newspapers Ltd; sub nom. Chase v Newsgroup Newspapers Ltd
[2002] EWCA Civ 1772; [2003] E.M.L.R. 11; (2002) 146 S.J.L.B. 279, CA (Civ Div)...... 40
Cheng v Tse Wai Chun Paul. See Tse Wai Chun Paul v Cheng
Clark v Associated Newspapers Ltd [1998] 1 W.L.R. 1558; [1998] 1 All E.R. 959; [1998]
E.C.C. 185, Ch D.. 102
Coco v AN Clark (Engineers) Ltd [1968] F.S.R. 415; [1969] R.P.C. 41, Ch D........ 109, 114, 127
Coulson & Sons v James Coulson & Co (1887) 3 T.L.R. 846...................................... 80
Cray v Hancock, unreported, November 4, 2005 38
Creation Records Ltd v News Group Newspapers Ltd [1997] E.M.L.R. 444; (1997) 16 Tr.
L.R. 544; (1997) 20(7) I.P.D. 20070, Ch D.. 116
Crossley v Newsquest (Midlands South) Ltd [2008] EWHC 3054 (QB), QBD 61

DPP v Whyte; sub nom. Corbin v Whyte (Patrick Thomas); Corbin v Whyte (Pearl
Rosemary); DPP v Whyte (Pearl Rosemary) [1972] A.C. 849; [1972] 3 W.L.R. 410; [1972]
3 All E.R. 12, HL... 138
Derbyshire CC v Times Newspapers Ltd [1993] A.C. 534; [1993] 2 W.L.R. 449; [1993] 1
All E.R. 1011, HL 45
Dering v Uris (No.2); Dering v William Kimber & Co Ltd; Dering v Purnell & Sons Ltd
[1964] 2 Q.B. 669; [1964] 2 W.L.R. 1298; [1964] 2 All E.R. 660 (Note, QBD............... 69
Donovan v Logan, unreported, April 1991 39
Douglas v Hello! Ltd (No.6); sub nom. Douglas v Hello! Ltd (Trial Action: Breach of
Confidence) (No.3) [2005] EWCA Civ 595; [2006] Q.B. 125; [2005] 3 W.L.R. 881; [2005] 4
All E.R. 128, CA (Civ Div); reversing in part [2003] EWHC 786 (Ch); [2003] 3 All E.R.
996; [2003] E.M.L.R. 31, Ch D 110, 113, 115, 117, 125
Duchess of Argyll v Duke of Argyll [1967] Ch. 302; [1965] 2 W.L.R. 790; [1965] 1 All E.R.
611, Ch D 115
Duke of Brunswick v Harmer , 117 E.R. 75; (1849) 14 Q.B. 185, QB 223
Durant v Financial Services Authority (Disclosure) [2003] EWCA Civ 1746; [2004] F.S.R.
28, CA (Civ Div)... 209

Easygroup IP Licensing v Athanasios Sermbezis, unreported, 2003, Ch D 206
Emlick v Al Nisr Publishing LLC, unreported, July 15 2009, EWHC......................... 227
Experience Hendrix LLC v Purple Haze Records Ltd [2007] EWCA Civ 501; [2008] E.C.C.
9; [2008] E.M.L.R. 10, CA.. 104

Faccenda Chicken Ltd v Fowler; Fowler v Faccenda Chicken Ltd [1987] Ch. 117; [1986] 3
W.L.R. 288; [1986] 1 All E.R. 617, CA (Civ Div) 121
Fallon v MGN Ltd [2006] EWHC 783 QB); [2006] E.M.L.R. 19, QBD 41
Ferguson v British Gas Trading Ltd [2009] EWCA Civ 46; [2009] 3 All E.R. 304; (2009)
106(8) L.S.G. 18, CA (Civ Div) 132
Fisher v Brooker [2009] UKHL 41; [2009] 1 W.L.R. 1764; [2009] Bus. L.R. 1334, HL....... 82
Football Association Premier League Ltd v Panini UK Ltd [2003] EWCA Civ 995; [2004] 1
W.L.R. 1147; [2003] 4 All E.R. 1290, CA (Civ Div) 96
Football Association Premier League Ltd v QC Leisure [2008] EWHC 1411 (Ch); [2008]
U.K.C.L.R. 329; [2008] 3 C.M.L.R. 12, Ch D 95
Fraser-Woodward Ltd v BBC [2005] EWHC 472 (Ch); [2005] E.M.L.R. 22; [2005] F.S.R. 36,
Ch D 91
F-Secure Corp Plc v Global Publications Ltd (DRS Case No.7578) 206

Galloway v Telegraph Group Ltd [2006] EWCA Civ 17; [2006] E.M.L.R. 11; [2006]
    H.R.L.R. 13, CA 60
Garry Flitcroft v MGN Ltd. *See* A v B Plc
Gillick v BBC [1996] E.M.L.R. 267, CA (Civ Div) 41
Godfrey v Demon Internet Ltd (Application to Strike Out) [2001] Q.B. 201; [2000] 3
    W.L.R. 1020; [1999] 4 All E.R. 342; [1999] I.T.C.L.R. 282, QBD 63, 221, 225
Goodwin v United Kingdom (17488/90) (1996) 22 E.H.R.R. 123; 1 B.H.R.C. 81, ECHR .. 199
Grappelli v Derek Block (Holdings) Ltd [1981] 1 W.L.R. 822; [1981] 2 All E.R. 272; (1981)
    125 S.J. 169, CA (Civ Div) 71
Green v Times Newspapers , unreported, 2001 66
Gutnick v Dow Jones [2002] HCA 56, HC (Aus) 225

Hamilton v Al-Fayed (No.1) [2001] 1 A.C. 395; [2000] 2 W.L.R. 609; [2000] 2 All E.R. 224,
    HL affirming 1999] 1 W.L.R. 1569; [1999] 3 All E.R. 317; [1999] E.M.L.R. 501, CA 53
Hartt v Newspaper Publishing (No.1), *The Times*, November 9, CA (Civ Div) 39
HRH Prince of Wales v Associated Newspapers Ltd; sub nom Associated Newspapers
    Ltd v HRH Prince of Wales [2006] EWCA Civ 1776; [2008] Ch. 57; [2007] 3 W.L.R. 222,
    CA affirming [2006] EWHC 522 (Ch); [2006] E.C.D.R. 20; [2008] E.M.L.R. 3, Ch D 88,
                                                            113, 116, 120, 124, 126, 129
Howlett v Holding [2006] EWHC 41; (2006) 150 S.J.L.B. 161, QBD 133
Hyde Park Residence Ltd v Yelland [2001] Ch. 143; [2000] 3 W.L.R. 215; [2000] E.C.D.R.
    275, CA (Civ Div) 94, 95, 96, 97

ICN Photonics Ltd v Patterson. *See* Patterson v ICN Photonics Ltd
Independent Television Publications Ltd v Time Out Ltd and Elliott; BBC v Time Out
    Ltd and Elliott [1984] F.S.R. 64, Ch D 78
Interbrew SA v Financial Times Ltd [2002] EWCA Civ 274; [2002] 2 Lloyd's Rep. 229;
    [2002] E.M.L.R. 24, CA (Civ Div) 200, 201
Ivereigh v Associated Newspapers [2008] EWHC 339 (QB) 189

Jameel v Dow Jones & Co Inc; sub nom. Dow Jones & Co Inc v Jameel [2005] EWCA Civ
    75; [2005] Q.B. 946; [2005] 2 W.L.R. 1614, CA (Civ Div) 36, 37, 46, 61, 226
Jameel v Wall Street Journal Europe SPRL (No.3) [2006] UKHL 44; [2007] 1 A.C. 359;
    [2007] Bus. L.R. 291, HL; reversing [2005] EWCA Civ 74; [2005] Q.B. 904; [2005] 2
    W.L.R. 1577, CA (Civ Div); affirming [2004] EWHC 37 (QB); [2004] E.M.L.R. 11, QBD   40
Jameel v Wall Street Journal Europe SPRL (No.3) [2006] UKHL 44; [2007] 1 A.C. 359;
    [2007] Bus. L.R. 291; [2006] 3 W.L.R. 642, HL 60
John v Associated Newspapers Ltd [2006] EWHC 1611; [2006] E.M.L.R. 27, QBD 116
John v MGN Ltd [1997] Q.B. 586; [1996] 3 W.L.R. 593; [1996] 2 All E.R. 35, CA (Civ Div) 67
Johnson v MGN Ltd [2009] EWHC 1481, QB 42
Joyce v Sengupta [1993] 1 W.L.R. 337; [1993] 1 All E.R. 897; (1992) 142 N.L.J. 1306, CA
    (Civ Div) 72, 111

K (A Child) v BBC; sub nom. BBC v K (A Child); K (A Child), Re [2001] Fam. 59; [2001] 2
    W.L.R. 253; [2001] 1 All E.R. 323, Fam Div 181
Kaye v Robertson [1991] F.S.R. 62, CA (Civ Div) 71, 72
Keays v Guardian Newspapers Ltd [2003] EWHC 1565, QBD 50
Kent CC v B (A Child); sub nom. B (A Child) (Disclosure), Re [2004] EWHC 411; [2004] 2
    F.L.R. 142; [2004] 3 F.C.R. 1, Fam Div 193
Kiam v MGN Ltd [2002] EWCA Civ 43; [2003] Q.B. 281; [2002] 3 W.L.R. 1036, CA (Civ
    Div) 68
Kidman v Associated Newspapers, unreported, 2003 70
Kimber v Press Association Ltd [1893] 1 Q.B. 65, CA 55
King v Lewis; sub nom [2004] EWCA Civ 1329; [2005] I.L.Pr. 16; [2005] E.M.L.R. 4, CA
    affirming [2004] EWHC 168 (QB); [2004] I.L.Pr. 31, QBD 46, 224, 225
Kingshott v Associated Kent Newspapers [1991] 1 Q.B. 88; [1990] 3 W.L.R. 675; [1991] 2
    All E.R. 99, CA (Civ Div) 55

Ladbroke (Football) Ltd v William Hill (Football) Ltd; sub nom. William Hill (Football)
    Ltd v Ladbroke (Football) Ltd [1964] 1 W.L.R. 273; [1964] 1 All E.R. 465; (1964) 108 S.J.
    135, HL 87

Lady Archer v Williams [2003] EWHC 1670 (QB); [2003] E.M.L.R. 38, [2003] F.S.R. 869,
QBD 121
Laurence Godfrey v Demon Internet. *See* Godfrey v Demon Internet Ltd (Application to
Strike Out)
Levi v Bates [2009] EWHC 1495 (QB), QBD.. 51, 58
Lion Laboratories Ltd v Evans [1985] Q.B. 526; [1984] 3 W.L.R. 539; [1984] 2 All E.R. 417,
CA (Civ Div)... 96, 129
Lonrho Plc (Contempt Proceedings), Re; sub nom. Lonrho Plc and Observer, Re [1990] 2
A.C. 154; [1989] 3 W.L.R. 535; [1989] 2 All E.R. 1100, HL.................................. 161, 162
Loutchansky v Times Newspapers Ltd (No.2) [2001] EWCA Civ 1805; [2002] Q.B. 783;
[2002] 2 W.L.R. 640; [2002] 1 All E.R. 652, CA 59, 60, 223, 225
Lowe v Associated Newspapers Ltd [2006] EWHC 320 (QB); [2007] Q.B. 580; [2007] 2
W.L.R. 595; [2006] 3 All E.R. 357, QBD... 49, 50

MGN Pension Trustees Ltd v Bank of America National Trust and Savings Association
and Credit Suisse [1995] 2 All E.R. 355; [1995] E.M.L.R. 99, Ch D 161,
192
McDonald's Corp v Steel (No.1) [1995] 3 All E.R. 615; [1995] E.M.L.R. 527, CA 48
McKennitt v Ash; sub nom. Ash v McKennitt [2006] EWCA Civ 1714; [2007] E.M.L.R. 4;
(2007) 151 S.J.L.B. 27, CA (Civ Div) 110, 113, 115, 116, 118, 120, 122, 123,
124, 126, 127, 129
McKerry v Teesdale and Wear Valley Justices; sub nom. McKerry v DPP (2000) 164 J.P.
355; [2001] E.M.L.R. 5; [2000] Crim. L.R. 594, DC.. 184, 185
Mandla v Dowell Lee [1983] 2 A.C. 548; [1983] 2 W.L.R. 620; [1983] 1 All E.R. 1062, HL   153
Marathon Mutual Ltd v Waters [2009] EWHC 1931 (QB); [2010] E.M.L.R. 3, QBD 72
Mardas v New York Times Co; Mardas v International Herald Tribune SAS [2008]
EWHC 3135 (QB); [2009] E.M.L.R. 8, QBD 226
Matthew Fisher v Gary Brooker. *See* Fisher v Brooker
Metropolitan International Schools Ltd (t/a SkillsTrain and t/a Train2Game) v
Designtechnica Corp (t/a Digital Trends) [2009] EWHC 1765 (QB); [2009] E.M.L.R. 27,
QBD 222
Monks v Warwick District Council [2009] EWHC 959, QB..................................... 42
Mosley v News Group Newspapers Ltd [2008] EWHC 1777 (QB); [2008] E.M.L.R. 20;
(2008) 158 N.L.J. 1112, QBD 113, 123, 124, 129, 130
Mosley v United Kingdom (Application 48009/08).. 111
Moss v Channel Five Broadcasting Ltd, February 3, 2006 49
Murray v Express Newspapers Plc; sub nom. Murray v Big Pictures (UK) Ltd [2008]
EWCA Civ 446; [2009] Ch. 481; [2008] 3 W.L.R. 1360, CA (Civ Div) 116, 118, 119

Nail v News Group Newspapers Ltd; Nail v Jones [2004] EWCA Civ 1708; [2005] 1 All
E.R. 1040; [2005] E.M.L.R. 12, CA (Civ Div); affirming [2004] EWHC 647 (QB); [2004]
E.M.L.R. 20, QBD... 65, 68
New York Times Co v Sullivan, 376 U.S. 254 (1964)... 45
Newspaper Licensing Agency Ltd v Marks & Spencer Plc [2001] UKHL 38; [2003] 1 A.C.
551; [2001] 3 W.L.R. 290, HL 81
Newstead v London Express Newspaper Ltd [1940] 1 K.B. 377, CA 44
Noorani v Calver (No.1) [2009] EWHC 561, QB 37
Norman v Future Publishing Ltd [1999] E.M.L.R. 325, CA (Civ Div) 33
Norowzian v Arks Ltd (No.2) [2000] E.C.D.R. 205; [2000] E.M.L.R. 67; [2000] F.S.R. 363,
CA 78
Norwich Pharmacal Co v Customs and Excise Commissioners; sub nom. Morton-Nor-
wich Products Inc v Customs and Excise Commissioners [1974] A.C. 133; [1973] 3
W.L.R. 164; [1973] 2 All E.R. 943, HL.. 228, 229
Nottingham City Council v October Films Ltd [1999] 2 F.L.R. 347; [1999] 2 F.C.R. 529;
[1999] Fam. Law 536, Fam Div 182

Patterson v ICN Photonics Ltd; sub nom. ICN Photonics Ltd v Patterson [2003] EWCA
Civ 343, CA (Civ Div)... 73
Peck v United Kingdom (44647/98) [2003] E.M.L.R. 15; (2003) 36 E.H.R.R. 41; 13 B.H.R.C.
669, ECHR.. 117, 123, 126
Pennwell Publishing (UK) Ltd v Ornstien [2007] EWHC 1570 (QB); [2008] 2 B.C.L.C. 246;
[2007] I.R.L.R. 700, QBD 235

Polanski v Condé Nast Publications Ltd [2005] UKHL 10; [2005] 1 W.L.R. 637; [2005] 1
All E.R. 945, HL.. 46
Polydor Ltd v Brown [2005] EWHC 3191 (Ch); (2006) 29(3) I.P.D. 29021, Ch D 232
Pro Sieben Media AG v Carlton UK Television Ltd [1999] 1 W.L.R. 605; [2000] E.C.D.R.
110; [1999] E.M.L.R. 109, CA (Civ Div).. 92

R. v Anderson (James); R. v Neville (Richard Clive); R. v Dennis (Felix); R. v Oz Pub-
lications Ink Ltd [1972] 1 Q.B. 304; [1971] 3 W.L.R. 939; [1971] 3 All E.R. 1152, CA
(Crim Div).. 137,
142, 155
R. v Bowden [2001] Q.B. 88; [2000] 2 W.L.R. 1083; [2000] 2 All E.R. 418, CA (Crim Div)   150
R. v Calder & Boyars Ltd [1969] 1 Q.B. 151; [1968] 3 W.L.R. 974; [1968] 3 All E.R. 644, CA
(Crim Div)... 138, 141
R. v Central Criminal Court, Ex p. Crook; sub nom. Crook, Ex p.; R. v Central Criminal
Court, Ex p. Godwin [1995] 1 W.L.R. 139; [1995] 1 All E.R. 537; [1995] 2 Cr. App. R.
212; [1995] 1 F.L.R. 132, CA (Crim Div).. 182
R. v Central Independent Television Plc [1994] Fam. 192; [1994] 3 W.L.R. 20; [1994] 3 All
E.R. 641; [1994] 2 F.L.R. 151, CA (Civ Div)... 182
R. v Edwards (1983) 5 Cr. App. R. (S.) 145; [1983] Crim. L.R. 539, CA (Crim Div)........ 155
R. v Evesham Justices, Ex p. McDonagh and Berrows Newspapers Ltd; sub nom. R v
Evesham Justices, Ex p. Mcdonagh [1988] Q.B. 553; [1988] 2 W.L.R. 227; (1988) 87 Cr.
App. R. 28, QBD... 180
R. v Gibson (Richard Norman); R. v Sylveire (Peter Sebastian) [1990] 2 Q.B. 619; [1990] 3
W.L.R. 595; [1991] 1 All E.R. 439, CA (Crim Div) 143
R. v Goring [1999] Crim. L.R. 670, CA (Crim Div)... 137
R. v Hicklin (1867-68) L.R. 3 Q.B. 360, QB.. 136
R. v Horsham Justices, Ex p. Farquharson [1982] Q.B. 762; [1982] 2 W.L.R. 430; [1982] 2
All E.R. 269, CA (Civ Div)... 162
R. v Mirza; R. v Connor; R. v Rollock [2004] UKHL 2; [2004] 1 A.C. 1118; [2004] 2 W.L.R.
201, HL.. 176
R. v Perrin [2002] EWCA Crim 747, CA (Crim Div).................................... 138, 149, 231
R. v Relf; R. v Cole (1979) 1 Cr. App. R. (S.) 111, CA (Crim Div) 155
R. v Secretary of State for National Heritage, Ex p. Continental Television BV [1993] 3
C.M.L.R. 387; [1993] E.M.L.R. 389; [1994] C.O.D. 121, CA (Civ Div); affirming [1993] 2
C.M.L.R. 333; [1993] C.O.D. 421, QBD 146
R. v Shayler (David Michael) [2002] UKHL 11; [2003] 1 A.C. 247; [2002] 2 W.L.R. 754, HL;
affirming [2001] EWCA Crim 1977; [2001] 1 W.L.R. 2206; [2002] H.R.L.R. 3, CA....... 196
R. v Taylor [1995] 1 Cr. App. R. 131; (1994) 158 J.P. 317; [1994] Crim. L.R. 527, CA (Crim
Div)... 140
R. v Twomey [2009] EWCA Crim 1035; [2009] 3 All E.R. 1002; [2009] 2 Cr. App. R. 25, CA15, 160
R. v Video Appeals Committee of British Board of Film Classification, Ex p. British
Board of Film Classification [2000] E.M.L.R. 850; [2000] C.O.D. 239, QBD................. 148
R. v Waddon unreported, 2000 149
R. v Walker unreported, 2009 135
Rantzen v Mirror Group Newspapers (1986) Ltd [1994] Q.B. 670; [1993] 3 W.L.R. 953;
[1993] 4 All E.R. 975, CA (Civ Div) 67
Reklos v Greece (1234/05) [2009] E.M.L.R. 16, ECHR... 119
Reynolds v Times Newspapers Ltd [2001] 2 A.C. 127; [1999] 3 W.L.R. 1010; [1999] 4 All
E.R. 609 HL, affirming [1998] 3 W.L.R. 862; [1998] 3 All E.R. 961; [1998] E.M.L.R. 723,
CA 41, 55, 58, 59, 60, 61, 69
Royal Aquarium & Summer & Winter Garden Society Ltd v Parkinson [1892] 1 Q.B. 431,
CA 54

S (A Child) (Identification: Restrictions on Publication), Re; sub nom. S (A Child)
(Identification: Restriction on Publication), Re [2004] UKHL 47; [2005] 1 A.C. 593;
[2004] 3 W.L.R. 1129, HL.. 113
Sanders v Percy & Ministry of Justice [2009] EWHC 1870, QBD....................................... 37
Scott (aka Morgan) v Scott [1913] A.C. 417, HL.. 181
Sheffield Wednesday Football Club Ltd v Hargreaves [2007] EWHC 2375 (QB), QBD... 228
Shetland Times Ltd v Wills, 1997 S.C. 316; 1997 S.L.T. 669; 1997 S.C.L.R. 160 OH 233
Silkin v Beaverbrook Newspapers [1958] 1 W.L.R. 743; [1958] 2 All E.R. 516; (1958) 102
S.J. 491, QBD.. 50

Slazengers Ltd v Gibbs & Co (1916) 33 T.L.R. 35.. 39
Slipper v BBC [1991] 1 Q.B. 283; [1990] 3 W.L.R. 967; [1990] 1 All E.R. 165; (1990) 134 S.J. 1042, CA (Civ Div).. 38
Solicitor General v Henry and News Group Newspapers Ltd [1990] C.O.D. 307, DC.... 168
Sony Music Entertainment (UK) Ltd v Easyinternetcafe Ltd [2003] EWHC 62 (Ch); [2003] E.C.D.R. 27; [2003] F.S.R. 48, Ch D 233
Stephens v Avery [1988] Ch. 449; [1988] 2 W.L.R. 1280; [1988] 2 All E.R. 477; [1988] F.S.R. 510, Ch D 115, 121
Stewart-Brady v Express Newspapers Plc [1997] E.M.L.R. 192, QBD.......................... 73
Sunday Times v United Kingdom (A/30) (1979-80) 2 E.H.R.R. 245; (1979) 76 L.S.G. 328, ECHR 7, 160

Theakston v MGN Ltd [2002] EWHC 137; [2002] E.M.L.R. 22, QBD.......................... 116
Thomas v News Group Newspapers Ltd; sub nom. Thomas v News Group International Ltd; Thomas v Hughes [2001] EWCA Civ 1233; [2002] E.M.L.R. 4; (2001) 98(34) L.S.G. 43, CA (Civ Div) 133
Tillery Valley Foods v Channel Four Television Corp [2004] EWHC 1075 (Ch); (2004) 101(22) L.S.G. 31, Ch D 127
Time Warner Entertainments Co LP v Channel Four Television Corp Plc [1994] E.M.L.R. 1, CA (Civ Div) 91
Todd v DPP [2004] All E.R. (D) 92 184
Tolley v JS Fry & Sons Ltd [1931] A.C. 333, HL 42
Totalise Plc v Motley Fool Ltd [2001] EWCA Civ 1897; [2002] 1 W.L.R. 1233; [2003] 2 All E.R. 872, CA.. 228
Tse Wai Chun Paul v Cheng; sub nom Cheng v Tse Wai Chun Paul [2001] E.M.L.R. 31; 10 B.H.R.C. 525; [2000] 3 H.K.L.R.D. 418, CFA (HK) 52
Turner v News Group Newspapers Ltd [2006] EWCA Civ 540; [2006] 1 W.L.R. 3469; [2006] 4 All E.R. 613, CA (Civ Div); affirming [2005] EWHC 892 (QB); [2005] E.M.L.R. 25, QBD 65
Tycon Energy Corp v Motley Fool Ltd unreported December 9, 2008 QBD................. 228

Veliu v Mazrekaj [2006] EWHC 1710; [2007] 1 W.L.R. 495, QBD 68
Venables v News Group Newspapers Ltd; Thompson v News Group Newspapers Ltd [2001] Fam. 430; [2001] 2 W.L.R. 1038; [2001] 1 All E.R. 908, Fam Div..................... 128
Vodafone Group Plc v Orange Personal Communications Services Ltd [1997] E.M.L.R. 84; [1997-98] Info. T.L.R. 8; [1997] F.S.R. 34, Ch D 72, 73
Von Hannover v Germany (59320/00) [2004] E.M.L.R. 21; (2005) 40 E.H.R.R. 1; 16 B.H.R.C. 545, ECHR 116, 117, 118, 123, 124, 126, 130

Wainwright v United Kingdom (12350/04) (2007) 44 E.H.R.R. 40; 22 B.H.R.C. 287; (2006) 156 N.L.J. 1524, ECHR 107
Watts v Times Newspapers Ltd [1997] Q.B. 650; [1996] 2 W.L.R. 427; [1996] 1 All E.R. 152, CA (Civ Div)... 44
Westcott v Westcott [2008] EWCA Civ 818; [2009] Q.B. 407; [2009] 2 W.L.R. 838, CA.... 54
Wood v Commissioner of Police of the Metropolis [2009] EWCA Civ 414; [2009] 4 All E.R. 951; [2010] E.M.L.R. 1, CA (Civ Div) 119

X v Dempster [1999] 1 F.L.R. 894; [1999] 3 F.C.R. 757; [1999] Fam. Law 300, Fam Div... 193
X v Persons [2006] EWHC 2783 (QB); [2007] E.M.L.R. 10; [2007] 1 F.L.R. 1567, QBD..... 127
X (formerly known as Mary Bell) v SO [2003] EWHC 1101; [2003] E.M.L.R. 37; [2003] 2 F.C.R. 686; [2003] F.S.R. 850, QBD 128
X (HA) v Y [1988] 2 All E.R. 648; [1988] R.P.C. 379; (1987) 137 N.L.J. 1062, QBD.......... 129
X Ltd v Morgan Grampian (Publishers) Ltd [1991] 1 A.C. 1; [1990] 2 W.L.R. 1000; [1990] 2 All E.R. 1, HL.. 198

TABLE OF STATUTES

1688 Bill of Rights
    art.9 .... 53, 194
1790 Treason Act (30 Geo.3 c.48)
    s.1.. 24
1911 Official Secrets Act (1 & 2 Geo.5
    c.28)............................. 180, 197
    s.1................................. 194, 195
    s.2.. 194
1925 Criminal Justice Act (15 & 16 Geo.5
    c.86)
    s.41 192
1933 Children and Young Persons Act
    (23 & 24 Geo.5 c.12)
    s.37 180
    s.39 .... 182, 183, 185
    s.47 180
    s.49 184
1952 Defamation Act (15 & 16 Geo.6 & 1
    Eliz.2 c.66)
    ss.1–3 285
    s.4....................................... 286
    s.5................................. 47, 286
    ss.6–11 286
    ss.12–15 287
    ss.16–18 288
1955 Children and Young Persons
    (Harmful Publications) Act (3
    & 4 Eliz.2 c.28) 151
1959 Obscene Publications Act (7 & 8
    Eliz.2 c.66) 144, 147, 149,
    151, 231
    s.1........................... 136, 137, 138
    (1) 231
    s.2........................... 140, 142, 152
    (5) 142

    s.4................................. 140, 152
1960 Indecency with Children Act (8 & 9
    Eliz.2 c.33) 131
    s.1(1) 150
    Administration of Justice Act (8 &
    9 Eliz.2 c.65)
    s.12 .... 181, 193
    (1) 181
1964 Obscene Publications Act (c.74) .. 137,
    140, 142, 147
1965 Murder (Abolition of Death Pen-
    alty) Act (c.71)..................... 24
1968 Theatres Act (c.54)............... 35, 283
1972 European Communities Act (c.68). 6
    s.2(1) 3
1974 Rehabilitation of Offenders Act
    (c.53)................................... 49
1976 Bail Act (c.63)..................... 20, 278
    Race Relations Act (c.74)
    s.3....................................... 154
    Sexual Offences (Amendment) Act
    (c.82)
    s.4(1)(a).............................. 186
    (b) 187
    (5A) 187
1978 Domestic Proceedings and Magis-
    trates Courts Act (c.22).......... 14
    Protection of Children Act
    (c.37)........................... 151, 230
    s.1....................................... 150
    s.1A 150
1979 Sale of Goods Act (c.54)
    s.14 18
1980 Magistrates Courts Act (c.43) 186
    s.6(1), (2)............................... 22

s.38 23
s.38A 23
1981 Contempt of Court Act (c.49) 8,
131, 159, 160, 161, 167, 168,
172, 174, 197, 198, 203, 279
s.2(2) 165, 177
s.3 .... 168, 170
s.4 190
(2) 189, 190, 191
s.5 .... 170, 171, 177
s.6(c) 172
s.8 .... 29, 159, 175, 176
s.10 .... 198, 200
s.11 .... 189, 191
Sch.2 167
Senior Courts Act (Supreme Court
Act) (c.54) 12
s.69 34
1983 Representation of the People Act
(c.2) 247, 358
s.66A 358
ss.92, 93 358
1984 Data Protection Act (c.35) 210, 211
Video Recordings Act (c.39) 147,
148, 151
s.2(3) 148
s.4 147
s.4A 148
s.9 147
Police and Criminal Evidence Act
(c.60) 197, 202
s.8 201
s.24 277
Sch.1 202
Sch.5 284
1985 Prosecution of Offences Act (c.23) . 29
1986 Public Order Act (c.64) 153, 154
s.17 153
s.18 .... 154, 155, 156
s.19 .... 155, 156
s.21 .... 155, 156
s.22 155
s.25 155
s.29A 154, 157
ss.29B–29N 157
1987 Criminal Justice Act (c.38) 187
1988 Criminal Justice Act (c.33)
s.159 .... 180, 192
Legal Aid Act (c.34) 282
Sch.2 Pt II para.1 72
Copyright, Designs and Patents
Act (c.48) 76, 77, 90, 95,
98, 99, 106, 234, 282
Pt 1 96
Pt 2 .... 99, 102, 105
s.1 279
s.3(1) 78
(2) 79
s.3A 78
(1) 235
s.4(1) 79
s.5A 80

s.5B 80
s.6 .... 80, 279
s.8 81
s.10(1) 82
s.11 82
ss.12–15 83
s.16 87
s.17 233
(2) 88
(4), (5) 88
s.18 233
(2) 88, 89
(3) 89
s.18A(2)(a) 89, 106
(b) 106
s.19 89
s.20 89
s.21 90
s.30(1) 90
(1A) 90
(2) 93
(3) 93
s.31(1) 95
(3) 95
ss.50A, 50B, 50BA, 50C 234
s.58 .... 98, 99
s.77 100
ss.78, 79 100
s.80 100
(2) 101
s.84 102
s.85 102
s.90 83
(2) 83
s.101 84
s.101A 84
ss.153–156 82
s.171(3) 96
s.178 92
s.180 102
(2) 103
s.182 103
ss.182A, 182B 103, 105
ss.182C, 182CA 103
ss.183, 184 103
s.191A 103
s.191G 103
s.205C 104
s.205F 104
s.296 234
s.296A 234
1989 Official Secrets Act (c.6) 180,
194, 197, 202, 282
ss.1–4 .... 195, 196
ss.5, 6 195
s.8 202
Children Act (c.41) 14
s.97 181
(2) 193
1990 Courts and Legal Services Act
(c.41) 28
s.8 67

Broadcasting Act (c.43)............... 35,
137, 140, 144, 239
s.201.................................. 283
1991 Criminal Justice Act (c.53)
s.53 186
Sch.6 186
1992 Sexual Offences (Amendment) Act
(c.34)................................. 187
1994 Criminal Justice and Public Order
Act (c.33)........................... 187
s.168................................. 231
1996 Criminal Procedure and Investigations Act (c.25)
ss.37, 38 188
ss.41, 42 188
Defamation Act (c.31) 2, 62, 221
s.1...... 38, 62, 63, 220, 221, 222, 289
(1)(b)................................ 221
(c)................................... 221
(6) 220
s.2............................ 63, 64, 290
s.3.................................... 291
s.4.............................. 64, 292
s.5.................................... 292
s.6.................................... 294
ss.7, 8 295
ss.9, 10.............................. 296
ss.11, 12 297
s.13 .... 53, 194, 298
s.14 .... 54, 298
(2) 54
s.15 .... 56, 299
(4) 57
s.16 299
ss.17, 18 300
ss.19, 20 301
Sch.1 .... 56, 302
Pt 1............................. 56, 302
Pt II 56, 302
Pt III 305
Sch.2 306
Broadcasting Act (c.55)
s.107(1) 362, 364
s.130............................. 362, 364
1997 Police Act (c.16) 197, 202
Protection from Harassment Act
(c.40)................................ 131
s.1(1), (2)............................ 132
Crime (Sentences) Act (c.43)........ 184
1998 Data Protection Act (c.29) 6, 198,
208, 209
Pt II 209
s.1.................................... 280
(1) 209
s.2.................................... 217
s.7.............................. 210, 219
(1)(d).............................. 211
s.8(5) 211
s.10 .... 212, 219
s.11(1)............................... 212
(3) 212
s.12 219

s.13 219
s.14 213
(1)–(3) 219
s.32 .... 215, 220
s.35(2)................................ 228
s.70(2)................................ 213
Sch.1 .... 213, 215, 218
Pt II para.2(3) 215
Pt II para.3(2) 215
Sch.2 .... 214, 215, 216
Sch.3 .... 214, 215, 216, 217, 218
Crime and Disorder Act (c.37)
s.51 24
Human Rights Act (c.42) 7, 17,
30, 67, 94, 107, 108,
135, 179, 242, 243
s.1..................................... 307
ss.2–4 308
ss.5, 6 309
s.7.................................... 310
s.8.................................... 311
s.9.................................... 312
s.10 .... 159, 312
s.11 313
s.12 .... 30, 69, 109, 177, 313
(3) 70, 111, 177
s.12A................................. 109
ss.13–16 314
s.17 315
ss.18, 19 316
ss.20, 21 317
s.22 319
Sch.1 319
Sch.2 324
Sch.3 326
Sch.4 328
1999 Youth Justice and Criminal Evidence Act (c.23) 183
s.25 189
ss.44, 45 183
s.46 .... 189, 190
s.48 187
s.52 189
2000 Financial Services and Markets Act
(c.8)
s.21(1) 370
Terrorism Act (c.11)
s.19 203
Regulation of Investigatory Powers
Act (c.23)..................... 197, 202
Political Parties, Elections and
Referendums Act (c.41)
s.144.................................. 358
2001 Criminal Justice and Police Act
(c.16)................................ 151
Anti-terrorism, Crime and Security
Act (c.24)........................... 155
2003 Communications Act (c.21) 144,
145, 146, 238, 241, 264
s.3(2)(f) 362, 364
(g) 351
(h) 346

(j) 354
(l) 351
s.319.............................. 241, 243
(2)(a) 346, 351
(b) 354
(c) 355, 358
(d) 355
(e) 354
(f) 351, 370
(i) 368, 370
(j) 368
(l) 351
(4) 144
(e), (f) 368, 370
(6) 354
(8) 355
s.320.............................. 355, 358
s.326.............................. 362, 364
s.329................................. 240
s.333................................. 358

Anti-social Behaviour Act (c.38)... 184
Courts Act (c.39) 160
Sexual Offences Act (c.42)..... 150, 230
Criminal Justice Act (c.44) 15, 160, 166
Pt 9 16
s.43 15
s.44 15
(5) 15
Sch.21................................... 15
2005 Constitutional Reform Act (c.4)..... 12, 28
Serious Organised Crime and Police Act (c.15)............ 197, 202
2006 Racial and Religious Hatred Act (c.1)...................... 153, 154, 157
2008 Criminal Justice and Immigration Act (c.4)
s.63 231

TABLE OF STATUTORY INSTRUMENTS

1982 Crown Court Rules (SI 1982/
      1109)................................. 180
1991 Family Proceedings Rules (SI
      1991/1247)
      r.16A(3) 193
1996 Copyright and Related Rights
      Regulations (SI 1996/2967)..... 89,
                                       106
1997 Copyright and Rights in Databases
      Regulations (SI 1997/3032).... 235
      reg.12(1)............................... 235
      reg.13(1)............................... 235
      reg.14 235
      reg.16 235
      reg.17 235
1998 Civil Procedure Rules (SI 1998/
      3132).............................. 2, 130
      r.5.4c 178
      r 6.37(3) 225
      r.31.17................................. 228
      r.48.1(2)............................... 228
2000 Data Protection (Processing of
      Sensitive Personal Data) Order
      (SI 2000/417)...................... 217
2002 Electronic Commerce (EC Direc-
      tive) Regulations (SI 2002/
      2013).............. 208, 222, 233, 328
      regs 1, 2............................... 330
      reg.3................................... 332
      regs 4, 5............................... 333
      reg.6................................... 334

      regs 7–9 335
      regs 10–14 336
      regs 15, 16........................... 337
      reg.17 .... 233, 337
      reg.18 .... 233, 338
      reg.19 .... 222, 233, 338
      reg.20 338
      regs 21, 22........................... 339
      Schedule 339
2003 Privacy and Electronic Commu-
      nications   (EC   Directive)
      Regulations (SI 2003/2426)... 209,
                                       212
      Copyright and Related Rights
      Regulations (SI 2003/2498).... 234
2004 Costs in Criminal Cases (General)
      (Amendment) Regulations (SI
      2004/2408)......................... 160
2005 Investment   Recommendation
      (Media) Regulations (SI 2005/
      382) 370
2006 Performances (Moral Rights, etc)
      Regulations (SI 2006/18)........ 99,
                                       102, 104
      Artists Resale Right Regulations (SI
      2006/346)
      reg.3(1) 105
      (3) 105
      reg.4................................... 105
      reg.12 105
      Sch.1 105

TABLE OF EUROPEAN LEGISLATION

TREATIES AND CONVENTIONS

1950 Convention for the Protection of
Human Rights and Funda-
mental Freedoms, Rome...... 1, 6,
7, 17, 67, 160,
181, 185, 243, 281
  art.6(1)................................. 179
  art.8 .... 107, 108, 109, 110,
114, 115, 118, 119, 120,
123, 124, 126, 130, 179,
243, 364
  art.9 .... 243, 354
  art.10........... 7, 30, 67, 70, 108, 109,
114, 121, 122, 124, 128,
149, 179, 196, 199, 223,
243, 267, 273, 346, 351,
354, 354, 355, 358, 362,
364, 368, 370
  art.13................................... 107
  art.14....................... 243, 351, 354
1957 EC Treaty establishing the European Community, March 25,
1957, Rome (Treaty of Rome) . 4,
5, 6, 16, 281
  art.226 17
  art.234 16
  art.243 12
  art.249 6
1986 Single European Act.................. 4, 5
1992 Treaty on European Union (Maastricht Treaty), February 7, 1992 4,
5, 6
2003 Treaty of Nice, 26 February 2001 .. 5

DIRECTIVES

1989 Dir.89/552 on the coordination of
certain provisions laid down
by Law, Regulation or
Administrative Action in
Member States concerning the
pursuit of television broadcasting activities [1989] O.J.
L298/23............................. 242
1995 Dir.95/46 on the protection of
individuals with regard to the
processing of personal data
and on the free movement of
such data [1995] O.J.L281/31.. 6,
209
1997 Dir.97/36/EC amending Council
Directive 89/552/EEC on the
coordination of certain provisions laid down by law,
regulation or administrative
action in Member States concerning the pursuit of
television broadcasting activities [1997] O.J. 202/60 242
2001 Dir.2001/29 on the harmonisation
of certain aspects of copyright
and related rights in the
information society [2001] O.J.
167/10 234
2007 Dir.2007/65/EC amending Council Directive 89/552/EEC on
the coordination of certain
provisions laid down by law,
regulation or administrative

action in Member States concerning the pursuit of
television broadcasting activities [2007] O.J. 332/27 242
art.1 .... 368, 370
art.3(b)................................ 354

(e), (f)........................... 368, 370
art.10(1) 368, 370
art.18................................... 370
art.22............................. 346, 247
art.23.................................. 362

1. INTRODUCTION TO THE LAW

Although this book is about media law, many of its readers will not be lawyers. This chapter is designed to enable all those engaged in media activities to become familiar with the essential basics of the English legal system. Such an understanding is of course necessary for all those involved directly with the law—such as journalists who report on court proceedings—but the information contained here will also be a useful foundation from which to better understand the remainder of this book.

SOURCES OF LAW

This section looks at the principal sources of the laws that are applicable to the jurisdiction of England and Wales. Scotland has its own legal system, as does Northern Ireland. An understanding of where laws come from is essential to gain a knowledge of the laws themselves, as well as how they apply and when, how and whether they are likely to be changed. There are two principal bodies which make law: Parliament and the judges. Recently those sources have had to be looked at in the light of European law, first in the form of law from the European Union and secondly from the European Convention for the Protection of Human Rights and Fundamental Freedoms, incorporated into English law in the Human Rights Act 1998.

Parliament

Parliament consists of three institutions: the House of Commons, the House of Lords and the Queen. Its significance is that it creates law, also known as "legislation" or Acts of Parliament.

Acts of Parliament

An Act of Parliament usually begins life as a Government proposal for a new law or a change to existing law. It is passed to a Parliamentary draftsman to produce a "Bill", the term given to a proposal for a new Act. Commonly, the Government's proposals are set out in a document called a "White Paper" which is circulated amongst various interested parties. The Bill must pass through various stages in each House of Parliament. This gives opportunity to the Members of each House (either in committee form or in plenary session) to discuss the proposed law in some detail. It can be amended or even discarded entirely at any of these stages. The length of time this process takes is dependent on the length of the Bill and the extent to which it is politically controversial. Once a Bill has passed through both Houses of Parliament it is sent for signature by the Queen, at which point it becomes law. The Queen's signature is called the "Royal Assent" and is something of a formality—no monarch has refused to sign since Queen Anne did so in 1707. An example of an Act of Parliament is the Defamation Act 1996 which appears in Appendix B. An Act has both a short title, commonly used by lawyers and others when referring to a statute, and a long title, which sets out the purpose or aim of the legislation. For example, in the case of the Defamation Act referred to above, the short title is the "Defamation Act 1996". The long title of this statute is as follows: "An Act to amend the law of defamation and to amend the law of limitation with respect to actions for defamation or malicious falsehood". An Act of Parliament will come into force on the date specified in its commencement section. If there is no such section then it will come into force on the day that it receives Royal Assent.

Delegated legislation

Legislation may also be created by specific bodies, such as government departments. The need for this is obvious where rules of great detail are required in a particular context and for a certain specified purpose. Parliament does not have the time to make such detailed rules. Further, where technical legislation is required, Parliament may not have the expertise to enact such matters. An example of delegated legislation is the Civil Procedure Rules which contains rules of court procedure. The body making delegated legislation must be acting under the authority of an existing Act of Parliament. If it attempts to exceed such authority then it will be acting beyond its delegated powers (ultra vires) and any such rules made will fail. Thus the courts can challenge the validity of a piece of delegated legislation (they cannot do so in respect of an Act of Parliament, see below).

Delegated legislation may take one of three forms:

(a) *Orders in Council.* The Government is permitted by Parliament, in certain circumstances, to create this type of legislation where there is a state of emergency. This would be the case, for example, where there is a war.

(b) *Statutory Instruments.* The most common form of delegated legislation, statutory instruments, arises out of the powers given to Ministers of the Crown to make law for a specified purpose. Many thousands of statutory instruments are issued every year and they are published in bound volumes available for inspection at any law library.

(c) Bye-laws. Local authorities are given the power by Parliament to make bye-laws, which are local laws affecting the local community. Examples of such laws are provisions preventing members of the public walking on the grass or playing ball games in community parks.

The Sovereignty of Parliament

Although there is no written constitution in the United Kingdom, the constitutional convention dictates that Parliament is "sovereign" and possesses unlimited legislative powers. This means that Parliament can create any law it likes and there is no other body or authority that can overturn or change such a law. The function of the courts is merely to interpret the law that Parliament has made. Such a constitutional position is in stark contrast to that of the US where the Supreme Court is able to overturn any law enacted by Congress where it considers such a law to be unconstitutional.

Since 1973, however, the sovereignty of Parliament has been subject to one exception. On January 1 of that year, the United Kingdom became a member of the European Economic Community (EEC) (as the European Union (EU) was then called). Since that time, the jurisdiction of England and Wales has been subject to Community law (see below). The precise constitutional effect of membership on the sovereignty of Parliament is the subject of much academic argument but it now seems clear that where a piece of European legislation conflicts with domestic legislation, it is the European legislation that will prevail and English legislation must be interpreted in line with it. Section 2(1) of the European Communities Act 1972 provides that:

> "All such rights, powers, liabilities, obligations and restrictions from time to time created or arising by or under the Treaties, and all such remedies and procedures from time to time provided for by or under the Treaties, as in accordance with the Treaties are without further enactment to be given legal effect or used in the United Kingdom shall be recognised and available in law, and be enforced, allowed and followed accordingly."

Section 2(1) has led to the position that certain Community law (notably treaty provisions and regulations (see below)) is directly applicable in the United Kingdom and that UK statutes shall be construed in such a way as to comply with Community law.

Judges

That judges create law is beyond doubt. They do so first by interpreting legislation. The construction given to any statutory provision will usually be followed by other judges in later cases (see below). The object of this consensus on construction is to ensure certainty in the application of the law. In extending a law to a new factual situation or in deciding that a law does not apply to a given set of facts the judge is thereby creating new law.

Secondly, a body of law known as common law has been developed by judges over the centuries. In order to understand judge-made law it is necessary to look at the system of "binding precedent", also known as stare decisis (the standing of decisions). As will be seen in the next chapter, each court has its own position in the court hierarchy. The position in the hierarchy determines the degree of authority of the decision made. Thus a decision of the Supreme Court, the highest appeal court in the jurisdiction (before October 1, 2009, this was the House of Lords—see below as to the creation of the new court), will have authority over all other courts. Those other courts are said to be "bound" by such a decision. For example, where a point of law arises in the High Court the judge in that court must look back at previously decided cases to see if there is a case dealing with the same point of law in relation to similar facts. If there is such a case and it is, say, a Supreme Court or House of Lords decision, the judge must follow that decision. The decision of the Supreme Court or House of Lords is a precedent which binds the lower courts. The position of each court in the hierarchy and the effect of its decisions on other courts are discussed in the next chapter.

The part of a judge's decision which binds judges in future decisions is known as ratio decidendi, or the "reason for deciding". This will usually amount to a very short part of the judgment, often only one sentence. It is the nub of the issue in the case, the principle of law which goes forward as binding precedent. Judges will often go on to speculate about what the legal position would be in a related but hypothetical set of circumstances. Such matters are known as obiter dicta, or "things said by the way". An obiter dictum does not bind judges in future cases but may be of persuasive authority, particularly where the judge who made the comments is a senior or respected judge.

THE EUROPEAN SOURCES

The European Union

The United Kingdom became a Member of the European Economic Community (as the EU was then called) on January 1, 1973. Since that time citizens of the United Kingdom, as well as the state itself, have been bound to follow the laws of the EU and the sovereignty of Parliament has been substantially curtailed. The Union was originally created as a free trade area with the aim of the abolition of customs duties and quotas for the original six members (Belgium, Luxembourg, France, Germany, Italy and the Netherlands). Four fundamental freedoms were envisaged as being necessary: the free movement between Member States of goods, capital, services and workers. These freedoms were set out in the Treaty of Rome, the founding constitution of the European Economic Community. A significant push towards closer integration was provided by the Single European Act of 1986 which provided a date for the completion of the single market: December 31, 1992. The Single European Act 1986 increased the types of activity that are within the legislative ambit of the EU to include matters relating to the environment and health and safety of workers. The Treaty on European Union of 1992 (the Maastricht Treaty) set an agenda which included a much closer union than that originally envisaged by the drafters of the Treaty of Rome. The Maastricht Treaty formally renamed the EC as the EU and made a number of important changes. It bestowed citizenship of the EU on each EC national, extended Union competence to include public health and consumer protection and proposed economic and monetary union with a single currency, the Euro, which came into existence on January 1, 2002. Most recently, the Treaty of Nice entered into force in February 2003. This provides for changes to all European institutions as a result of the enlargement of the EU to include 10 more countries, known as the "Accession countries", which joined in May 2004. Romania and Bulgaria joined the EU on January 1, 2007, bringing the total number of Member States to 27. Any further enlargement of the EU would very likely require further changes to the Treaty. A draft constitution of the EU was unveiled in 2003 which would establish a constitutional framework for the Union, but this has run into problems with ratification by Member States and, as a result, there is no scheduled date for adoption. In order to understand the effect that "European law" has on the United Kingdom, it is necessary to consider the constitution of the EU and to look at the different types of laws that come from it. The Union is administered by four main institutions. The Commission, which sits in Brussels, is responsible for initiating EU policy and legislation by making recommendations to the Council. It acts as the Union watchdog by ensuring that Member States comply with treaty provisions and it develops and enforces competition and states aid law. The Commission is made up of a number of Directorates-General, each having responsibility for a particular matter such as the environment, transport, communications, competition law and policy and external affairs. Each Directorate-General is headed by a Commissioner who is appointed by Member States. The number of Commissioners that each Member State is entitled to appoint depends on the size, in terms of population, of the state making the appointment. Larger Member States appoint two Commissioners, smaller Member States only one. Commissioners, once appointed, are required to give up their national loyalties and exercise independent judgment on matters before them.

The Council is the law-making body. It consists of one government representative from each Member State. The representative chosen for this purpose will vary with the subject-matter being discussed at each meeting. For example, when discussing the Common Agricultural Policy the representative from each Member State will be the Agriculture Minister. When the government representative from each country is the Head of State, the meeting is known as the "European Council". The Treaty of Rome requires the European Council to meet at least twice a year.

The Parliament, which sits in Strasbourg and Brussels, consists of a number of directly elected members (MEPs) from each Member State. The number of MEPs that each country is entitled to elect depends on the population of the country. The United Kingdom has 78 members, fewer than previously as a consequence of the arrival of new Member States. The original role of the Parliament was limited. It had to be "consulted" by the Commission and Council on proposed legislation, but the Council was not bound by any comments which the Parliament made. The Single European Act 1986 and the Treaty on European Union (the Maastricht Treaty) increased the functions of the Parliament to the extent that it now enjoys a "co-decision" function with respect to legislation and, in certain areas of law-making, the Parliament can veto legislation where the Council refuses to adopt its recommendations.

The European Court of Justice (ECJ) is the judicial body of the EU and is located in Luxembourg. It consists of one judge from each Member State plus a president. The court ensures the uniform application of European law throughout the Community. Cases may be brought before the court in one of three ways: by a reference from a national court on a point of European law; by an action brought by the Commission against a Member State for breach of a treaty obligation; or by an action brought by one Member State against another. The parties to a case do not themselves decide to initiate a reference to the ECJ. Therefore, it is wrong to refer to an "appeal to the European Court". The ECJ is not bound by its own previous decisions but it has developed a consistent body of case law which can be regarded as authoritative. The ECJ is discussed further below.

There are three main types of European legislation which must be considered:

(a) Treaty provisions.   The Treaty of Rome was incorporated into English law by the European Communities Act 1972. The provisions of the Treaty are therefore an immediately binding and directly applicable part of the law of England and Wales. Any amendments to the Treaty, such as those incorporated by the Treaty on European Union (the Maastricht Treaty), are immediately binding in the United Kingdom by virtue of European law.

(b) Regulations.   The Treaty makes provision for the creation of legislation by the Council and Commission in the form of (amongst others) regulations and directives. Article 249 of the Treaty states that a regulation will be directly applicable in all Member States and thus no action needs to be taken on a national basis to implement its provisions. A regulation is analogous therefore to an Act of Parliament. However, it is a rule of European law that any national law that conflicts with European law will be overridden by it. Thus an Act of Parliament generally takes second place to a regulation.

(c) Directives.   Directives are issued by the Council and Commission in the same way as regulations. A directive differs from a regulation in that it is "binding as to the result to be achieved, upon each Member State to which it is addressed, but shall leave to the national authorities the choice of form and methods". Thus, a directive must be implemented by each Member State. In the United Kingdom, an Act of Parliament will usually be passed to give effect to the provisions of the directive. A time-limit, usually two years, is given to the Member States to carry out the task of enactment. An example is European Directive 95/46 on "the protection of individuals with regard to the processing of personal data and on the free movement of such data". The United Kingdom passed the Data Protection Act 1998 to give effect to this directive.

European Convention on Human Rights

The European Convention for the Protection of Human Rights and Fundamental Freedoms (ECHR) was drafted in 1950 with the aim of achieving a certain minimum standard of treatment of human beings in Europe. The Convention sets out a number of fundamental rights including the right to liberty and security of the person, the right to respect of one's family and private life, the right to freedom of thought and religion and, of particular significance to media law, the right to freedom of expression (see art.10 of the Convention in Appendix C). It came into force in 1953, with the United Kingdom being one of the first members. There are now 45 members of the Convention, situated mainly in Europe. It can be seen then that there are many more members of the ECHR than of the EU and the two institutions must not be confused. Breaches of the ECHR are ruled upon by the European Court of Human Rights (ECtHR) which sits in Strasbourg. Applications, in the form of a petition, to the ECtHR, may be made by a member country as against another country or, where a member country has declared itself willing to give such a right, by an individual within any member country. The United Kingdom made such a declaration in 1966 and has renewed it every five years since then. Where a petition is brought by an individual, it will not be entertained until all national remedies (e.g. an application for judicial review or, in appropriate cases, an appeal to a minister) have been exhausted.

The United Kingdom passed the Human Rights Act 1998 to give greater effect to the ECHR. Since the Act came into force on October 2, 2000, the decisions of the ECtHR have been binding on the courts of England and Wales. This has had and continues to have significant impact on English law, especially in the field of media law. Decisions of the court predating the Human Rights Act 1998 and the provisions of the Convention remain of persuasive authority and political significance (the Contempt of Court Act 1981 was passed as a result of the decision of the ECtHR in *Sunday Times v United Kingdom* (1979) 2 E.H.R.R. 245). The ECJ has also said that, in interpreting and applying European law, it will take the provisions of the Convention into account. The Convention has thus been an indirect source of European law (and hence English law) for many years, and since 2000 a direct source of law. For a further examination of the impact of the Human Rights Act 1998 on the media see below.

THE COURTS

It is necessary for those working in the media to have an understanding of the court system and a basic grasp of the function and type of work that each court deals with. Students of the law, including those studying media law, will obviously need to understand the working of the court system. What follows then is a basic introduction to the courts of the legal jurisdiction of England and Wales, as well as of two European Courts which affect the laws of the jurisdiction.

The courts of England and Wales are divided into two broad sets: those that deal with civil cases and those that are concerned with criminal matters (for a distinction between civil law and criminal law see below). This section will look at the courts on the basis of this division. It should always be borne in mind, however, that there is some overlap between the work undertaken by the criminal courts on the one hand and the civil courts on the other—this will be pointed out where relevant.

Civil Courts

The diagram below shows the structure of the civil courts. The arrows represent lines of potential appeal from one court to the next in the court hierarchy. Generally speaking, the higher the court in the hierarchy, the greater the weight of its decision. A decision of a court is said to be binding on all inferior courts. This means that a judge ruling on a point of law in a case must follow the decision of a judge of a higher court where there has been an earlier decision on the same point. Thus the High Court will be bound by a decision of the Court of Appeal where it has to consider a similar case to one decided by that higher court.

There are two trial (or first instance) courts in the civil court hierarchy and thus all civil trials will take place in either one or the other. The County Court generally deals with cases that are less important than those dealt with by the High Court. From April 26, 1999, the rules determining which court will try a civil case have been simplified. All cases are divided into three categories: small claims (those cases with a value of less than £5,000), fast-track cases (£5,000–£25,000, with trial length estimate under a day) and multi-track cases (all cases not suitable for small claims or fast-track, including non-money claims).

Diagram of Civil Court structure

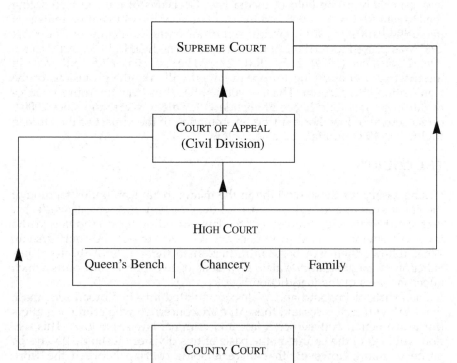

Although the value of the claim is the most important factor in determining which track a particular case will be allocated to, other considerations include the following:

- the nature of the remedy sought;
- the complexity of the case;
- the number of parties;
- the value of any counterclaim;
- the amount of any oral evidence which may be required;
- the importance of the claim to persons who are not parties to the action;
- the views expressed by the parties; and
- the circumstances of the parties.

Money claims may not be started in the High Court unless the value is over £25,000, but in practice the High Court is likely to transfer to the County Court any claim with an estimated value of less than £50,000. Non-money claims should generally be commenced in the High Court, and the rules dictate that certain types of cases, such as defamation actions, should always be commenced in the High Court. Following commencement and the completion of an allocation questionnaire by the parties, the case will be allocated by the court to one of the three tracks.

EXAMPLE 1

Susie enters into a contract with James to build an extension on her house. The extension falls down and the cost to put the damage right is £75,000. The action, brought by Susie against James when he refuses to pay, should normally be commenced in the High Court. It will be allocated by the court to the multi-track.

EXAMPLE 2

As a result of the above incident, Susie tells a journalist working for a local newspaper that James is a "charlatan and incompetent workman". The story, with the quote from Susie, is published in the paper the following week. James sues Susie and the newspaper for libel and claims that he has lost a valuable decorating contract worth £15,000. The case should be commenced in the High Court as it is a defamation action—such actions will also be allocated to the multi-track.

County Court

There are approximately 200 County Courts and one can be found in most towns in England and Wales. A single judge (a district or circuit judge) will sit to hear each case.

Where an action commenced in the County Court is worth less than £5,000, it will be usually allocated to the small claims track. The procedure for small claims is quicker and less formal than the other tracks and the participation of lawyers is not encouraged. The referral to the small claims track is not automatic and will generally not occur where:

- the case involves a difficult question of law or complex facts;

- the case involves fraud;

- the parties have agreed that the reference should not be made; or

- it would be unreasonable for the claim to proceed to small claims having regard to the circumstances of the parties, the interest of any other person or the subject-matter of the dispute.

Decisions of the County Court do not bind other County Courts.

High Court

The High Court, the other trial court (as opposed to an appeal court) in the civil court structure, generally hears cases of higher value and all defamation actions. For administration purposes, the High Court is divided into three divisions. The subject-matter of each case will determine which division conducts the trial. The three divisions and their workload are as follows.

Queen's Bench Division (QBD).   The QBD hears contract and tort cases (including all defamation actions), as well as certain commercial and admiralty matters. Actions are commonly heard by a single judge with the exception of defamation cases which may be tried by judge and jury. The president of the QBD is the Lord Chief Justice.

Chancery Division.   The Chancery Division hears disputes relating to the sale or ownership of land, the execution of trusts or administration of estates, intellectual property and bankruptcy.

Family Division.   The Family Division hears matters relating to divorce as well as wardship and adoption of children.

The Central Office of the High Court is The Royal Courts of Justice in The Strand, London. In addition, most of the larger towns in England and Wales will have a High Court, called a District Registry. In most cases, a single High Court judge will preside over the trial.

Each division has a special court within it confusingly called a "Divisional Court". The Divisional Court of the QBD is of particular importance. It has special power over and above that of other courts: it reviews the functioning of other courts (and also of certain public bodies) on the basis of the legality of their decisions (judicial review). Where the Divisional Court finds that a court has reached its decision in an illegal way (e.g. because the judge had a personal interest in the outcome of the case or because the court did not have proper jurisdiction to hear it), it will quash that decision. In this way, the Divisional Court of the QBD plays a supervisory role in respect of inferior courts (the Magistrates' Court, Crown Court and County

Court). In addition to the power to grant judicial review of an administrative action of a public body or inferior court, the Divisional Court hears:

- applications for the writ of habeas corpus from a person who alleges that they are being unlawfully imprisoned;
- applications for punishment for a "contempt of court" (see Chs 7 and 8) committed in an inferior court; and
- appeals on points of law either directly from the Magistrates' Court or via the Crown Court (see below).

Appeals from a decision of the High Court, whether of a divisional or ordinary court, lie to the Court of Appeal. However, in exceptional cases an appeal can be taken directly from the High Court to the Supreme Court. Such an appeal, known as "leapfrogging" (see diagram above), will be allowed only where:

(a) the trial judge has granted a "certificate of satisfaction"; and

(b) the Supreme Court has given permission to appeal.

A certificate of satisfaction is rare and will only be granted where all parties consent and the case involves a point of law of general public importance.

Decisions of a single judge in the High Court will bind the County Court but will not bind other High Court judges. Decisions of the Divisional Court (which usually consists of two judges) bind other courts within the same division but not the Divisional Court itself.

Court of Appeal (Civil Division)

There are two divisions of the Court of Appeal: the Civil Division and the Criminal Division. The Civil Division, headed by the Master of the Rolls, hears appeals from decisions of the County Court and all three divisions of the High Court.

The procedure in the Court of Appeal is essentially as follows: a barrister for each party will make representations to the court based on documentary evidence alone (there are no "live" witnesses in appeal proceedings); the judges, of which there are usually three, will then either allow (in which case the decision of the trial court is effectively reversed) or dismiss the appeal.

In theory, the Court of Appeal can sit anywhere in England and Wales. However, it normally sits at The Royal Courts of Justice, The Strand, London. This is the same building that houses the Criminal Division of the Court of Appeal and the Central Office of the High Court.

Decisions of the Court of Appeal bind the High Court and the County Courts. The courts' decisions will also bind itself, i.e. judges in future cases in the Court of Appeal must follow previous Court of Appeal decisions, except where:

(a) a later decision of the House of Lords/Supreme Court applies;

(b) there are previous conflicting decisions of the Court of Appeal; or

(c) where the previous decision was made per incuriam, i.e. in error because some relevant statutory provision or precedent was not considered by the court.

Supreme Court

The Supreme Court is the final Court of Appeal in both civil and criminal cases in England and Wales and Northern Ireland and the final court of appeal in civil cases for Scotland. It took over the judicial functions of the former highest court in the land, the House of Lords, on October 1, 2009. According to the Ministry of Justice website, "The introduction of a Supreme Court for the United Kingdom will provide greater clarity in our constitutional arrangements by further separating the judiciary from the legislature."

To underline that separation, the judges of the Supreme Court are no longer called Law Lords, but Justices (except for two who will be called President and Deputy President) of the Supreme Court. The Supreme Court is housed in its own building on the southwest corner of Parliament Square. Detailed information is available on the Supreme Court's own website: *http://www.supremecourt.gov.uk/index.html*.

According to the Constitutional Reform Act 2005 which created it, the Supreme Court will be made up of an uneven number of Justices, not less than three. It is likely that five Justices will be the usual number (following the practice of the previous House of Lords). A decision of the Supreme Court is binding on all other courts in the jurisdiction.

Where a point of European law is before the Supreme Court and the parties cannot agree on its interpretation or application, the Supreme Court (as the final appeal court) must refer the point to the ECJ for a decision (art.243 EC—see below).

Since the Practice Direction of 1966, the House of Lords was not bound by its own previous decisions—the House stated, however, that it would only depart from such decisions in exceptional circumstances (for an example of such a case see *British Railways Board v Herrington* [1972] 1 All E.R. 749 where the House overruled its earlier decision in *Addie v Dembreck* [1929] A.C. 358), thus preserving the certainty that is necessary in the legal system. It is likely that the Supreme Court will adopt the same approach.

One change in terminology is pending: to avoid confusion with what has hitherto been referred to as the "Supreme Court of England and Wales", the collective description for the Court of Appeal, the High Court of Justice and the Crown Court, the latter are to be called the Senior Courts of England and Wales. At the time of writing, this change (via an amendment to the now-misleadingly titled Supreme Court Act 1981) has yet to be brought into force.

Criminal Courts

The criminal court structure (see diagram below) is similar to the civil court structure in that there are two first instance courts and a system of appeals culminating in the Supreme Court.

Criminal Court structure

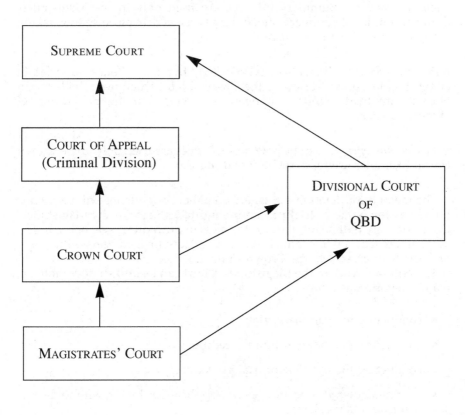

Magistrates' Court

The Magistrates' Court is the lowest court in the criminal court hierarchy. There are approximately 400 Magistrates' Courts located all over the country. The court is presided over by three judges called Justices of the Peace (JPs). These are persons appointed from members of the local community and are not lawyers. They work part-time and are compensated for the work they do in the court by receiving expenses and a payment representing loss of earnings. JPs are assisted on matters of law and procedure by a legal adviser called the clerk. The legal adviser sits immediately in front of the justices in the courtroom and will be a qualified solicitor or barrister.

Occasionally a very busy Magistrates' Court (particularly in London) will have a single judge deciding upon cases. He will be a qualified lawyer and so will not need a court clerk. Such judges are called district judges.

In the same way that there are two trial courts in the civil court structure, there are two courts where a trial can take place on the criminal side: the Magistrates' Court and the Crown Court. The type of offence that the defendant is accused of committing will determine in which court the case will be tried. For this purpose, all offences are divided into three categories. They are as follows:

Summary offences.   Summary offences are tried only in the Magistrates' Court. Examples of summary offences are careless driving, speeding, taking a conveyance and common assault.

Either way offences.   Either way (also called "hybrid") offences are tried in either the Magistrates' Court or the Crown Court. Examples of either way offences are theft, burglary, dangerous driving and the publication of obscene articles.

Indictable only offences.   Indictable only offences are tried only in the Crown Court. Examples are rape, robbery and murder.

The method for determining where an either way offence will be tried is known as the mode of trial procedure and takes place in the Magistrates' Court (for an outline of the mode of trial procedure, see below). The Magistrates' Court will conduct committal proceedings for those either way offences that are sent to the Crown Court for trial.

The criminal work of the Magistrates' Court can be broken down into six main categories, as follows:

- conducting the summary trial;

- conducting the mode of trial procedure;

- conducting the transfer for trial procedure;

- hearing Crown Prosecution Service applications for the withholding of bail from a defendant;

- hearing applications from police officers for arrest and search warrants; and

- conducting proceedings in the Youth Court (the name given to the Magistrates' Court when it is hearing criminal trials of defendants under the age of 18).

Where a defendant is found guilty in the Magistrates' Court, he or she will be sentenced in the same way as a defendant in the Crown Court (see below). The Magistrates' Court only has power to impose sentences of imprisonment of up to six months (or, if a defendant is found guilty of two or more 'either way' offences, 12 months by way of consecutive sentences), or a fine up to £5000 for each offence. In cases triable either way, the offender may be committed by the magistrates to the Crown Court for sentencing if a more severe sentence is thought necessary.

Somewhat confusingly, the Magistrates' Court has some, albeit limited, civil function. Briefly, the civil jurisdiction consists of the power to hear certain types of matrimonial or family proceedings (see the Domestic Proceedings and Magistrates' Courts Act 1978 and the Children Act 1989), actions for the recovery of local council tax and appeals from applications to local authorities for liquor licences.

Decisions of the Magistrates' Court do not bind any other court.

Crown Court

The Crown Court will try all indictable only offences and those either way offences that are transferred to it from the Magistrates' Court. It will also sentence those defendants who are sent to it by the magistrates after a trial of an either way offence in the Magistrates' Court where the justices are of the view that their sentencing powers are insufficient.

Trial in the Crown Court is by judge and jury. The judge will decide issues of law and the jury will decide issues of fact. The jury of 12 people will decide upon the guilt or innocence of the defendant.

It should be noted that the Criminal Justice Act 2003 provides restrictions on the right to trial by jury by identifying two situations in which a trial on indictment might be conducted by a judge sitting alone. However, the first situation is controversial and the relevant section (s.43, covering long and/or complex fraud trials) is not yet in force at time of writing. The second situation is where there is a danger of jury tampering: this is in s.44 which is in force. It was deployed for the first time in England and Wales when in June 2009 the Court of Appeal made the historic ruling in *R. v Twomey* [2009] EWCA Crim 1035 that the trial of four men could go ahead without a jury because the two necessary conditions were fulfilled (i.e. under s.44(4) that there was evidence of a real and present danger that jury tampering would take place, and under s.44(5) that, notwithstanding any steps—including the provision of police protection—which might reasonably be taken, the likelihood that jury tampering would take place would be so substantial as to make it necessary in the interests of justice for the trial to be conducted without a jury).

The judge in a Crown Court trial is usually a circuit judge, but some cases are dealt with by recorders—part-time judges who are practising lawyers. The judge will proceed to sentence the defendant where they are found guilty, often after an adjournment following conviction to allow the Probation Service to prepare a report. This adjournment is sometimes mandatory (e.g. youths facing imprisonment for the first time).

The Crown Court hears appeals from a defendant convicted in the Magistrates' Court against the sentence imposed by that court. It will also hear appeals against conviction where the defendant in the Magistrates' Court pleaded not guilty. The prosecution has no right of appeal to the Crown Court.

Unlike the Magistrates' Court there is no general upper limit on the amount of fine or length of imprisonment that the Crown Court can impose. Under the Criminal Justice Act 2003, judges must now fix the "minimum term" to be served when imposing mandatory life sentences for murder, to be determined according to various factors set out in Sch.21 of the Act.

Decisions of the Crown Court do not bind any other court.

Court of Appeal (Criminal Division)

The principal function of the Criminal Division of the Court of Appeal is to hear appeals from the Crown Court. The defendant may appeal (with permission) to the Court of Appeal against conviction or sentence.

The prosecution cannot appeal to the Court of Appeal against the acquittal of a defendant or against the sentence imposed on the defendant (although under the Criminal Justice Act 2003, Pt 9, it can appeal against certain rulings of law made by a trial judge in a trial on indictment). However, if it appears to the Attorney General that the sentencing of a person in the Crown Court has been unduly lenient he may, with the permission of the Court of Appeal, refer the case to the Court of Appeal to review the sentencing of that person. On such a referral the Court of Appeal may quash any sentence passed on the defendant and pass such sentence as it thinks appropriate for the case.

The president of the Criminal Division is the Lord Chief Justice who is assisted by several Lords Justices of Appeal.

The Criminal Division of the Court of Appeal binds all inferior courts. However, unlike the Civil Division, it does not bind itself.

Supreme Court

The role of the Supreme Court as the final court of appeal in the jurisdiction has been discussed above in connection with the civil court structure. It will be remembered that for an appeal to lie to the Supreme Court, permission must first be obtained from either the Court of Appeal or from the Supreme Court itself. In criminal cases there is an additional requirement that the appeal must involve a point of law of general public importance.

European Courts

Although not part of the court structure of England and Wales, there are two further courts that have an effect on English law and thus need consideration.

The European Court of Justice

The European Court of Justice (ECJ) is the court of the European Union (EU). Since the United Kingdom joined the European Economic Community (as the EU was then called) in 1973, it has been subject to Community law (the law of the EU is confusingly called "Community law"). The court is made up of 15 judges, one from each Member State.

The ECJ interprets Community law and makes sure that it applies uniformly throughout the Member States. This uniformity of application is ensured by a provision in the constitution of the EU (the EC Treaty) which provides that any court in any Member State may refer a piece of Community law arising in a case that it is dealing with to the ECJ for interpretation. A court would do this where the parties disagree on how Community law affects their case. Where a disputed point of Community law arises in the final court of appeal in each Member State, that court must refer the point to the ECJ for a decision. Thus, in the jurisdiction of England and Wales, any court may refer, but the Supreme Court must refer a point of EC law to the ECJ. Such a reference (called an art.234 reference after the relevant provision in the EC Treaty) is not an appeal as such, and thus does not form part of the appeal structure of the courts of England and Wales. Therefore, it is incorrect to talk of parties "appealing" a case to Europe, as the decision for a case to be referred to the ECJ lies not with the parties to it, but with the English court itself. Once the ECJ has interpreted the piece of

Community law which is causing difficulty, the case is remitted back to the referring court which continues with the case where it left off. The ECJ is not empowered to determine matters of fact in a case, only to rule on the aspect of EC law which is referred to it. It is for the national court then to apply the law to the facts of the relevant case and reach a decision.

In addition, the ECJ will hear applications by the EC where it considers that a Member State has failed to comply with Community law. Article 226 of the Treaty states that:

> "If the Commission considers that a Member State has failed to fulfil an obligation under this Treaty, it shall deliver a reasoned opinion on the matter after giving the State concerned the opportunity to submit its observations. If the State concerned does not comply with the opinion within the period laid down by the Commission, the latter may bring the matter before the Court of Justice."

A Member State may also bring action against another Member State for acting contrary to the treaty obligations.

This is the procedure whereby the Commission can force the United Kingdom (or any other Member State) to comply with Community law or to enact a piece of legislation that it is required so to do by the Community.

The other main jurisdiction of the ECJ is to hear applications for a declaration that the Council or Commission has acted illegally. Such applications may be brought by the Council, the Commission or by a Member State.

The European Court of Human Rights

The European Court of Human Rights (ECtHR) sits in Strasbourg. It is not part of the EU. The court decides upon alleged human rights abuses that are referred to it by individuals in states that are signatories to the European Convention for the Protection of Human Rights and Fundamental Freedoms (ECHR).

Since the coming into force of the Human Rights Act 1998 in October 2000, all courts in the United Kingdom must take into account relevant judgments of the ECtHR. Even before that date the courts had shown a willingness to consider the Convention rights, as a result of the principle that, where possible, English law should be construed in line with international treaty obligations. In order for an individual to make an application to the ECtHR, they have to show that they have exhausted all national remedies that are open to them. This normally involves bringing proceedings in a national court and making all the appeals that it is possible to make. The admissibility of the complaint will then be determined by the Human Rights Commission (see Glossary) which may then refer the matter on to the ECtHR for a final decision.

THE LEGAL ACTION

This section looks at the nature of a legal action. Journalists and reporters should be aware of the law and procedure of any case that may come before the courts. In addition to those persons who report court proceedings, knowledge of the legal process is essential to anyone who may be actually engaged in litigation, for example the producer of a film or video being prosecuted for the offence of obscenity or the proprietor or editor of a newspaper being sued for defamation.

In the same way that the court system is divided into those courts that deal with civil cases and those that deal with criminal matters, it is most useful to look first at the civil legal action and then at the criminal one.

It seems obvious to say it, but criminal law is concerned with crimes. A crime is a wrong committed by an individual (or company) against society which may result in a prosecution. It may be that there is only one individual "victim" of the criminal conduct, but in a wider sense it can be seen that the criminal act can affect society as a whole. For example, a street mugging affects primarily the victim, but may result in a general fear of walking the streets being instilled into the community.

Whilst criminal law involves purely crimes, civil law concerns everything else. Examples of civil law will therefore be those laws dealing with the family, with employment, with safeguarding one's reputation and with enforcing one's contractual rights.

The civil action

Civil actions involve one person (or company) suing another. The way that lawyers write the title of the action is as follows: *Jones v Brown*. The claimant (the person who brings the action) is listed first, followed by a "v" and then the name of the defendant. In lawyerspeak the "v" is spoken as "and". Most civil actions will arise out of a dispute between two parties in either contract or tort (the nature of these two causes of action is considered below). As we have seen, all civil actions will begin in either the County Court or the High Court and will be allocated to one of three tracks depending on the value of the case. Contract and tort actions should be commenced in the High Court whatever their value where the case is unusually complex or where it involves a difficult point of law. When commenced in the High Court, most contract and tort actions will be dealt with by the Queen's Bench Division (see above).

Contract

A contract will exist between two people where they have a legally enforceable agreement between them. For example, you made a contract with the bookseller to buy this book. The agreement was that the bookseller gave you the book and you gave the bookseller the price. Contracts always give each party certain rights. These rights may be specifically laid out in the contract (express terms) or made a part of the contract by the operation of law (implied terms). An example of an implied term is that the purchased item must be of "satisfactory quality". This term is incorporated in a business seller's contract by s.14 of the Sale of Goods Act 1979.

EXAMPLE

Upon getting home, you discover that half the pages in this book are blank. This is clearly a breach of the contract that you have with the bookseller, and so you would have a right to get your money back. If the bookseller refused to give your money back you could sue them to get the price you paid for the book returned to you.

A person claiming breach of contract will not always confine their application merely to a return of the contract price. There are occasions when the claim will be for more than the mere price of the contract.

EXAMPLE
Soap City Ltd is a manufacturer of soap powder and enters into a contract with Primetime for the broadcasting of Soap City Ltd's advertisement on Primetime's television channel. Primetime makes a mistake and broadcasts the advertisement at the wrong time: the advertisement is transmitted during a documentary programme about the harmful effects of soap powder on clothes and skin. As a result Soap City Ltd suffers a fall in sales of the soap powder. Here, Soap City Ltd will claim not only for the return of the broadcasting fee but also for the loss of profit experienced as a result of Primetime's breach of contract.

Tort

Tort is a collective term that incorporates several different ways for one person to sue another. Each cause of action is a tort in its own right.

The tort of nuisance, for example, is a tort that allows neighbouring landowners to sue each other where they feel that their right to enjoy their land (which term in a legal context includes houses and other buildings) is being adversely affected. You might consider bringing such an action where the clothes on your washing line are frequently damaged by smoke from your neighbour's barbecue.

Battery is a tort which can be used to sue a person who physically applies force or violence to another. Y would have such a cause of action where he is punched by X in the head during a drunken brawl in a pub. Of course, in this example, X would also find himself subject to a criminal legal action— he could be prosecuted for assault.

By far the most frequently litigated tort is negligence. A person commits the tort of negligence where they cause damage or injury to another as a result of acting in a way which the law judges to be below the standard of a normal (or reasonable) person. For example, Ben is walking down The Strand on his way to the theatre when a motorist mounts the pavement and crashes into him. As a result of the motorist's negligence, Ben sustains injuries and his clothes are torn. Ben will be able to sue the motorist for damages representing compensation for his injuries together with the cost of a new set of clothes.

A further tort, and one that will be discussed in greater detail in Ch.2, is the tort of defamation. This tort is committed where one person publishes a statement about another which tends to lower that other in the estimation of people generally. Thus where a newspaper publishes an article about Simon, calling him a thief and a liar, Simon will have a cause of action in defamation against the newspaper and the journalist who wrote the article.

The criminal action

Most criminal actions begin with the police arresting a person whom they suspect has committed an offence. The arrest may be with or without a warrant to arrest. A warrant is not needed where the police have reasonable grounds to believe that an arrestable offence (see Glossary) has been committed, is being committed or is about to be committed. A warrant for arrest may be issued to the police upon application to a magistrate. Once arrested, the suspect will be taken to the police station and interviewed. When the police have enough evidence they will consult the Crown Prosecution Service which will decide whether to charge the suspect with the offence.

Once charged, the suspect (who should from this point be referred to as "the defendant") will be either released on bail or held in custody until the time that they have to appear in court. Where they are released on bail, they will be given a date and time to appear at the court. If they fail to appear, they can be found guilty of the offence of absconding. In certain cases, the police may impose conditions on bail, for example that the defendant must reside at a certain address, that they must report to the police station each day or that they must not go out at night.

Where police bail is refused, the defendant must be brought before the next available sitting of the local Magistrates' Court where they may make an application for court bail. The court can only withhold bail for certain specified reasons (set out in the Bail Act 1976), the most common of which are that there are substantial grounds for believing that the accused will:

- fail to appear at court in answer to bail;
- commit further offences whilst on bail; or
- interfere with witnesses in the case against them or obstruct the course of justice.

The Crown Prosecution Service (see below) will take over the case from the police at an early stage and will prosecute the defendant at bail hearings in court and at trial.

The name of the case will be written "*R. v Smith*". In criminal actions there is no claimant. The "R" stands for Regina (or Rex), meaning the Crown.

Mode of trial procedure.   In the previous section it was stated that all criminal offences are divided into three categories for the purposes of determining the mode of trial, i.e. whether the case will be tried in the Magistrates' Court or the Crown Court. Summary offences will be tried in the Magistrates' Court. Indictable only offences will be tried in the Crown Court. The so-called "either way" offences, for example burglary, theft and dangerous driving, may be tried in either the Magistrates' Court ("summarily") or the Crown Court ("on indictment"). Where an either way offence comes before the court, the justices will be told of the nature of the offence and will make a decision as to where the case should be tried. In doing so, they will take account of:

- the nature of the offence;

Commencement of proceedings

Either

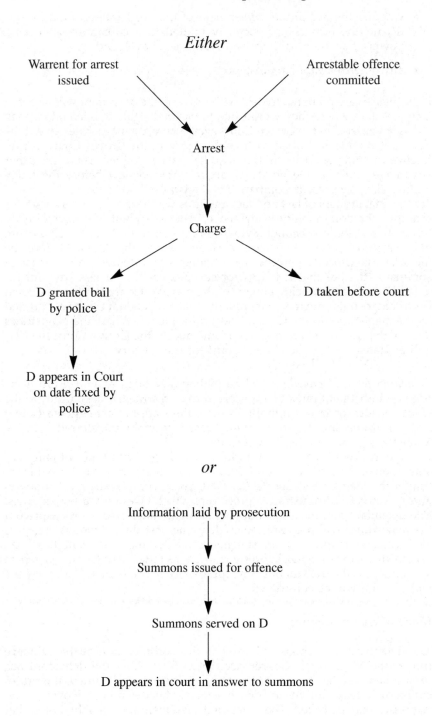

Warrent for arrest
issued

Arrestable offence
committed

Arrest

Charge

D granted bail
by police

D taken before court

D appears in Court
on date fixed by
police

or

Information laid by prosecution

Summons issued for offence

Summons served on D

D appears in court in answer to summons

- whether it is serious;

- whether the maximum punishment of the magistrates would be sufficient (the justices are normally limited to a maximum sentencing
power of six months' imprisonment—see above); and

- any other relevant circumstances.

If the justices are prepared to deal with the case, the defendant will be given
a choice as to where they would like to be tried. Thus the defendant may
choose to be tried in the Crown Court even where the magistrates accept the
case. Defendants will often elect trial by jury in the Crown Court in pre-
ference to summary trial as the acquittal rate is higher. There are other
advantages such as the ability to argue points of law before the judge
without the jury present (compare the Magistrates' Court where the justices
are the final arbiters of law and fact and thus will hear arguments about, for
example, the admissibility of evidence). The defendant will have already
had notice of the prosecution evidence in the form of Advance Disclosure
(the service of prosecution witness statements on the defence before the
mode of trial procedure in the case of either way offences). Advantages of
summary trial are that it is less formal, less costly and less stressful for
defendants. The sentencing powers of the magistrates are less than a Crown
Court judge, but it must be remembered that a defendant can be committed
by the magistrates to the Crown Court for sentence. Where the magistrates
decline the case or where the defendant chooses the Crown Court the case
will be transferred to the Crown Court for trial by jury.

Committal for trial procedure.   Those either way offences which are to be
tried on indictment must be transferred from the Magistrates' Court to the
Crown Court for trial. Committal proceedings are the name given to that
stage of proceedings where a criminal case is formally transferred from the
Magistrates' Court to the Crown Court.

There are two types of committal proceedings: with and without consideration of the evidence. Committal without consideration of the evidence
(under the Magistrates' Courts Act 1980, s.6(2)) is by far the most common
and is a largely administrative procedure which takes only a few minutes.
The defendant and their solicitor will normally attend such procedure but
the magistrates will not read the evidence against the defendant (which is
all contained in prosecution statements). After the defendant has been
asked whether they want reporting restrictions to be lifted (see Ch.8), a date
will be set for the defendant's first appearance in the Crown Court and the
bail position will be considered.

Mode of trial procedure

The defendant may choose committal with consideration of the evidence
(under the Magistrates' Courts Act 1980, s.6(1)). After the defendant has
been asked whether he wants reporting restrictions to be lifted, the prosecution will read out the evidence against the defendant. However, no
witnesses may be called. The defendant may then make a submission that
there is no case against them which is sufficient to be sent to the Crown

Mode of trial procedure

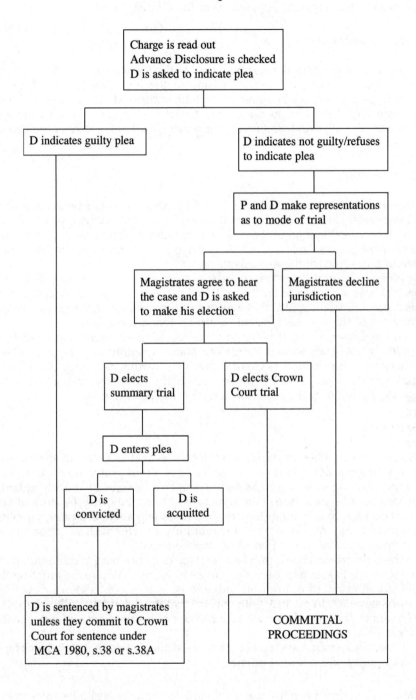

Court. If no submission is made, or if such a submission fails, the defendant is given a date for their appearance at the Crown Court.

Indictable only offences

Indictable only offences must be heard at the Crown Court. All indictable only offences will have a first hearing at the local magistrates' court at which the defendant's bail position will be addressed. The matter will then be transferred directly to the Crown Court under s.51 of the Crime and Disorder Act 1998 and all subsequent hearings will take place at the Crown Court.

Criminal trials

As stated above, a criminal trial may take place in one of two courts—the Magistrates' Court or the Crown Court—depending on the type of offence involved (see the diagram below). A trial will only be necessary where the defendant pleads "not guilty". A guilty plea will result in the court proceeding to sentence the defendant.

Where the trial takes place in the Magistrates' Court, it will be the magistrates who decide on the guilt or innocence of the defendant. If they find the defendant guilty they will then go on to pass sentence (see below for a list of the various types of sentences that are available).

In the Crown Court it is the jury that decides whether the defendant is guilty or not. They should decide the matter unanimously. In some cases, where all 12 jury members cannot agree on a verdict, the judge will allow a majority decision of 11:1 or even 10:2. If the jury produces a verdict of guilty, the judge will proceed to sentence the defendant.

Sentencing

There are a number of different sentences available to the magistrates or judge where a defendant pleads guilty or is found guilty after a trial. In a simple driving case (e.g. careless driving or speeding) the defendant's licence may be endorsed with penalty points or they may be disqualified from driving. In non-motoring criminal cases (e.g. theft, burglary, rape) the defendant may receive a fine, a community penalty such as probation or community service, or a period of imprisonment.

The only criminal case in which a judge does not have a discretion as to the sentence he can impose is the offence of murder. Where the jury find the defendant guilty of murder the judge must sentence the defendant to "life imprisonment". In practice "life" means that the defendant will serve about 14 years in prison and spend the remainder of his life term on licence to the Home Office.

Set out below are the sentences that are available where a person has been found guilty of a criminal offence.

Death. The death penalty was abolished for murder and other offences of homicide by the Murder (Abolition of Death Penalty) Act 1965. The Crime and Disorder Act 1998 (s.36) abolished the last instances of the death penalty in English law, for treason and piracy, substituting the penalty of life imprisonment.

Criminal offences—trial court

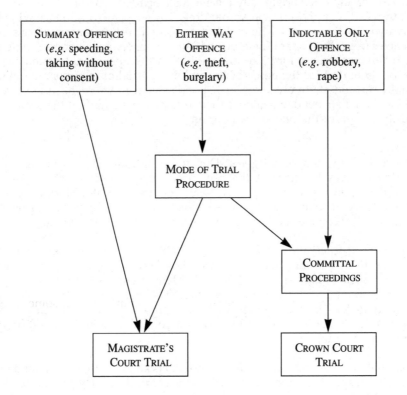

Imprisonment. Each criminal offence (except those that are not serious enough to warrant imprisonment) will have a certain maximum period of imprisonment that may be imposed by the judge where a defendant is found guilty. For example, the maximum period of imprisonment for theft is seven years and for burglary 10 years. As mentioned above, the magistrates are subject to their maximum punishment which is usually six months' imprisonment. Exceptionally, where a defendant is found guilty by the magistrates of two or more either way offences, the magistrates may give up to 12 months' imprisonment. Normally a sentence of imprisonment means that the defendant will serve a proportion of his sentence in prison and will be released on licence to the Home Office for the remainder. If the defendant commits any further offence while on licence, they can be returned to prison without further court appearance to serve the remainder of their sentence. Defendants sentenced to life imprisonment are often released on licence after serving a number of years' imprisonment. They remain on licence to the Home Office for the rest of their lives and can be recalled to prison at any time.

A person under the age of 21 who is given a custodial sentence will not go to an adult prison. Instead they will attend a Young Offenders' Institution. A person under the age of 15 cannot be given a custodial sentence unless convicted of an offence for which the maximum period of punishment for an adult would be 14 years or more imprisonment.

In rare cases, a defendant may receive a suspended sentence. This means that they will not go to prison at that time. The suspended sentence will be activated by the courts where the defendant commits an imprisonable offence during the "operational period" of the suspended sentence. Where the defendant does commit an offence within the operational period they will be sentenced for the new offence and any period of imprisonment will usually run consecutively to the suspended sentence. Where the judge gives a defendant a suspended sentence they will state the length of the sentence and the length of the operational period.

EXAMPLE

Mark is convicted of burglary. Due to exceptional circumstances, the judge decides to suspend the sentence. He gives Mark two months' imprisonment, suspended for one year. Five months later Mark commits the offence of robbery and is given a sentence of four months in prison. Mark will receive a total sentence of six months' imprisonment.

Community Rehabilitation Order (CRO).   A CRO will often be made where the court finds that the circumstances of the offence are not serious enough to merit a custodial sentence. The defendant must visit their probation officer, a trained social worker, at certain specified intervals and may be required to live in a certain place or undergo psychiatric treatment. A Community Rehabilitation Order may be combined with a Community Punishment Order.

Community Punishment Order (CPO).   A CPO is an order that the defendant do a certain specified amount of work in the community. They will often be required to participate in community projects of various kinds, such as the painting of houses or the cleaning of a community centre. A CPO will be expressed to be for a certain number of hours, the maximum being 240.

Fine.   Before making an order that the defendant pay a fine, the court will inquire into the defendant's financial circumstances. The level of fine imposed by the court should reflect the defendant's financial standing.

Penalty points/driving ban.   Motoring offences (e.g. careless/dangerous driving or driving with excess alcohol) carry a variety of possible punishments. In addition to the above, the court can order that the defendant be disqualified from driving for a certain period of time or that their driving licence be endorsed with a certain number of penalty points. When a defendant commits a driving offence for which they are given points, which, when taken together with other points endorsed on their licence in the past three years, total 12 or more they will be disqualified from driving for at least six months. (This is known as "totting".)

Absolute or conditional discharge.   To impose an absolute or conditional discharge the court must be satisfied that no punishment is required. This may be due to the petty nature of the offence (particularly where it is a first offence) or to the nature of the defendant's circumstances. A conditional discharge is expressed to be conditional for a certain period—where the defendant commits an offence during that period they may be sentenced for the original offence. An absolute discharge is often given where the court finds that, although the defendant committed the offence, they are morally blameless.

LAWYERS

This section looks first at the types of lawyers who work within the jurisdiction and, secondly, at some particular lawyers who are of interest to the legal system in general and to media law in particular.

Barristers

The legal profession is traditionally thought of as being divided into two, with barristers doing the court work and solicitors doing everything else. Until 1990, barristers had exclusive rights of audience in all superior courts (the High Court, Crown Court, Court of Appeal and the then House of Lords). However, this monopoly is slowly being eroded by the increase in solicitors' rights of audience (see below).

The training of a barrister usually begins with a law degree, followed by a one-year vocational training course which takes place at the Inns of Court Law School in London or one of the designated Bar Vocational Course training centres. A trainee barrister must be a member of one of the four Inns of Court: Gray's Inn, Lincoln's Inn, Middle Temple or Inner Temple. During the vocational year each trainee barrister must frequent the Inn at which he is a member to learn the ways of the profession. This requirement is met by attending a number of dinners at the Inn's dining room. Upon completion of the vocational training course the student will be "called to the Bar" and must undergo a period of pupillage for a term of 12 months, during which they must spend a good deal of time watching and learning from another barrister (called a "pupil master").

The professional body to which all barristers belong is the Bar Council. There are approximately 12,000 practising barristers in England and Wales. Around two-thirds of these work in London, the remainder in various trial centres around the country such as Leeds and Norwich.

A senior barrister (one of at least 10 years' standing) may be invited by the Queen's Counsel Selection Panel to become a Queen's Counsel. This is known as "taking silk", named after the material used in making the robe that the barrister thereby becomes entitled to wear. A Queen's Counsel can be recognised by their use of the letters "QC" after their name. There are around 1300 QCs in England and Wales.

Members of the public are now permitted to consult a barrister directly, following the coming into force of the Public Access Rules in July 2004. It is usual, however, for the former practice to be followed, of a client's solicitor instructing the barrister, and attending meetings (called "conferences") with the barrister.

Solicitors

There are over 108,000 practising solicitors in England and Wales. For professional purposes they usually group together in solicitors' firms, of which there are approximately 10,000. Solicitors engage in a great variety of legal work from buying and selling houses (conveyancing) to drafting wills and defending persons accused of a criminal offence. Solicitors have long been able to attend the Magistrates' Court and the County Court to represent a client. Following pressure from the Law Society, the solicitors' professional body, Parliament ended the barristers' monopoly on rights of audience in the higher courts in the Courts and Legal Services Act 1990. Solicitors may now, in certain circumstances, be granted audience rights in the higher courts.

The training of a solicitor usually consists of a law degree followed by a one-year vocational course called the Legal Practice Course. Following successful completion of the Legal Practice Course, the student must undergo a two-year period of employment with a firm of solicitors under a "training contract", following which the trainee may be called a solicitor and will be admitted to the Roll of Solicitors maintained by the Law Society.

Legal executives

A legal executive is a junior form of lawyer who can be found working in the offices of solicitors. Legal executives are members of the Institute of Legal Executives which regulates their conduct. They are involved in most forms of legal work but do not have any rights of audience in court. They can, however, make interim applications (see Glossary) in chambers.

In order to become a legal executive one must undergo a four-year training course which can be undertaken part-time or by distance learning while employed in a solicitors' firm. The minimum entry requirements to undertake such a course is normally four GCSEs—there is no such requirement for a mature student. Upon satisfactory completion of the examinations, a trainee legal executive becomes a Member of the Institute of Legal Executives. Five years' experience working in a solicitors' practice entitles a Member to be called a Fellow of the Institute of Legal Executives, a title which carries with it certain privileges such as the ability to witness the swearing of affidavits.

Many legal executives go on to qualify as solicitors by taking the one-year Legal Practice Course. In most cases, a legal executive who passes the LPC will be exempt from the need to undertake a training contract.

Lord Chancellor

The role of Lord Chancellor has existed for hundreds of years, surviving attempts at abolition which were announced in June 2003. The Constitutional Reform Act 2005 left the role in existence but in modified form, coupling the post with that of Secretary of State for Constitutional Affairs. The latter post was renamed in 2007 and is now that of Secretary of State for Justice. The Lord Chancellor is no longer head of the judiciary and Speaker of the House of Lords (removing in some measure the traditional overlap between the three branches of government, namely the executive, legislative and judicial functions, generally considered undesirable in a modern democracy). The Lord Chancellor's duties include advising the Queen on the appointment of members of the judiciary from amongst the ranks of barristers and, to a more limited extent, solicitors, and dealing with constitutional issues. Further detail is available from the Ministry of Justice website (*http://www.justice.gov.uk*).

Crown Prosecution Service (CPS)

The CPS was created by the Prosecution of Offences Act 1985 to undertake criminal prosecutions. The CPS employs solicitors and barristers who are specialists in criminal law and procedure to conduct prosecutions and carry out other court functions (such as making an application for bail to be withheld) in the criminal courts. The CPS also unusually employs non-legally qualified people to present simple guilty pleas in the Magistrates' Courts. These "lay presenters" have limited rights of audience and are known as Designated Case Workers. Where a criminal trial is to take place in the Crown Court, the CPS may instruct counsel to act on its behalf. It has recently been suggested that the CPS may change its name to the Public Prosecution Service (PPS) to make its role more readily understandable to the general public and to bring its title into line with the Office of the Director of Public Prosecutions.

Director of Public Prosecutions (DPP)

The DPP is appointed by the Government to advise on matters of criminal law. Police chief constables should consult the DPP on such matters so as to achieve geographical consistency of application of the law.

The DPP is the head of the CPS and will take the decision whether to prosecute in the case of important or politically sensitive offences.

Attorney General

The Attorney General is the senior legal officer of the Government. He is appointed by the Prime Minister from among the ranks of MPs who were practising lawyers before their election to the House of Commons. The Attorney General represents the Crown in important legal cases, acting through the Treasury Solicitor's Department which he supervises. Certain prosecutions, for example for the offence of publishing jury deliberations under s.8 of the Contempt of Court Act 1981, cannot be undertaken without the consent of the Attorney General.

2. REPUTATION

INTRODUCTION

The history of the law of the media has featured a constant battle between, on the one hand, the desire—indeed, the right—of society to be fully informed of events and matters which are in the public interest and, on the other hand, the need for suitable remedies to be available where the media unwarrantably threaten or cause damage to reputation. (Another vital area of conflict, between the right to information and the right to personal privacy, has assumed acute importance in recent years—this is dealt with in Ch.4.)

Unlike the written constitution of the US (specifically the First Amendment guaranteeing freedom of speech as an unassailable right of the American people), there is no current provision of English law which guarantees such freedom. But the United Kingdom has a vigorous and competitive free press protected by the various legislative and common law defences which have arisen over time. The media is generally free to publish what it likes, but may of course find itself being sued for doing so and will then seek to rely on those defences. Since the coming into force of the Human Rights Act 1998 (HRA) on October 2, 2000, there is now enshrined in English law the qualified right to freedom of expression. The HRA gives effect to the European Convention on Human Rights (see Ch.1), art.10 of which provides that everyone has the right to freedom of expression. The media can now seek to rely on this right and the courts are bound to act in a way which upholds it. Section 12 of the HRA requires courts to have specific regard to the importance of this right when it considers a remedy which would affect journalistic, literary or artistic material. However, crucially the art.10 right is subject to a number of restrictions, such as conditions imposed by law in the interests of national security or public safety, for the prevention of disorder or crime, and (relevant to this chapter) restrictions "for the protection of the reputation or rights of others."

The media's freedom of publication must be seen in the light of the individual's right to redress for damage caused to his or her reputation.

A person's reputation is protected by the action known as defamation. A related, but less significant, action is that of malicious falsehood. This chapter considers both defamation and malicious falsehood in some detail.

DEFAMATION

All communicators must be aware of the tort of defamation. The threat of such an action is probably the most serious curb to media freedom in this country. Those working in the media must be alert to the risk of defamation at every stage of the publishing or broadcasting process.

Several factors make the risk of a defamation action a particularly serious influence on the media.

It is possible (see further below) to commit the tort even where one is unaware that a person's reputation is affected by the communication in question. Every person in the chain of communication may be sued for damages by the claimant. If a journalist writes a defamatory article, not only is the journalist at risk of being sued but so is the newspaper company which publishes the article, the editor of the newspaper, the proprietor of the newspaper and even, in theory if not in practice, the newsagent shop where the newspaper is sold.

Libel proceedings present a very significant financial commitment for even wealthy media organisations (likewise of course for privately-funded claimants). The costs involved in defending a full-scale libel action may be prohibitive, commonly running into hundreds of thousands of pounds (see below for further details). It is true that the successful defendant will often be awarded a significant percentage of their costs. However, the money for the defence must still be found as the case progresses and there is no guarantee, even where the judge orders the defendant's costs to be paid by the claimant, that the claimant will be in a position to pay.

In the event of losing, the amount of money that a media organisation will have to pay by way of damages and costs to a successful claimant may be very large indeed, even though the very large damages awards of the 1980s seem to be a thing of the past. With guidance from the Court of Appeal, juries have been persuaded to award claimants more sensible sums, but of course, a defendant who loses at trial will usually be ordered to pay the claimant's legal costs, in addition to funding their own. As damages have become more moderate, costs have risen, and as the first decade of the 21st century comes to an end, debate is focusing very much on the lack of proportionality as far as libel costs are concerned.

The financial consequences for media defendants have been exacerbated in recent years by the introduction of conditional fee agreements (CFAs, commonly called "no win, no fee" agreements) between claimants and their solicitors which permit a successful claimant's lawyers to recover a "bonus" of up to 100 per cent of their fees as a "success fee" in addition to their base costs in the event of winning at trial. This sum is ultimately paid by the unsuccessful media defendant, together with the premium (often a hefty five or even six figure sum) for the litigation insurance that many CFA-backed claimants and their solicitors are able to secure.

The way in which CFAs have been used by certain firms of solicitors acting for claimants has been the subject of considerable controversy in the media industry, alarm being caused by a tendency for them to be less a way of giving the impecunious access to justice, and more a tactical weapon to deter the media from seeking to defend libel actions.

The courts have the power to regulate costs by imposing orders capping costs, but it can be a complicated procedure and is regarded as an exceptional measure.

The whole area of libel costs has recently been the focus of intense scrutiny by various official bodies. During 2009, the House of Commons Culture, Media and Sport Select Committee conducted a detailed enquiry into "Press Standards, Privacy and Libel" in which issues of libel costs featured heavily. At the same time, Lord Justice Jackson spent 2009 conducting a review of Civil Litigation costs as a whole, and among his proposals was the abolition of recovery of insurance premiums and success fees from unsuccessful defendants. It remains to be seen if these proposals will be acted upon by the new parliament elected in the May 2010 General Election.

Furthermore, early in 2009 the Government issued a consultation paper (CP4/09, published February 24, 2009) suggesting measures for the application of more stringent limits on costs in libel litigation by means of fixed rates of charging, mandatory capping of overall costs to ensure proportionality, and more transparency as regards CFAs and litigation insurance premiums. This led to the introduction of a pilot scheme in the High Court in London and Manchester from October 2009 to September 2010, the "Defamation Proceedings Costs Management Scheme", making provision for "costs management based on the submission of detailed estimates of future base costs. The objective is to manage the litigation so that the costs of each party are proportionate to the value of the claim and the reputational issues at stake and so that the parties are on an equal footing".

The best advice for the media would obviously appear to be to avoid making defamatory statements which might lead to a successful action. This is not to say that the media should never publish matter that is defamatory, for to do so would instantly prohibit vast tracts of our current reading and listening material. Much defamatory matter is printed or broadcast on a daily basis, with the publishers being safe in the knowledge that one of the many defences to an action in defamation would be likely to apply to any action by a would-be claimant, which would normally deter any libel action. There is always a chance, however, that the would-be claimant, if he or she (or it—companies can sue for libel) can afford to do so, might try and use the libel law to suppress criticism by launching an unmeritorious claim which the defendant cannot afford to fight. There have been examples of this over the years (the late Robert Maxwell was a notorious instance), and 2009 saw the launch of a campaign by freedom of speech groups in the UK for a wholesale reform of the libel law (see website *http://www.libelreform.org*). One of the arguments used by the campaign is that even where would-be publishers are confident of their case, fear of the crippling costs of a libel claim by a well-resourced claimant will give them no option but to dilute what they wish to say, or not publish at all. This argument reflects the loud protest in the US about the perceived contradiction between English libel law and the First Amendment of the US constitution, resulting in several states (including New York and California) enacting legislation to bar the enforcement of English libel judgments there.

It remains to be seen whether the law-makers in this country will take steps to address what the reformers refer to as the 'chilling effect' of English libel law on freedom of speech. Taking the law as it now stands, the following section looks at the types of publications that will amount to defamation and considers the defences that may potentially be available to publishers of defamatory material.

Definition

Defamation is a cause of action which seems incapable of precise definition. Many judges in many cases have offered definitions, only to be criticised later by other judges or by academics. In 1975, the Faulks Committee on defamation (Cmnd.5909 (1975)) recommended the following definition:

"The publication to a third party of matter which in all the circumstances would be likely to affect a person adversely in the estimation of reasonable people generally."

Whatever definition is used the following principles are certainly true:

1. the statement which is alleged to be defamatory must be made to someone other than the claimant—it will not be defamation to call someone a thief and a liar if no one else hears the conversation;

2. the claimant must be alive—it is not possible to defame the deceased;

3. the statement must be in a form of words which tend to do one or more of the following:

   - lower the claimant in the estimation of normal right-thinking people;
   - expose the claimant to hatred, contempt or ridicule; or
   - cause the claimant to be shunned or avoided.

The first of the categories under principle 3 above is by far the most common. The claimant will be lowered in the estimation of right-thinking people where the ordinary reader or viewer would think less of them after reading or hearing the publication in question.

The second and third categories were considered in the case of *Berkoff v Burchill* [1997] E.M.L.R. 139. The defendant, a journalist and film critic, wrote an article in *The Sunday Times* on the following lines:

"Film directors from Hitchcock to Berkoff are notoriously hideous-looking people."

A further article stated that the creature in the film Mary Shelley's Frankenstein was: "a lot like Stephen Berkoff, only marginally better-looking."

On an application for a determination as to whether the words used were capable of being defamatory, the Court of Appeal held that although a statement that a person was hideously ugly was clearly subjective and therefore could not lead to that person being shunned or avoided, the words could expose the claimant to ridicule and therefore could be defamatory.

In *Norman v Future Publishing Ltd* Unreported November 19, 1998 CA (Civ Div) Jessye Norman, the internationally renowned American opera singer, tried to take the *Berkoff* case a stage further when she complained of an article which appeared in the November 1994 edition of *Classic CD* maga- zine. The particular passage that was the subject of her complaint read as follows:

> "While her Salome is released this month on Philips, it is still hard to envisage the grand, statuesque 49-year-old as the libidinous adolescent on stage stripping off the seven veils. This is the woman who got trapped in swing doors on her way to a concert, and when advised to release herself by turning sideways replied: 'Honey, I ain't got no sideways'."

Ms Norman stated that the words meant that she had used a mode of speech which was vulgar and undignified and which conformed to a degrading racist stereotype of a person of African-American heritage. On a preliminary application for a determination as to whether the words used were capable of being defamatory, the Court of Appeal was not prepared to "strip society and journalism of all humour" and found that the words could not have the meaning attributed to them by the claimant.

However, it must be borne in mind that:

- an imputation may be defamatory even where it is true (although this will provide a defence to an action); and

- an imputation is not necessarily defamatory where it is untrue.

EXAMPLE 1
An item on the 10 o'clock news reports that an MP has lied to his con- stituents. The MP will have a cause of action in defamation against the journalist and the broadcaster—his reputation will have been lowered in the thoughts of reasonable people. The statement may be true but will still be defamatory (the journalist and broadcaster may, however, be able to use the defence of justification—see below).

EXAMPLE 2
A magazine article states that a famous pop star is too ill to perform at his next concert and may not ever be able to make another live appearance. This is not defamation even where the statement is untrue. It does not lower the estimation of the pop star in the minds of reasonable people (it is clearly not defamatory to suggest that a person is ill—although there may be an action in malicious falsehood).

Trial by judge and jury

Defamation is a civil action but it differs from other civil actions in one important way: there is still a presumption (under s.69 of the Supreme Court Act 1981) that a jury rather than a judge will decide who wins the case. If they find that the claimant wins, the jury will go on to decide the amount of compensation that should be paid.

However, the right to jury trial is qualified under s.69 in cases involving any prolonged examination of documents, accounts or any scientific or local investigation which cannot conveniently be made with a jury.

In *Beta Construction Ltd v Channel Four TV Co Ltd* [1990] 2 All E.R. 1012, the defendants had admitted liability in a libel action and the only issue that remained to be tried was that relating to quantum of damages. The claimant wanted damages to be assessed by a jury while the defendant applied for trial by judge alone. The Court of Appeal, upholding the first instance decision that damages should be quantified by judge alone, stated that the question as to whether a libel action involving prolonged examination of documents or accounts should properly be tried by a jury depends upon a consideration of such factors as:

(a) the extent to which the presence of a jury might add to the length of the trial;

(b) the extent to which the presence of a jury might add to the cost of the trial by reason of its increased length and the necessity of photocopying a multitude of documents for use by the jury;

(c) any practical difficulties which a jury trial might cause, such as the physical problem of handling in the confines of a jury box large bundles of bulky documents; and

(d) any special complexities in the documents or accounts which might lead a jury to misunderstand the issues in the case.

It should be noted that there is a trend on the part of the "jury list" judges to be more and more open to applications by the parties to libel cases for trial by judge alone on the grounds that jury trials are inevitably longer and more expensive and best avoided if possible. Further, the parties may consent to trial by judge alone. The availability of a reasoned judgment will mean that (notwithstanding the tendency of damages awards by judges to be lower than those by juries), parties are more likely to consent to trial without a jury in cases where it is a point of principle that is at stake rather than a desire to obtain damages.

Libel or slander?

There are two forms of defamation in English law: libel and slander. Libel is defamation in a permanent form, for example writing. Slander is defamation in a transitory form, for example speech. For some years it was not certain whether defamatory matter contained in television and radio broadcasts would be libel or slander. The Broadcasting Act 1990 made the position clear: any broadcast material will be subject to an action in libel. Theatre productions are defamation in a permanent form (Theatres Act 1968). Films are subject to libel actions and the same will apply to video and to publication of words or pictures on the internet and hence defamatory statements conveyed by those media will (in the same way as material contained in printed matter such as books, newspapers and magazines) be subject to a libel action.

It is clear then that, for the purposes of media law, we will be concerned only with libel. All forms of publication and broadcast are in a permanent form.

The legal distinction between libel and slander is important because a claimant who brings a libel action does not have to prove that he or she has suffered any loss or injury as a result of the statement—in legal terminology libel is said to be actionable per se—and damage is presumed to have occurred.

By contrast, the basic position with slander (resulting from the more transitory nature of the allegations involved) is that in order to succeed in an action for slander, a claimant must allege and prove actual material loss as a result of the defamatory statement.

For the sake of completeness, it is worth noting that this rule does not apply where certain serious allegations are involved: e.g. a slander action concerning

(a) imputations of criminal conduct punishable by imprisonment;

(b) imputations of a contagious or infectious disease;

(c) imputations of sexual immorality; or

(d) imputations injurious to another's official, professional or business reputation (the most widely invoked in practice),

can be brought without proving actual damage i.e. like a libel case, those slanders are actionable per se.

Publication

For a libel to be actionable (i.e. for the claimant to be able to sue the defendant), it must be communicated to a third party, i.e. some person other than the claimant. A strange rule provides that communication of a defamatory statement between a defendant and his or her spouse is not publication (although there will be publication where there is communication to the claimant's spouse).

As will be examined later in Ch.9, a refinement to this basic rule has been developed, arising out of a claim over an alleged libel on the internet: the Court of Appeal decision in *Jameel v Dow Jones & Co Inc* [2005] EWCA Civ 75 established that where publication is not "substantial" (e.g. only a handful of internet 'hits'), the court may exercise its discretion to strike out a claim as an abuse of the process. In that case, the evidence showed that there had been really trivial publication in England—just five hits on a website, three of which were by associates of the claimant. In the words of Lord Phillips M.R. giving the Court of Appeal's judgment:

"It would be an abuse of process to continue to commit the resources of the English court, including substantial judge and possibly jury time, to an action where so little is now seen to be at stake. The game will not merely not have been worth the candle, it will not have been worth the wick."

Note that all the circumstances will be taken into account in determining "substantiality". The number of publications is not the sole criterion but it will be an important factor when a foreign claimant seeks to use the English court to sue a foreign publication.

The *Jameel* principle is clarified by two 2009 slander cases, which highlight what constitutes "substantiality". In *Noorani v Calver (No.1)* [2009] EWHC 561 (QB) a libel claim over a letter published by the defendant to council members of the local Conservative Association was accompanied by a slander claim because the claimant alleged that his wife and daughter had been told by the defendant verbally that he (the claimant) was an "Islamic terrorist". The judge held that this allegation was more than mere abuse and was actionable per se (under category (a) above). However, with no evidence at all that these particular publishees had thought worse of the claimant, the tort was not a real and substantial one, and the slander claim was struck out as an abuse on *Jameel* principles.

In *Sanders v Percy & Ministry of Justice* [2009] EWHC 1870, the claimant sued a County Court official and the Ministry of Justice for slander (among other things), over a telephone conversation between the official and the claimant's solicitor in connection with some other case. There was no proof of any specific loss to the claimant. Sanders claimed that the official had made a number of allegations, including:

- that he had committed benefit fraud;
- that he was a chancer and a vexatious litigant;
- that he drove an untaxed car; and
- that he worked as an Ali G impersonator but bore no resemblance to Ali G.

Should the claim be struck out because the allegations were not in categories (a) to (d) above, and there was no proof of specific loss? And if not, should it be struck out under the *Jameel* rule? The judge decided that the only element of the slander claim which could go ahead was the benefit fraud allegation. It came under category (a) and was sufficiently serious to stand under *Jameel* principles (even though the words had only been heard by one person). The other allegations failed to come within categories (a)–(d), except for the Ali G allegation which did tend to injure his 'professional' reputation (category (d)). But the judge struck out the "Ali G" claim following the rationale of *Jameel*, because it was not a serious allegation, and the recipient, the solicitor, would not be affected by this slight on the claimant's professional capabilities. (It might have been different had the call been to the claimant's agent, or someone thinking of booking an Ali G impersonator).

So the *Jameel* test is not simply one about how many people have received the defamatory allegations—it could be just one recipient, if the allegation is serious enough in all the circumstances to warrant legal action.

A person will be liable for any publication which:

- they intend;
- they can reasonably anticipate; or

- where there is unintentional publication, it is published due to a want of care on their part.

EXAMPLE 1

A person carrying a defamatory placard at a demonstration that he knew was being televised will be liable not only for his own publication but may also be liable for the broadcast depicting the placard.

EXAMPLE 2

A person sending a fax to Sasha's place of business will be liable for any matter defamatory of Sasha contained therein which is read by the fax operator and other employees at Sasha's place of work.

The latter scenario formed part of the issues in *Cray v Hancock* Unreported, November 4, 2005 EWHC (QBD). The claimant was a solicitor, who was on the receiving end of a campaign of complaints by two disgruntled clients, Mr and Mrs Hancock, who (among many other things) sent a letter and two faxes to the claimant's firm where they were seen by three of his colleagues. It was found that the correspondence was sent with no restriction as to who could read it, and that the defendants were therefore liable to the claimant for the publication to the claimant's colleagues of the libels which the correspondence contained.

To take another example from case law, in *Slipper v BBC* [1990] All E.R. 165, the BBC was potentially held to be responsible by the Court of Appeal not only for its own broadcast, but also for published reviews of the programme appearing in daily newspapers. The claimant was held to be entitled to claim additional general damages from the BBC in respect of the newspaper reviews. The commercial publishing process may frequently involve a series of publications: each repetition will be treated as a fresh publication creating a new cause of action in defamation. For example, a journalist who writes a newspaper article about the speech of a politician may be sued in respect of any defamatory matter contained in the speech which he reproduces. Similarly the editor, sub-editor, printer, distributor and retail seller of the newspaper (as well as the politician!) may be sued— the printer, distributor and newsagent may, however, be able to use the defence of innocent dissemination contained in s.1 of the Defamation Act 1996 (see below).

In the modern communications era, this situation is a particular problem for internet service providers and other operators of communication systems who may be liable for defamatory material communicated using their systems. The huge rise in the use of the internet for blogging and social networking, through sites such as Facebook and Twitter, and the "user-generated content" ("UGC") that this produces, makes this issue ever more important. The providers and operators of such sites will, in most cases, be unaware of any defamatory material—in the same way that telecoms providers are unaware of the content of telephone conversations which take place using its lines. The defence in s.1 of the 1996 Act will be available to such an "operator of or provider of access to a communications system" in certain circumstances—above all, in the absence of any notification that there is defamatory material on a site. They may lose that protection if they receive such notification and fail to react (although it has recently been decided that this proviso does not apply to, for example, Google, in relation to defamatory material in search results generated by its search engine technology—see Ch.9 for further detail about defamation and the internet).

Words must be defamatory

The words used must be capable of bearing a defamatory meaning. The jury should consider the natural and ordinary meaning that the words would have to the "ordinary, reasonable and fair minded-reader". Such a reader, said one judge, is not unduly suspicious but nor are they unduly naive. They can and do read between the lines. They can read an implication more readily than a lawyer, and may indulge in a certain amount of loose thinking. But they must be treated as a person who is not avid for scandal and someone who does not, and should not, select one bad meaning where non-defamatory meanings are available (Neill L.J. in *Hartt v Newspaper Publishing Plc, The Times*, November 9, 1989).

It should be noted that what the ordinary, reasonable and fair-minded reader regards as defamatory may change from time to time. For example, it was at one time defamatory to call someone a "German", i.e. during both World Wars and the tendency, at that time, to denigrate Germans (*Slazengers Ltd v Gibbs & Co* (1916) 33 T.L.R. 35). Further, the meaning of words may change over time. To call someone "gay" 30 years ago meant that the person being described was happy or carefree. Today a different meaning is common and calling someone gay could well be defamatory in certain circumstances (*Donovan v Logan* Unreported April 1991—although not actually deciding whether alleging gayness is defamatory per se) produced a successful outcome for Jason Donovan who claimed that calling him gay was defamatory because he had always held himself out as being heterosexual—the statement therefore meant that he was dishonest).

In *Lewis v Daily Telegraph Ltd* [1963] 2 All E.R. 151, the claimant claimed damages for libel as a result of an article appearing on the front page of *The Daily Telegraph*:

"INQUIRY ON FIRM BY CITY POLICE Officers of the City of London Fraud Squad are inquiring into the affairs of Rubber Improvement Ltd and its subsidiary companies. The investigation was requested after criticisms of the chairman's statement and the accounts by a shareholder at the recent company meeting. The chairman of the Company, which has an authorised share capital of £1 million, is Mr John Lewis, a former socialist MP for Bolton."

The claimant argued that the words used meant that the firm was actually guilty of fraud or was suspected by police of being guilty of fraud and that any statement which described police investigations into a person was usually defamatory of that person. The defendants admitted the article could be defamatory, but only to the extent that it meant there was a police investigation and that this did not suggest actual guilt to the ordinary reader. The House of Lords thought the ordinary man would not necessarily infer fraud by the mere existence of an inquiry. One paragraph of the judgment provides an analysis of who the ordinary reader might be:

"The ordinary man does not live in an ivory tower and he is not inhibited by a knowledge of the rules of construction. So he can and does read between the lines in the light of his general knowledge and his experience of worldly affairs. Ordinary men and women have different temperaments and outlooks. Some are unusually suspicious and some are unusually naive. One must try to envisage people between these two extremes and see what is the most damaging meaning that they would put on the words in question."

The meaning to be attributed to an article may thus be extremely complex and must in each case be decided solely on the basis of the words used. The question of imputation of guilt of offences by reference to police investigations into an individual's conduct is one of the most hazardous areas for the media.

The courts have identified that such a story may carry one of the following three tiers of meaning:

(a) that an individual is guilty of criminal conduct (the most serious meaning);

(b) that there are reasonable grounds to suspect that an individual is guilty of criminal conduct; or

(c) that there are grounds merely for an investigation into whether there has been criminal conduct (the least serious meaning).

Since the case of *Chase v News Group Newspapers* [2003] E.M.L.R.11, the current terminology is to refer to these meanings as *Chase* Levels 1, 2 and 3 respectively.

It can be seen that the differences between these Levels are subtle. Indeed in *Charman v Orion Publishing (No.2)* [2005] EWHC 2197, Gray J. (having ordered that he should try the issue of meaning himself as a preliminary issue) seemed to introduce an intermediate Level, somewhere between *Chase* Levels 1 and 2, of "cogent grounds" to suspect an individual. However Eady J. has subsequently (in *Armstrong v Times Newspapers* [2005] EWHC 2816) expressed doubt as to whether there is any difference between "cogent" and "reasonable". This serves to indicate the difficulty of this area at the moment.

However, these distinctions will be important for a newspaper that is seeking to prove the truth of its story, as a great deal more evidence will be required in court to prove the truth of a *Chase* Level 1 meaning over a *Chase* Level 2 meaning. In *Jameel v Wall Street Journal* [2004] EWHC Civ 37, the claimants brought an action over an article headlined "Saudi Officials Monitor Certain Bank Accounts" and "Focus is on those with Potential Terrorist Ties". The article said that bank accounts belonging to the claimants were being monitored "in a bid to prevent them from being used wittingly or unwittingly for the funnelling of funds to terrorist organisations". The jury held that this was defamatory and that it meant that the claimants were possibly involved in funnelling funds to terrorists. Journalists should therefore be alert to this danger when reporting on crime. However, fortunately for the *Wall Street Journal*, the trial judge's ruling that the privilege defence known as the *Reynolds* defence did not protect them was overturned by the House of Lords in 2006—highlighting the value for journalists of ensuring wherever possible that another defence, such as qualified privilege, may be available to them, to mitigate the dangers and difficulties of having to prove the truth of *Chase* Level 1 or 2 meanings (see further below on *Reynolds*).

Those dangers were underlined in *Fallon v Mirror Group (No.2)* [2006] EWHC 783, where the defendant (which had published an article about a police investigation into race-fixing) had pleaded a defence to *Chase* Levels 2 and 3 meanings. Eady J. ruled that their statement of case was defective: the article could not bear a Level 3 meaning, and the defence did not support a Level 2 meaning.

As far as a television broadcast is concerned, the Court of Appeal has laid down the principle that the court should give to the material complained of the natural and ordinary meaning which it would have conveyed to the ordinary reasonable viewer watching the programme once. Such was the judgment of Neill L.J. in *Gillick v BBC* [1996] E.M.L.R. 267. The case concerned the broadcast of a live television programme on the 25th anniversary of the opening of the first Brook Advisory Centre. Mrs Gillick, who had previously fought a lengthy court battle to restrict a GP's right to offer contraceptives to girls under 16, appeared in the programme and was questioned by the presenter in the following terms: "But after you won that battle there were at least two reported cases of suicide by girls who were pregnant." Mrs Gillick alleged that the words meant that she had caused or was morally responsible for the deaths of at least two young girls. On the preliminary issue of whether the words were capable of bearing a defamatory meaning, the Court of Appeal held that they were so capable. Neill L.J. said that within the spectrum of meanings of which the words were reasonably capable was the meaning alleged by the claimant.

The broadcast media should thus be aware that the meaning which may be attached to words and phrases by viewers sitting comfortably at home and who are not necessarily focusing their whole attention on the television may be somewhat different from the meaning which they would attach to similar words appearing in a newspaper.

If the publication is in the form of an article, the claimant must show that the statement is defamatory in the context of the article as a whole. The case of *Charleston v News Group Newspapers Ltd, The Times*, March 31, 1995 involved the early *Neighbours* characters Harold and Madge. The two actors, Ian Smith and Anne Charleston, sued the *News of the World* because of an article which contained the following headline: "Strewth! What's Harold up to with our Madge?" Immediately beneath the headline was a large photograph of a naked man and woman engaged in a sexual act. The faces of the man and woman were those of the claimants. Beneath the photograph the article went on to describe a new computer game in which the faces of soap stars were superimposed over the bodies of others. The claimants accepted that no defamatory meaning could be conveyed by the article as a whole but contended that it was legitimate to identify a group of readers who read only part of a publication, i.e. the headline and photograph alone, the point being that some readers of the newspaper would look at the headline and photograph (which were clearly defamatory on their own) without reading the small print beneath. The House of Lords, somewhat surprisingly, held that it was not possible to divide the readership of a publication into different groups for the purposes of deciding what was defamatory: the article must be read as a whole. The claimants thus lost their case.

There has been some question as to whether this rule ought to be reviewed in the light of the growth of the internet in the fifteen years since *Charleston* was decided. Headlines, introductory paragraphs, photos and photo captions assume greater prominence on news websites where people surf and read webpages without necessarily clicking through to the full article. However, the rationale of *Charleston* continues to govern the approach of the court: for instance, in *Monks v Warwick District Council* [2009] EWHC 959 (QB), the claimant sought to sue in respect of an extract from an email published in a newspaper. That claim was struck out by the judge on the basis that the claimant was not permitted to select passages of an article to assert a defamatory meaning which, taken as a whole, the article did not bear.

Innuendo

Often the words used by the defendant will appear innocent in themselves, but have a hidden meaning which would be recognised in light of other facts. In these cases, the claimant will try to show that in their particular case the ordinary, reasonable and fair-minded reader ought to be endowed with some special knowledge. They will need to show this where the words complained of are not defamatory in themselves, but become defamatory in the light of certain facts known to certain people. This is known as true innuendo and is a separate cause of action (which can be made on its own or in addition to an action based on the natural meaning of the words) for which separate damages should be awarded.

In *Tolley v Fry & Sons Ltd* [1931] All E.R. 131, the claimant, an amateur golfer, was depicted in an advertisement for the defendant's chocolate. He successfully showed that certain people familiar with the golfing world would think that he had been paid for the advertisement and that therefore he had prostituted his amateur status, even though on the face of it, there was nothing defamatory about the advert itself. In cases of true innuendo it is essential for the claimant to show as part of their case against the defendant that the statement was published to persons who had the special knowledge that they are relying on.

The operation of the rule on innuendo was considered by Eady J. in the summer of 2009 in *Johnson v MGN Ltd* [2009] EWHC 1481 (QB). The claimant was the footballer Glen Johnson: an article in "The People" had alleged that he had missed his side Portsmouth's Boxing Day match against West Ham, not for the reported reason of injury, but because in fact he had already signed to play for Liverpool. Johnson claimed that the natural and ordinary meaning of the article was that he had lied about the real reason for missing the match; and that by innuendo it also meant he had breached Premier League Rules concerning contact with other clubs during the currency of a player contract. There was no suggestion that what had been printed in the paper was true, but the defendant applied for a ruling that the article could not bear the alleged meanings. Its application failed. Eady J. ruled that innuendo meaning should remain, even though the number of readers who would have the requisite special knowledge was "very small indeed". He also allowed the natural and ordinary meaning to stand, as the wording in the article was ambiguous and allowance should be made in favour of the claimant because it could not be said that *no* reader would have understood them in the meaning claimed.

So-called "false innuendo" arises where the claimant alleges that the words in themselves bear a particular meaning (usually in addition to their plain and ordinary meaning) which is discernible without the need for additional evidence. In other words, a false innuendo is simply an inference that can be drawn from the statement as it stands, i.e. from the words themselves which is the usual meaning of an "innuendo". The court will look at what the "ordinary reader" would have understood by the words complained of.

EXAMPLE

An article in *Slap Magazine* states that a particular MP "must have been telling the truth because, as we all know, MPs always tell the truth". The words themselves are not defamatory on the face of them. It is not defamatory to say of a person that she is honest. But the article is written in such a way as to suggest that the MP concerned is lying. This is an example of false innuendo.

Words must refer to the claimant

The claimant must show that the words were published of and concerning them. It will be no defence that the claimant is not referred to by name if they would be capable of being identified by the reasonable person. Thus it will be libel to broadcast a defamatory statement about "the MP for Canterbury" or "the President of the Royal Television Society".

The words used may be taken to refer to the claimant where they are mentioned by name, even if the defendant did not intend to refer to the claimant. In one case (*Hulton v Jones* [1910] All E.R. 29), a newspaper carried a humorous account of the events at a motor festival in Dieppe, casting doubt on the moral standing of one Artemus Jones, a churchwarden from Peckham: "There is Artemus Jones with a woman who is not his wife, who must be, you know—the other thing...". A barrister by the name of Artemus Jones was successful in his action against the newspaper despite the fact that he was not a churchwarden, had not been in Dieppe and was not from Peckham.

The usual disclaimer at the end of films (e.g. "this work is entirely fictitious and any similarity between the characters and any other person is entirely coincidental") will not protect the producers if viewers can identify the claimant from the work. The use of the phrase is just one factor that the jury may look at in determining whether the work, taken as a whole, is defamatory.

The defendant may be liable where the statement is true of one person but defamatory of someone else with the same name. For this reason great care must be taken by journalists when reporting proceedings in the criminal courts, particularly where the accused has a common name. In *Newstead v London Express Newspapers* [1940] 1 K.B. 377, the defendant published an article stating that Harold Newstead, a 30-year-old Camberwell man, had been convicted of bigamy. The claimant, a different Harold

Newstead, also of Camberwell and aged about 30, was successful in his libel action. Journalists should thus provide as much information as is reasonable to ensure that this problem does not arise.

Care must also be taken when publishing photographs that the correct photograph is used! In *Watts v Times Newspapers* [1996] 1 W.L.R. 427, an article in *The Sunday Times* accused Nigel Watts of plagiarism. It was mistakenly illustrated with a photograph of a different Nigel Watts who was an artist. Nigel Watts, the artist, was successful in his allegation that many people who read the article would have understood it to refer to him. Note that a useful statutory defence now provides some protection for defendants where a mistake of this kind is made: see below, under "Offer of amends".

In general, the test for identification is whether reasonable readers generally, or a reasonable reader with specific knowledge, would understand the statement to refer to the claimant. Identification may additionally arise from publication of a photograph (as in the *Watts* case above), nickname or physical description of the claimant.

Defamation of a "class"

There cannot be a successful action for defamation of a class (or group) of persons unless the claimant, as an individual, can be identified. This will largely depend upon the size of the relevant class and the nature of the allegation. The narrower the class and the more specific the allegation, the more likely it is that readers could reasonably take it to refer to each member of the group. For example, to say of the readers of the book *Media Law* that they cheat at exams is not defamatory as no individual reader can be identified from the statement. To say it of students in a particular seminar group at a particular university would be actionable because it would be likely that the right-minded reader would believe that the statement reflected on the integrity of the individual claimant, i.e. everyone in the group.

In *Aiken v Police Review Publishing Co Ltd* Unreported April 12, 1995 CA (Civ Div) the Court of Appeal had to consider the application of the defendant to have the action struck out (terminated) on the ground that "the claimants would not have been identifiable to readers of the words complained of as the individuals to whom the said words were directed". The case concerned an article in the *Police Review* magazine published under the headline "Nazi 'humour' forces Jewish PC to quit" and alleged anti-semitism among some of the officer's colleagues. The officer worked as a dog handler.

The 10 claimants were the long-serving dog handlers in Area 8 Dog Section (located at Hyde Park Police Station) of the Metropolitan Police Force who had all served with PC Nigel Brown at the relevant time. The evidence was that there were 60 officers at Hyde Park Police Station of whom up to 35 worked in the dog section. The judge said that it was not obvious that the words were incapable of referring to each or any of the individual claimants. The application to strike out therefore failed.

Defamation of an entity

An individual responsible for running a corporation may have a cause of action where there is a defamatory statement published of and concerning the corporation. The reasonable reader is capable of concluding that any negative allegation against a corporation will reflect badly on the person or persons who run it. In addition, the company itself may be able to sue in its own right, as a company has a legal personality and is therefore entitled to bring an action in the same way as an individual. However, a local authority or government department cannot sue for libel (*Derbyshire CC v Times Newspapers* [1993] 1 All E.R. 1011) as it is against the public interest for organisations of government to have such a right. Note though that such an organisation's individual officers or councillors may be defamed by an article about a council's actions and may sue in their own right.

Forum shopping

Cases involving claimants from abroad have been a particular feature of libel law in recent years. The rules on jurisdiction are complicated, but in a nutshell the position is as follows: as well as showing publication of the words complained of in the jurisdiction of the court (England and Wales), the claimant must also have a reputation within the jurisdiction which can be damaged by those words.

It may sometimes suit a foreign libel claimant to choose the English court, rather than the courts of their own country. For example, in the USA public figures face a very high hurdle of having to prove "actual malice" on the part of the publisher before they can sue for libel (as a result of the Supreme Court decision in *New York Times Co v Sullivan*, 376 U.S. 254 (1964))—bringing a claim if possible in the High Court in London is an attractive option.

The early years of the twenty-first century have seen the English courts being generally welcoming to such claims. The most publicised example of this trend was probably Roman Polanski's successful libel action against the American magazine *Vanity Fair*. The claimant was resident in France (but of course had an international reputation as a film director) and the defendant was based in New York (but 55,000 copies of its magazine were published in England and Wales). The jurisdiction of the English court was clear. However, the most remarkable feature of the case was that the claimant declined even to set foot in England to attend and give evidence at the trial, due to the danger of arrest and extradition to the USA (whence he had fled to France in the late 1970s) on charges of having unlawful sex with an underage girl. The House of Lords granted him permission to give his evidence by video link from Paris, on the basis that there is no rule of law which justifies depriving a fugitive from justice of the opportunity to enforce his legal rights through the English courts (*Polanski v Condé Nast* [2005] 1 W.L.R. 637). Polanski went on to secure a jury award of £50,000 damages in July 2005.

The jurisdiction issue often arises in relation to allegations on the internet (see further in the Ch.9) since if the website concerned is accessed in England, that constitutes sufficient publication. In *Don King v Lewis* [2005] E.M.L.R. 45, the well-known boxing promoter resident in Florida was allowed to sue a New York lawyer in this country over allegations on a California-based boxing website concerning legal proceedings in New York. This was because Mr King could show a reputation in England, having strong business connections here, and the website had been accessed in the jurisdiction of the English court.

The case of *Jameel v Dow Jones* referred to above, however, shows the court attempting to place some restriction on particularly tenuous cases by striking out an action as an abuse of process.

The Court of Appeal's decision in the summer of 2006 in the case of *Al-Koronky v Time Life* [2006] EWCA Civ 1123 showed an alternative form of protection from claimants from non-EU jurisdictions where a successful defendant might have trouble pursuing a claim for costs against the defeated claimant: in this case, the claimant was from the Sudan. The defendant had applied for an order that the claimant make a payment of security for costs, to be deposited in the court's account in London, before being allowed to pursue his action. Eady J. had applied the tests required to establish to what extent the defendants would find enforcing a claim for costs in the Sudan to be difficult or impossible, and the answer was clear from the resulting order that £375,000 should be paid by the claimant as security for costs. The Court of Appeal upheld his decision.

Defences

An understanding of the defences to a defamation action is crucial to all those engaged in the media business. Despite the "publish and be damned" philosophy which, though noble, can be very expensive, many defamatory statements would be unpublished were it not for the mind's eye view of a suitable defence to any potential action.

The principal defences used by media defendants are:

- justification (or truth);

- fair comment on a matter of public interest;

- privilege (absolute and qualified);

- innocent dissemination;

- offer of amends; and

- consent to publication.

Where the claimant is able to prove that the defendant acted maliciously (see below), the defendant will be unable to succeed in the defences of fair comment and qualified privilege.

Justification

It is a defence for the defendant to show that the allegation complained of is true. This is the case even where the words are published out of spite, purely for financial gain or for any other malicious motive.

Once the claimant shows that the statement is defamatory it is presumed, at that point, that the statement is not true. The defendant, to be successful in their defence of justification, must then prove:

- the truth or substantial truth (the so-called "sting") of each defamatory statement;

- the truth of any reasonable interpretation which may be understood of the words complained of; and

- the truth of any innuendoes lying behind the words.

Proof of this defence may be no easy task and many a defendant has backed down at some point in the litigation process even though they considered their statement to be true. It may be, for example, that the defendant is unable to bring enough admissible evidence to court to convince the jury of the truth of the statement. Therefore, even where the statement is true, the claimant may succeed in their defamation action.

The decision to plead the defence of justification will not be an easy one. The media defendant is not helped by the fact that the nature of jury trials makes their outcome impossible to predict. Further, an unsuccessful plea of justification will aggravate any damages awarded (due partly to the rigorous cross-examination to which the claimant will have been subject and partly to the necessary repetition of the libel by the defendant during the course of the trial).

The harshness of the rule that each and every allegation must be proved to succeed in the defence of justification is lessened somewhat by s.5 of the Defamation Act 1952:

"in an action for libel or slander in respect of words containing two or more distinct charges against the claimant, a defence of justification shall not fail by reason only that the truth of every charge is not proved, if the words not proved to be true do not materially injure the claimant's reputation, having regard to the truth of the remaining charges."

Thus, it may well be worth using the defence of justification not only where the statement contains defamatory material of a comparatively minor nature (where the sting is proved, such minor material may be effectively ignored), but also where there is defamatory matter present which, whilst incapable of proof, is of a less serious nature than that which can be justified.

EXAMPLE

A daily newspaper reports that Mr X is responsible for the murder of his wife and for never getting his children to school on time. Provided that the newspaper can prove that Mr X murdered his wife, s.5 will allow the defence of justification to be successful even where it cannot be proved that his children are always late for school.

Evidence of justification

Where the defendant pleads justification he must show that the statement that is alleged to be defamatory is in fact true. It is not enough to prove that many people believe the statement to be true. The meaning to be attributed to the words is crucial in this respect as the journalist will need evidence to prove the truth of the meaning the jury decides the words have. A defendant is required to set out what precise meaning it intends to prove is true in its defence document. Therefore, a whole string of witnesses who testify as to their belief in the words complained of, will not lead to the defendant being found not liable. The practical result for journalists is that they cannot assume they will not be sued merely because they preface their statement with the words, "Many people believe that...".

The proof of the truth of the statement complained of must be shown at trial by putting appropriate evidence before the court. In *McDonald's Corp v Steel*, *The Times*, April 14, 1994 (CA), the court considered the question of evidence of justification. The defendants had distributed leaflets, entitled "What's wrong with McDonald's?", setting out details of serious health risks associated with eating McDonald's food. McDonald's applied to have various parts of the defence of justification in the defence struck out. The High Court judge granted the application to strike out various passages on the basis that there was no evidence before the court supporting those passages. The Court of Appeal reversed this decision stating that it was perfectly proper for a defendant to plead particulars of justification which he was in anticipation of being able to prove at the date of the trial. It was inappropriate to strike out such particulars before trial unless it was clear at the time of the application for striking out that no other admissible evidence was ever going to be forthcoming.

The practical result of this decision is that before a plea of justification is included in a defence, the following criteria should normally be satisfied:

(a) the defendant should believe that the words complained of are true;

(b) the defendant should intend to support the defence of justification at trial; and

(c) the defendant should have:

    (i) reasonable evidence to support the defence; or
    (ii) reasonable grounds for supposing that sufficient evidence to prove the defence would be available at the trial.

It is clearly an inadvisable gamble for a journalist to try to defend an action in the mere hope that evidence of justification will be found before trial.

Evidence arising after publication

In *Moss v Channel Five Broadcasting Ltd* (February 3, 2006), Eady J. made clear that a defendant can rely on events which happen *after* the publication complained of and which fortuitously help bolster the justification defence.

The case had been brought by Kate Moss over a programme broadcast by the defendants in January 2005 which she complained alleged that in 2001 she had rendered herself comatose by excessive cocaine consumption. After she sued, the *Daily Mirror* ran articles about her cocaine abuse which led to Moss issuing a public apology for her conduct. The defendant duly relied as part of its defence of justification on the matters which the *Mirror* had reported and on the admission which seemed implicit in her public statement.

The claimant applied to strike this material out on the basis her complaint was about a specific incident in 2001, and that it would be wrong to allow justification of a more general charge.

The judge ruled that the defendants were allowed to justify the words in any meaning they were capable of bearing—here, the meaning which the defendants were justifying (that the claimant was "a serious cocaine abuser") was one that the words complained of (in context) were capable of bearing. Further, the defendants were allowed to rely on events subsequent to broadcast.

Contrast the situation with the defence of fair comment: the case of *Lowe* illustrates that, because the state of mind of the defendant is relevant to fair comment, events relied on to support that defence must pre-date publication and have been known to the defendant to some extent (see below).

Relevance of malice

Malice (proof that the defendant acted out of ill-will towards the claimant— see further below in fair comment) will generally be irrelevant to the defence of justification. If the statement was true it does not matter that it was published maliciously.

There is one exception to the rule that malice is irrelevant to the defence of justification: the Rehabilitation of Offenders Act 1974. This statute provides that certain previous criminal convictions become "spent" after the expiry of a certain number of years from the date of conviction. The number of years depends upon the punishment for the crime in question. The effect of a conviction being spent is that it should never be referred to in any court proceedings and ought not to be referred to in any communication. The Act states that a malicious motive will defeat the defence of justification in relation to the publication of details of such spent convictions.

Fair comment

It is clearly one of the necessary elements of a free society that the media should be able to comment without constraint on matters of public interest. The courts will give protection to such comment as long as it could arise from an honestly held belief. Newspapers tend to rely more frequently on the defence of fair comment than on justification. However, the complex nature of the defence makes it a potential minefield for journalists and their editors.

The defence of fair comment will attach to:

- a statement;

- in the form of opinion;

- which is based on true facts;

- on a matter of public interest; and

- without malice.

Opinion based on fact

The comment must be an expression of opinion, not a statement of fact. It is not always easy to draw the distinction and one must be aware that a set of words might be comment in one context, when the defence of fair comment may be available, and fact in another, when it will have to be justified. Where the words state explicitly "I think that" or "It seems to me that", or other such words, then this will be indicative that they are comment. This is not necessary though. The statement may make an observation about a fact—for example, X's behaviour was disgraceful or Y's conduct was exemplary.

In *Keays v Guardian Newspapers Ltd* [2003] EWHC 1565, the judge ruled that the article was only capable of being regarded as comment and could not be held as being factual in character. The claimant Sara Keays was known to the public as a result of having an affair with a Tory politician and giving birth to his daughter. The article in the *Observer* was published in the "Comment" section and speculated about the decision of the claimant to publish her story and that of her daughter in the press. The author drew her inferences about the state of mind and motives behind the claimant's decision. The judge held that the article was clear that it did not purport to be a statement of fact—indeed, the author could not verify the claimant's state of mind, and a reader would understand that this was an opinion.

The opinion or comment may be extreme, prejudiced or biased and still fall within the bounds of the defence. The language used may also be rude or offensive and may still properly be legitimate criticism (*Silkin v Beaverbrook Newspapers* [1958] 1 W.L.R. 743). A defendant does not have to persuade the court to agree with their opinions, nor to demonstrate that they are "reasonable" or "fair". The Court of Appeal in *British Chiropractic Association v Singh* [2010] EWCA Civ 350 reached a surprising conclusion, which illustrates that care must be taken to consider the context of the allegation complained of. Here, the defendant had written that the claimant promoted treatments which were "bogus" and made medical claims for which "there is not a jot of evidence". At first instance, Eady J. ruled that these were allegations of fact, indeed "the plainest allegation of dishonesty". The Court of Appeal disagreed, and ruled that in the specific scientific context of the case, the true nature of the words was that they expressed value judgments, and were hence comment. The Court of Appeal also gave its view that it would be more helpful if the defence were called "honest opinion", since "fair comment" is somewhat misleading.

The comment must be based on true facts and these facts must be known to the writer at the time of the article being published. Thus, comment based on facts which are incorrect cannot be the subject of this defence even where honestly made. For example, one can say of X that he is unfit to attend public houses if X has a record of causing fights in public places. One could not say it of Y whom X had provoked into fighting with him. A defendant will be required to prove that the facts upon which the comment has been made are substantially true.

These matters were considered in *Lowe v Associated Newspapers Ltd* [2006] 3 All E.R. 357, a case concerning an article which subjected the claimant (the chairman of Southampton FC) to criticism in relation to his takeover of the club in 1997, calling it "a repellent piece of financial chicanery", and in relation to a former manager whom the claimant was accused of having treated "shabbily". The judge made clear that the defence may rely on facts which were not stated in the article complained of, but such facts must have: (a) existed at the time of the publication; and (b) been known at least in general terms at the time to the individual making the comment. A general fact which *was* within the commentator's knowledge may be supported by specific examples even if the commentator had *not* been aware of them.

In *Levi v Bates* [2009] EWHC 1495 (QB) the claimant, a former director of Leeds Utd FC, sued the club's chairman Ken Bates over allegations in match programmes and a letter to club members. They were to the effect that the claimant was a "shyster" who had tried to "blackmail" the club. Defences of justification, fair comment and qualified privilege (see below) were pleaded. It was held by the judge that on the facts, the defence of justification failed, and so did the defence of fair comment. Even though the allegations were largely expressed in terms of comment, and they were views that could have been held by an honest person, the judge found that the factual basis for them was lacking (the articles complained of were held to be "riddled with material inaccuracies" and "such facts as have been proved by Mr Bates to be true fall well short of amounting to a sufficient sub-stratum for the comments"). As will be seen below, the defence of qualified privilege was held not to protect the defendant in relation to the articles in the match programmes, and as a result the judge (trying the case without a jury) awarded £50,000 damages to the claimant.

Public interest

For the defence of fair comment to be available, the defendant must prove that the allegedly defamatory statement was made concerning a matter of public interest. A comment will be on a matter of public interest if it concerns a matter which affects people at large, so that they may be legitimately interested in it, or concerned at what is going on or what may happen to them or to others. It will thus include, amongst other matters, opinions on the conduct of public figures, local and national government and public and private companies in so far as it affects people or the administration of justice. Where people enter the public arena, they are considered to invite comment upon themselves, and this may include scrutiny concerning their motives. Older cases suggest that the private life of a public figure may not properly be the subject of comment where it is not relevant to their public role.

Recent court decisions concerning "public interest" show a tendency towards the expansion and development of its breadth of application. Where people have voluntarily put aspects of their private lives into the public domain or hold themselves out as role models, they may thereby be the subject of comment. Per Eady J. in *Branson v Bower* [2002] 2 W.L.R. 452:

"In a modern democracy all those who venture into public life, in whatever capacity, must expect to have their motives subjected to scrutiny and discussed. Nor is it realistic today to demand that such debate should be hobbled by the constraints of conventional good manners—still less of deference. The law of fair comment must allow for healthy scepticism."

Malice

A defence that a defamatory statement is one of fair comment may be defeated by proof of malice on the part of the defendant. Malice in this context does not have its usual language meaning of a person's motives or interest and is, therefore, rather misleading. At its simplest, malice in the defence of fair comment, means the defendant did not have an honest belief in the opinion expressed. To defeat an otherwise successful fair comment defence, a claimant must therefore show that the individual's state of mind was such that he did not believe the opinions represented. This is summarised in the Hong Kong Court of Final Appeal judgment in *Cheng v Tse Wai Chun* [2000] 3 HKLRD 418:

> "A comment which falls within the objective limits of the defence of fair comment can lose its immunity only by proof that the defendant did not genuinely hold the view he expressed. Honesty of belief is the touchstone. Actuation by spite, animosity, intent to injure, intent to arouse controversy or other motivation, whatever it may be, even if it is dominant or sole motive, does not of itself defeat the defence. However, proof of such motivation may be evidence, sometimes compelling evidence, from which lack of genuine belief in the view expressed may be inferred."

In summary, therefore, to succeed in a fair comment defence, the defendant must:

(a) have expressed opinions honestly; and

(b) have done so based upon facts which are accurately stated.

Absolute privilege

Statements made on an absolutely privileged occasion cannot be the subject of a defamation action. This is the case even where the defendant is motivated by malice (see below). Absolute privilege is relevant to reports of the following events:

- parliamentary proceedings; and
- judicial proceedings.

Parliamentary proceedings

Statements made during the course of parliamentary proceedings, as well as the publication of official reports of those proceedings, are absolutely privileged. This does not extend to statements of MPs made other than in the course of a parliamentary debate or proceeding. Work by select committees is generally regarded as being included within the definition of parliamentary proceedings.

EXAMPLE

An MP calls the Prime Minister a liar during Prime Minister's Question Time in the House of Commons. Despite the statement by the MP being defamatory of the Prime Minister, no action in defamation will be available. The statement was made on an occasion to which the defence of absolute privilege attaches.

This privilege comes originally from art.9 of the Bill of Rights 1689 (for a statement as to the precise nature of art.9 see Lord Woolf's judgment in *Hamilton v Al Fayed*, *The Times*, March 30, 1999), which precludes any court from impeaching or questioning proceedings in Parliament:

"That the freedom of speech and debates or proceedings in Parliament ought not to be impeached or questioned in any court or place out of Parliament."

Reports of parliamentary proceedings

The media will not be able to use the defence of absolute privilege in publishing reports of parliamentary proceedings (though the defence of qualified privilege may be available—see below). The media had previously been able to use art.9 as a shield against a libel action brought by an MP. Parliamentary privilege prevented the defendants putting forward the defence which they wished to put forward. For example, the defence was one of justification and the matter requiring proof was contained in parliamentary debates. However, following the judicial stay (i.e. halting of an action) of the libel claim brought by Neil Hamilton, the former MP for Tatton, against the *Guardian*, preventing him from having the opportunity to clear his name, the law was changed. This case led in part to the passing of s.13 of the Defamation Act 1996 which now provides that, for the purposes of defamation proceedings only, a person may waive the protection of parliamentary privilege. Thus, in a similar case today the MP could allow the media defendant to bring evidence of statements that were made on a privileged occasion. Section 13 provides as follows:

"Where the conduct of a person in or in relation to proceedings in Parliament is in issue in defamation proceedings, he may waive for the purposes of those proceedings, so far as concerns him, the protection of any enactment or rule of law which prevents proceedings in Parliament being impeached or questioned in any court or place out of Parliament."

The waiver of the protection will result in the court conducting defamation proceedings being able to hear evidence which otherwise would have been inadmissible. Of course, it is only the person who is afforded parliamentary privilege who can waive it—such a person may very well choose not to do so. In fact, the House of Lords ruled that s.13 permitted such waiver in Neil Hamilton's subsequent libel action against Harrods' owner Mohamed Al Fayed (*Hamilton v Al Fayed* [2000] 2 All E.R. 222).

Judicial proceedings

Any statement made by any person in the course of proceedings before any court or tribunal is absolutely privileged. This does not apply to administrative proceedings such as local authority meetings (*Royal Aquarium & Summer & Winter Garden Society v Parkinson* [1892] 1 Q.B. 431).

Reports of judicial proceedings

Absolute privilege will attach to a fair and accurate report of court proceedings where it is published contemporaneously with those proceedings (Defamation Act 1996, s.14). The court proceedings to which this defence relates are those of:

(a) any court in the United Kingdom;

(b) the European Court of Justice or Court of First Instance of the European Union;

(c) the European Court of Human Rights; and

(d) any international criminal court established by the United Nations Security Council or by an international agreement to which the United Kingdom is a party.

A newspaper or other media report will be published contemporaneously if it is published as soon as is reasonably practicable after the court proceedings concerned. Thus the precise time frame in which a report must be published will depend upon the nature of the publication. If it is the nine o'clock news on BBC1 then arguably it must be published the same day. Publication one month after the court report could be contemporaneous in the case of a monthly magazine or periodical. Where the media is prevented from publishing details of a court proceedings by an order of the court or a statutory provision, any publication of a report of those proceedings will be treated as being published contemporaneously if it is published as soon as practicable after the restriction comes to an end (s.14(2)). This is obviously a valuable defence to the media in reporting the proceedings of the courts.

Complaints to the police

An important case in 2008 clarified that absolute privilege also applies to complaints to the police. Previously, in the absence of clear authority, it was thought that such complaints would be protected by qualified privilege (see below). The decision of the Court of Appeal in *Westcott v Westcott* [2008] EWCA Civ 818 was that absolute privilege should apply. The case concerned a family dispute—the defendant was married to the claimant's son but the marriage had broken down. She had visited the claimant with her baby, and subsequently made oral and written complaints to the police that the claimant had attacked and hit them both. The police investigated but did not prosecute. The claimant (a JP) sued for libel and slander but the preliminary issue of whether the complaints to the police were absolutely privileged went against him, both before Richard Parkes QC sitting as a

Deputy High Court Judge, and on appeal. Ward L.J. summarised the rationale for the decision as being a necessity "for the due administration of justice that complaints of alleged criminal conduct should always be capable of being made to the police free from fear that a person accused will subsequently involve the complainant in costly litigation".

Qualified privilege

Statements made on an occasion to which the defence of qualified privilege attaches cannot be the subject of a successful libel action unless it can be shown that the defendant acted with malice in publishing the statement complained of (it is this requirement of the absence of malice that is one of the key distinguishing features between absolute and qualified privilege, malice being irrelevant to the former). The claimant will usually be able to prove malice where they can show that the defendant did not believe the truth of the statement they published (see further below).

There are two principal types of qualified privilege that are relevant to the media:

- reports of proceedings; and

- duty and interest.

The first is largely statutory and the second is an old common law defence that has received recent invigoration as a result of the case of *Reynolds v Times Newspapers Ltd* [1998] 3 W.L.R. 862 (see below).

Reports of proceedings

Fair and accurate reports of certain proceedings will attract the defence of qualified privilege. The defence was common law in origin but has now been all but superseded by statute.

Common to all reports seeking to benefit from qualified privilege is the requirement that the defendants must prove that the reports are fair and accurate. The test is whether or not the report gives a balanced and substantially accurate impression of the proceedings. Minor inaccuracies will be ignored in determining whether the report is fair and accurate (*Kimber v Press Association* [1893] 1 Q.B. 65). A substantial inaccuracy or a failure to report something which contradicts information in the part of the proceedings reported will make the defence unavailable (see, e.g. *Kingshott v Associated Kent* [1991] 1 Q.B. 88).

EXAMPLE
During the trial of James and others for assault, a witness states that James was in the pub where the assault took place. James's defence is that, despite being in the pub, he took no part in the offence. In cross-examination the witness admits that he did not actually see James hit the victim. A newspaper report on the trial the following day states that, "an eye witness has placed James at the scene of the crime", but fails to mention the information elicited from cross-examination. The report will be unable to benefit from the defence of qualified privilege.

Statutory privilege for reports under the Defamation Act 1996

Section 15 provides that a report will be protected by qualified privilege unless it is shown to be made with malice. Sch.1 contains a comprehensive list of "publications" to which this qualified privilege relates and is set out in full in Appendix B. The Schedule lists a number of different types of reports of proceedings and divides them into two sub-categories. The first category (Pt I) contains a list of those reports of proceedings to which the defence attaches "without explanation or contradiction" (see below). The principal types of publications in this category are fair and accurate reports of:

- proceedings in public of a legislative body anywhere in the world;
- proceedings in public before any court anywhere in the world;
- proceedings in public of a government-appointed public inquiry anywhere in the world;
- proceedings in public of an international organisation or international conference anywhere in the world;
- a copy of or extract from any register or other document required by law to be open to public inspection; and
- a notice or advertisement published by or on the authority of a court anywhere in the world.

Part II of the Schedule contains a list of occasions where fair and accurate reports are privileged "subject to an explanation or contradiction". Examples of such statements are fair and accurate reports of:

- proceedings at any public meeting or sitting in the United Kingdom of:
  (a) a local authority or local authority committee;
  (b) a justice or justices of the peace acting otherwise than as a court exercising judicial authority;
  (c) a commission, tribunal, committee or person appointed for the purposes of any inquiry by any statutory provision, by Her Majesty or by a Minister of the Crown or a Northern Ireland Department;
  (d) a person appointed by a local authority to hold a local inquiry in pursuance of any statutory provision;
  (e) any other tribunal, board, committee or body constituted by or under, and exercising functions under, any statutory provision;
- any public meeting held in a Member State of the EU; or
- proceedings at any general meeting of a UK public company.

Importantly, it also includes a fair and accurate copy of, or extract from, a notice issued for the information of the public by the government of any EU Member State or any authority performing governmental functions, including police functions. Therefore, a journalist provided with a notice by a government or local authority press officer or police press officer will be able to rely on qualified privilege for a report based on the contents of the notice, provided it is fair and accurate and published without malice.

The words "subject to an explanation or contradiction" mean that qualified privilege will not be a defence to fair and accurate reports of proceedings of the bodies in the second of the two lists above if it is proved that the defendant has been requested by the claimant to publish in the newspaper in which the original publication was made a reasonable letter or statement by way of explanation or contradiction, and has refused or neglected to do so, or has done so in a manner not adequate or not reasonable having regard to all the circumstances. Thus the defence of qualified privilege will fail where the medium in question has refused the claimant's reasonable request to publish a statement in reply.

Where such a request is made, the claimant must be given sufficient space (in the case of a newspaper or similar medium whether electronic or otherwise) or air time (in the case of a broadcast) to make an adequate response.

Common law privilege for reports

Section 15(4) of the 1996 Act guarantees the survival of the common law defence of privilege for fair and accurate reports of proceedings (as well as the "duty or interest" privilege at common law) by providing that the statute is not to be taken as limiting or abridging any subsisting privilege.

Duty or interest

Qualified privilege attaches to communications (so long as they are not malicious) where:

(a) the statement is made by a person who has:

   (i) a duty to make the statement; or
   (ii) an interest in making the statement;

   and

(b) the recipient or recipients of the statement have a duty or interest in receiving it.

EXAMPLE
Alan is managing director of A Ltd. The finance director of A Ltd, Zach, decides to leave and take up a similar post with B Ltd, whose managing director, Brenda, asks Alan for an employee reference for Zach. Alan gives a positive reference. Soon after, Alan discovers financial irregularities in A Ltd's accounts which suggest that Zach may have been stealing large amounts of money from A Ltd. The evidence is not at that stage 100 per cent cast-iron, but Alan calls Brenda to tell her that contrary to the reference, he has reason to doubt Zach's honesty. Thanks to the reciprocal duty and interest in the communication between the two managing directors, Alan will have a defence of qualified privilege in the event that Zach tries to sue him for defamation (slander, in this instance) over what he told Brenda on the phone.

A real-life instance of these principles being applied was the case of *Levi v Bates* [2009] EWHC 1495 (QB) referred to earlier in relation to the defence of fair comment. Allegations were published by the defendant, the chairman of Leeds Utd FC, in a letter to club members and in match programmes. The judge held that privilege protected the defendant in respect of the letter, due to the reciprocal duty and interest element in the limited publication to those particular recipients. However similar allegations more widely published in the programmes were not so protected. The case illustrates how the privilege focuses on the specific features of the way the allegations are published, more than on the allegations themselves.

For this reason, this type of qualified privilege had historically been unavailable to the media, despite their attempts to the contrary, due either to the absence of a sufficient duty on the part of the publisher or a lack of sufficient interest on the part of each individual publishee that make up the "readership".

However, the judgment of Lord Bingham in *Reynolds v Times Newspapers Ltd* [1998] 3 W.L.R. 862 altered this position considerably. The case itself concerned an article in *The Sunday Times* concerning the political crisis in Ireland in 1994 which culminated in the resignation of the claimant, Albert Reynolds, as Taoiseach (Prime Minister). Mr Reynolds claimed that the words used meant that he had deliberately and dishonestly misled the Irish Parliament and lied to his cabinet colleagues. The defendant claimed that it was entitled to the defence of qualified privilege on the basis that the public interest in the general publication of information and discussion relating to political issues and the public conduct of elected politicians entitled it to such protection. The trial judge ruled that such a defence was not available and the jury found the article to be defamatory. On appeal, the Court of Appeal ruled that although the defence of qualified privilege was not available in this case, it would be available to the media where three tests were satisfied. Speaking for the entire court Lord Bingham said:

"In our judgment, when applying the present English common law of qualified privilege, the following questions need to be answered in relation to any individual occasion.

1. Was the publisher under a legal, moral or social duty to those to whom the material was published (which in appropriate cases may be the general public) to publish the material in question? (We call this the duty test.)
2. Did those to whom the material was published (which again in appropriate cases may be the general public) have an interest to receive that material? (We call this the interest test.)
3. Were the nature, status, and source of the material, and the circumstances of the publication, such that the publication should in the public interest be protected in the absence of express malice? (We call this the circumstantial test.)"

It is clear from this judgment that the defence of qualified privilege may now apply to the media generally. It is the third requirement (the "circumstantial test") that will cause most difficulties in practice—it effectively sets out a standard of responsible journalism which must be demonstrated to fall within the defence.

The court set out 10 guiding principles, now known as the *"Reynolds factors"*, which would be considered in deciding the question of whether a particular publication had acted responsibly and may avail itself of a qualified privilege defence, notwithstanding that the defamatory allegations may be false or at least that the newspaper is unable to prove their truth.

The 10 factors are as follows:

- seriousness of the allegation;
- matter of public concern;
- source;
- steps taken to verify the information;
- status of the information;
- urgency of the matter;
- comment sought from claimant;
- whether the gist of the claimant's side of the story is published;
- tone; and
- circumstances of the publication.

The importance of this new defence to the media should not be underestimated, but it can be seen that it firmly shifts the focus of the libel action onto the conduct of the publication and, indeed, the individual journalist. It will entail a full exploration, under cross-examination, of the journalist's working habits and practices in relation to preparation of the article. On the occasions when this defence has been considered by the courts since the *Reynolds* case, frequently the standard of journalism has been found wanting and the court has ruled that the protection of qualified privilege would not be available. The standard is, therefore, a high one to attain; otherwise it would be too wide a license for the media. Per Lord Phillips in *Loutchansky v Times Newspapers Ltd* [2002] 1 All E.R. 652:

> "Setting the standard of journalistic responsibility too low would inevitably encourage too great a readiness to publish defamatory matter. Journalists should be rigorous, not lax, in their approach. It is in the interests of the public as well as the defamed individual that, wherever possible, truths and no untruths should be told."

In that case, *The Times* had published allegations that the claimant was the boss of a Russian criminal organisation and involved in money laundering and the smuggling of nuclear weapons. They relied upon various pieces of information that they argued they were entitled to treat as reliable, including media reports of involvement of the Bank of New York in money-laundering activity in Russia, reports of the claimant's exclusion from the United Kingdom, three unidentified sources and one named source who was the author of a book on organised crime. Considering the *Reynolds* factors, Gray J. held that the story was serious and on a matter of public concern, but that some of the sources were unsafe and that there was little evidence of the steps taken to verify the information. More effort should have been made to contact the claimant—simply publishing a bare denial as the claimant's only side of the story was insufficient. For these reasons, he ruled that *The Times* could not rely on the qualified privilege defence and was liable to the claimant.

The defence also failed in the notorious case of *Galloway v Telegraph* [2006] E.M.L.R. 221 (Court of Appeal), but there the key factor was the extent to which the paper had strayed from simply reporting neutrally on the discovery of some apparently incriminating documentation, and had instead adopted a highly critical tone which in effect deprived it of the defence.

By contrast, the defendant newspaper did succeed in a qualified privilege defence in *Al-Fagih v HH Saudi Research & Marketing (UK) Ltd* [2001] All E.R. (D) 48. The defamatory allegation was made by a political rival of the claimant, to the newspaper's journalist, and it was subsequently found to be untrue. It was important that the newspaper made clear who had made the allegation and did not adopt the statement itself. The newspaper had not made an attempt to verify the information, but it was a matter of public concern and the newspaper sought to fully and fairly report both sides to a political dispute in their allegations and counter-remarks. As such, it could claim the protection of qualified privilege for its report.

In *Jameel v Wall Street Journal SPRL (No.3)* [2006] 3 W.L.R. 642, a key House of Lords ruling which represents the current state of play as regards the *Reynolds* defence, the defendants were ultimately successful (having lost in front of Eady J. and a jury, and in the Court of Appeal). This was yet another of the many recent cases of a foreign claimant coming to this country to sue over allegations of organised crime (*Loutchansky*) or, as in this case, terrorism. The *Wall Street Journal* had reported on Saudi–US co-operation post-9/11 in monitoring certain named bank accounts on the grounds of "potential" terrorist links. It had no means of proving the truth of the *Chase* Level 2 meaning (see above) pleaded by the claimant, so sought to rely on the *Reynolds* defence. But all the journalist had to go on were anonymous sources (in US and Saudi intelligence circles), a disability which had previously tended to be fatal to the defence.

The House of Lords said that the article in question was measured and neutral in tone, on matters of high public interest and importance, in short just the sort of piece that the *Reynolds* privilege exists to protect. The decision in the *Wall Street Journal's* favour signals a move away from the box-ticking approach of the 10 "*Reynolds* factors", towards a broader three-part test, as set out by Lord Hoffmann:

1. Is the subject-matter of the article as a whole of public interest?

2. If so, was the inclusion of the defamatory statement justifiable?

3. If so, were the steps taken to obtain and publish the material fair and responsible?

Lord Hoffmann also considered that it was misleading to see the *Reynolds* defence as a branch of qualified privilege because, viewed properly, it is the material which is "privileged" (not the occasion of communication, as in the "duty and interest" situation). He favoured calling it "the *Reynolds* public interest defence". It remains the case that what is required of the journalist will depend on the circumstances and nature of the story. There is no doubt, though, that if their publication is to stand any chance of succeeding in a *Reynolds* defence, it is in any event of critical importance for a journalist to maintain and retain proper records and notes of research, conversations and attempts to contact the subject of the allegation so as to maximise the chances of getting through the third element of Lord Hoffmann's *Jameel* test.

Malice and qualified privilege

A defence of qualified privilege will be unavailable if a claimant can prove that the defamatory material was published with "malice". The meaning of malice here is different to the usual understanding of someone's motives, and will usually mean a claimant demonstrating that a defendant did not have an honest belief in the truth of the material. If a defendant publishes defamatory material without caring whether it is true or not, then this is equated to him knowing it was false. The meaning of malice in relation to qualified privilege is summarised by May L.J. in *Alexander v Arts Council of Wales* [2001] 1 W.L.R. 1840, as follows:

> "To entitle a person to the protection of qualified privilege, he has to have a positive belief in the truth of what he published. Such a belief is presumed unless the contrary is proved, and so the burden of establishing malice lies on the person who asserts it, in this instance the claimant. What the claimant has to establish is a dominant and improper motive on the part of the defendant comprising a desire to injure the claimant. This dominant motive can only be inferred from what the defendant did or said or knew. If it is proved that he did not believe that what he published was true, that is generally conclusive evidence of express malice. But a person may have an honest belief in what he publishes despite imperfection of the mental process by which the belief is arrived at."

Last, it is worth noting that a case in December 2008 established that where a publication is protected from libel litigation by absolute or qualified privilege, there is likely to be protection from a privacy claim too (privacy will be dealt with in detail in Ch.4). *Crossley & Crossley v Newsquest (Midlands South) Limited* [2008] EWHC 3054 (QB) concerned a press report of a neighbour dispute which had ended up in the county court (the case concerned sewage disposal). The Crossleys had lost and been ordered to pay costs. They later applied to court to vary the costs order, and this application and the previous court case were covered in the local paper. To a libel complaint against the paper, the Crossleys sought to add a complaint for breach of their privacy, in relation to details of their financial affairs which had been referred to in open court and included in the press report. Eady J. ruled that the privacy claim could not be added to the complaint. He found that the press do enjoy protection from litigation over a report containing information which would otherwise be private but had been mentioned in open court, where the report satisfies the test for qualified and/or absolute privilege under the law of libel.

Innocent dissemination

Liability for each defamatory publication extends to a list of potential defendants who fall within the category of publishers. As discussed above, a libellous newspaper article will be "published" by the journalist, editor, printer, publisher and the distributor. Many persons within the list of potential defendants will not know of the existence of the statement alleged to be defamatory and will, at least morally, be blameless. The old common law defence of innocent dissemination did little to help defendants who found themselves in this position due to a burden of proof that was unhelpful and impractical.

When addressing the unfairness caused to printers and others by the common law defence, Parliament took the opportunity, in the Defamation Act 1996, to extend and widen the old defence. Section 1 of the Act contains a new innocent dissemination defence which is designed to benefit a range of persons including broadcasters of live television programmes and distributors of sound recordings. It also attempted to deal with some of the challenges presented by new technology and effectively added internet service providers to the list of potential beneficiaries of the new defence (see Ch.9).

Section 1 provides that a person has a defence to defamation proceedings where they are able to show that:

(a) they were not the author, editor or publisher of the statement complained of;

(b) they took reasonable care in relation to its publication; and

(c) they did not know, and had no reason to believe, that what they did caused or contributed to the publication of a defamatory statement.

The defence to defamation proceedings is thus available to a person who can show that they were not the author, editor or publisher of the statement complained of. In this context, a "publisher" is a "commercial publisher whose business is issuing material to the public". "Author" means the originator of the statement, but does not include a person who did not intend that their statement be published at all. "Editor" means a person having editorial or equivalent responsibility for the content of the statement or the decision to publish it.

According to s.1, a person shall not be considered to be the author, editor or publisher (and thus the defence becomes potentially available to them) if they are only involved in one or more of the following:

(a) printing, producing, distributing or selling printed material containing the statement;

(b) processing, making copies of, distributing, exhibiting or selling a film or sound recording containing the statement;

(c) processing, making copies of, distributing or selling any electronic medium in or on which the statement is recorded, or in operating or providing any equipment, system or service by means of which the statement is retrieved, copied, distributed or made available in electronic form;

(d) broadcasting a live programme containing the statement in circumstances in which they have no effective control over the maker of the statement; or

(e) operating or providing access to a communications system by means of which the statement is transmitted, or made available, by a person over whom they have no effective control.

This list is not exhaustive. The courts are able to find that other persons are not authors, editors or publishers and are able to have regard to the above provisions by way of analogy in deciding whether such persons are to be so considered.

Once a person has proved that they are not the author, editor or publisher, they must go on to show that they took all reasonable care in relation to the publication and that they did not know and had no reason to believe that they caused or contributed to the publication. In determining whether a person took such reasonable care or whether what they did caused or contributed to the publication, the court shall bear in mind:

(a) the extent of their responsibility for the content of the statement or the decision to publish it;

(b) the nature or circumstances of the publication; and

(c) the previous conduct or character of the author, editor or publisher.

It is the two-stage test of the defence in s.1 that will cause defendants difficulties. It is not enough for the defendant to show that they were not the author, editor or publisher—they must go on to prove that they took reasonable care and did not know (or have reason to believe) that they contributed to the defamatory publication. In *Laurence Godfrey v Demon Internet Ltd* [1999] I.T.C.L.R. 282, the judge did not hesitate to find that an internet service provider (ISP) was not an author, editor or publisher. But in that case the ISP could not show either that it had taken reasonable care or that it had the requisite lack of knowledge due to having been informed by fax of the defamatory content and subsequently failing to remove the offending article (see Ch.9 for further detail).

The judgment of Eady J. in *Bunt v Tilley* [2006] EWHC 407 (QB) reaffirms that s.1 affords ISPs a complete defence to any claim brought over postings of which they have not been put on notice.

Offer of amends

In an attempt to promote the more swift resolution and settlement of defamation actions, Parliament has replaced the old 1952 Act offer of amends provisions (which were rarely used) with a new defence contained in s.2 of the 1996 Act.

The defendant may make a so-called "offer of amends" to the claimant and the refusal by the claimant to accept such an offer will be a defence to the action. The offer may be made in relation to the statement generally or in relation to a specific defamatory meaning which the person making the offer accepts that the statement conveys (the latter being called a "qualified offer").

The offer itself must be in writing, must be expressed to be made as an offer pursuant to s.2 of the Defamation Act 1996, and must state whether or not it is a qualified offer and, if so, set out the meaning to which the offer relates. The offer of amends provisions state that the offer must be made before the offeror serves any defence in the proceedings on the person allegedly defamed.

An offer to make amends is an offer:

(a) to make a suitable correction of the statement complained of and a sufficient apology to the aggrieved party;

(b) to publish the correction and apology in a manner that is reasonable and practicable in the circumstances; and

(c) to pay to the aggrieved party such compensation (if any), and such costs, as may be agreed or determined to be payable.

Where an offer under the 1996 Act is not accepted by the aggrieved party, it will be a defence to the proceedings (a qualified offer is a defence only in respect of the meaning to which the offer related) unless the offeror knew or had reason to believe that the statement complained of:

(a) referred to the aggrieved party or was likely to be understood as referring to them; and

(b) was both false and defamatory of that party.

There is a presumption, for the purposes of the defence, that the defendant did not know or have reason to believe these matters. Thus the burden of proving them rests with the claimant. The effect of the claimant successfully doing so is that the defendant will be disqualified from using the defence. This may raise a problem where a journalist has contacted the subject of the allegations in preparing the article and the subject has stated that the allegation is untrue. In order to still be able to use the offer of amends, the journalist would have to show why, notwithstanding the claimant's comment, they still had reason to believe the truth of the allegations.

Where the defendant makes an offer of amends which is not accepted by the claimant, the defendant may then choose to use the fact of their offer as a defence to the subsequent proceedings (a qualified offer is only a defence in respect of the meaning to which the offer related). However, by virtue of s.4 of the 1996 Act, if they do so they will be unable to rely on any other defence.

Although not strictly relevant to this section on defences, it may be useful to set out here the consequences of accepting an offer of amends. The party who accepts the offer may not bring (or continue where already commenced) an action in defamation in relation to the publication to which the offer relates. Where the parties are in agreement on the steps to be taken to fulfil the offer (such as the content of the correction or the amount of compensation to be paid), the party who has accepted the offer may, where the other party fails to carry out such steps, apply to the court for an order forcing the publisher to carry out the terms of the offer.

However, it may be that, although the offer has been accepted in general terms, the parties do not agree on the steps to fulfil the offer. In such a situation, the party who made the offer may take such steps as they think are appropriate and may publish a correction or apology in terms agreed by the court. This is extremely unusual, as the court is not able to award the publication of an apology to a successful litigant in a defamation action. The court intervening on terms of an apology may, therefore, only arise under the offer of amends procedure. The court will determine the amount of compensation and costs and, in doing so, will take into account the sufficiency of the published correction or apology.

The operation of the offer of amends procedure as far as damages and costs are concerned can be illustrated by a number of recent cases. In *Nail v News Group Newspapers* [2004] EWHC 647 (QB), the claimant Jimmy Nail sued over lurid allegations, originally published in a biography about him called "Nailed" published in 1998, which surfaced again in the *News of the World* in 2002. Memorable elements (recorded with admirable restraint by Eady J. in his judgment) included "loud nookie in a broom closet" and the improvised use of fat from a chip-pan as lubricant during a "hammer and tongs" kitchen sex session. There was renewed interest in the book (over which Nail had not sued in 1998 on legal advice) and a small number of further copies were sold.

The newspaper had made an apology under the offer of amends procedure. In fixing damages, Eady J. applied a two-stage test, assessing damages against the newspaper at £45,000 but then applying a "discount" to reflect the mitigating effect of the newspaper's conduct, in particular the apology. He thought 50 per cent appropriate, and hence awarded damages of £22,500. (Against the book publisher, the very low sales figures of the book within the limitation period led to a modest award of £7,500.)

Significantly, the newspaper's discount took the level of damages below the amount of a settlement offer which Nail had previously rejected, leaving him bearing a serious costs burden. This only increased when he subsequently lost an appeal to the Court of Appeal which upheld Eady J.'s approach ([2005] 1 All E.R. 1040).

The amount of the offer of amends discount will vary depending on the circumstances. In *Campbell-James v Guardian Media Group* [2005] E.M.L.R. 24, false allegations of links between the claimant and the abuse of prisoners at Abu Ghraib prison were eventually followed by an apology, after a three-month delay which the judge found "remarkably casual". A basic damages figure of £90,000 was thus reduced by only 35 per cent to £58,500.

In *Turner v News Group Newspapers* [2005] E.M.L.R. 25, allegations involving "swingers" and sex parties resulted in an award of £15,000 reduced by 40 per cent to £9,000. An interesting feature of this case was the defendant's use of an approach developed in the case of *Burstein v Times Newspapers Ltd* [2001] 1 W.L.R. 579 whereby a defendant can adduce evidence of "background context directly relevant to the damage which the claimant claims has been caused by the defamatory publication"—in other words, material about the claimant which will tend to mitigate damages. The *News of the*

World sought to deploy this in front of the judge who ruled that a proper Burstein plea (despite the possibility of it causing additional hurt to the claimant's feelings) did not automatically reduce the discount. The Court of Appeal upheld the judge's finding ([2006] E.M.L.R. 703).

A final example is *Angel v Stainton* [2006] EWHC 637 (QB). An elderly company director was accused of serious wrongdoing in a letter of limited circulation. The defendants did apologise but not very promptly and in a grudging manner—the discount applied was 40 per cent, reducing a basic award of £40,000 to £24,000.

In *Green v Times Newspapers* Unreported January 17, 2001 EWHC (QBD), the court held that an offer of amends could not protect a defendant from a separate action arising from a new publication of the same article. In that case the claimants had accepted an offer of amends in relation to an article which accused them of insider trading. The court was still to decide the amount of damages the newspaper must pay, although an apology had been published. The claimants complained that the original article was still available on the website and rejected a further offer of amends by the newspaper. The judge ruled that it was possible for the claimants to reject the offer if they wished and continue with the separate libel action over the website publication. This emphasises the importance for a newspaper to properly maintain its archives online (see Ch.9 for more detail).

If an offer of amends is accepted by the aggrieved party, then no further action in libel or slander can be taken by that party against the person who made the offer over the publication which is the subject of the offer. This does not affect the right of the aggrieved party to take action in defamation against a different party who may be jointly responsible for the publication. For example, a journalist may make an offer of amends to a person who is defamed by their published article. The acceptance of this offer by the defamed person does not prevent them bringing an action against the editor and/or proprietor of the newspaper in which the defamatory article was published.

Consent

The fact that the claimant has consented to a defamatory publication will be a complete defence to a defamation action. Thus, where a famous personality is informed of the proposed content of a magazine article about her and she agrees to the inclusion of such material, she will be unable to sue the magazine for libel as a result of the publication. However, there would have to be agreement to the specific defamatory allegations and the actual words used, rather than general agreement to the subject of the article.

Remedies

The following remedies are available to a claimant who is successful in a libel action against the defendant:

- damages (money); or
- injunction.

Damages

The principal remedy for defamation is damages. The object of damages is to compensate the claimant for the lowering of their reputation that they have suffered as a result of the publication and for any consequent loss that is recoverable (e.g. loss of earnings).

Awards often seem to go further than this however. Part of the reason for this is inherent in the nature of the jury system itself. Juries typically find it irresistible to give someone else's money away and perceive media defendants to be "able to afford it". They often have a greater sympathy with the defamed person than with the newspaper. This tendency has been offset in recent years by a number of factors, not least the trend noted above for libel trials to take place before judge alone.

After a series of very high jury awards in the 1980s, many commentators felt that the level of libel damages was too high. Section 8 of the Courts and Legal Services Act 1990 empowered the Court of Appeal to substitute its own award of damages for that made by the jury at trial. However, the Court of Appeal may only intervene to vary the level of a damages award where an award was so high that it was "divorced from reality" to a degree that no reasonable jury could have thought appropriate.

However, various decisions in the 1990s led to a reduction in the amount of compensation that a claimant can expect to obtain as a result of a libel against them. In *Rantzen v Mirror Group Newspapers (1986) Ltd* [1993] 3 W.L.R. 953, the Court of Appeal, having regard to the Human Rights Convention (later enshrined in the Human Rights Act 1998), found that the sum of £250,000 awarded by the jury in *Rantzen* was excessive because it was not proportionate to the damage suffered by the claimant. It reduced the award to £110,000.

In 1994, the European Commission of Human Rights found unanimously that the size of the damages awarded to Lord Aldington (the jury found in the case of *Aldington v Watts and Tolstoy (The Times*, December 1, 1989) that Count Tolstoy should pay £1,500,000 as a result of his distributing copies of a pamphlet stating that Lord Aldington was involved in repatriating Russian prisoners of war to their certain death from Yugoslavia at the end of the Second World War) was a violation of the right to freedom of expression under art.10 of the European Convention for the Protection of Human Rights and Fundamental Freedoms (FCHR).

In December 1995 the Court of Appeal reduced the amount of damages that the *Sunday Mirror* had to pay Elton John from £350,000 (awarded by the jury at the end of the High Court trial) to £75,000. The court took the opportunity to set down some guidelines of which the jury should be made aware before assessing the size of any award. This important case (*John v MGN Ltd, The Times*, December 14, 1995) concerned a report in the *Sunday Mirror* which claimed that the pop star was on a diet which required that he chew food and then spit it out rather than swallow it. The paper described this as a "diet of death" which was a form of the eating disorder bulimia nervosa.

The Court of Appeal, in reducing the damages to less than a quarter of those awarded by the jury, pointed out that it was offensive to public opinion that a claimant could recover compensation for injury to his reputation that was heavily in excess of that which was recoverable for serious personal injury. It proposed a system whereby the jury:

- should be told of damages found to be acceptable by the Court of Appeal in previous cases;

- should be informed of the maximum amount of awards in personal injury actions for the sake of comparison; and

- should be directed, where possible, by the judge to an appropriate bracket for awards which they should be encouraged to take into account.

The trend since then has demonstrated that juries have been more sensibly restrained, but on occasion are still capable of awarding apparently punitive sums. In *Kiam v MGN Ltd* [2002] 3 W.L.R. 1036, the jury awarded £105,000 in spite of the fact that the judge indicated a bracket of £40,000 to £80,000 would be appropriate. The Court of Appeal held it could not interfere with the decision of the jury unless it was outside what a reasonable jury could have awarded, but notably, Sedley L.J. disagreed with this outcome. He said it was indecent that the damage to Kiam was put on a compensatory par with the wreckage of human life by brain damage or the loss of both legs below the knee.

In the late 1990s, prudent advice tended to be that any libel award above £150,000, however serious the libel, was susceptible to being reduced by the Court of Appeal. Then in the 2004 case considered earlier, *Nail v News Group Newspapers* [2004] EWHC 647 (QB), Eady J. referred to the then "current conventional overall ceiling for damages of £200,000". There have been signs in the mid-2000s that damages levels are creeping up, and that even with cases tried by judge alone, we may be moving back into an era when six-figure sums may become the norm rather than the exception.

In the section above dealing with the offer of amends defence, the illustrative cases referred to show that we are not there yet. However, three 2006 decisions seem to point the way. First, in January 2006, the Court of Appeal ([2006] E.M.L.R. 221) upheld the award by Eady J. of £150,000 to George Galloway after the *Telegraph*'s *Reynolds* defence failed—the allegation was a serious one of making personal profit from dealings with Iraq. A few days later, a jury awarded Rupert Lowe £250,000 for allegations that were arguably less serious than that award would indicate (see details of case above in section on fair comment). Then in the summer of 2006, Eady J. had to assess damages under the offer of amends procedure in the case of *Veliu v Mazrekaj* [2006] EWHC 1710, where a serious allegation of involvement in the 7/7 London bombings was made in a small circulation Albanian-language newspaper: he took the starting point for damages to be £180,000.

The actual or potential audience of the defamatory material will affect the size of the award together with the seriousness of the allegation made. The statement of claim in a newspaper libel action will often state the circulation of the issue in question. Consequently, a successful claim against a newspaper with national circulation should (but does not always!) result in a much higher damages award than that against a local paper with limited readership. For this reason *Veliu* is a striking decision.

Proof of a malicious motive on the part of the defendant will aggravate a damages award, as will an unsuccessful plea of justification, particularly where it has been accompanied by rigorous cross-examination of the claimant. Damages may be reduced where the claimant's name has been "cleared" in public prior to the judgment or where they have been successful in actions against other defendants in respect of similar defamatory statements.

For eager and wealth-hungry claimants there is another side of the coin that must always be considered before embarking on the lengthy and expensive process of suing someone in defamation: a jury is not bound to award a large sum by way of damages. In *Dering v Uris* [1964] 2 Q.B. 669, the claimant, a doctor and ex-prisoner of Auschwitz concentration camp who had been forced by the Nazis to perform experimental surgical operations on other prisoners, successfully sued the defendant in respect of a reference to him in the defendant's book, *Exodus*. The jury, in an expression of their disapproval of the claimant, went on to award nominal damages of a halfpenny. In the *Reynolds* case (see qualified privilege above), the jury awarded the sum of £1 to the former Prime Minister of Ireland whom the defendant had accused of lying.

Injunction

An injunction is an order granted by the court to prevent publication, or further publication, of the matter complained of. Injunctions are often sought at trial in addition to a claim for damages and they are discretionary. It is common for judges to grant such injunctions at trial to prevent any repetitive publication of the defamatory material. The Human Rights Act 1998, s.12 ascribes special status to information published by the media and to the right of "freedom of expression". The section provides that where the court is considering granting an injunction it must have particular regard to:

"the importance of the Convention right to freedom of expression and, where the proceedings relate to material which the respondent claims, or which appears to the court, to be journalistic, literary or artistic material (or to conduct connected with such material), to—

(a) the extent to which—

(i) the material has, or is about to, become available to the public; or

(ii) it is, or would be, in the public interest for the material to be published;

(b) any relevant privacy code."

Interim injunctions (those obtainable before trial) will rarely be granted to prevent publication of defamatory matter (or to restrain malicious falsehood). The case of *Bonnard v Perryman* [1891] 2 Ch. 269 is usually cited as the leading authority for what has come to be regarded as a rule. In that case, the Court of Appeal said that "it is wiser... in all but exceptional cases... to abstain from interference until the trial and determination of the plea of justification". Recent decisions have confirmed this approach, since interim

injunctions tend to be inconsistent with the freedom of expression principle
contained in art.10 of the ECHR.

However, if the claimant is able to show that the defendant is intending
to publish matter which is clearly untrue and that there is no arguable
defence, an injunction may exceptionally be granted. Such an injunction
was unusually awarded in 2003 to restrain the *Mail on Sunday* from publishing untrue allegations about the sexual conduct of the Prince of Wales.
In exercising its inherent discretion as to whether to grant an interlocutory
injunction the court will, as a result of relevant case law, take into account
the following four principles:

(1) where the defendant states that they intend to rely on a defence, an
    injunction will not be granted unless it can be shown that the
    defendant is acting in bad faith or that the defence is certain to fail;

(2) the claimant should be able to show that the defendant intends to
    publish or further publish the defamatory or similar words;

(3) an injunction will not be granted unless the claimant is able to show
    that the words to be published are clearly defamatory of him (this
    principle is repeated in the Human Rights Act 1998, s.12(3)); and

(4) the claimant may be obliged to make an undertaking to meet the
    defendant's costs of complying with the injunction where it is found
    at trial that the injunction should not have been granted. A failure by
    the claimant to provide such an undertaking or a doubt about his
    ability to meet such costs may be detrimental to his application.

The unwillingness of the court to grant interim injunctions in defamation
cases has led claimants to make their application for an injunction on the
grounds of breach of confidence or breach of contract where an interim
injunction may be granted even though the defendant has a defence which
may succeed at trial.

Statement in open court

Where libel proceedings are brought and the defendant subsequently settles
the action, it is common for a claimant to seek a statement in open court as
part of the settlement agreement. This is where the defendant will formally
admit in court that the allegations it made were untrue and apologise for
them. For example, in March 2003 the *Daily Mail* carried an article which
suggested that the actress Nicole Kidman had had an adulterous affair with
the actor Jude Law, while he was married. The *Daily Mail* subsequently
made a statement in open court apologising for the distress and embarrassment caused by its untrue allegations (*Kidman v Associated Newspapers*
Unreported 2003). The purpose of the statement in open court is to give a
formal record of the fact that the allegations are untrue, and to provide an
opportunity for other media organisations to publicise such a statement so
that the claimant obtains widespread coverage of the correction and
apology.

MALICIOUS FALSEHOOD

A false statement will be actionable in defamation only where it leads to a lowering of the claimant in the estimation of right-thinking members of society. Statements may be made about the claimant which, whilst untrue, are not defamatory. In such cases it may be possible for the claimant to bring an action in malicious (or injurious) falsehood.

An example is provided by the case of *Grapelli v Derek Block (Holdings) Ltd* [1981] 2 All E.R. 272. The claimant, Stephane Grapelli, employed the defendants as his managing agents. The defendants arranged, without the claimant's authority, for the claimant to give concerts at various venues in England. When the concerts had to be cancelled, the defendants stated that the reason for the cancellation was that Mr Grapelli was seriously ill and that it would be doubtful if he would ever tour again. Such a statement was clearly damaging to Mr Grapelli's career but not defamatory as it is not damaging to reputation to say that someone is ill. The claimant's action in slander was accordingly dismissed but his alternative plea of malicious falsehood was successful.

A further reason for bringing an action in malicious falsehood, as opposed to defamation, is that legal aid has traditionally been available where the claimant is able to show that they have a good case on the merits. This has been less significant since the advent of "no win, no fee" agreements for claimants in defamation actions.

An action in malicious falsehood survives the death of either party, whereas the cause of action in defamation ceases with the claimant's (or the defendant's) death.

Definition

In order to succeed in an action in malicious falsehood the claimant must generally prove that the defendant has:

(a) published about the claimant words which are false;

(b) published those words maliciously; and

(c) save in the special circumstances described below, thereby caused special damage which followed as the direct and natural result of the publication.

Malicious falsehood is therefore concerned with protecting the claimant's economic interests rather than his reputation.

Untrue statement about the claimant

In *Kaye v Robertson* [1991] F.S.R. 62, the claimant was a well-known actor and star of a television series called *'Allo 'Allo*. He had undergone very extensive surgery on his head after part of an advertisement hoarding had fallen through his car windscreen in a storm. The first defendant was the editor of the *Sunday Sport*, a tabloid renowned for far-fetched "scoops", and was responsible for journalists who interviewed and photographed the claimant in his hospital bed. The claimant sought an interlocutory injunction to prevent publication, alleging inter alia malicious falsehood. He claimed that he had not consented to the interview and had anyway (to the defendants' knowledge) not been in a fit state to consent; shortly after the interview he had no recollection of the incident. As to the requirement that the words complained of be false, Glidewell L.J. said:

> "I have no doubt that any jury which did not find that the clear impli-cation from the words contained in the defendants' draft article were false would be making a totally unreasonable finding. Thus the test is satisfied in relation to this cause of action."

In *Vodafone Group Plc v Orange Personal Communications Services Ltd* [1997] E.M.L.R. 84, the defendant had run an advertising campaign stating, inter alia, that: "On average, Orange users save £20 per month". The comparison was being made with the telephone services of Vodafone and Cellnet. In determining that the words used meant that if Orange users had been on Vodafone or Cellnet they would have had to pay £20 more per month, Jacob J. in the Chancery Division stated that, for the purposes of malicious fal-sehood, the court had to decide the single natural and ordinary meaning of the words. In doing so the court can be guided by libel principles but should not consider innuendo. The courts have been reluctant to prevent fair competition by way of comparative advertising and did not allow Vodafone to succeed in its malicious falsehood claim.

As regards the extent to which the words complained of have to be "about" the claimant, the case of *Marathon Murual Ltd v Waters* [2009] EWHC 1931 (QB) confirmed that there only has to be some reference, direct or indirect, in the words complained of to the claimant or to its business or other economic interest—there is no need for it to be proved that the clai-mant had been identified in the minds of recipients of the words.

Malice

Malice in the context of malicious falsehood means to act without just cause or excuse and with some indirect, dishonest or improper motive. It is for the claimant to prove malice.

The requirement of malice in the *Kaye* case was made out because there was no doubt from the evidence that it was apparent to the reporter from the *Sunday Sport* that Mr Kaye was in no condition to give any informed consent to an interview. Even if there had been any doubt as to this, the defendant could not have been in any such doubt after he read the affidavit sworn by Mr Kaye in the proceedings. Any subsequent publication would therefore inevitably have been malicious.

The definition of malice in this context was arguably broadened by *Joyce v Sengupta* [1993] 1 All E.R. 897. The *Today* newspaper published an article on its front page headed "ROYAL MAID STOLE LETTERS". The article was based on police suspicions and went on to describe how Linda Joyce had stolen the Princess Royal's intimate letters and handed them to a national newspaper. Instead of suing in defamation for which legal aid is unavail-able (Legal Aid Act 1988, Sch.2, Pt II, para.I), the claimant brought a claim against the defendants claiming damages for malicious falsehood and obtained legal aid to pursue her claim. On appeal from a decision of the

High Court striking out her claim, the Court of Appeal reversed the decision and held that the publication was capable of being malicious in that:

"The defendants went ahead and published the police suspicions as though they were fact and did so without taking any steps to check or verify them. This showed a calculated, reckless indifference to the truth or falsity of the allegations. Malice is to be inferred from the grossness and falsity of the assertions and the cavalier way they were published." (per Sir Donald Nicholls V.C.)

Special damage

In most cases, the claimant must prove that they have suffered special or actual damage in order to succeed in an action in malicious falsehood. The *Vodafone* case (above) confirmed that in the context of malicious falsehood, special damage means actual pecuniary loss. Such special damage must have been incurred by the claimant as a direct result of the publication. Proof of special damage will not be required where:

(a) the words used are calculated to cause financial loss and are published in writing or other permanent form (e.g. broadcasts); or

(b) the words used are calculated to cause financial damage to the claimant in respect of any office, profession, calling, trade or business held or carried on by him at the time of the publication.

In *Stewart-Brady v Express Newspapers Plc* [1997] E.M.L.R. 192, the claimant unsuccessfully argued that he had suffered pecuniary loss as a result of an article in the *Sunday Express*. The article stated that the claimant, one of the Moors murderers who was a patient at Ashworth hospital, had assaulted a female visitor by grabbing her face and sticking his tongue down her throat. The claimant argued that the words would cause financial loss in two ways: (1) he received privileges such as visits and gifts, making and receiving telephone calls, sending and receiving letters or making purchases in the hospital shop which were likely to be withdrawn; and (2) he received a discretionary weekly allowance from the hospital which was likely to be withdrawn or reduced. The judge held that the first claim of financial loss could not "by any stretch of the imagination" amount to pecuniary loss for the purposes of malicious falsehood and the second claim was unfounded as there was no reason to believe that the allowance would be withdrawn.

Defamation and malicious falsehood compared

Where a company's products are criticised, it can be difficult to analyse whether the allegations are tantamount to a libel on those running the company. The issue is likely to arise when a defendant to a libel claim (brought to avoid the need to prove malice as part of the grounds of action) applies for a ruling disallowing the meaning pleaded by the claimant. This is what happened for instance in *ICN Photonics v Patterson* [2003] EWCA Civ 343. The claimant had brought libel proceedings over a letter written by the defendant criticising its Nlite laser product. The defendant made an interim application to the judge, arguing that the letter was incapable of bearing any meaning defamatory of the claimant, and that, if anything, the claim was one of malicious falsehood. The judge disagreed, and the defendant appealed to the Court of Appeal.

The defendant was successful. The court ruled that, where the words complained of relate to a product, the issue on an application for a ruling as to meaning was whether those words were capable of reflecting adversely on the manufacturer or his conduct of his business as opposed to being disparaging merely of the product. In the current action, the statement that the product was unsafe unless used with medical supervision was not by itself capable of being defamatory of the manufacturer.

Despite the fact that the torts of defamation and malicious falsehood both enable the claimant to bring an action as a result of statements made about him, there are hence significant differences between the two causes of action. The table below highlights those differences.

Differences between Libel and Malicious Falsehood

	Libel	Malicious falsehood
Proof of damage required	✗	✓
Right to jury	✓	✗
Proof of loss of reputation required	✓	✗
Presumption of falsity of statement	✓	✗
Proof of malice required	✗	✓
Legal aid available	✗	✓
PR's action after death	✗	✓

PRESS COMPLAINTS COMMISSION (PCC)

Although providing no cause of action in law, the PCC receives complaints from members of the public about, amongst other matters, infringement of personal privacy. The Commission has published a Code of Practice (see Appendix E) which provides appropriate professional standards in respect of reporting in the printed media. The code covers all newspapers, whether daily or weekly and whether national or local. It also covers most magazines, but not those which are available only on subscription.

Complaints should be made in writing to the Commission (address listed in Appendix H) and should include:

- a cutting of the complete article;
- a summary of the complaint and how it has breached the code; and
- copies of any relevant correspondence.

The Commission will make an initial determination as to whether the complaint shows a breach of the code. If it does not show such a breach the Commission will write to the complainant informing him of that decision and will send a copy of the complainant's letter to the editor of the newspaper concerned. If the complaint does reveal a potential breach, the Commission will send a copy of the complainant's letter to the relevant editor and investigate the matter further. The PCC will usually attempt to broker a resolution acceptable to both sides. If that proves impossible, the complaint will be adjudicated on by a panel from the Commission. If the complaint is upheld the newspaper concerned will be asked to publish the adjudication of the Commission with "due prominence".

Reputation

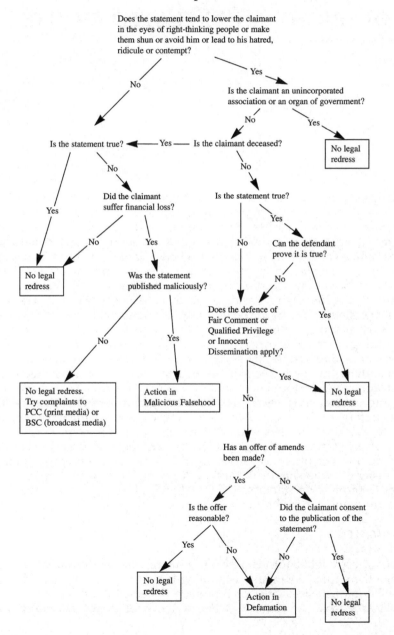

3. COPYRIGHT AND RELATED RIGHTS

This chapter concerns the rights of, amongst others, authors, producers, publishers, directors and composers to exploit their works and to prevent infringement by third parties. Particular rights discussed here are copyright, moral rights, performers' rights, artists' resale rights and rental and lending rights. The legal regulation in this field is largely statutory in nature and derives, in the main, from the Copyright, Designs and Patents Act 1988, as amended by various EU directives in recent years.

Copyright, the first right considered in this chapter, protects a creator's interest in certain works by virtue of a property right that is deemed to exist in the work as soon as it is created, and that exists for a certain number of years during which the owner of the copyright may bring actions for infringement. *Moral rights* are a loose category of rights that generally protect authors' and performers' interests in the desire to be associated with their creations and performances, and to object to alterations to those works and performances. *Performers' rights* benefit performers and those with whom performers have exclusive recording contracts allowing them to object to the unauthorised exploitations of recordings containing their performances. *Artists' resale rights* allow the author of a work to claim a royalty on any sale of his or her work which is a resale subsequent to the first transfer of ownership by the author. *Rental rights* allow performers and authors to prohibit or authorise the rental or lending of works containing their performances or including their works.

COPYRIGHT

The law of copyright protects a person's interest in their creation by preventing others from unlawfully exploiting the work that is protected. The desirability of the existence of such protection stems from the premise that few would choose to create a work if they could not guarantee for themselves a monopoly in the commercial realisation of profits from their creation. The universal recognition of this need for protection has led most developed countries to create laws that protect this most important of intellectual property rights. Harmonisation of such laws throughout the EU has produced a substantially similar legal regime throughout Member States: some very similar; others, particularly France, less so.

It is generally true to say that the law of copyright prohibits any person from reproducing the copyright work of another without the owner's consent. Copyright is a property right and will be owned by a person in a similar way to the ownership of a house or a car. Thus a journalist whose article is copied by another journalist has a right of action in the courts and may obtain damages for the infringement. Similarly, a broadcaster that finds that its broadcast material is recorded and re-broadcast by another will have a claim. An author of a novel who finds that his or her work has been made into a film may sue the production company and others, and a composer of a song will have an action against an illicit cover version of their song.

This chapter considers the creation and existence of copyright as well as the different types of copyright that may subsist in various works. It looks at the duration of copyright and analyses the rules of ownership and the ability to transfer ownership or allow others to exploit the protected work. Lastly, it considers when a seeming act of infringement (such as copying a newspaper article) may not, in fact, be an infringement of copyright.

The creation of a copyright work

Unlike other forms of intellectual property right (such as trade marks and patents), there are no registration requirements for the legal existence of copyright. The right will automatically arise as soon as a copyright work is created (provided it is original and meets the qualifying conditions—see below), and will subsist for the prescribed duration.

EXAMPLE
Sasha decides to give up a career in law to write a novel about lawyers and their daily lives. Copyright will exist in the work the moment the words are written or typed.

The Copyright, Designs and Patents Act 1988 divides all copyright works into the following three categories:

- original literary, dramatic, musical or artistic works;

- sound recordings, films or broadcasts; and

- the typographical arrangements of published editions.

Thus unless a work falls into one of the above categories, it will not be protected by copyright.

Literary, dramatic, musical and artistic works

The fundamental requirement for the existence of copyright in literary, dramatic, musical and artistic works is that the work in question must be original. The requirement of originality does not import a concept of inventiveness. There are two aspects to originality. First, the work must not be copied from another work. Secondly, more than a minimal amount of skill, labour and judgement must have been expended in creating the work. Thus a mere list of information compiled from other information will be entitled to copyright protection (see *Independent Television Publications Ltd v Time Out Ltd* [1984] F.S.R. 64 where it was held that the *TV Times* programme listings were an original literary work) where some effort has been expended in arranging the material by the author. In practice, the threshold is rather low. The mere fact that one work is similar to another does not mean that the second is not protected by copyright, so long as there has been no copying—two composers may create a strikingly similar piece of music without ever hearing each other's work and copyright will exist in each. Literary, dramatic and musical works are defined in s.3(1).

A *literary* work is defined as:

"any work, other than a dramatic or musical work, which is written, spoken or sung, and accordingly includes—

(a) a table or compilation other than a database,
(b) a computer program,
(c) preparatory design material for a computer program, and
(d) a database."

"A database" is defined in s.3A as:

"a collection of independent works, data or other materials which—

(a) are arranged in a systematic or methodical way, and
(b) are individually accessible by electronic or other means."

The definition of originality is different for databases. A literary work consisting of a database is original if "by reason of the selection or arrangement of the contents of the database the database constitutes the author's own intellectual creation".

Common examples of literary works include books, articles and newspapers as well as interviews, speeches and song lyrics. Despite the word "literary", this type of copyright does not require the work to have any literary merit (and thus it applies to a table of numbers just as much as it does to a great work of English literature). The work must be more than minimal though and, therefore, names or slogans alone will probably not attract copyright protection.

A *dramatic* work "includes a work of dance or mime". Examples of dramatic works include plays written for the theatre, works of choreography, pantomimes, operas and screenplays. The expression "dramatic work" has to be given its natural and ordinary meaning (see *Norowzian v Arks Ltd (No.2)* [2000] F.S.R. 363 where it was held that the expression meant a work of action, with or without words or music, which was capable of performance).

A *musical* work means "a work consisting of music, exclusive of any words or action intended to be sung, spoken or performed with the music", i.e. the musical composition itself, excluding any lyrics, which will attract literary copyright. Copyright in a musical work should not be confused with that in a sound recording (see below), and thus the music played in the sound recording, and the sound recording itself, are separate copyright works.

Copyright does not subsist in a literary, dramatic or musical work until the work is recorded in a material, or tangible, form (s.3(2)). Thus the law of copyright does not protect a mere idea but the form of expression of an idea (for the protection of ideas by the law of confidentiality see Ch.4). It is thus essential to record an idea for copyright protection in the expression of that idea to be gained. For example, a novel or speech will be recorded for the purposes of s.3(2) as soon as it is written down. An interview will be recorded where it is taped or videoed. In certain cases (particularly where ownership of copyright is disputed) it may be crucial to ascertain the date upon which the copyright in a work came into existence. Authors of novels and other works could send by post or email a sealed (in the case of a hard copy) and date stamped copy of their work to themselves or a solicitor or trusted friend as soon as it is completed, but this is not automatically deemed conclusive proof of the date of creation and, contrary to popular belief, this is not a necessary prerequisite to the existence of copyright.

EXAMPLE
In the example above, Sasha writes the novel and it is so successful that she is invited to receive an award. She rehearses what she is going to say in her acceptance speech in front of the mirror. She repeats the speech at the awards ceremony, which is televised. Copyright exists in her speech only at the ceremony because the speech was not recorded when rehearsed in front of the mirror.

An *artistic* work is defined in s.4(1) as:

"(a) a graphic work, photograph, sculpture or collage, irrespective of artistic quality,
(b) a work of architecture being a building or a model for a building, or
(c) a work of artistic craftsmanship."

As mentioned above, an artistic work must be original, but the statute does not specifically impose a requirement that it be recorded. Of course, it will be relatively rare for a work that falls within the above definition not to exist in a material form. It is possible for a work to gain protection as both a literary and artistic work (see, e.g. *Anacon Corp Ltd v Environmental Research Technology Ltd* [1994] F.S.R. 659, a case relating to circuit diagrams).

Sound recordings, films and broadcasts

Such works are often called *derivative works* because they consist of (or derive from) other copyright works. The works upon which derivative works are based are called "underlying works". For example, a film (derivative work) will be based on a screenplay or novel (underlying work).

A *sound recording* is defined in s.5A as:

> "(a) a recording of sounds, from which the sounds may be reproduced, or
> (b) a recording of the whole or any part of a literary, dramatic or musical work, from which sounds reproducing the work or part may be produced,

> regardless of the medium on which the recording is made or the method by which the sounds are reproduced or produced".

Sound recordings are, of course, familiar to us and we all own many types, such as cassettes, CDs and mini discs and, increasingly, without their having any separate physical existence at all, as part of, say, the memory of a computer or iPod. It is important to realise that the copyright in the sound recording is separate and distinct from the physical item itself. Although I own my CD of "Dreaming Out Loud" by OneRepublic, the copyright in the sound recording is owned by Aftermath Entertainment/Interscope Records (and the copyright in the underlying musical work is owned by Mosley Music/Interscope Records). All that I actually own is the metal and plastic that comprises the physical CD. The soundtrack of a film is protected as part of the film but may also exist separately as a sound recording.

A film is defined in s.5B as "a recording on any medium from which a moving image may by any means be produced" and includes the soundtrack. This is a wide definition that will cover all technical methods of recording moving images. Examples include video cassettes, CD-ROM and DVD.

Copyright will not exist in relation to a sound recording or film where it is a copy taken from a previous sound recording or film.

EXAMPLE

Production company A makes a documentary about the business of importing bananas called *Yellow Peril*. Production company B uses, by consent, a 40-second section of *Yellow Peril* in its 90-minute film about drug smugglers. Production company A owns the film copyright in *Yellow Peril*. Production company B owns the film copyright in its film about drug smugglers but could not sue for infringement in relation to the 40-second section.

A broadcast is defined in s.6 as:

> "an electronic transmission of visual images, sounds or other information which—

> (a) is transmitted for simultaneous reception by members of the public and is capable of being lawfully received by them, or
> (b) is transmitted at a time determined solely by the person making the transmission for presentation to members of the public."

The definition of broadcast does not include internet transmission, unless it is a transmission taking place simultaneously and by other means, is a concurrent transmission of a live event, or is part of a programme service where programmes are transmitted at scheduled times. A broadcast includes reception of a broadcast that is relayed by means of a tele-communications system. It can be seen that the definition of broadcast is wide enough to capture all electronic transmissions—both wired and wireless.

Typographical arrangement

The typographical arrangement of published editions is a protected form of copyright. Published edition is defined in s.8 as "a published edition of the whole or any part of one or more literary, dramatic or musical works". Copyright exists in the typographical arrangement of published editions. Typographical arrangement is not defined in the Act but is taken to mean the way in which the printed page is set out. In *Newspaper Licensing Agency Ltd v Marks and Spencer Plc* [2003] 1 A.C. 551, the House of Lords held that, in the context of a newspaper, the typographical copyright protected the design layout and presentation of the newspaper page. However, a single article, when copied from the page, did not reveal how the page looked as a whole and could not by itself be protected by typographical copyright. Marks and Spencer was therefore not liable for infringement of typographical copyright as a result of its practice of circulating internally relevant individual press articles copied from newspapers. Whether it infringed copyright in the stories themselves was a separate issue.

Copyright in the typographical arrangement of published editions exists to protect publishers' investment in the publishing process. Thus any photocopy made of one or more of the pages of this book would potentially infringe the typographical arrangement copyright of Sweet & Maxwell (and the authors' literary copyright in the underlying work). This form of copyright is particularly important when copyright does not exist in the underlying literary work itself.

EXAMPLE
Xenos Publishing produces a book containing the complete works of Charles Dickens. There is no copyright in the literary work because Charles Dickens died in 1870 and therefore the copyright has expired. Any person photocopying the pages will nevertheless be infringing the typographical arrangement copyright of Xenos Publishing.

Practicalities

The practical upshot of the above is that all media works must be "cleared" prior to publication. The process of clearing includes checking whether the work concerned, for example a film, contains other works, for example a song. It is perhaps best to think of copyright as existing in many layers, with each layer coming into existence at a different time and potentially being owned by a different person. All of these layers may exist concurrently and protect the different creative talents that the individual copyright owners invested in the creation. The need to clear works is, of course, extremely common in the media industries and, unless one of the defences to copyright infringement exists (see below), consent must be obtained from the copyright owner (which might include payment of a fee) for use of a copyright work.

Qualification

Even if a work is original, copyright does not subsist in it unless the qualification requirements of the 1988 Act are satisfied (s.153). The basic position is that a work will qualify for copyright protection in the UK if at the time the work was created either where:

(a) the author (see below) was British, domiciled or resident in the UK or another country to which the 1988 Act extends, or a body incorporated in the UK or another country to which the 1988 Act extends (s.154); or

(b) the work was first published in, or in the case of a broadcast the broadcast was made in, the UK or a country to which the 1988 Act extends (s.155 and s.156).

Duration, authorship and ownership

There are a number of rules in the 1988 Act that deal with the question of who owns each particular type of copyright that is created and for how long that copyright is to last. The tables below show each type of copyright work and set out the basic rules on authorship and duration.

The first owner of copyright in a work is the author unless the work is a literary, dramatic, musical or artistic work or a film and is created in the course of employment in which case the employer is the first owner (unless agreement has been reached to the contrary—*see Burrows v Smith* [2010] EWHC 22 (Ch), which concerned the ownership of copyright in a document relating to a computer game. The court held that the wording of the designer's employment contract was such that copyright in a work (i.e. the document relating to a computer game) created in the employer's time and at its expense would vest in the employer. The court rejected the submission that the contract could be read as enabling the designer to retain copyright) (s.11). This means that if a work is commissioned, the person creating the work (not the commissioner) will be the first owner of the copyright in the work. After the copyright work has been created, the author may transfer the ownership to another (see below).

EXAMPLE

Two journalists each write an article for a national daily newspaper. The first journalist is employed by the newspaper, whilst the second is freelance. Copyright will exist in both articles but whereas the first will automatically be owned by the newspaper, copyright in the article written by the second journalist will be owned by the journalist herself. It is common therefore, for contracts with freelance writers, to include an assignment or licence (see below) of the copyright.

Where more than one person has created a work, the work may be classed as a work of joint authorship if the contribution of each author is not distinct from that of the other authors (s.10(1)). (See *Matthew Fisher v Gary Brooker and Onward Music Limited* [2009] 1 W.L.R. 1764 concerning ownership of the musical copyright in the song "A Whiter Shade of Pale", where the court held that the organist's contribution was sufficiently different from the basic composition as to qualify as an original element of the work, and therefore the organist was entitled to a share in the ownership of the musical copyright in the work).

In some instances it can prove difficult to get to the bottom of who jointly owns a copyright work. For example, in *McPhail v Bourne* [2008] EWHC 1235 the court upheld the terms of a settlement agreement between the former members of the band Busted in respect of ownership of copyright in various songs. The court suggested that if it had been unable to uphold the terms of the settlement it would have been very difficult for it to determine each parties' contribution to the songs and therefore where copyright ownership should lie.

The duration of copyright is usually either 50 or 70 years (depending on the type of copyright) from the end of the year in which a particular event occurs, commonly the death of the author or the release to the public of the copyright work, depending on the type of work concerned (ss.12–15).

Dealings and transfers

It is most likely, in the context of the media, for the owner of copyright to part with possession of it, either wholly or partially, for the purposes of exploitation. A book publisher, for example, would be unable lawfully to publish a novel if the author of that novel had not given copyright permission. All dealings in copyright fall into one of two categories:

- assignment
- licence.

Assignments and licences are dealt with in s.90. Whereas an assignment is a transfer of ownership (a so-called "property right"), a licence merely constitutes an arrangement between two or more persons for the use of a copyright work for a certain duration (a "contractual right"). Whether a particular dealing is to be by way of licence or assignment will have a considerable impact on the relationship between the parties concerned.

Assignments

All assignments of copyright must be in writing and signed by, or on behalf of, the owner (assignor). Although an assignment will constitute a transfer of ownership, it does not have to be a transfer of the ownership of the entire copyright. This rather confusing aspect of copyright law distinguishes it from transfers of the ownership of tangible property. Unlike tangible property, copyright can be divided into a number of rights, each of which may be separately assigned or retained (s.90(2)). Assignments of copyright may thus relate to one or more of the following:

(a) duration—copyright may be assigned for the whole remaining duration of the copyright concerned or for any lesser period.

(b) type of act—a copyright owner has the exclusive right to exploit the work in a number of ways, e.g. the right to issue copies of the work to the public or the right to perform the work in public, each of which may be assigned separately.

Thus, copyright comprises a complex multitude of rights. One could liken the exploitation of copyright to a family tree, which commences at the base with one unit, but which subdivides into many different branches with each branch having a different lifespan and existing for a different purpose. Those sub-branches can potentially each be assigned or licensed and, therefore, may be owned by many different people who can end up far removed from the creator of the original work. With assignment of just part of the remaining duration of the copyright work, it would be worth making specific provision in the assignment document for the reassignment of the work at the end of the term to the original assignor. Provision should also be made for what, if anything, the assignee can do with articles made by him/her during the term.

EXAMPLE

Robert, an English novelist, writes a work of fiction (*Exeter Nights*) which proves to be very popular. He is approached by Sordid Films Ltd, an independent production company, which wants to make a film of the book. Robert assigns the film rights to the production company for 15 years for exploitation of the film. The author has made an assignment of part of his entire copyright ownership limited by type of act and duration. He may still assign one or more of the many other rights that comprise his copyright ownership, for example the right to produce a theatrical play of the work. Upon the expiry of 15 years, the film right reverts to Robert who will own it for the remaining duration of copyright. Separately, when Sordid Films Ltd makes the film of *Exeter Nights*, numerous new copyrights will be created that exist in the film itself.

Licences

A licence is a permission to exploit a copyright work in a certain specified way. It is not a property right but merely a contractual right, which cannot be passed on by the licensee to a third person unless agreed. A licence may be oral or in writing and can even be implied from the relationship between the licensor and licensee.

EXAMPLE

X Promotions Ltd, an advertising agency, produces a television advertisement for Y Manufacturing Ltd. In the absence of any express contractual provision, there will be an implied licence for Y to use the advertisement. The ownership of the copyright in the advertisement will remain with X. It would be preferable for X and Y to have expressly entered into a licence agreement (or an assignment—see above) so that

Authorship

COPYRIGHT WORK	AUTHOR
Literary, dramatic, musical, artistic	The creator of the work
Sound recording	The producer (the person by whom the arrangements necessary for the making of the sound recording are made)
Film	The producer and the principal director
Broadcast	The person making the broadcast
Published editions	The publisher of the edition

Duration of protection

COPYRIGHT WORK	DURATION	TIME STARTS TO RUN
Literary, dramatic, musical, artistic	70 years	From the end of the calendar year of the death of the author
Sound recording	50 years	From the end of the calendar year in which it was made
Film	70 years	From the end of the calendar year in which the death occurs of the last to die of: (a) the principal director (b) the author of the screenplay (c) the author of the dialogue, or (d) the composer of music, specially created for the film
Broadcast	50 years	From the end of the calendar year in which the broadcast was made
Published editions	25 years	From the end of the calendar year in which the edition was first published

each would know the limits of the potential use of the advertisement and avoid later disputes.

Licences of copyright may be *exclusive* or *non-exclusive*. An exclusive licence, which must always be in writing, is similar to an assignment in that it gives the licensee a right to sue others for infringement of the copyright concerned (s.101). A non-exclusive licence is merely a contractual right and carries with it no automatic right to sue for infringement. For this reason it is important for non-exclusive licence-holders to obtain a contractual promise from the licensor to take action against infringers of the licensed right, or insist that the licence is in writing and signed by the copyright owner and that it expressly grants the licensee a right of action, in which case s.101A would allow the licensee to bring an action for infringement. Where a licensee wishes to take a monopoly in a particular type of exploitation, they should insist on an exclusive licence. A licensor of an exclusive licence cannot then grant a licence of the same rights to any other person during the period that the exclusive licence is in existence. A non-exclusive licence holder does not enjoy such a guarantee, and may find that one or more similar licences may arise thus affecting the profitability of his or her exploitation.

EXAMPLE
In the example above, Sordid Films decides to grant an exclusive licence for rental of videos of *Exeter Nights* in the US to Video Star Corporation and a non-exclusive licence to Omar Films of Caracas for video rental in Venezuela. Whereas Video Star is guaranteed exclusivity in the US, Sordid could grant another licence for exploitation in Venezuela, thus potentially damaging Omar Films' business.

Licences will commonly be limited to exploitation for a particular length of time ("licence period") and geographical area where the licensed activity can be carried out ("licensed territory"). In the above example, the licensed territory for Omar Films will be Venezuela.

This is essential to prevent Omar Films renting videos in the US and encroaching on the territory of Video Star.

Infringement of copyright

The law of copyright gives the owner of a copyright work the right to prevent others doing certain things (the "restricted acts") in relation to that work. A person who does an act that constitutes a restricted act without the consent of the copyright owner will commit *primary infringement* of copyright whether or not they knew of their infringement (so-called "strict liability"). A further set of acts (*secondary infringement*) will amount to copyright infringement where the person committing the act knew or had reason to believe that what he was doing infringed the owner's copyright.

Section 16 sets out the restricted acts as follows:

- copying the work;
- issuing copies of the work to the public;

- renting or lending copies of the work to the public;

- performing, showing or playing the work in public;

- communicating the work to the public; and

- making an adaptation of the work or doing any of the above in relation to an adaptation.

Primary infringement will be committed where any person does, or authorises the doing of, one of the above acts in relation to the *whole or any substantial part* of the copyright work without the consent of the copyright owner. The issue of what amounts to a "substantial part" is a matter of degree in each case and all the circumstances have to be considered. The quality or importance of what has been taken is much more important than the quantity (see *Ladbroke (Football) Ltd v William Hill* [1964] 1 W.L.R. 273). Thus a single paragraph or extracts from a larger piece of text may amount to a substantial part if it contains the most memorable passages or otherwise contains the whole creative essence of the work (see *HRH Prince of Wales v Associated Newspapers Ltd* [2006] E.W.H.C. 522 in which it was held that extracts of the journal of His Royal Highness The Prince of Wales, which were printed in *The Mail on Sunday*, amounted to a substantial part of the journal). When assessing what amounts to a substantial part it must be remembered that copyright does not protect ideas but the expression of ideas (see *Michael Baigent and Richard Leigh v The Random House Group Limited* [2007] E.W.C.A. Civ 247 in which it was held that the material copied in the book *The Da Vinci Code* did not amount to a substantial part because it was at too high a level of abstraction and amounted to ideas only and not an expression of those ideas).

EXAMPLE
   The annual lawn tennis tournament at Wimbledon is televised live by the BBC. An ITV news broadcaster re-broadcasts some of the BBC's footage (the aces and match points) on its evening news programme. Whilst the clips shown amount to only 45 seconds in total (out of a whole day's televised play), they will amount to a substantial part because it is the most vital part. Such use may however attract the defence of "fair dealing" (see below).

Copying

Copying in relation to a literary, dramatic, musical or artistic work means reproducing the work (or a substantial part of it) in any material form (s.17(2)). Examples include photocopying, rewriting long hand, reproducing extracts and photographing. Section 17(2) specifically provides that the storing of any work in any medium by electronic means is an act of copying—downloading information from a web page will thus constitute copying. Copying also includes making any copy that is transient or incidental to the main purpose.

In relation to films or television broadcasts, copying will not only include video recording or making an electronic copy but also "making a photograph of the whole or any substantial part of any image forming part of the film or broadcast" (s.17(4)). Reproducing a still from a film would thus constitute copying.

As far as typographical arrangements are concerned, copying means "making a facsimile copy of the arrangement" (s.17(5)).

Increasingly, copyright works are created, processed, distributed and accessed through the medium of computers, and every time that happens the work is copied, for the purposes of the 1988 Act. As a result, many more uses of a work are caught by the law than was the case in the pre-digital era.

Issuing copies to the public

Section 18(2) provides that the following will constitute infringement:

(a) the act of putting into circulation in the European Economic Area (EEA) copies not previously put into circulation in the EEA by or with the consent of the copyright owner; or

(b) the act of putting into circulation outside the EEA copies not previously put into circulation in the EEA or elsewhere.

However, specifically excluded from the above provisions are the following (as specified in s.18(3)):

(a) any subsequent distribution, sale, hiring or loan of copies previously put into circulation (subject to rental or lending right); or

(b) any subsequent importation of such copies into the UK or another EEA State;

except as far as paragraph (a) of s.18(2) applies to, "putting into circulation in the EEA copies previously put into circulation outside the EEA".

Actions for infringements of this type are relatively rare. Infringement would occur where copies of a copyright work are brought into the UK (or other EEA country) for the first time and sold. It is not necessary that such copies themselves be infringing copies.

Rental or lending

Rental is defined (s.18A(2)(a)) as "making a copy of the work available for use, on terms that it will or may be returned, for direct or indirect economic or commercial advantage". Lending means "making a copy of the work available for use, on terms that it will or may be returned, otherwise than for direct or indirect economic or commercial advantage, through an establishment which is accessible to the public". The most common example of rental is DVD hire. Lending would include the activities of public libraries.

Rental and lending rights apply to literary, dramatic and musical works and artistic works (save for architecture in the form of a building or a model for a building or a work of applied art) as well as films and sound recordings. The Copyright and Related Rights Regulations 1996 created a right to "equitable remuneration" where rental rights are transferred (see below).

Performing, showing, playing

Performance includes any method of visual or acoustic presentation (including sound recordings, films and broadcasts) and applies to literary, dramatic and musical works (s.19). There is no definition of showing or playing a work in public in the Act, but this type of infringement is limited to copyright in sound recordings, film or broadcasts.

Communicating to the public

Any copyright work (except the typographical arrangement of a published edition) will be infringed where it is communicated to the public in an electronic transmission (s.20). That includes broadcasting the work to the public generally, or making it available in a way that members of the public can choose how and when to access the work (such as video-on-demand).

Adapting

Adaptation includes the translation of a work, and the conversion of a dramatic work to a non-dramatic work and vice versa and relates only to literary, dramatic or musical works (s.21). Examples of adaptations include producing a play from a novel, creating a picture book from a story and transcribing a musical work.

PERMITTED ACTS

The Copyright, Designs and Patents Act 1988 allows a person to undertake certain activities in relation to copyright works without obtaining prior permission from the copyright owner. It follows that evidence that activities fall within one of the "permitted acts" will constitute a defence to an action for infringement of copyright. The defences of most relevance to the media are the following:

- fair dealing
- incidental inclusion
- public interest
- reproduction of speeches and interviews.

Fair dealing

The activities that are permitted by virtue of the fair dealing provisions in the Act are of enormous significance to the media. The courts have demonstrated a flexible approach to the interpretation of such provisions, thus facilitating the dissemination of information that would otherwise constitute copyright infringement.

There are two types of activity relevant to the fair dealing provisions:

- criticism or review; and
- reporting current events.

Criticism or review

A critic or reviewer is allowed the freedom to copy a work for the purpose of criticism or review where such criticism or review is "fair". Section 30(1) provides that:

> "fair dealing with a work for the purpose of criticism or review, of that or another work or of a performance of a work, does not infringe any copyright in the work provided that it is accompanied by a sufficient acknowledgment and provided that the work has been made available to the public."

A work will have been made available to the public where (s.30(1A)):

- copies have been issued to the public;
- the work is made available by means of an electronic retrieval system;
- copies have been loaned or rented to the public;
- the work has been performed, exhibited, played or shown in public;
- the work has been communicated to the public.

However, importantly, a work will not have been made available to the public by an unauthorised act. Thus, where a leaked copy of a copyright work becomes available, it will not be lawful to then review or criticise such a work.

EXAMPLE
The eagerly awaited sixth novel in a thrilling series is due to be published in two months' time when several chapters of the novel, entitled *A Day in the Life of a Junior Wizard*, appear on an internet site without the publisher's knowledge. Hundreds of people access the site and read the chapters, but it will not be lawful for Hazel to review the work for her publication *Bewitching Bimonthly*. Even though many people have read the work and it has been made available, it has only become so by means of an unauthorised act (the leak to the site).

Many of the principles of the defence of fair dealing for the purposes of criticism or review can be best illustrated by reference to case law. *Fraser-Woodward Ltd v BBC* [2005] EWHC 472 concerned use by the BBC of 14 photographs of a celebrity and his family which were originally published in various tabloid newspapers by licence. Images of the newspaper pages in which the photographs were published were shown in a programme made for the BBC which they said was to criticise and/or review tabloid journalism. The court held that there was fair dealing in respect of the photographs and set out the basic principles on which fair dealing is to be assessed:

(a) regard should be had to the motives of the user;

(b) fair dealing is a matter of impression;

(c) the amount of the work used is relevant and excessive use could render the use unfair; and

(d) the court can have regard to the purpose of the use made.

In *Time Warner Entertainments Co v Channel Four Television Corp Plc* [1994] E.M.L.R. 1 the claimant owned the copyright in Stanley Kubrick's film *A Clockwork Orange*. The film had not been available in the UK for over 20 years after it had been withdrawn by the claimant due to allegations of copycat violence. The defendant made a television programme about the film and used 12 extracts taken from a copy of the film that was lawfully obtained in Paris. The clips used varied in length between 10 seconds and 115 seconds and amounted to 12.5 minutes in total, or 8 per cent of the film. An injunction was obtained by the claimant preventing broadcast of the programme by Channel 4 on the basis of copyright infringement. The Court of Appeal lifted the injunction, holding that the use made of the clips constituted fair dealing for the purposes of criticism or review. It may be useful to consider the following observations from the Court of Appeal's judgment, which clearly demonstrates the judges' wide interpretation of the fair dealing defence:

(a) the defence of fair dealing will not be unavailable merely because the chosen sample of extracts has the effect of misrepresenting the film taken as a whole (only the violent scenes from the film were reproduced in the programme);

(b) the taking of a substantial proportion of a copyright work (here 8 per cent) would not prevent the defence applying unless the use amounted to "illegitimate exploitation" of the work;

(c) the criticism or review need not relate to the copyright work itself but could relate to decisions taken concerning the copyright work (in this case the programme was not a criticism of *A Clockwork Orange* itself but a criticism of the decision to withdraw the film from public showing), to the thought and philosophy behind the work or indeed to another work.

The question of what will amount to a "sufficient acknowledgment" was not in issue in the *Time Warner* case due to the fact that the origins of *A Clockwork Orange* were clear. Section 178 of the Act provides as follows:

"'sufficient acknowledgment' means an acknowledgment identifying the work in question by its title or other description, and identifying the author unless:

(a) in the case of a published work, it is published anonymously;
(b) in the case of an unpublished work, it is not possible for a person to ascertain the identity of the author by reasonable inquiry."

A sufficient acknowledgment was held by the Court of Appeal to have been given in a case concerning the broadcast by an English broadcaster of extracts from a German television programme. *Pro Sieben Media AG v Carlton UK Television Ltd* [1999] E.M.L.R. 109 concerned a programme made about Mandy Allwood, a single mother who became pregnant with octu-plets following a course of fertility treatment. The claimant obtained the exclusive right to broadcast in Germany an interview with Mandy Allwood and did so (via satellite receivable in the United Kingdom) in one of its daily magazine programmes called *Taff*. The defendant later broadcast a pro-gramme entitled *Selling Babies*, which contained extracts from the *Taff* broadcast and was ostensibly on the subject of cheque-book journalism.

The two exceptions in s.178 not being relevant to the *Pro Sieben* case, it was necessary for Carlton to show that it had identified the work and its author. Laddie J., at first instance, held that by displaying the word "Taff" in the *Selling Babies* programme, Carlton had identified the work. Carlton argued that the author had been identified by virtue of the fact that all Taff broadcasts depicted the Pro Sieben logo (a stylised "7") at the top right corner of the screen. The judge held that, by virtue of the fact that such a symbol was meaningless to the general viewing public in the United Kingdom, the defendants had failed to identify the author of the copyright work. The Court of Appeal overturned this decision on the basis that it was irrelevant that the logo was meaningless to the bulk of the UK audience if it constituted the normal means by which the claimant identified itself. In the *Fraser-Woodward* case the court held that sufficient acknowledgment of the author did not require express identification.

Reporting current events

Provided the use is fair, a copyright work can be copied, broadcast, etc., for the purpose of reporting current events. This defence is heavily relied on by publishers of newspapers and producers of news programmes. It allows news readers to quote verbatim from newspaper headlines and allows news programmes to use extracts from other broadcasts. But its use is wider than reliance being placed by news gatherers on other organisations' news coverage. It is vital for the republication of primary documents, such as memos or CCTV footage, where news outlets do not own the copyright themselves and would find it impossible in the circumstances to "clear" its use. It is important to bear in mind that it is the allegedly infringing act that must constitute reporting current events—the copyright work used for such reporting does not need to be "current" itself. Thus an interview with a Hollywood actor that was originally broadcast in 1960 could be broadcast on the date of the actor's death in 2007 without obtaining copyright per-mission. Section 30(2) of the Act provides:

"Fair dealing with a work (other than a photograph) for the purpose of reporting current events does not infringe any copyright in the work provided that (subject to subsection (3)) it is accompanied by a sufficient acknowledgment."

Section 30(3) states that:

"No acknowledgment is required in connection with the reporting of current events by means of a sound recording, film or broadcast where this would be impossible for reasons of practicality or otherwise."

The statutory provisions do not make it clear what is meant by *current* events nor what will amount to *fair* dealing and so for that we must turn, once again, to case law. In *British Broadcasting Corp v British Satellite Broadcasting Ltd* [1992] Ch. 141 the claimant had paid substantial sums for the right to broadcast live coverage of the World Cup matches played in Italy in 1990. It also owned the copyright in the broadcasts it transmitted of those matches. The defendant used a number of clips (lasting from 14 to 37 seconds each) from the footage in its news broadcasts on its satellite sports channel. The court held such use to be fair notwithstanding that the clips amounted to the most significant parts of the whole (the goals). It went on to say that the defence was not limited to the reporting of current events in a general news programme but extended to the reporting of current events in sport in a sports news bulletin. In light of this decision, many UK broadcasters signed up to a voluntary News Access Code of Practice, which sets out the terms on which each broadcaster can record, and include in their news broadcasting, extracts from sports footage, which were initially broadcast on another broadcaster's service. This is not binding on broadcasters and so a broadcaster could depart from the code and still be acting within the fair dealing defence. However, in practice, most broadcasters abide by the terms of the code.

Following the *BBC v BskyB* case some commentators suggested that an item would cease to be "current" for the purpose of the Act where it was more than one day old. More recent case law shows that the meaning of "current" is not to be interpreted quite so strictly, but there is a need on the part of the news organisation to be able to demonstrate what exactly is current about the events it is reporting and the use being made of the copyright work.

In *Hyde Park Residence Ltd v News Group Newspapers* [2000] 3 W.L.R. 215, the *Sun* newspaper published stills taken from a security video that showed the Princess of Wales and Dodi Fayed at the Villa Windsor in Paris on August 30, 1997—the day before their deaths. On September 2, 1998, the *Sun* published a story including the stills that it had obtained, without permission, from a security guard who had worked at the Villa Windsor. The purpose of the story was to contradict public accounts given by Mohammed Al Fayed of events that had taken place that day at the Villa Windsor. Mr Al Fayed's company, which brought the action, claimed that it was impossible to describe the events of August 30, 1997 as being "current" on September 2, 1998, and also that the publication was not about reporting the current events of that day, but about attacking Mr Al Fayed. The court held that the stills were not reporting the events of August 30, 1997, but that they were part of subsequent media coverage of Mr Al Fayed's comments on the death of his son (the most recent pronouncement being made on August 31, 1998), and that such coverage could be a "current event" on a wide interpretation of those words. Per Aldous L.J.:

"It would be astonishing if works, for example parts of films of events or statements of eye witnesses, ceased to be available for lawful use for the purposes of reporting such events at some arbitrary moment during the time when, as in this case, they were still enormously and unceasingly in the news."

The *Hyde Park* case demonstrated the importance of establishing the purpose of the article before considering whether the use being made of the copyright work could be within the reporting of current events exception.

The point was further developed in *Ashdown v Telegraph Group* [2001] 4 All E.R. 666, where the *Sunday Telegraph* published a leaked secret minute written by the former Liberal Democrat leader, Paddy Ashdown. The Court of Appeal was required to consider whether the Human Rights Act 1998 had had any impact on the existing copyright legislation, and, in particular, the defences available to journalists when exercising their right to freedom of speech. The court found that, exceptionally, the narrowness of the s.30 defence for reporting "current" events might mean that the court had to construe the term in light of the right of freedom of expression. Per Phillips L.J.:

"It is possible to conceive of information of the greatest public interest relating not to a current event, but to a document produced in the past. We are not aware of any provision of the [1988] Act which would permit such publication in such circumstances, unless the mere fact of publication and any controversy created by the disclosure, is sufficient to make them 'current events'. This will often be a 'bootstraps' argument of little merit. For these reasons, we have reached the conclusion that rare circumstances can arise where the right to freedom of expression will come into conflict with the protection afforded by the [1988] Act."

It is, of course, essential that news and current events are reported to the public and the courts are surely correct in their liberal interpretation of the Act, which allows great freedom for the media when conveying information generally. But the use made of the relevant copyright material must, of course, be considered to be fair, and this is often not easy for a newspaper to demonstrate. It is an essential element of the defence of fair dealing for the purpose of reporting current events and must be objectively applied to the facts on a case-by-case basis. In the *Hyde Park* case, the newspaper was held not to have a fair dealing defence because the use of the stills could not objectively be said to be "fair". The article amounted to an attack on the truthfulness of statements made by Mr Al Fayed, but the stills themselves did not show anything significant in contradicting his pronouncements that was not available from other public sources. It was said that a fair-minded and honest person would not pay for and use dishonestly taken stills which were not previously published to make such an attack, where the stills did not contain essential information. Where there is an issue of commercial exploitation, this may weaken a fair dealing defence for a newspaper. In *Ashdown* (above) the extensive use of Mr Ashdown's own words was held to have made the *Sunday Telegraph* article more commercially valuable in attracting readership and, further, capable of detracting from the value of the memoirs that Mr Ashdown intended to publish and sell in his own right. Where the purported fair dealing is, in fact, commercially competing with the copyright owner's legitimate exploitation of the copyright work, then a fair dealing defence will almost certainly fail.

Incidental inclusion

It is not uncommon for media publications to include copyright works that are not central to the main theme of the publication. An example would be the inclusion of an advertisement on the side of a bus caught on camera during an on-street interview. Such incidental inclusion of any kind of copyright in an artistic work, sound recording, film, broadcast or cable programme does not infringe the copyright in such work (s.31(1)).

A musical work is treated slightly differently. Where a musical work, or that part of a sound recording, broadcast or cable programme as includes a musical work, is deliberately included it cannot be incidentally included (s.31(3)). In *Football Association Premier League Ltd v QC Leisure* [2008] E.W.H.C. 1411 (Ch) the inclusion of the sound recording and musical work embodied in the Premier League anthem, in the context of the filming and broadcasting of a sporting event, which had been played over the public address system at the stadium and picked up by microphones, was held to be entirely incidental.

EXAMPLE

A production company produces two pieces of film footage. The first is a cinema advertisement for a new alcoholic drink that shows a group of young people laughing and drinking at a party. The second is a fly-on-the-wall documentary at a night club. Whereas the copyright in the musical works played at the night club would not be infringed, not being deliberately included by the production company, there would be infringement of the copyright in any music at the party (deliberate inclusion).

The Panini football stickers case illustrated that too great a reliance may not be placed on incidental inclusion, particularly where commercial exploitation is at stake (*Football Association Premier League Ltd v Panini UK Ltd* [2003] 4 All E.R. 1290). Panini was selling collectable football stickers showing footballers wearing team strips showing the Premier League logo or the logo of their Premier League club. The Premier League had entered into an official merchandising agreement with another sticker manufacturer and sought an injunction to stop Panini selling its stickers on the basis that the stickers infringed the copyright in the club logos. It was clear that the logo (which was protected by copyright) was an integral part of the photograph of the player, but the Court of Appeal said that the fact that it was so integral did not shed light on whether something included in that way was incidental or not. To decide whether something was incidentally included, it was right to consider why the copyright work had been included in the other work, and that included any commercial reason as well as an aesthetic one. Here, in order to produce a collectable sticker, the player had to be in authentic club strip and, therefore, the inclusion of the club logo was essential to the purpose of creating the stickers and could not be said to be incidental.

Public interest

Although likely to be relatively rare, it is possible for a seemingly infringing act to be given immunity where the publication of the material concerned is

Fair dealing

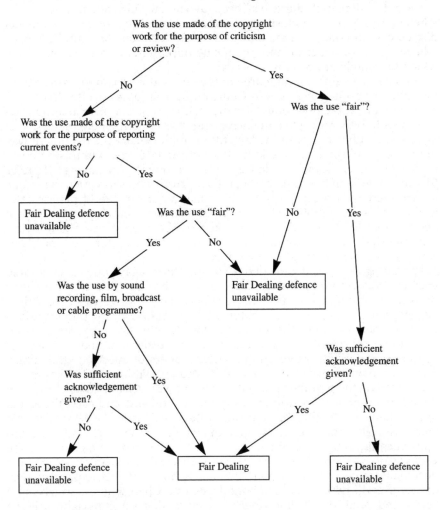

in the public interest. There is no test for public interest in the Act nor is any such defence set out there. But the Act did foresee the potential application of such a defence. Section 171(3) provides that nothing in Part I (copyright provisions) "affects any rule of law preventing or restricting the enforcement of copyright, on the grounds of public interest or otherwise".

This provision in the Act has been pressed into service in two high-profile copyright cases in recent years—the *Hyde Park* case and the *Ashdown* case (both above)—and has redefined the available scope of a public interest defence in copyright.

The possibility of a public interest defence under modern copyright law arose in *Lion Laboratories v Evans* [1984] 2 All E.R. 417, where the claimant made breathalysers used by the police. The defendants gave secret memoranda to a newspaper, which showed that there was some considerable doubt about the accuracy of the breathalysers. The court held that there was a potential public interest available to the defendant in the infringement of copyright action, but there has been debate in subsequent cases as to whether this public interest was available only because the documents disclosed wrongdoing on the part of the claimants (the "iniquity" rule), or whether it was a wider defence of making important information available, which the public has a right to receive.

This has been a developing area of the law and can be demonstrated by the different approaches of two Court of Appeal judges in the *Hyde Park* case (above). Aldous L.J. opted for the stricter, first interpretation that the court would only refuse to enforce copyright protection where to do so was against the public policy of the law, for example, where the document was immoral, or injurious to public health and safety or the administration of justice. However, Mance L.J. left the question more open, saying: "I prefer to state no more in this case than that the circumstances in which the public interest may override copyright are probably not capable of precise categorisation or definition." Ultimately on the facts, the Court of Appeal decided that the *Sun* could not rely on a public interest defence, notwithstanding that the background events of the death of the Princess of Wales were of considerable public importance.

The Court of Appeal considered the questions again only a short time later in *Ashdown* (above) and preferred the view that the public interest defence to copyright infringement was not capable of precise categorisation. However, it was clearly stated that it will be very rare for the public interest to justify the copying of the form of a work to which copyright attaches.

It should be noted, however, that there is a difference between matters that are in the public interest and matters that are of interest to the public. The defence will be available only rarely and the disclosure should only be proportionate to the public interest. In some cases, it will suffice to disclose the information contained in the copyright documents and copy the actual documents only to the relevant authorities. This may be less attractive journalistically, and the newspaper may take the view that it needs to reproduce the actual document or words, to give credible evidence of the veracity of its story. However, by only disclosing the information of a document, rather than its format, the only action available to prevent such disclosure will be in breach of confidence (see Ch.4) where a much more broad and well-trod public interest defence than in copyright, will be available to a journalist.

Reproducing Speeches and Interviews

The Copyright Designs and Patents Act 1988 confers copyright on spoken words as soon as they are recorded. The owner of the copyright in an unprepared speech will usually be the speaker of the words. Where the words of a speech are spoken in the course of employment, the speaker's employer will be the copyright owner.

Section 58 of the 1988 Act provides that it will not be an infringement of any copyright in the words as a literary work where the media reproduce a record of speeches for the purpose of reporting current events provided that:

(a) the record is a direct record of the spoken words and not taken from a previous record or from a broadcast;

(b) the making of the record was not prohibited by the speaker and it did not infringe any existing copyright;

(c) the use being made of the record, or material taken from it, is not of a kind prohibited by or on behalf of the speaker or copyright owner before the record was made; and

(d) the use being made of the record is by or with the authority of the person who is lawfully in possession of it.

EXAMPLE
A verbatim account of a politician's speech at a party conference is taken down by a journalist and reproduced in a newspaper the following day. The politician will own the copyright in their speech but there will be no infringement by publication.

When interviews are conducted for the purpose of broadcast, it is common for the interviewer to request the interviewee to sign a "Contributor's Consent Form" which gives the broadcaster the express consent of the interviewee for all broadcast and editing purposes. This is done for clarity of understanding between the parties but is not necessary in law. Clearly, there will be circumstances where a journalist cannot obtain the express consent of his or her interviewee to reproduce his or her words, but the journalist will still be at liberty to report them as the journalist's record is a direct record of spoken words in accordance with s.58.

Other defences

There are several other defences available under the 1988 Act, but which are of much less importance for the media. These include fair dealing for the purpose of private research or study, recording for the purposes of time-shifting (i.e. home video use) and a defence for transient copies. This latter defence was introduced mainly to clarify the law concerning information technology and the fact that computers often make copies of copyright works as a part of their technical operation. Provided there is no monetary significance to such a temporary copy, and it is only a part of a lawful activity, then there will not be a copyright infringement (this does not apply to a computer program or a database).

MORAL RIGHTS

Moral rights were introduced into English law for certain authors and film directors by the Copyright, Designs and Patents Act 1988. Certain moral rights have also been created for performers by The Performances (Moral Rights, etc.) Regulations 2006. Since the Regulations deal with these rights under Part 2 of the 1988 Act (the part which deals with performers' rights), performers' moral rights are similarly dealt with below.

Sharing some similarities with copyright, but distinct from it, moral rights are certain rights of individuals in relation to copyright works, infringement of which gives rise to an action for breach of statutory duty. One key difference to copyright is that such rights may not be assigned, but are personal to the creator of the work. Largely absent from English law prior to the 1988 Act, moral rights can be subdivided into four distinct and individual rights:

- to be identified as the author or director (the *paternity* right);
- to object to derogatory treatment of a work (the *integrity* right);
- not to be falsely attributed as the author of a work (the *false attribution* right); and
- to privacy of certain photographs or films (the *privacy* right).

The right to be identified

All authors of literary, dramatic, musical and artistic works and directors of films have the right to have their identity brought to the attention of readers or viewers of the work in question in a clear and reasonably prominent fashion (s.77). The paternity right subsists for the same duration as the copyright in the work concerned. However, the paternity right will not apply unless the right has been *asserted*. The right may be asserted by virtue of a statement in a document that assigns copyright in a work or by an "instrument in writing signed by the author or director" (s.78). It is not uncommon, at the beginning of a book, to see the following words:

> "[The Author] asserts [his/her] moral rights in accordance with ss.77–80 of the Copyright, Designs and Patents Act 1988."

In many cases, the exact method of identification will be the subject of contractual arrangement between the author and publisher or director and producer (e.g. the size of lettering and duration of appearance of the director's name at the front and back ends of a motion picture) in which case the protection that the paternity right provides is rendered less significant.

There are a number of exceptions to the right of paternity, those likely to be of most relevance to the media being as follows:

(a) computer programs, the design of a typeface or computer-generated works;

(b) anything done by the author as a result of the work having been made in the course of the author's employment;

(c) fair dealing for the purpose of reporting current events by means of a sound recording, film or broadcast;

(d) works made for the purpose of reporting current events;

(e) the incidental inclusion of a work in an artistic work, sound recording, film or broadcast;

(f) works published in magazines, newspapers or similar periodicals, encyclopedias, dictionaries, yearbooks or other collective works of reference, provided that they are made for the purposes of such publication, or made available with the consent of the author.

It follows that in each of the above exceptions, the author cannot insist on being identified even where he or she purports to assert such a right.

The right to object to derogatory treatment

The author of a literary, dramatic, musical or artistic work and the director of a film has the right not to have his or her work subjected to derogatory treatment (s.80). The integrity right subsists for the same duration as the copyright in the work concerned. Unlike the paternity right, the integrity right need not be asserted by the author or director. The application of this moral right is limited by the definitions in the Act.

"Treatment" is defined in s.80(2) as:

"any addition to, deletion from or alteration to or adaptation of the work, other than a translation of a literary or dramatic work or an arrangement or transcription of a musical work involving no more than a change of key or register."

Such a treatment will be "derogatory" where it amounts to:

"distortion or mutilation of the work or is otherwise prejudicial to the honour or reputation of the author or director."

There is no relevant case law on the integrity right, but it seems clear that a book will be the subject of derogatory treatment, and the author's moral rights will be infringed, where a film made from the book alters the plot or characters in such a way as to affect negatively the views of the public about the author. Similarly, a director's moral rights would be infringed where, post director's cut, alterations are made to a film that reflect badly on the director, such as the digital addition of commercial items into various scenes by way of product placement or the addition of scenes that make it a pornographic work.

The exceptions to the integrity right that are of most relevance to the media are as follows:

(a) computer programs or computer-generated works;

(b) works made for the purpose of reporting current events;

(c) works published in magazines, newspapers or similar periodicals, encyclopedias, dictionaries, yearbooks or other collective works of reference, provided that they are made for the purposes of such publication, or made available with the consent of the author;

(d) anything done for the purpose of avoiding the commission of an offence (e.g. the editing of a film to remove an obscene item prior to broadcast);

(e) anything done to comply with a duty imposed by or under an enactment (e.g. editing a film to comply with the "taste and decency" provisions in the ITC Programme Code); and

(f) expressly for the BBC, anything done to avoid the inclusion of material which offends taste or decency, which may incite crime, lead to disorder or be offensive to public feeling.

For exceptions (d), (e) and (f), where the author or director is identified there must be a sufficient disclaimer.

The false attribution right

The false attribution right is the right not to be attributed as the author of a literary, dramatic, musical or artistic work or the director of a film (s.84). Such a right would be infringed by, for example, selling copies of a book that stated that the author was a person who was, in fact, not the author. An attribution may be express or implied, and the right expires 20 years after a person's death.

Although a relatively unusual cause of action, it is relevant to works of parody. In *Alan Clark v Associated Newspapers* [1998] 1 All E.R. 959, Alan Clark MP brought an action against a satirical column called *Alan Clark's Secret Election/Political Diar(y/ies)* published in the *Evening Standard*. Mr Clark was well known both as an MP and author of his diaries of his political life, which he had published, and which had become bestsellers. The column had a heading that introduced the piece, identified its real author as Peter Bradshaw and suggested that it was his imaginary diary entry. The court found that the false attribution right was no bar to publishing parodies, but that it was necessary to make clear that it was such a parody. In this case, the column did not go far enough, nor have sufficiently prominent antidote, to contradict the general impression being given that Mr Clark was its author.

The privacy right

The person who commissions the taking of photographs or the making of a film for private and domestic purposes has the right to prevent the photographs being issued to the public, exhibited or shown in public or communicated to the public (s.85). This is so despite the fact that the copyright in the photographs, in the absence of an agreement to the contrary, will belong to the photographer. The privacy right subsists for the same duration as the copyright in the work concerned. The right will not be infringed where a photograph or film is incidentally included in an artistic work, film or broadcast. Note that this only applies to *commissioned* works for private and domestic purposes, and will not therefore affect the situation where a photojournalist takes a photograph of another person in the course of his or her work engaged by a newspaper or broadcaster. See Ch.4 for further information on the laws relating to privacy generally.

PERFORMERS' RIGHTS

Performers' rights, which exist independently of copyright (s.180), benefit individual performers in certain works. The reason for this protection for performers lies in the lack of copyright protection for performers generally (unless they happen to be the copyright owner). Thus, whilst performers (e.g. session musicians, singers, actors) will not own the copyright in works in which they perform merely by virtue of their performance, they are nevertheless afforded protection in Part 2 of the 1988 Act. The Performances (Moral Rights, etc.) Regulations 2006 have divided Part 2 of the 1988 Act into four chapters. Chapter 1 is an introduction, Ch.2 deals with "economic rights", Ch.3 deals with moral rights and Ch.4 deals with qualification for protection. Economic rights exist in the form of both property and non-property rights in relation to the performances.

The *property rights* are infringed by a person who, without the consent of the performer:

(a) makes a copy of a recording of the whole or any substantial part of a performance (the *reproduction* right) (s.182A);

(b) issues to the public copies of a recording of the whole or any substantial part of a performance (the *distribution* right) (s.182B);

(c) lends or rents to the public copies of a recording of the whole or any substantial part of a performance (the *rental or lending right*) (s.182C); and

(d) makes available to the public by electronic transmission, in such a way that members of the public may access the recording from a place and at a time chosen by them, a recording of the whole or any substantial part of a performance (the *making available right*) (s.182CA).

Performers' property rights may be transferred by assignment which must be in writing (s.191A), but a performer will always retain the right to equitable remuneration for rental and lending of works containing his or her performances (s.191G). The right to equitable remuneration may not be assigned (other than to a collecting society) nor waived.

The performer's *non-property rights* will be infringed by a person who, without the consent of the performer:

(a) makes a recording of the whole or any substantial part of a live performance, or broadcasts live the whole or any substantial part of a performance, or makes a recording of the whole or any substantial part of a performance directly from a broadcast of a live performance (s.182);

(b) shows or plays in public the whole or any substantial part of a performance or communicates to the public the whole or any substantial part of a performance, by means of a recording which was (and which that person knows or has reason to believe was) made without the performer's consent (s.183);

(c) imports into the UK otherwise than for his private and domestic use, or in the course of business possesses, sells or lets for hire, offers or exposes for sale or hire or distributes, a recording of a performance which is (and which that person knows or has reason to believe is) an illicit recording (s.184).

By virtue of s.180(2), performers' rights attach to any of the following types of performances (which must be live but do not need to be in front of an audience):

- dramatic (including dance and mime);
- musical;
- a reading or recitation of a literary work;
- a variety act or similar presentation.

There are two categories of person who are entitled to rights in performances and hence are able to bring infringement actions: the performers themselves and the person who has recording rights in relation to the performance.

EXAMPLE

Ray attends a live rock concert and, unknown to the organisers, records the concert. He then makes and sells copies of his recording. Ray has breached the performers' rights (in this case the reproduction right) of the musicians and vocalists. If the rock group's recording company is contractually entitled to make a recording of the concert then it too has an action against Ray for infringement of performers' rights.

By virtue of The Performances (Moral Rights, etc.) Regulations 2006, the following *moral rights* have also been conferred on performers (see chapter 3):

- to be identified as performer (s.205C); and
- to object to derogatory treatment of a performance (s.205F).

As with authors and directors, the right to be identified must be asserted in writing, and there are exceptions, including incidental inclusion and news reporting. The performer's right is to be identified in a manner likely to bring his or her identity to the notice of the person seeing or hearing the performance, such as, in the case of a concert, in the concert programme.

A performer's right to object to derogatory treatment is infringed if the performance in question is broadcast live, or if a recording of the performance is played in public or is communicated to the public with any distortion, mutilation or other modification that is prejudicial to the performer's reputation. Exceptions to the right include in relation to a performance given for purposes of reporting current events and to modifications "which are consistent with normal editorial or production practice". Additionally, acts done to avoid commission of an offence, to comply with a statutory duty or, in the case of the BBC, to avoid inclusion in a programme "of anything which offends against good taste or decency or which is likely to encourage or incite crime or lead to disorder or to be offensive to public feeling" will not infringe the performer's right if there is "sufficient disclaimer". A sufficient disclaimer is, in effect, a clear statement that the modification is made without the performer's consent.

The duration of all performers' rights is 50 years from the end of the calendar year in which the performance takes place, or, if during that period a recording of the performance is released, 50 years from the end of the calendar year of release. The definition of performer is not limited to a living performer and rights subsist in live performances by performers who have died before the commencement of the 1988 Act (see *Experience Hendrix LLC v Purple Haze Records Ltd, Lawrence Miller and John Hillman* [2007] E.W.C.A. Civ 501 in which the court held that there was infringement of sections 182A and 182B of the 1988 Act as a result of Purple Haze Records selling nine albums of various live performances given by Jimi Hendrix between 1967 and 1970).

In order to fall within the provisions of Pt 2 of the 1988 Act relating to performers' rights, a performance must be a qualifying performance. It will be a qualifying performance if given by a "qualifying individual" or takes place in a "qualifying country". A *qualifying country* means the UK or another member state of the EEA, or a country enjoying reciprocal protection. A *qualifying individual* means a citizen or subject of, or an individual resident in, a qualifying country.

ARTISTS' RESALE RIGHTS

The Artist's Resale Right Regulations 2006 create a new intellectual property right ("resale right"). Regulation 3(1) states that the author of a work in which copyright subsists shall have a right to a royalty on any sale of the work which is a resale subsequent to the first transfer of ownership by the author ("resale royalty"). The right continues for as long as copyright subsists in the work and cannot be assigned.

Works means "any work of graphic or plastic art such as a picture, a collage, a painting, a drawing, an engraving, a print, a lithograph, a sculpture, a tapestry, a ceramic, an item of glassware or a photograph" (reg.4). This is not an exhaustive list. A copy of a work is not to be regarded as a work for these purposes unless the copy is one of a limited number which have been made by the author or under his authority.

A resale right may be exercised only by a person who, at the contract date, is a "qualifying individual" or a "qualifying body". A *qualifying individual* means a national of an EEA state or a national of a country otherwise listed in the Regulations. A *qualifying body* broadly means a charity.

"Resale" is defined in reg.12 as:

"(a) the buyer or the seller, or (where the sale takes place through an agent) the agent of the buyer or the seller, is acting in the course of a business of dealing in works of art; and
(b) the sale price is not less than 1,000 Euro".

A sale will not be regarded as a resale if the seller previously acquired the work directly from the author less than three years before the sale.

The royalty shall be an amount based on the sale price which is calculated in accordance with Sch.1 of the Regulations (reg.3(3)) which is set out in the table below. However, the total amount of royalty payable shall not exceed €12,500.

PORTION OF THE SALE PRICE	PERCENTAGE AMOUNT
From 0 to €50,000	4%
From €50,000.01 to €200,000	3%
From €200,000.01 to €350,000	1%
From €350,000.01 to €500,000	0.5%
Exceeding €500,000 Euro	0.25%

RENTAL RIGHTS

Performers and authors have the right to authorise or prohibit the rental or lending of works containing their performances or including their works. Such a right is an important source of income for authors and performers, which is likely to grow in significance in the coming years. It was added to the provisions of the Copyright, Designs and Patents Act 1988 by the Copyright and Related Rights Regulations 1996. A "performer" is defined above. An "author" for these purposes is:

(a) the author of a literary, dramatic musical or artistic work; or

(b) the director of a film.

Lending is defined by s.18A(2)(b) as meaning:

"making a copy of the work available for use, on terms that it will or may be returned, otherwise than for direct or indirect economic or commercial advantage, through an establishment which is accessible to the public."

Rental is:

"making a copy of the work available for use, on terms that it will or may be returned, for direct or indirect economic or commercial advantage" (s.18A(2)(a)).

Although rental and lending rights may be assigned (and in some cases there will be a deemed assignment by operation of law), they will be replaced with an unwaivable right to equitable remuneration. There is no definition in the Act of equitable remuneration, but it is unlikely to be sufficient to pay authors and performers a lump sum prior to exploitation of the work concerned even if it is a genuine pre-estimate of the work's commercial success.

The "database right" is discussed in Ch.9.

4. PRIVACY AND CONFIDENTIAL INFORMATION

In certain circumstances, disclosure of information that is either confidential or private will be unlawful and a duty will be imposed by the law on the recipient of such information to keep it secret. This duty is an obvious constraint on the media industry generally and on current affairs reporting and investigative journalism in particular. However, the law of confidence is now of much wider application and has developed rapidly since the coming into force of the Human Rights Act 1998 in October 2000. The law in this area has been in a state of flux and clearly defined principles are still emerging. The categorisation of what is private and/or confidential and therefore falls outside the realm of that which can be legitimately published or broadcast has changed significantly. Whilst recent cases have helped to clarify the approach that will be taken by the courts, some areas still remain uncertain.

It was always believed that English law contained no right of privacy as such and that the developing law of breach of confidence could provide protection in appropriate circumstances.

It is also interesting to consider the view of the European Court of Human Rights (ECHR) in *Wainwright v UK* (App. No.12350/04), which concerned the strip-search of a mother and her son when visiting another son who was being held on remand at a prison in Leeds. The European Court declared in 2006 that the lack of a general tort—or civil wrong (see p.22)—of invasion of privacy in English Law was a violation of art.13 of the European Convention for the Protection of Human Rights and Fundamental Freedoms (ECHR) because there was no remedy available for the interference with the Wainwrights' art.8 privacy rights. (It should be noted, however, that the case concerned events that took place *prior to* the coming into force of the Human Rights Act.)

However, the law has leapt on apace, tested and championed by an army of celebrities wrestling with the media over the extent to which their lives should be exposed to the public gaze.

Recent authorities have expanded the law of confidence to cover scenarios that can only rightly be described as "invasions of privacy". Although the courts have remained at pains to maintain the semantic position that there is no free-standing tort of invasion of privacy, England has moved towards a fully fledged privacy law in all but name.

There is no absolute right to keep personal information confidential. But, as this chapter explains, the courts are operating a series of checks and balances on what types of information and in what circumstances privacy should prevail, and when the competing interest of dissemination of information to the public should win out.

HUMAN RIGHTS

The Human Rights Act 1998 (HRA) (see also Ch.1 and its text at Appendix C) incorporated into English law the European Convention for the Protection of Human Rights and Fundamental Freedoms (ECHR). Many heralded the Act as the advent of the first stand-alone privacy right in the United Kingdom, and the way it has been applied in recent times tends to support that view. The HRA provides the context in which all legal rights and obligations must be understood.

Article 8 of the Convention, entitled "Right to respect for private and family life", provides as follows:

"1. Everyone has the right to respect for his private and family life, his home and his correspondence.

2. There shall be no interference by a public authority with the exercise of this right except such as is in accordance with the law and is necessary in a democratic society in the interests of national security, public safety or the economic well-being of the country, for the prevention of disorder or crime, for the protection of health or morals, or for the protection of the rights and freedoms of others."

Contrast against this, the right to freedom of expression contained in art.10, which provides that:

"1. Everyone has the right to freedom of expression. This right shall include freedom to hold opinions and to receive and impart information and ideas without interference by public authority and regardless of frontiers. This Article shall not prevent States from requiring the licensing of broadcasting, television or cinema enterprises.

2. The exercise of these freedoms, since it carries with it duties and responsibilities, may be subject to such formalities, conditions, restrictions or penalties as are prescribed by law and are necessary in a democratic society, in the interests of national security, territorial integrity or public safety, for the prevention of disorder or crime, for the protection of health or morals, for the protection of the reputation or the rights of others, for preventing the disclosure of information received in

confidence or for maintaining the authority and impartiality of the judiciary."

In terms of the relative weight that should be attached to the potentially conflicting rights in arts 8 and 10, s.12(A) of the HRA (which applies where "a court is considering whether to grant any relief which, if granted, might affect the exercise of the Convention right to freedom of expression") provides that the court must:

"have particular regard to the importance of the Convention right to freedom of expression and, where the proceedings relate to material which the respondent claims, or which appears to the court, to be journalistic, literary or artistic material (or to conduct connected with such material), to:

(a) the extent to which:

(i) the material has, or is about to, become available to the public; or

(ii) it is, or would be, in the public interest for the material to be published;

(b) any relevant privacy code."

Section 12 was intended to give comfort to media organisations, in that the courts would be obliged to give special consideration to their rights under art.10. However, art.10 is not an absolute right and allows that the right to freedom of expression will still be subject to laws that are necessary for, amongst other things, the "protection of the reputation or rights of others". It is now clearly established that art.10 does not carry greater weight than art.8. In each case, s.12 only requires the court to conduct a balancing exercise between the two competing rights. This balancing between competing rights features time and again in recent privacy cases and is a central reason for the continuing degree of uncertainty in this area of law.

Confidential information

As explained in Ch.1, the HRA requires that English law must now be interpreted in light of the Convention rights which it enshrines. In the law affecting the media, the existing legal right to which the "gloss" of the HRA has been most frequently applied is the law of confidence. The law of confidential information should be thought of, at its most traditional, as the law that protected commercial secrets, such as secret recipes or business plans.

Traditionally, confidence will be breached (and thus an action for breach of confidence will lie) where, as Megarry J. stated in *Coco v AN Clarke (Engineers) Ltd* [1968] F.S.R. 415:

(a) the information has the necessary quality of confidence;

(b) the information has been imparted in circumstances importing an obligation of confidence; and

(c) there is an unauthorised use of the information to the detriment of the original communicator of the information.

These relatively simple elements, which constitute the law of confidence, have been applied to a myriad of different circumstances and stretched in new directions. These three fundamental principles still form the legal basis for the traditional, commercial, breach of confidence action.

However, the advent of the HRA and the widening in the scope of actions for breach of confidence has resulted in a restraint on the media from publishing certain personal information as well as the more traditionally recognised business or "trade secrets". In *Douglas v Hello!* (see below) it was recognised that the existing law of breach of confidence needed to be developed to give proper effect to the art.8 right to respect for an individual's privacy.

Most significantly, in May 2004, the House of Lords handed down its judgment in the case brought by the supermodel Naomi Campbell against the *Mirror* newspaper (see below). This remains a leading authority on the law of confidence in the field of personal privacy. In fact, it is now correct to say that there is the traditional breach of confidence action, and then there is *Campbell* confidence: misuse of or unjustified publication of private information. This new type of action has been developed as a distinct type of confidence and is considered separately in greater detail below.

The basic principles of confidence, which were traditionally conceived in the commercial world, were elaborated to give a contemporary use against the mass media. With the advent of the modern approach espoused in *Campbell* and developed more recently by the Court of Appeal, in particular in *McKennitt* (see below), it is important to remember that the cases discussed below dealing with the protection of private information under the "classic" breach of confidence heads, and which precede the judgment in *Campbell*, would be analysed on a slightly different basis if they were brought today.

The principal method of media restraint in this branch of the law is the injunction. Unlike other areas of the law, for example defamation, a breach of confidence action will allow the claimant to obtain an *interim* injunction. Thus, where a person or company learns that a newspaper or other publication is about to publish information which is, in that person's view, confidential or private, an application may be made immediately for an injunction to restrain such publication. Generally, a journalist will need to put his allegations to the person who is the subject of the story. This is because if the allegations are defamatory of the individual, the journalist will need to check their truth or to give the subject an opportunity to respond, in order to demonstrate responsible journalism. In defamation cases there is a longstanding rule (established in the 19th century case of *Bonnard v Perryman* [1891] 2 Ch. 269) that the courts will not normally grant an injunction to restrain the publication of defamatory allegations where the defendant contends that the allegations are true. However, where the article involves the disclosure of private information, this rule does not apply and the journalist who approaches the subject of a story in advance runs a risk that the subject might seek an injunction and halt the publication of the article. This explains why, in practice, such allegations are frequently put to the subject a very short time before publication or sometimes not at all, thus depriving them of a realistic opportunity to seek an injunction preventing publication. An injunction restraining the publication of private information will be granted by the court where the "balance of convenience" requires it and where the applicant can show that it is likely to (in the sense of "probably will") establish if the action came to trial that publication should not be allowed (s.12(3) HRA). Of course, the injunction may be lifted at the trial but many months may by then have elapsed, thus potentially rendering the original story un-newsworthy. The media has raised concerns that in recent years celebrity claimants have sought to bypass the rule in *Bonnard v Perryman* and obtain interim injunctions by dressing up what are in reality defamation claims (primarily intended to protect reputation not privacy) as privacy claims. While it is clear that a claimant is free to choose his own cause of action (*Joyce v Sengupta* [1993] 1 W.L.R.), the courts have emphasised that where the nub of a complaint is the falsity, not the private nature of the alleged facts, it will be an abuse of process to bring a cause of action in privacy to defeat the rule in *Bonnard v Perryman*. Such a distinction may be difficult to operate in practice as intrusive allegations about an individual's private life will often also be defamatory (e.g. allegations about an adulterous affair). The courts have recognised that in privacy cases an interim injunction preventing publication is often the only effective remedy. After publication has taken place and the "cat is out of the bag" an award of damages after a contested trial cannot restore the privacy that has been breached. At the time of writing we await the result of an application by former FIA chairman Max Mosley (see below) to the European Court of Human Rights seeking the introduction of a legal requirement for journalists across Europe to notify the subjects of stories before the publication of articles that could intrude on their private lives (*Mosley v United Kingdom* App.48009/08).

CAMPBELL CONFIDENCE: MISUSE OF PRIVATE INFORMATION

The coming into force of the HRA stimulated a development away from the traditional notion that a duty of confidence could only be enforced in the context of a pre-existing relationship in equity or contract. As referred to above, the House of Lords' judgment in *Campbell v MGN Ltd* [2004] UKHL 22 in May 2004 has established a different sub-set of the traditional breach of confidence action, shifting the focus from violation of a confidential relationship by unauthorised disclosure to the actual nature of the information disclosed and the protection of personal autonomy, dignity and self esteem.

The model Naomi Campbell brought an action against the *Mirror* newspaper for its publication of the fact that she had, and was receiving treatment for, a drug addition. The article was accompanied by a photograph of her on the street leaving a therapy session which, on its own, was an ordinary street scene. The faces of those she was with had been pixellated but she was clearly recognisable. The article included details about the fact that she was receiving treatment at Narcotics Anonymous (NA), the nature of that treatment and how often she attended.

At first instance, the Court held that both the fact of the addiction and the additional details of her attendance at NA sessions were capable of protection under the law of confidence. On appeal, the newspaper successfully argued that the fact that she was a public figure and a role model made a difference to the status of the information. Ms Campbell had previously denied having a drug addiction and, therefore, had conceded at the outset that the newspaper was entitled to expose her misconduct and subsequent hypocritical concealment by stating that she had a drug addiction and that she was receiving treatment. What she had objected to was the publication of details of where and how she was receiving treatment and the photograph of her at the specific NA centre she attended. The Court of Appeal decision ([2003] E.M.L.R. 2) held that where a public figure made false statements about their private life, the press was allowed to set the record straight and the peripheral details (such as where and how she was receiving treatment) were part of the detail required to give the overall story credibility. Ms Campbell had courted publicity during her career, and the press was entitled to set the record straight about her untruthful statements. Where the publication was in the public interest, then the journalist should be allowed some latitude as to how to convey the information.

But this approach of the Court of Appeal was narrowly overturned (three to two) in the House of Lords. Finding for Ms Campbell, the Lords decided that the disclosure of the additional information conveyed in the story about where and when she attended for treatment and the photograph of her leaving NA was a breach of confidence. However, their Lordships analysed the case slightly differently from the classic breach of confidence construction outlined above and emphasised instead the detrimental effect unlawful disclosure of such private information would have on the subject of the disclosure. In deciding whether the information contained in the article was of a nature that should be protected, their Lordships laid down a two-stage test:

- Is the information obviously private?

- Where it is not, is the information of a nature where its disclosure would be likely to give substantial offence to the subject of the information?

This was crucial in relation to the photograph of Ms Campbell. On the face of it, the photographs simply showed the model on a busy London street. However, when coupled with the commentary in the article it was clear that they conveyed an image of how she looked on the occasion of her attendance for treatment and an image of the place that she had visited. The information in the picture alone was not "obviously private", but the Lords held that disclosure of the image, which conveyed to the reader where Ms Campbell went for treatment, was likely to cause substantial offence to her. An important distinction was drawn between this and a photograph of a person engaged in some everyday activity. Per Baroness Hale L.J.:

"We have not so far held that the mere fact of covert photography is sufficient to make the information contained in the photograph confidential. The activity photographed must be private. If this had been, and had been presented as, a picture of Naomi Campbell going about her business in a public street, there could have been no complaint. She makes a substantial part of her living out of being photographed looking stunning in designer clothing. Readers will obviously be interested to see how she looks if and when she pops out to the shops for a bottle of milk. There is nothing essentially private about that information nor can it be expected to damage her private life."

However, an affirmative answer to either of the questions above is not the end of the story. This brings into play the balancing exercise of the competing rights under the HRA. The test will be whether the benefit of the publication is proportionate to the harm done by the disclosure of the information, which interferes with the right of privacy. It is then for the newspaper to demonstrate that there is public interest in each element of the private information that the publication will disclose (see below).

Here, the majority of their Lordships did not give the journalistic leeway that had been allowed by the Court of Appeal. The Lords found that the newspaper could not demonstrate public interest in the additional facts of the story, and although there was public interest in exposing Ms Campbell's deceit, this was insufficient to justify the ancillary points. Importantly, the judgment indicates that journalists are to be required to demonstrate public interest in each and every item of information contained within a story—not just the story as a whole.

Campbell-type privacy has been developed and applied by the Court of Appeal in *Douglas v Hello!* [2005] EWCA Civ 595, *McKennitt v Ash* [2006] EWCA Civ 1714, *HRH Prince of Wales* [2006] EWCA Civ 1776 and more recently *Mosley v News Group Newspapers Limited* [2008] EWHC 177 (QB).

The landmark decision of the Court of Appeal in *McKennitt* has had significant consequences for the media not only in relation to the publication of tabloid "kiss and tell" stories but also unauthorised biographies and paparazzi photographs.

Loreena McKennitt, a Canadian citizen, folk singer and songwriter, sued Niema Ash, once a friend and employee of hers. In 2005, Ash had published a book entitled *Travels with Loreena McKennitt: My Life as a Friend*. The book disclosed, amongst other things, private information about the claimant relating to a number of matters including her personal and sexual relationships, her feelings about the death of her fiancé and the circumstances of his death, matters concerning her health and diet, matters concerning her emotional vulnerability, and details concerning a dispute between the claimant and the defendant arising out of a property purchase in 1997, which was the subject of litigation that had subsequently settled. The claim was brought on the basis that some of this information had been disclosed in breach of confidence and in breach of the claimant's privacy.

Whilst maintaining that there is no tort of "invasion of privacy" in English domestic law, and that the development of a right to protect private information must be through the developing action of breach of confidence, it was accepted that this does not sit easily in those cases where there is no pre-existing relationship of confidence between the parties (as in the *Douglas* and *Campbell* cases). This "verbal difficulty" is now avoided by rechristening the tort as "misuse of private information".

In complaints of wrongful publication of private information, a revised two-step test (considered in detail below) will now be applied. In turn, that test will be informed by the following four propositions as distilled (by their Lordships in *Re S (A Child)* [2005] 1 A.C. 593) from *Campbell*:

- Neither art.8 nor art.10 has precedence over the other.

- Where the values under the two articles are in conflict, an "intense focus" on the comparative importance of the specific rights claimed is required.

- The justifications for interfering with or restricting each right must be taken into account.

- The proportionality test must be applied to each (the ultimate balancing test).

TWO-STEP TEST

The first question is whether the information is private, i.e. did the person in question have a reasonable expectation of privacy?

If so, the second step is to conduct the balancing exercise and ask whether in all the circumstances the art.8 right of the owner of the private information must give way to the publisher's art.10 right of freedom of expression.

These stages have to be followed for each piece of information complained of (and each photograph, which requires additional, separate, justification).

STEP ONE: ARTICLE 8—IS THE INFORMATION PRIVATE?

The first stage of the test, determining whether information complained of is in fact private, may in many instances be dealt with easily. It must also be assessed objectively from the point of view of the reasonable bystander standing in the claimant's shoes.

This is similar to the first requirement of *Coco v AN Clarke* (above) for traditional confidentiality cases. The courts apply an objective test in determining whether information has a confidential character: would the reasonable person, in the position of the defendant, have realised that the information they have in their possession is confidential? This was relatively straightforward when applying the law to a commercial setting: clearly the "secret recipe" or new marketing strategy were valuable items of information that should be exploited only by those who legitimately know of them.

A distinction must be drawn between information that is confidential (i.e. secret) and information that is private. The latter is difficult to define, as it relies in part on a subjective view—what is private information about oneself for one person, may be of no particular sensitivity to another. This difficulty in categorising what type of personal information ought to be protected by virtue of being private is a fundamental problem with the emerging law of privacy. Before *Campbell*, the Court of Appeal had perceived this as a test of instinct rather than law, when it said that "usually the answer to the question of whether there exists an interest worthy of protection will be obvious" (*A v B & C; sub nom. Garry Flitcroft v MGN Ltd* [2002] 2 All E.R. 545). In fact it is often far from obvious; the courts have regularly disagreed—in *Campbell* the Court of Appeal disagreed with the first instance judge and the House of Lords disagreed with the Court of

Appeal (and indeed with each other) as to some of the principles to be applied. In *Douglas*, the Court of Appeal defined what is private as including information that is personal to the person who possesses it and that they do not intend it to be imparted to the general public.

Who is doing what and with whom is the staple diet of tabloid newspapers. Whether details of an individual's sex life is the type of information that should be protected by the law has been, and will continue to be, a controversial area. The courts have long held that mutual confidences of a marriage should be protected from disclosure (*Argyll & Argyll* [1965] 1 All E.R. 611). This was extended to protect details of sexual conduct outside of a marriage as well (*Stephens v Avery* [1988] 2 All E.R. 477). As Mr Justice Eady remarked in Mosley:

"There is now a considerable body of jurisprudence in Strasbourg and elsewhere which recognise that sexual activity engages the rights protected by Article 8...there must exist particularly serious reasons before interferences on the part of public authorities can be legitimate".

Interference with private life has to be of some seriousness before art.8 becomes engaged. The information may be unimportant or it may be of considerable gravity. Both are capable of protection, but it should not be so unimportant as to be trivial.

If the content is "anodyne", imprecise or already known to the public, it cannot usually be protected (though photographs may be an exception, as discussed below). However the categories of information that may be capable of being protected by the law of confidence and the emerging law of privacy are almost limitless. A brief review of cases in recent years includes information relating to sex life, health and medical treatment, family, household details, the contents of diaries, correspondence and emails, corporate financial dealings, wedding photographs and pictures of the inside of someone's home. In one recent case (*Author of a Blog v Times Newspapers Limited* [2009] EWHC 1358) the real name of an anonymous internet blogger was claimed to be private, though the courts disagreed. Here the author of a blog called "The Night-Jack" applied to the court to prevent the *Times* newspaper from publishing his real name. The blogger was a serving police officer and the blog set out his opinions regarding various social and political issues relating to the police and the justice system. The blogger accepted that the *Times* had discovered his identity by a process of deduction from material publicly available on the internet but argued that nonetheless the newspaper was under a duty of confidence not to publish his identity, and that he had a reasonable expectation of privacy regarding his true identity. In an important decision for bloggers wishing to maintain their anonymity the court dismissed the application on the basis that "blogging is essentially a public rather than a private activity".

Triviality

Trivial information will not usually engage art.8. However, there are exceptions. In *McKennitt* even anodyne descriptions of the inside of a cottage were held to attract protection given the particular emphasis in art.8 on the respect to be accorded to a person's home.

There has been a divergence of opinion on this issue between the English courts and the European approach. As noted above, Baroness Hale remarked in *Campbell* that there is nothing private in a picture of someone "popping out for a pint of milk" and a claim for an injunction brought by Elton John involving photographs of him walking, casually dressed, from his Rolls Royce to the front gate of his home was rejected on similar grounds (*John v Associated Newspapers Ltd* [2006] EWHC 1611 (QBD)).

Yet that is precisely the sort of photograph that was the subject of protection in the important European case of *von Hannover v Germany* ([2005] 40 EHRR 1 (see below). The continuing tension between the leading domestic decision in *Campbell* and the European Court in *von Hannover* was acknowledged by the Court of Appeal in *Murray v Big Pictures (UK) Limited* [2008] EWCA Civ 446 (below) and has not yet finally been resolved.

In another Court of Appeal decision following hot on the heels of *McKennitt*, this was taken further and the question of triviality is now to be established, it would seem, by asking what *intrusive effect* the material in question has, rather than its *informational content* (see generally *HRH Prince of Wales v Associated Newspapers Ltd* [2006] EWCA Civ 1776).

Photographs

The courts have drawn some distinction between the confidential nature of information when conveyed in text form only, when compared to photographs. It is recognised that photographs may be especially intrusive and can be protected against publication, when the information conveying the same set of facts, in text form, may lawfully be made known.

Although photographing persons or objects will generally not constitute a breach of confidence, in *Creation Records Ltd v News Group Newspapers* (*The Times*, April 29, 1997), a successful action resulted from the publication of a photograph of a set for a photo shoot. In making arrangements for the taking of photographs for a forthcoming album by Oasis, a swimming pool was drained and a white Rolls Royce lowered into it. An official photographer was present and took photographs over several hours. Although secrecy was an important issue, some fans turned up at the location and took photographs of the proceedings. One of these "fans" was a *Sun* photographer who also took photographs, one of which was very similar to the shot chosen by Noel Gallagher for the album cover. That and two others were published in the *Sun* and readers were invited to send £1.99 for a glossy poster of the world exclusive picture of the new Oasis album shoot. The Court held that the nature of the photo shoot, together with the imposition of security measures made it an occasion of confidentiality as far as photography was concerned.

In *Theakston v MGN* ([2002] E.M.L.R. 22) the TV presenter, Jamie Theakston, sought to restrain publication both of the fact that he had been to a brothel and photographs taken of him there. Whilst the Court allowed publication of the information about his visit, it granted an injunction over the photographs, on the grounds that they were more intrusive into a person's private life than was justifiable. Per Ouseley J.:

"The courts have consistently recognised that photographs can be particularly intrusive and have shown a high degree of willingness to prevent the publication of photographs, taken without the consent of the person photographed but which the photographer or someone else sought to exploit and publish. This protection extended to photographs, taken without their consent, of people who exploited the commercial value of their own image in similar photographs, and to photographs taken with the consent of people but who had not consented to that particular form of commercial exploitation, as well as to photographs taken in public or from a public place of what could not be seen with the naked eye, then at least with the aid of powerful binoculars. I concluded that this part of the injunction involved no particular extension of the law of confidentiality and that the publication of such photographs would be particularly intrusive into the claimant's own individual personality."

This reference to special protection for information in photographic form (more recently approved in *Douglas* and *Mosley*) was accepted by the judge in granting an interim injunction in 2005 to Elizabeth Jagger restraining further publication of a CCTV recording from a nightclub in Soho, which included stills of her engaging in sexual activity with Calum Best. The pictures were captured in an area where they could be seen by security staff or passers by. She did not seek to prevent publication of any information by verbal description, merely the recording itself or stills taken from it. Bell J. accepted that the mere fact that the incident took place in a somewhat public place did not preclude the claimant from succeeding in a privacy claim (following *Campbell* and the European cases of *Peck* and *von Hannover* (see below)).

Indeed, in some cases, a photograph alone could found an action in confidence, as the confidential information sought to be protected was the very fact of what the occasion looked like. This was the case in *Douglas v Hello!*, where the claimants wanted to protect the images of what the bride and groom had actually looked like on the day. The official photographs were the subject of an exclusive deal between the celebrity couple Michael Douglas and Catherine Zeta-Jones and glossy magazine *OK!*.

However, a paparazzi photographer managed surreptitiously to take some unauthorised photographs and sold them to rival *Hello!*, which published them—ruining *OK!*'s exclusive. In the case, which went to the House of Lords, it was held that *Hello!*'s publication was a breach of confidence. The Court of Appeal ([2005] EWCA Civ 595) upheld the first instance judge's decision and awarded £14,600 in favour of the Douglases. The House of Lords [2007] UKHL 21 (which was concerned only with *OK!*'s claim, this having been rejected by the Court of Appeal), by a majority of three to two, overturned the Court of Appeal decision and reinstated the first instance award of £1,033,156 in favour of *OK!*. (*OK!*'s claim was not concerned with art.8, or protection of privacy, but was brought in order to protect a commercial confidence and so the traditional analysis was appropriate.) The confidential/private information in question in this case consisted of photographic images of how the wedding looked. Had certain guests merely described what the couple were wearing and what they had done on the wedding day to *Hello!*, this would have been unlikely to threaten *OK!*'s exclusive as the public would have wanted still to see the pictures of the celebrity pair.

If a photograph conveys some private information, its publication must be separately and specifically justified. In *Campbell*, their Lordships were divided on the approach to be taken. The minority focused on whether the photograph concerned showed its subject in an undignified, distressed, humiliating or embarrassing situation. However, the majority focused on whether it was apparent from the photograph itself (or taken together with the accompanying text) that the activity captured was of a private nature.

The European Court has injected into English law a further dimension. Its landmark decision in the case of *von Hannover v Germany* ([2005] 40 EHRR 1) has been firmly adopted by the Court of Appeal in *McKennitt* (and in so doing the Court of Appeal went further by refusing to accept the media's submission that *von Hannover* was decided on the basis of many years of media intrusion and press harassment, rather than the publication of the specific photographs that in themselves would not otherwise have been an invasion of privacy).

This was a claim that was brought by Princess Caroline of Monaco arising out of the publication of various photographs of her engaged in activities such as practising sport, out walking, leaving a restaurant or on holiday.

It was held that the concept of private life extends to aspects of personal identity, such as a person's name or a person's picture; that it includes a person's physical and psychological integrity, and that art.8 is primarily intended to ensure the development of the personality of each individual in their relations with other human beings:

"There is therefore a zone of interaction of a person with others, even in a public context, which may fall within the scope of 'private life'."

The Court drew a distinction between occasions on which the princess was pursuing private leisure activities in public places such as restaurants and beaches, and occasions when she was appearing in a more official capacity. The decisive factor was what contribution the photographs made to a debate of general interest.

The case is of significant impact and publication of long-lens photographs of individuals (whether celebrities or not) engaging in ordinary activities in public places is unlikely to be justifiable. According to the principles established in *von Hannover* the mere fact that photographs are taken in a public place does not of itself mean there can be no reasonable expectation of privacy. It was hoped that the case of *Murray v Big Pictures (UK) Limited* would help to resolve the element of uncertainty in domestic law about whether the publication of photographs of individuals involved in ordinary activities in public places should be considered off limits (by extension of the logic in *von Hannover*); or permissible under the principles identified by Baroness Hale in *Campbell*, to the effect that there must be some areas of innocuous behaviour in public places such as "popping out for a pint of milk" that did not attract a legitimate expectation of privacy. *Murray* was a case brought on behalf of David Murray, the infant son of author JK Rowling, in respect of long lens photographs taken of him in his buggy on an Edinburgh street. At first instance the claim was struck out by Patten J. on the basis that "there remains an area of innocuous public conduct in a public place which does not raise a reasonable expectation of privacy". In striking out the claim the judge sought to distinguish between routine activities, such as a trip to the shops, from more organised recreational activities. However, the claim was reinstated by the Court of Appeal which noted that:

"[The] question of whether there is a reasonable expectation of privacy is a broad one, which takes account of all the circumstances of the case. They include the attributes of the claimant, the nature of the activity in which the claimant was engaged, the place at which it was happening, the nature and purpose of the intrusion, the absence of consent and whether it was known or could be inferred, the effect on the claimant and the circumstances in which and the purposes for which the information came into the hands of the publisher".

On the basis of the above test the Court of Appeal felt that the case should proceed to trial because it was "at least arguable that David had a reasonable expectation of privacy. The fact that he is a child is in our view of greater significance than the judge thought." Unfortunately (at least for media lawyers) the case settled before trial thereby depriving us of a detailed judicial analysis of its facts. While it is clear that the courts will attach particular importance to the art.8 rights of children, it remains an open question as to whether in the future pictures of celebrities in public places will only be permissible in England if they contribute to a genuine public debate rather than simply to satisfy the readers' curiosity about the subject. The outcome of this debate may have significant impact on the future of the paparazzi and tabloid celebrity reporting in this country.

Since the Court of Appeal decision in *Murray*, the European Court of Human Rights judgment in *Reklos and Davourlis v Greece* (1234/05 [2009] ECHR 200 January 15, 2009) has established that there are circumstances in which the mere *taking* of a photograph without consent (but with no immediate plans to publish) may both engage and breach the subject's art.8 rights. In this case a Greek clinic had allowed a professional photographer to enter a restricted area of the clinic and take two photographs of a newborn baby without the consent of its parents, to whom the photographs were subsequently offered for sale. There had been no current intention by the clinic to publish the photographs to the world at large but the baby's parents complained about the failure to seek their consent and asked for the negatives to be handed over, which the clinic refused. The ECHR found that the lack of parental consent and the refusal to deliver up the negatives constituted a breach of art.8. The decision in *Reklos* should be compared with that of the domestic courts in *Wood v Commissioner for Police for the Metropolis* [2009] EWCA Civ 414, which also considered the question of whether the bare taking of a photograph with no intention to publish it more widely could engage art.8. Mr Wood was an anti-arms trade campaigner who had been photographed by the police outside the Annual General Meeting of a company whose subsidiary arranged a trade fair for the arms industry. The photographs were taken by the police to identify potential offenders at the meeting and the subsequent trade fair but at the time officers refused to make clear the purposes for which the images would be used. The Court held that the mere taking of a photograph in a public place did not of itself engage a subject's art.8 rights without further aggravating circumstances. Although it ultimately decided that on the facts of the case the actions of the police were in breach of Mr Wood's art.8 rights, the Court warned that:

> "It is important that this core right protected by Article 8, however protean, should not be read so widely that its claims become unreal and unreasonable. For this purpose I think there are [three] safeguards, or qualifications. First, the alleged threat or assault to the individual's personal autonomy must (if Article 8 is to be engaged) attain 'a certain level of seriousness'."

Pre-existing relationship

Whether there is a relationship of confidence involved is still a factor that is to be taken into account under the new tort. Both *McKennitt* and the *Prince of Wales* cases were different from *Campbell*, *Douglas* or *von Hannover* in that there was already a pre-existing relationship of confidence between the parties. These two claims fell within the already established cause of action of breach of confidence. Nevertheless, the Court of Appeal took the view that in "misuse of private information" claims against the media, the two-step test is to be applied.

The traditional approach (whether the information has been imparted in circumstances importing an obligation of confidence) and cases decided using that approach may still inform how any pre-existing relationship fits into the new cause of action.

Information will be imparted in circumstances imposing an obligation of confidence where there is a relationship between the parties that would lead the reasonable man to conclude that the information should be kept secret. Even in the pre-*Campbell* era such a "relationship" did not have to exist already between the parties and it was often implied in the circumstances. Thus, a clearly audible exchange between A and B in a crowded marketplace would not lead to an obligation of confidence no matter how confidential the information. Others present in the market place hearing the conversation would not be under an obligation of confidence either as there was no expectation of confidence between the parties. However, where a diary was dropped on the street and a stranger picked it up, although there is no pre-existing relationship between the diary-writer and the stranger, the stranger can be in no doubt that the information he has received is confidential and an obligation of confidence would be implied.

Several types of relationship will obviously give rise to an automatic obligation of confidence, for example the relationship that exists between an employer and their employee, between two commercial concerns undertaking a business negotiation with each other and between one family member and another.

EXAMPLE

Roxana has an idea for a new television game show. She secretly tells Rose of the idea. Rose is under a duty to keep the idea confidential and may be sued by Roxana if she does not do so.

As far as the employer–employee relationship is concerned, the obligation of confidence may arise by virtue of an express provision in an employment contract. But this does not mean that such an obligation cannot arise where there is no such provision. In *Faccenda Chicken v Fowler* [1986] 1 All E.R. 617 the Court established that, in appropriate circumstances, there would be an implied contractual provision to keep confidential information obtained by virtue of the employment.

EXAMPLE

James is employed by Barnes in Barnes's factory. He discovers that Barnes is making twice the profit that he is declaring in the annual accounts. James is under a duty to keep the information secret and not to tell the story to a journalist.

The employment contract issue has begun to arise more and more as an issue for the media, notably where employees of famous or powerful individuals seek to reveal their story (often in return for substantial payment) about the time they spent as an "insider". Lady Archer, the wife of the disgraced peer Jeffrey Archer, was awarded £2,500 damages and obtained an injunction against her former PA, Jane Williams (*Archer v Williams* [2003] F.S.R. 869). The PA had contacted various national newspapers with the aim of selling her story. As a result of these communications, one Sunday newspaper ran a story about Lady Archer having cosmetic surgery. The Court held that the PA remained bound by the obligation of confidence, which in this case had arisen expressly in her employment contract, and her own desire to tell the story (and, therefore, her right to freedom of expression under art.10 of the Convention) did not override the duty of confidence.

There is no denying that the existence of, and intimate details from, sexual relationships of people in the public eye is of great curiosity to the public at large. The last decade has seen the creation and growth of the "celebrity magazine" which regales stories of the lives of the stars, including their relationships, appearance, family and lifestyle. Inevitably, the law has become embroiled in trying to identify where disclosure of information about a sexual relationship is lawful and where it is not.

As mentioned above, where details of a relationship are capable of being treated as confidential and between spouses, there will be a presumption that this is the case. Thus, where a husband proposes to reveal secrets about his wife, she will be likely to succeed in obtaining an injunction to prevent this. This is because the courts recognise the married relationship as being a repository of confidential information, which both parties are entitled to expect to be protected. However, in considering disclosures of secrets about other kinds of relationships, the courts have been willing to apply the laws of confidence. In *Stephens v Avery* [1988] 2 All E.R. 477 a newspaper carried a report that the claimant had had a lesbian affair with the wife of a notorious criminal. The newspaper obtained the information from a friend of the claimant's in whom the claimant had confided. The Court held that the fact that the claimant had passed on the information to her friend did not prevent her bringing an action against the friend to restrain its further dissemination. This case made it clear that the law of confidence could protect relationships other than between husband and wife, although it may not operate in the same way.

The question of whether the nature of the relationship between the parties gave rise to confidential circumstances was considered in the *Garry Flitcroft* case (above). The newspapers had bought the kiss-and-tell stories of two women, who had both had affairs with the footballer Garry Flitcroft. The women had met him at a bar where one worked as a lap dancer and had had clandestine sexual relationships with him for some months. Mr Flitcroft, who was married with two children, sought an injunction to prevent publication of the story. A significant factor in this case was that the women wanted to tell their stories and it was asserted that preventing them from doing so would be to infringe their art.10 rights to freedom of expression. The Court of Appeal discharged the injunction, saying that whilst the nature of the relationships concerned were the "outer limits of relationships which require protection of the law", in this instance to stop publication would be an unjustified interference with the freedom of the press.

In the light of recent decisions it seems unlikely that the English Courts would follow the decision in *Flitcroft* today either in granting greater protection to marital confidences than to a footballer's one night stand, or in allowing one party to such an encounter to tell their story if by doing so it would encroach unacceptably on the other party's reasonable expectation of privacy (see *McKenitt*). In *CC v AB* [2006] EWHC 3083 (QB), Eady J. recognised that in personal and sexual relationships (even adulterous ones) there is a reasonable or legitimate expectation of privacy. This was in many ways a surprise decision for the media. An injunction was granted to a sports celebrity who had conducted an adulterous relationship for some months with the defendant's wife, despite the Judge acknowledging that it was "a striking proposition that a spouse whose partner has committed adultery owes a duty of confidence to the third party adulterer". However, this was not a case of one party to a private relationship seeking to exercise their art.10 rights. Unlike in *Flitcroft*, neither of the parties to the sexual relationship wanted it to be made public. Furthermore, the injunction did not prevent the defendant from telling close friends, members of the family, the family doctor, counsellor or lawyers—it was the threatened sale of the story to the tabloids that was prevented.

Browne v Associated Newspapers Ltd [2007] EWHC 202 (QB) concerned a claim for an interlocutory injunction. Lord Browne of Madingley, the claimant and Group Chief Executive of BP, sought an injunction against the publishers of the *Mail on Sunday* to restrain it from publishing details of his relationship with Mr Jeff Chevalier, and confidential or private information that Mr Chevalier had obtained during the course of their relationship. The Court of Appeal ([2007] EWCA Civ 295), upholding for the most part the first instance decision of Eady J., commented that the mere fact that the information was imparted in the course of a relationship of confidence does not in itself satisfy the test of "expectation of privacy". The test must be applied to each item of information communicated to, or learned by, the person concerned in the course of the relationship. The nature of the relationship is of considerable importance. A detailed examination of all the circumstances on a case-by-case basis is required, including the nature of the information itself, and the circumstances in which it has been imparted or obtained. In short, each case must be decided on its own facts.

The question of whether the circumstances in which the information is imparted give rise to an obligation of confidentiality also overlaps with the issues discussed below in relation to public domain. The previously received wisdom was that where an activity takes place in public and in view of others, then these circumstances will not usually create an obligation of confidence. However, this rule may be varied by factors such as whether the information (or photograph) was obtained using a long lens or where a person is in a public place but with a reasonable expectation of privacy (which itself now has to be re-evaluated in light of the attitude of the ECJ in the *Peck* and *von Hannover* cases, both of which require a stricter approach as to whether an event in a public place could still be considered private).

In *McKennitt*, the fact that many of the matters were disclosed to Ash by virtue of her longstanding friendship with McKennitt made it far more difficult to argue that the defendant's rights should prevail. In fact, the book itself explicitly recognised that much of the material was confidential: for example, Ash stated that McKennitt "confided to me" and "revealed her innermost self to me".

The state of a person's health is any event a private matter, and the Court found that it was "doubly private when information about it is imparted in the context of a relationship of confidence".

One of the most significant aspects of the *McKennitt* judgment is the recognition of the European jurisprudence, in particular the *von Hannover* case. Whilst holding that McKennitt did not really need to rely on *von Hannover* to prove her case, the Court of Appeal nevertheless made comments on it that were far reaching. It found that *von Hannover* extends the reach of art.8 beyond what had previously been understood and that the English courts should give respectful attention to it; that art.8 jurisprudence did in this case, and will in the future, shape the test of "reasonable expectation of privacy".

The judgment of Eady J. in *Mosley v News Group Limited* [2008] EWHC 1777 (QB) provides a useful compendium of the current law in this area. In *Mosley*, the claimant, a married man and president of the Federation Internationale de l'Automobile (FIA), was secretly filmed on private property by one of five women with whom he was engaged in various sexual and sado-masochistic activities. Stills and images were published by *News of the World* in its newspaper and online (where they were viewed over a million times) together with allegations that Mr Mosley had taken part in a "depraved Nazi-style orgy" with girls "wearing mock death camp uniforms". The images quickly became available to millions via other websites around the world. Mr Mosley was not approached for comment before publication and subsequently vehemently denied that there had been any Nazi element. He immediately sought an interim injunction to have the offending material removed from the *News of the World* website. Although the Court accepted that the claimant's art.8 rights were engaged it was not prepared to grant an injunction against *News of the World* because in the circumstances it would have been a futile gesture to injunct one newspaper when the material would still be widely accessible on the internet. While expressing sympathy with the claimant's predicament the Court was not prepared to play "King Canute" by granting an injunction where it would make no practical difference to the availability of the material worldwide. Perhaps unusually, Mr Mosley continued with his privacy case despite his initial failure to obtain the most effective remedy of an injunction. At trial the Court found that it was "fairly obvious that the clandestine recording of sexual activity on private property must be taken to engage Article 8". It also found that the woman paid to make secret recordings by *News of the World* had breached an old-style duty of confidence to the other participants to whom trust and discretion were very important. In deciding the case in Mr Mosley's favour the judge went on to reject the public interest justifications put forward by the newspaper as part of the "balancing exercise" set out at step two below.

STEP TWO: ARTICLE 10—THE BALANCING EXERCISE

As set out above, it is now well established that neither article takes precedence over the other and that the art.10 right is not a trump card. Where conflict arises, an "intense focus" is necessary upon the comparative importance of the specific rights being claimed in the individual case. This involves weighing the interference with the art.8 rights of the claimant by allowing publication against the interference that will be caused to the publisher's art.10 rights if an injunction is granted. The proportionality test must be applied to each.

In carrying out this exercise, factors that will be relevant include how private the material is and the level of intrusion, as well as the type of speech (political at one end of the spectrum and "vapid tittle-tattle" at the other). This inevitably involves moral judgements. The decision of the European Court in *von Hannover* and in particular the following remarks, which were specifically cited by the Court of Appeal both in *McKennitt* and *HRH Prince of Wales*, will be critical to how the balancing exercise is to be conducted:

> "The decisive factor in balancing the protection of private life against freedom of expression should lie in the contribution that the published photos and articles make to a debate of general interest."

Where the competing art.10 rights are those of the person telling the story (rather than the media itself) the position may be slightly different. In *Flitcroft*, it was both relevant and one of the decisive factors, that the two women involved in the "relationship" were exercising their own art.10 rights to tell their own story. This can be contrasted with the case of *CC v AB* (see above).

In *McKennitt*, the defendant argued that her right to freedom of expression, to tell her own story, should be taken into account. She relied on *Flitcroft* but this argument was dismissed on the basis that the information complained about was not in fact her story at all but rather the claimant's— she was merely a spectator and much of the content of the book would only be of interest by virtue of the fact that the claimant was the central character.

Furthermore, she had only obtained the information concerned by virtue of the nature of her relationship with the claimant, which was miles away from the "relationship of casual sex" between the footballer and the two women. "The footballer could not have thought that when he picked the women up they realised that they were entering into a relationship of confidence with him". The same clearly could not be said about this relationship.

Information in the public domain

The general principle is that information that is already known cannot claim the protection of private life. Thus, even where information is confidential, it is generally understood the media will not be prevented from publishing it where it has already been published elsewhere if it relates to commercially confidential information.

EXAMPLE

A waiter leaks to a local free newspaper details of a scam at the restaurant where he works to pass off supermarket plonk as vintage wine. The newspaper publishes an article about this but the restaurant does not take any action against the newspaper, believing that its reputation is so poor and that it is so little read no one will believe the story. A national newspaper then publishes the story about the fraud, but the restaurant cannot now take any action in confidence against the national newspaper as the information is already in the public domain.

In the long-running *Spycatcher* case, the House of Lords held that the UK Government could no longer prevent publication of the book by Peter Wright because it had been so widely published abroad it was now public knowledge (*AG v Guardian Newspapers Ltd (No.2)* [1988] 3 All E.R. 545). The Court said it was less likely to reach the same conclusion where the information was private details about an individual resident in the United Kingdom, as the effect of publication in their residential locality might still be markedly different to publication overseas.

In trade secret and commercial confidence cases a straightforward approach applies. Once the information in question is made "generally accessible" it can no longer be protected as confidential. The House of Lords in *Douglas v Hello!*, having held that photographic information about the wedding could properly be the subject of a confidence, addressed the question whether that obligation of confidence could be enforced *after* the approved photographs had been published. It was held that it could, on the basis that the publication of one photograph did not destroy the obligation of confidence in respect of other photographs of the same event. The "secret" consisted of images of the wedding as a whole and not just individual images of it.

In personal privacy cases, however, the position is more complex. Even if material is not secret, it can still be private. As with so much else in this area of law, it will depend on the particular factual circumstances. It is clear that an act done in a private place, such as an individual's home, will have the necessary quality of confidence—even where several or many other people are present. In *Douglas v Hello!* [2003] 3 All E.R. 996 this "private event" was taken to extremes when a wedding attended by several hundred people was still held to be a private occasion and images of the married couple were capable of being confidential. It is important to note though that guests were told that the wedding was private, and photography and cameras were forbidden (for further background detail on this case, see *Privacy & Data Protection*, Vol.1, Issue 8, p.6).

In *Browne v Associated Newspapers Ltd* (see above), the Court of Appeal commented in passing that there is potentially an important distinction between information which is made available to a person's circle of friends or work colleagues, and information which is widely published in a newspaper.

The situation becomes more complex when an individual is in a public place, but claims that they had a reasonable expectation of privacy there. As we have seen, the European Court has said that even where the events take place in public, an individual's art.8 right may still be engaged. The case of *Peck v United Kingdom* [2003] E.M.L.R. 15 dealt with the disclosure of council CCTV footage to media organisations, which showed an individual on a main road in Brentwood town centre carrying a knife. It later became known that the individual had just attempted suicide. The UK Government argued that this individual's action was already in the public domain, taking place as it did on a street and capable of being witnessed by anyone present at the time. But the Court held that there is a "zone of interaction of a person with others, even in a public context, which may fall within the scope of 'private life'". Whilst the CCTV recording itself was lawful, as it was to prevent and detect crime (indeed, the fact he was being recorded had saved his life), the further disclosure of the CCTV footage to the media and its subsequent broadcast to millions of people was held to be an invasion of Mr Peck's privacy.

As we have seen, a similar approach was taken by the European Court more recently in *von Hannover v Germany* in connection with photographs published of Princess Caroline of Monaco. This European case was considered by the Court of Appeal in *HRH Prince of Wales v Associated Newspapers Ltd* (2006) EWCA Civ 1776 which concerned a journal (the Hong Kong journal) kept by HRH Prince Charles that contained a personal description of his participation in an event that marked the handing over of Hong Kong, including a banquet attended by the Chinese president, and was described by him in a disparaging manner. He referred to the Chinese entourage as "appalling waxworks". The *Mail on Sunday* published extracts from the journal following a State visit to London by the Chinese president. It was argued that he had opened up a "zone" of his life to public scrutiny. Disappointingly for the media, however, the fact that information about a particular "zone" of an individual's private life is put in the public domain (even if put there by the claimant) will not open up that whole area to public scrutiny.

It has been argued previously that information falling within a particular "zone" once revealed would mean that a person has a greatly reduced expectation of privacy in relation to any other information that fell within that zone. That argument has been rejected.

The Court of Appeal in *McKennitt* explained "if information is my private property, it is for me to decide how much of it should be published. The 'zone' argument completely undermines that reasonable expectation of privacy".

The fact that the claimant passes on information to another will be taken into account by the court in determining whether the information is still confidential, but the mere fact of such dissemination does not automatically prevent an action in breach of confidence. Where the information is known to a greater group of people, it raises the question of whether it has passed into the public domain.

The courts have also concluded, in respect of a celebrity who is in the public eye, that there is a distinction between a person who is a "publicity seeker" and someone who is contractually bound to give interviews by virtue of what they do (*X&Y v Persons Unknown* [2006] EWHC 2783 (QB)).

In the circumstances, the public domain defence will succeed in the face of a personal privacy claim where it relates to what is in effect a re-publication of information previously made known to the public in almost identical terms (but see also **Photographs** above where the re-publication of a photograph may still infringe in some circumstances given the special treatment of photographs).

False private information

It was previously thought that false personal information could not be protected. It is now clear from *McKennitt* that this approach is wrong and the question is not whether the information objected to is true or false, but rather whether it is private. As Longmore L.J. observed:

> "The question in a case of misuse of private information is whether the information is private not whether it is true or false. The truth or falsity of the information is an irrelevant inquiry in deciding whether the infor-mation is entitled to be protected".

So as long as the false material does not deprive the true material of its intrusive quality or overall significance, a remedy is available.

It is not yet settled what the position would be if wholly false information is the subject of complaint. In the traditional breach of confidence scenario no claim can be brought for false information. Even under the new tort, if the heart of a claim is a complaint about *false* allegations and the privacy claim is brought in order to avoid what should rightly be a claim in defa-mation and in order to obtain an interim injunction, then an abuse of process argument could be raised. The courts have rejected applications for interim injunctions on these grounds e.g. *Tillery Valley Foods Ltd v Channel Four* [2004] EWHC 1075 (Ch). In *Browne v Associated Newspapers Ltd* (see above), which concerned an application for an interlocutory injunction, the Court of Appeal observed that if a case was brought on the basis of breach of confidence, but the true object of the complaint was to protect reputation, then the higher burden of proof that applies to injunction applications in defamation (namely, that the claimant must demonstrate that the proposed defence of justification would be bound to fail and the words complained of were manifestly untrue) would probably be applied.

UNAUTHORISED USE

The traditional three-step test from *Coco v AN Clarke* also required a clai-mant to establish that the use of the information complained of was an unauthorised use. This seldom presents much difficulty (and did not fall to be considered in the post-*Campbell* cases considered above) as in many cases the unauthorised use will be publication by the media. It will rarely be difficult to show that the dissemination of the information complained of, for example to a journalist or to the public generally, is an unauthorised use.

Two highly unusual breach of confidence cases deal with preventing the unauthorised disclosure of confidential information solely by the media because of particular problems that may cause—even before a particular publication is envisaged. Both were exceptional cases concerning child killers: Jon Venables and Robert Thompson, who were the killers of toddler Jamie Bulger, and Mary Bell, who had murdered two children when aged only 11 herself.

In *Venables and Thompson v News Group Newspapers* [2001] 1 All E.R. 908, an application was made for a permanent injunction to prevent the media from publishing details of any information that might lead to the identification, appearance or whereabouts of either of the killers. Venables and Thompson were then aged 18 and the press raised the question as to whether the reporting restrictions that had protected them as juveniles would now be lifted. On release from detention, it was proposed that both would be given new identities. The Court granted the injunction on the grounds that widespread dissemination of the new names, addresses and appearance of the pair could have potentially disastrous consequences for them, not only by means of intrusion and harassment but that it might pose a serious risk of physical harm and even death from vengeful members of the public or their victim's family. Unusually, the Court here seemed to place considerable reliance on the potential effect that the unauthorised disclosure by the media may have on the claimants. Similarly in *X, a woman formerly known as Mary Bell & Y v News Group* [2003] F.S.R. 850 the Court placed emphasis on the consequences that such unauthorised disclosure might have, particularly on Y, the daughter of Mary Bell. Unlike *Venables and Thompson*, it was not considered that the unauthorised disclosure might pose a threat to life, but the protective injunction was still granted on the basis that X and Y would lose much through publicity and it could undo the rehabilitative progress that had been made. The court held that the physical and psychological well-being of X and Y was protected by art.8 and that in this instance that outweighed the art.10 rights of the media.

DISCLOSURE IN THE PUBLIC INTEREST

A newspaper or broadcaster fighting an attempt at restraint for breach of confidence may, in appropriate circumstances, be able to use the public interest defence. If successful, an injunction may be avoided at both the interlocutory stage and at trial. The publisher must show that the public interest in preventing disclosure is outweighed by the public interest in its publication. "Public interest" is not specifically defined but appears to be narrowly construed and it is for the newspaper to demonstrate what it claims is the positive effect for the public on it being able to publish the confidential information.

Mere fame does not render a claimant a public figure and the mere fact that the public may have interest in a claimant does not necessarily mean that intrusion into their private lives is justified.

The courts are wary of the public interest defence being used where in fact what is being argued is merely that the public is interested in the information: there is a distinction between information that is truly of public interest and that which is of interest to the public. In order for the public interest defence to be considered and to succeed, it must focus on the specifics of the information that is published and how the disclosure of each piece of information serves the public interest.

In *Lion Laboratories Ltd v Evans* [1984] 2 All E.R. 417 the claimant was a company that made intoximeter devices used by the police to conduct roadside breath tests. The defendant was an ex-employee who disclosed to the press certain documents relating to the unreliable nature of the devices made by the claimant. An action by the claimant company for breach of confidentiality failed on the basis that it was in the public interest for information relating to the reliability of such devices, and the corresponding positive effect on the administration of justice, to be widely available.

In *X v Y* [1988] 2 All E.R. 648 an employee of the claimant health authority supplied the first defendant, a reporter with a national newspaper (one of the other defendants), with information obtained from hospital records, which revealed that two doctors working in the area had AIDS. On hearing that the defendants wished to publish an article identifying the doctors, the claimant applied to the court for an injunction restraining any such publication. The defendants contended that it was in the public interest that the names of doctors carrying the AIDS virus who were continuing to practise should be disclosed. However, the Court held that the public interest in preserving the confidentiality of hospital records identifying actual or potential AIDS sufferers outweighed the public interest in the freedom of the press to publish such information, because victims of the disease ought not to be deterred by fear of discovery from going to hospital for treatment. Accordingly, a permanent injunction was granted preventing publication.

Where the confidential information involves government secrets, the court will be reluctant to grant an injunction restraining publication unless it is clearly in the public interest to do so. *Att Gen v Guardian Newspapers Ltd (No.2)* [1988] 3 All E.R. 545 concerned Peter Wright's book *Spycatcher*. Various extracts appeared in the *Guardian* and *The Sunday Times*, following which the government obtained an injunction preventing any further publication until the trial. Various appeals followed, culminating in a final application to the House of Lords to have the injunction lifted. The House confirmed that Peter Wright was under a life-long duty to keep secret information relating to his work but stated that, unlike private individuals and organisations, the government had the additional burden of being required to show that the public interest would be harmed by publication.

Revealing crime or iniquity is in the public interest and to that extent freedom of expression will override most claims to privacy. The modern position extends beyond iniquity and can include correction of a false public image, as in *Campbell* where she had specifically denied taking drugs and so the media was entitled to inform the public of the true position. Thus, if a public figure misbehaves then the public have the right to have the record put straight. Doubt was cast, however, in *McKennitt* on the role model argument (espoused in *Flitcroft*) that those who are role models have lesser rights and their otherwise private actions are more susceptible to the public interest defence.

The correct question that needs to be asked in cases involving information received in confidence, according to the *Prince of Wales* case, is "whether in all the circumstances it is in the public interest that the duty of confidence should be breached". In the *Mosley* case the court rejected the newspaper's arguments that the publication of the obviously intrusive clandestine images could be justified by reference to a countervailing public interest in exposing that there had been a Nazi theme to Mr Mosley's activities and that he had "mocked the humiliating way Jews were treated". Had these facts been proved the judge conceded that there might have been a public interest in revealing them (at least to those in the FIA to whom Mr Mosley was accountable, though not necessarily the public at large). Nor did the court accept that any significant criminal offence had been committed the exposure of which would justify the publication. Trivial wrongdoing is not enough:

> "It is not for the state or the media to expose sexual conduct which does not involve any significant breach of the criminal law".

REMEDIES

The available remedies are damages and injunctive relief. Until recently the damages awards in this area have been low (such as £3,750 (for the privacy aspect of the claim) to each of the Douglases, £3,500 to Naomi Campbell, £5,000 to Loreena McKennitt). However these figures are on the rise and more recently Max Mosley was awarded £60,000 in general damages although the court made it clear that exemplary (or punitive) damages were not available in a claim for infringement of privacy.

Injunctions

Despite the rise in damages there is little doubt that an injunction will remain the most effective form of relief in privacy cases. The Court recognised in *Mosley* that no award of damages could fully compensate the claimant:

> "Whereas reputation can be vindicated by an award of damages, in the sense that the claimant can be restored to the esteem in which he was previously held, that is not possible where embarrassing personal information has been released for general publication. As the media are well aware, once privacy has been infringed, the damage is done and the embarrassment is only augmented by pursuing a court action."

Recognising that an injunction is often the only effective remedy in privacy cases, Max Mosley's current application to the ECHR argues that in order effectively to protect a citizen's art.8 rights there must be a legal requirement for journalists to notify the subject of a potentially intrusive story prior to publication. This would allow the subject an opportunity to seek an injunction rather than being left simply with the unsatisfactory remedy of damages if (as is often the case) the newspaper gives no warning prior to publication. Mosley was given no prior warning and he claims that the lack of a legal duty on the newspaper to do so means that the UK has failed in its obligation to provide an effective remedy for a breach of his art.8 rights. The ECHR's decision is not available at the time of writing but one can identify some practical difficulties in applying such a requirement. For instance if the English courts adopt a radical interpretation of the European decision in *von Hannover* the notification requirement might become extremely onerous. It could be necessary for journalists to notify the subjects of every single photograph taken in a public place without specific consent (with the possible exception of occasions when the subject is on some strictly defined "public business" such as a news conference). The consequences of such a development for the celebrity and tabloid media in this country would clearly be far-reaching and there is already some evidence of celebrities (see Sienna Miller below) using the law to control by agreement the occasions on which photography will be permitted.

"Super injunctions"

There has been much public debate about the rise of the so called "super-injunction". This is an ominous but somewhat vague term used to describe injunctions where an order has been made (using the court's various powers under the Civil Procedure Rules (CPR), the Contempt of Court Act 1981 and the Administration of Justice Act 1960) to place restrictions on the reporting of the injunction proceedings, e.g. the names of the parties and sometimes even the fact that an injunction has been made at all. The justification for such restrictions is to avoid the purposes of the injunction being defeated by publicity, but concerns have been raised that such orders may be becoming dangerously routine, contrary to the principles of open justice. It has been complained, for instance, that due to the wholesale anonymisation of the parties' names (which are normally replaced by letters of the alphabet) case dockets can often begin to look like "Alphabet Soup".

Sometimes attempts to enforce and obtain the terms of such orders can prove counter productive. In 2010 footballer John Terry sought to obtain a super injunction (*LNS v Persons Unknown* [2010] EWHC 119 (QB)) preventing publication of details of an alleged extramarital relationship with the former partner of England teammate Wayne Bridge. When the injunction was overturned, Terry was stripped of the England captaincy amid intense media scrutiny of the affair which could now be reported in time-honoured fashion as the "story they tried to ban". In 2009 an injunction was obtained on behalf of multi-national energy company Trafigura against the *Guardian* newspaper preventing the publication of a leaked confidential draft report about alleged waste dumping in West Africa. The *Guardian* was also prevented from reporting the fact that Trafigura had obtained an injunction and the case was referred to in court documents simply as *"RJW and SJW v Guardian News and Media"*. The *Guardian* subsequently complained that the terms of the order restrained it from even reporting a parliamentary question about the injunction. This sparked a high profile media debate about super-injunctions and their supposed ability to fetter the reporting of parliamentary democracy. The media storm whipped up by the injunction brought the underlying allegations against Trafigura to the top of the news agenda in the UK and around the world. Many overseas websites, beyond the reach of the English courts, went so far as to publish the draft report, forcing Trafigura to acknowledge that there was no longer any point to the injunction remaining in place. This is a telling illustration of the "King Canute" principle, by which obtaining an injunction in the English courts against a newspaper will sometimes be of little practical effect in the age of the internet where information can be available around the world in minutes via blogs and global social networking sites such as Twitter or Facebook.

PROTECTION FROM HARASSMENT

The Protection from Harassment Act 1997 was originally designed to cope with the problem of "stalkers". It is clear, however, that the civil and criminal actions created by the Act may be used by individuals to curb the activities of journalists and others engaged in media activities. This has led to criticism on the basis that freedom of expression has suffered another knock in an already restricted environment.

Section 1 provides:

> "(1) A person must not pursue a course of conduct:
>
> (a) which amounts to harassment of another, and
> (b) which he knows or ought to know amounts to harassment of the other.
>
> (2) For the purposes of this section, the person whose course of conduct is in question ought to know that it amounts to harassment of another if a reasonable person in possession of the same information would think the course of conduct amounted to harassment of the other."

Such conduct is a criminal offence and, if an actual or apprehended breach of s.1, may also give rise to civil proceedings for an injunction and/or damages. Harassment is not defined in the Act, but it is clear that it must mean conduct that has occurred on two or more occasions. The conduct need not be physical. For example, conduct such as the sending of many, or offensive, letters could constitute harassment. In *Ferguson v British Gas Trading Limited* [2009] EWCA Civ 46 the claimant was a former British Gas customer who, after changing suppliers, continued to be sent bills (which she claimed were unjustified). She was also sent sequence upon sequence of computer-generated letters threatening to cut off her gas supply, take legal proceedings or report her to a credit reference agency. The claimant contacted British Gas many times by letter and by telephone and though most of her letters went without reply she did receive apologies and assurances that the matter would be dealt with. However the threatening letters kept on coming causing the claimant great distress. British Gas said that the claim should be struck out on the basis that the course of conduct complained of was not of sufficient gravity to constitute harassment. The Court of Appeal disagreed stating that it was strongly arguable that the company's conduct was sufficiently serious to satisfy the gravity test and capable of causing real anxiety. The fact that the letters were computer generated did not make the conduct any less serious. British Gas also argued that there had been a failure by the claimant to identify a senior employee with knowledge of the course of conduct who could represent the "directing mind" of the company, or an employee responsible for the course of conduct and for whose acts the company was vicariously liable. The Court of Appeal did not agree. It noted that there was no defence of accidental harassment and or any good reason why a corporation should be exonerated for conduct which, if carried out by an individual, would amount to harassment. A company should be taken to have knowledge of material within the knowledge of its employees, even if its top management knew nothing of the particular case. It was only necessary to prove that the company ought to know that its conduct amounted to harassment.

Harassment by journalists

It is likely that a court would hold that the "doorstepping" activities of a journalist could be harassment, where such behaviour crossed the boundary of what a person might think reasonable. Conduct can include speech.

The Press Complaints Comission (PCC) Code requires journalists to desist from persisting with questioning, telephoning or pursuing individuals once asked to desist. Journalists must also identify themselves and the company they represent if asked to. There are similar provisions in the Ofcom Broadcasting code. Some celebrity claimants have gone a step further and brought civil harassment claims against the media. In 2008 Sienna Miller accepted £37,000 damages in settling her harassment claim against photographic agency Big Pictures Limited brought following incessant and "intolerable" pursuit by photographers. As part of the settlement the agency undertook not to pursue Ms Miller by car, motorcycle or on foot, or doorstep her at her family home, but it was agreed that pictures could be taken when she attended bars, nightclubs or red-carpet events.

In one case, brought against the *Sun* newspaper, the court held that publication may amount to harassment where the journalist's article was not considered reasonable (*Thomas v News Group Newspapers Ltd* [2002] E.M.L.R. 4). The *Sun* had published an article about disciplinary proceedings against police officers which had arisen after a complaint was made by a clerk at the police station, Esther Thomas. In its article, the *Sun* referred to Ms Thomas as "a black clerk" and gave details of her place of work. It also subsequently published a number of readers' letters that complained about the disciplining of the officers, and some of which blamed Ms Thomas. She said she later received hate mail and was afraid to go to work. The court held that, in general, press criticism of someone would not usually constitute unreasonable conduct amounting to harassment. However the newspaper would be required to show that its conduct was reasonable. In this instance, it was arguably not reasonable to refer to Ms Thomas's colour in the reporting and the newspaper had not disassociated itself from the readers' letters. The test for a publisher would be whether a proposed series of publications that was likely to cause distress to an individual was an abuse of freedom of the press.

Thomas was referred to in *Howlett v Holding (No.4)* [2006] EWHC 41 (QB). The defendant had instituted a campaign of harassment against the claimant who was a former Labour councillor, which involved flying banners behind his aircraft and dropping leaflets making various untrue allegations such as shoplifting. The claimant had brought two successful libel actions but the defendant continued to fly the banners. The claimant brought a claim for harassment under the Act, seeking an injunction, during the course of which it also transpired that the defendant had put the claimant under surveillance.

In granting a permanent injunction against the defendant, the court followed *Thomas*, holding that the exercise of the right of free speech can constitute harassment. The impact of the defendant's exercise of his right to freedom of expression in this instance was objectionable because of the impact it had on the claimant's privacy and psychological well-being. Balancing the Convention rights and using the principle of proportionality, the claimant's rights took precedence.

FURTHER READING

- M. Tugendhadt and I. Christie, *The Law of Privacy and the Media*, (Oxford: Oxford University Press)

- Professor Gavin Phillipson, "Max Mosley goes to Strasbourg: Article 8, Claimant Notification and Interim Injunctions" (2009) 1 Journal of Media Law 73–96

- *Privacy and the Press: Where Are We Now?* [Keynote speech of Mr Justice Eady, Justice Conference December 1, 2009]

- PCC Code of Practice: *http://www.pcc.org.uk/cop/practice.html*

- Ofcom Broadcasting Code: *http://www.ofcom.org.uk/tv/ifi/codes/bcode/privacy/* (see Appendix F)

- Privacy & Data Protection Journal: *http://www.pdpjournals.com*

5. OBSCENITY AND INDECENCY

INTRODUCTION

The twenty-first century may be seeing libel tourism but the twentieth saw obscenity tourism, with "dirty books" by English speaking authors published abroad to avoid censorship at home.

The novel *Lady Chatterley's Lover* by DH Lawrence was first published in 1928 in Italy because it could not be published openly in the United Kingdom due to its explicit descriptions of sex and its use of (then) unprintable words. In 1960 the Crown prosecuted Penguin books for its publication (albeit with deletions) in the UK, and Penguin won a dramatic and highly publicised trial, giving the firm the right to publish the book in its entirety. The battle for freedom of speech was assisted by the naivety of the prosecutor who posed the famous question "is it a book you would wish your wife or servants to read?" Within a year a previously obscure novel had sold 2 million copies, although it was to be many more years before it was realised that prohibition produces sales, from racy pop lyrics (Frankie Goes to Hollywood's "Relax") to dull spy trivia ("Spycatcher"), and even to works of real literary merit.

Although capable of somewhat easier challenge after the implementation of the Human Rights Act in 2000, the criminal offence of indecency remains on the statute book and applies to theatres showing provocative works and even museums showing images of daily bodily functions.

Obscenity brings fascinating insights into society's acceptance of "shocking" material, as was highlighted in 2009 when a blogger who wrote a fantasy internet blog about the kidnap, rape and murder of members of the Girls Aloud pop group was cleared of obscenity charges. To the blogger, former civil servant Darryn Walker (*R. v Walker*, June 2009, Newcastle Crown Ct), it was not vile pornography but adult celebrity parody that was meant to be for an audience of like-minded people. The prosecution collapsed when an expert report concluded that the blog was not easy enough to find by young fans of the group and could only be read by those prepared to search for such pornographic material on his Girls (Scream) Aloud blog, which had been taken off the website by Walker as soon as the blogger was aware of the upset and fuss created.

Darryn Walker, then 35, from South Shields, did not restrict himself to graphic detail about the kidnap, torture and murder of the five band members as well as rape and mutilation, but had told visitors to his blog that his words were "imaginary descriptions" of "a World in which women are disposable sex objects that exist solely for the pleasure of men". His words were fantasy but undoubtedly would cause real offence to some.

DEFINITION

Obscenity causes a number of problems for the law, not least of which is the difficulty in its definition. The vast majority of people agree that certain types of material should not be published generally or at least not published in places to which children have access. But these people rarely agree on precisely what obscene actually amounts to. What to one person might be blatantly pornographic and objectionable will inevitably be merely "a bit risqué" to another, and coffee table reading to yet another.

The law tries to steer a course between the extremes of opinion and to provide a workable system whereby pornographic material is prohibited without the corresponding infringement to civil liberties and freedom of expression. There are two separate systems of regulation which attempt to achieve this result. Statutory offences of obscenity lead to criminal liability and possible forfeiture of offending material. Indecent items, while not illegal as such, may fall foul of certain media codes of practice or other industry self-regulation.

Statutory obscenity—definition

The original test for obscenity was laid down by a judge in 1868 (*R. v Hicklin* (1868) L.R. 3 Q.B. 360). He said that the court must consider:

> "Whether the tendency of the matter charged as obscenity is to deprave and corrupt those whose minds are open to such immoral influences, and into whose hands such a publication might fall."

This definition was closely followed by the drafters of the Obscene Publications Act 1959. Section 1 provides that:

> "an article shall be deemed to be obscene if its effect or (where the article comprises two or more distinct items) the effect of any one of its items is, if taken as a whole, such as to tend to deprave and corrupt persons who are likely, having regard to all relevant circumstances, to read, see or hear the matter contained or embodied in it."

It should be noted that this definition, which still provides the current law on obscenity, is dependent on the type of person who may have access to the material and whether he is likely to be depraved and corrupted by it. There is thus a subjective element which must be considered in every case.

The definition in s.1 above refers to an article. This may be anything which contains matter to be read or looked at as well as records, films and videos. The Broadcasting Act 1990 adds matter recorded in television programmes to the list of "articles".

Section 1 of the 1959 Act specifically states that a work should be "taken as a whole" in considering whether it is obscene. The decision in *R. v Anderson* [1971] 3 All E.R. 1152 means that magazines should be taken item by item and not read as a whole. The case concerned the publishers of *Oz*, a magazine read by adults and children and published in bright and attractive colours. In *Oz*, No.28, "School Kids Issue", the subject of the prosecution, there were a number of innocent and innocuous articles, dealing with such matters as school affairs and the system of education in this country. In addition, two further items dealt with the objectionable matter. The first was an advertisement for a magazine called *Suck* which described the joys from the female aspect of an act of oral sex. A second item was an article which showed a picture of children dressed in school clothes engaging in various sexual activities. The Court of Appeal held that the publishers were not guilty of the offence (see below) but also said that the fact that the magazine contained a number of harmless items did not mean that the remaining items could not be obscene. *Oz* was a counter culture underground magazine that intended to be fun, provocative and push boundaries, including stronger (artistic as well as gynaecological) images of naked women that were then readily available. Realistically it was read by students and older persons rather than school kids. The conviction (at least until it was overturned) was a bit of a "last hurrah" for the establishment. *Oz* did not perhaps deserve to be treated too seriously: in the "School Kids" issue the head of Rupert Bear was superimposed on a character having sex in an explicit cartoon! But the sentences of 15 months imprisonment (had they not been overturned on appeal) was no joke.

A magazine comprises a number of distinct items and the fact that a number of such items are of innocent character should not detract from the objectionable nature of only one. Following *Anderson*, the Court of Appeal has held that the principle of one obscene item tainting a work as a whole, where the work comprises a number of distinct parts, can also apply to film. In *R. v Goring* (1999) Crim. L.R. 670, the defendant was charged with offences under the Obscene Publications Act 1964 in relation to three pornographic films. One of the films consisted of eight different scenes, each with its own title. At trial, the jury had found that one or more of these scenes were obscene and the judge directed that if the film was made up of distinct items, then any one of those items being obscene could mean the whole film was deemed obscene. The Court of Appeal agreed that a film, like a magazine, could be comprised of a package of distinct items.

Most prosecutions for obscenity result from material which is of a sexual or pornographic nature but the offence could equally apply to material depicting in detail acts of, for example, extreme violence or precise details of drug-taking. Obscenity law was used to ban David Britton's graphic and extremely violent book "Lord Horror". A magistrate had ordered the entire remaining print run to be destroyed, but the ban was eventually overturned in 1992 by the Court of Appeal. Descriptions of or images of drug taking, e.g. as found in films *Trainspotting* or *Pulp Fiction*, fall on one side of the line, but the programme (in a boxed set of season two of the TV series) *Weeds* was not granted classification by BBFC (see later) to be shown as the film due to information about drug taking it contained. What is clear is that for an article to be obscene, it must deprave and corrupt. In the *Oz* case (above), the trial judge had told the jury that if they found the article to be repulsive, filthy, loathsome or lewd then they should find the publishers of *Oz* guilty of the offence of obscenity. The Court of Appeal quashed the conviction on the basis that the trial judge had misinformed the jury. An article is not necessarily obscene under the Act merely because it is "repulsive, filthy, loathsome or lewd". It appears from more recent case law that to deprave and corrupt means to make morally bad or to pervert or corrupt morally. Whether material which is the subject of a prosecution does tend to pervert or corrupt morally is entirely a matter for the jury.

Section 1 of the 1959 Act deems an article obscene only where it tends to deprave and corrupt persons who are likely to read, see or hear it. The test is thus more subjective than the test for defamatory material which centres on the views of the reasonable, fair-minded reader. Under the test for obscenity, both the reasonable reader and the particularly sensitive reader are excluded unless they are likely readers. Indeed, it is possible for material to be considered to have a corrupting effect even where the likely reader is familiar with indecent material of a lesser nature.

In *DPP v Whyte* [1972] A.C. 849, the House of Lords said that even those already depraved and corrupted could be corrupted further and that the Act was not only concerned with protecting the wholly innocent but also the less innocent from further corruption. Different tests should be applied depending on the likely reader of the material. A further issue that has arisen concerning this part of the definition (*R. v Calder and Boyars Ltd* [1968] 3 All E.R. 644 was about the publication in the United Kingdom of a book entitled *Last Exit to Brooklyn*. The book gave a graphic description of the depths of depravity and degradation of life in Brooklyn including homosexual acts and drug-taking, but it was a serious work genuinely believed by its publishers to be in the interests of literature. The appeal against conviction was allowed because, inter alia, the trial judge gave no guidance to the jury on the question of what the Act meant by persons who were likely to read the book. Salmon L.J., in the Court of Appeal, said that the jury should have been directed to consider whether the effect of the book was to tend to deprave and corrupt a "significant proportion" of those persons who were likely to read it. What is a significant proportion is a matter for the jury to decide.

The question of a "significant proportion" of readers being corrupted by material has been reconsidered recently in the light of internet publication. In *R. v Perrin* [2002] EWCA Crim. 747, a prosecution was brought concerning an obscene web page which was openly accessible on the internet as a preview page for an adult subscription site. A police officer with the obscene publications unit viewed the site, but there was no evidence of who else may have visited it. On the basis of *Last Exit to Brooklyn* the defendant appealed his conviction saying that the jury needed to be satisfied that a significant proportion of those visiting the web pages were vulnerable. But the Court of Appeal decided that the *Last Exit to Brooklyn* case was different because it concerned a defence of public good (see below) where there had been mass publication. Here, there was no conceivable public good for pornographic images on the internet and "persons" likely to view the material must mean only some persons, which is a more than negligible number. The court said that if a seller of pornographic books had a lot of customers who were not likely to be corrupted by an obscene publication, that did not mean it was acceptable for him to sell such books to a small number of customers who were likely to be corrupted.

Is an article obscene?

When determining whether an article may be obscene, the following questions should be asked:

Consider the article "taken as a whole" (but where it is in distinct sections then look at any one of those sections)

$\downarrow$

Who is likely to read, see or hear the article?

$\downarrow$

Considering that audience, will those likely viewers tend to be morally depraved or corrupted by it? If yes,

$\downarrow$

Will those who tend to be corrupted be a more than negligible number?

If yes,

$\downarrow$

Is the article so repulsive that, in fact, it is likely to discourage such behaviour?

If no,

$\downarrow$

ARTICLE MAY BE OBSCENE

THE OFFENCES

There are two offences that may be committed in respect of obscene publications.

The first (which is now a "serious arrestable offence") is under s.2 of the Obscene Publications Act 1959, which provides that any person who, whether for gain or not, publishes an obscene article shall be liable to prosecution. A person publishes an article where they:

(a) distribute, circulate, sell, let on hire, give, or lend it, or where they offer it for sale or for letting on hire; or

(b) in the case of an article containing or embodying matter to be looked at or a record, shows, plays or projects it.

The Broadcasting Act 1990 provides that publication extends to matter included in a programme service (see Glossary for definitions of "programme" and "programme service"). The courts have construed the term "publication" widely enough to include the development and printing and return to a customer of a photographic film (*R. v Taylor* (1994) 158 J.P. 317, CA).

The second, introduced by the Obscene Publications Act 1964, provides that a prosecution may be brought in respect of the "possession, ownership or control of an obscene article for publication for gain". This offence does not require proof of publication but the prosecution will have to prove that the obscene article was owned, possessed or controlled for gain. In appropriate circumstances, a bookshop or newsagent could be found guilty of this offence (they will not be guilty under the 1959 Act because, due to a technicality in the law, the display of goods in a shop window or on a shop's shelf does not constitute "offering for sale" as required by s.2) as could a television company which had possession of a programme containing obscene material.

In addition to the normal criminal sanctions for these two offences (persons convicted can receive up to three years' imprisonment), an order for forfeiture of the offending material may be made.

DEFENCES

The defences relevant to the media are the following:

- that the article is for the public good;

- innocent publication or possession; and

- that the activities portrayed in the article are so depraved as to cause repulsion ("aversion").

Public good

Section 4 of the 1959 Act provides that a person shall not be convicted of the offence in s.2 and an order for forfeiture shall not be made where it is proved that publication of the article was justified as being for the public good.

The definition of public good depends on the identity of the medium in question:

- in the case of books and magazines, where it is in the interests of "science, literature, art or learning, or of other objects of general concern";

- as far as films and plays (for a definition of "play" see Glossary) are concerned, the definition of the public good is a little different: they must be in the interests of "drama, opera, ballet or any other art, or of literature or learning";

- in the case of television and radio publication will be for the public good where it is in the interests of "drama, opera, ballet or any other art, science, literature or learning or any other objects of general concern". The defence is therefore wider for broadcasts.

The word "learning", which appears in all three definitions of public good, has a somewhat narrower meaning than may at first sight be imagined. For something to be in the interests of learning, it must relate to scholarly activity. It will not, therefore, include material alleged to be of use for the purposes of sex education (*Attorney-General's Reference (No.3 of 1977)* [1978] 1 W.L.R. 1123).

In *R. v Calder and Boyars Ltd* [1968] 3 All E.R. 644, the court stated that the proper direction that should be given in cases where the defence is raised was that the jury must consider on the one hand:

- the number of (readers) they believed would tend to be depraved and corrupted by the article;

- the strength of the tendency to deprave and corrupt; and

- the nature of the depravity or corruption.

- On the other hand they should assess:

- the strength of the literary, sociological or ethical merit which they consider the article to possess.

The jury should then weigh up these factors and decide whether on balance the publication was proved to be justified as being for the public good.

Innocent publication or possession

It is a defence for a person charged with publishing obscene material to show that they did not know nor should have known that they would be liable to prosecution. The precise wording of the defence is as follows:

"A person shall not be convicted of an offence if he proves that he had not examined the article in respect of which he is charged and had no reasonable cause to suspect that it was such that his publication of it would make him liable to be convicted of an offence against this section." (s.2(5) of the Obscene Publications Act 1959)

The objective element of this defence means that the defence will not be available to a person who did not know they could be prosecuted but should have known. Thus a newsagent who states that they did not realise that a magazine they displayed in their shop contained obscene material will not be able to use the defence (the 1964 Act includes a similarly worded defence) where a reasonable newsagent would have had that realisation—this may be due, for example, to the nature of the magazine in question or because there was a picture on the front cover which would have led to the suspicion of the presence of such material. The objective element in this defence has led many newsagents to choose not to stock certain magazines which have a reputation for publishing potentially obscene material—the reputation of the magazine will defeat the newsagent's defence in s.2.

Aversion

Although not actually a defence, the practical result of the decision in *R. v Anderson* (above)—that merely repulsive, loathsome or lewd articles were not obscene—means that material that is shocking or disgusting may not be obscene because it has the effect of discouraging readers or viewers from engaging in the activity in question. The judge said:

> "Many of the illustrations in *Oz* were so grossly lewd and unpleasant that they would shock in the first instance and then they would tend to repel. In other words, it was said that they had an aversive effect and that far from tempting those who had not experienced the acts to take part in them they would put off those who might be tempted so to conduct themselves."

This "defence", if successful, would result in a finding that the article was not obscene because it did not tend to deprave or corrupt.

COMMON LAW OFFENCES

So where are we now? What can be obscene these days?

The line between permissiveness and obscenity continues to move, aping the assertion by the lawyer Louis Sirkin during the trial of American pornographer Larry Flynt in the 1970s in the US that "One man's obscenity is another man's art". According to the police bestiality, necrophilia, extreme rape and torture would still be considered obscene as would depictions of sexual gratification through lavatorial functions. In R18 material purchased from licensed sex shops you can somewhat bizarrely see images of people urinating on others, but not people drinking urine. In a sex film you cannot show a woman "evacuating her bowels" but in the context of a legitimate photographic exhibition at a museum (with appropriate warnings to keep children out of the relevant rooms) one could display such images. It seems quite a lot depends on context and upon whether the media gets het up about it. Tate Modern can display work by American artist Jeff Koons of graphic images and sculptures of him having sex with his then wife Italian porn star Cicciolina (e.g. his "Dirty-Jeff On Top" statue), but an image of naked 14-year-old Brooke Shields (who appeared in the 1980 film The Blue Lagoon) described by the Museum as "challenging" might have fallen on the wrong side of the line. The Tate Modern removed the image, which was a photograph taken by Richard Prince of an original photograph of Brooke Shields taken by Gary Gross. She may have been aged 10 or perhaps aged 14, and in the movie producers used a body double for some of her naked scenes but not others. Confused? The law is!

There are a number of common law offences relating to obscenity, which are now mainly defunct, although occasionally used by prosecutors where no other offence seemingly fits the bill. These include "conspiracy to corrupt public morals" and "outraging public decency". The latter has been raised recently in connection with a number of controversial art works—both the artist and the gallery proprietor were convicted of the common law offence after an exhibition of a sculpture which had earrings made from freeze-dried human foetuses (*R. v Gibson* [1990] 3 W.L.R. 595). The jury found by a majority that this was an outrage of public decency, but unlike the statutory obscenity offence, there is no artistic or "public good" defence. There is no real definition of this offence, but it is suggested that indecency must mean something different to the statutory definition of obscene and must be more akin to shocking and offending.

The effectiveness of the offence of outraging public decency, when other crimes just don't seem to fit, was demonstrated in 2009 when a man with a website devoted to Spandex-clad women was given a suspended jail term after secretly filming participants at a gala in Sheffield's International Sports Centre. Somewhat foolishly, the secret cameraman later watched footage of the female swimmers on his laptop on a commuter train to London from his home in Essex and was observed by a fellow commuter offended enough to notify the police. The defendant had zoomed in on young swimmers, concentrating on their genitals, breasts and buttock areas—although it turned out that the swimmers were actually over age 18. The "victims" were of course completely unaware of what was happening, but when they were notified became "distressed and violated" (the court subsequently was told). The offender was banned from public swimming pools until 2012 and ordered to attend a sex offender's rehabilitation course. Outraging public decency has also been considered when individuals have stood naked on a plinth on Trafalgar Square (not a breach) or stripped off for long walks from one end of the country to the other. Prosecutors have to bear in mind if they are likely to achieve a conviction: in 2007 two young women who flashed their breasts in front of a CCTV camera (both aged 21) were charged but had the court case against them dropped. The CPS had justified the criminal proceedings because the incident took place near a children's play area. The young women's defence was that it was "it was just a little joke, one of those spur-of-the-moment-things" and the CPS Crown Prosecutor reviewed the case and dropped the charges as it would not be in the public interest to pursue it. One suspects that the CPS appreciated that they might have been laughed out of the Crown Court...

Terrestrial television

The Broadcasting Act 1990 removed the exemption of television for the purposes of the Obscene Publications Act 1959. Thus a broadcaster who publishes an obscene programme will be liable to prosecution in the same way as a newspaper or magazine publisher. For the purposes of the Act, a person publishes an article:

"To the extent that any matter recorded on it is included by him in a programme service."

Further, the 1990 Act charged the Independent Television Commission (ITC) (now Ofcom) with doing everything within its power to ensure that television programmes do not offend against good taste or decency.

Ofcom (see Ch.10) enforces a code for its television licence holders (ITV, Channel 4, Five, GMTV, Sky, the various cable companies and digital service providers) to observe in their broadcasting business. The Broadcasting Code, revised in 2009 and which took effect from December 16, 2009 (see Appendix F) lists a number of types of viewing material to be regulated. It does not refer specifically to obscenity but provides that the regulator is required under the Communications Act 2003 to cover standards in programmes:

"when applying the Code content, broadcasters should be aware that the context in which the material appears is key. In setting this Code, Ofcom has taken into account (as required by Section 319(4) of the [Communications] Act [2003]) the following:–

(a) the degree of harm and offence likely to be caused by the inclusion of any particular sort of material in programmes generally where programmes of a particular description;

(b) the likely size and composition of the potential audience for programmes included in television and radio services generally or in television and radio services of a particular description;

(c) the likely expectation of the audience as to the nature of a programme's content and the extent to which they nature of a programme's content can be brought to the attention of potential members of the audience;

(d) the likelihood of persons who are unaware of the nature of a programme's content being unintentionally exposed, by their own actions, to that content;

(e) the desirability of securing that the content of service identifies when there is a change affecting the nature of a service that is being watched or listened to and, in particular, a change that is relevant to the application of the standard set under this section.

(f) the desirability of maintaining the independence of editorial control over programme content.

These criteria have informed Ofcom's approach to setting the Code and therefore must be taken into account by broadcasters when interpreting the rules."

Protecting Children

Section 1 of the Ofcom Broadcasting Code, "Protecting the Under-Eighteens", is to ensure that people under 18 years of age are protected from material that might seriously impair their physical, mental or moral development and that broadcasters take all reasonable steps to protect people under eighteen. For television services, this is in addition to broadcaster's obligations resulting from the Audiovisual Media Services Directive. The "watershed" must be observed and material unsuitable for children (under the age of 15 years) should not, in general, be shown before 9pm or after 5.30am.

The Code regulates the appearance in programmes of drugs, smoking, solvents and alcohol, violence and dangerous behaviour, offensive language, sex and nudity. Films, premium subscription film services, pay-per-view services, adult-sex material on premium subscription services are covered by specific rules.

The old "taste or decency" test has been replaced by one of "harm and offence": to ensure that generally accepted standards are applied to the contents of television and radio services so as to provide adequate protection to members of the public in the inclusion in such services of harmful and/or offensive material.

Ofcom's Code also protects children from seeing or hearing violence and dangerous behaviour through the broadcast media. The Code makes clear that violence, its after-effects and descriptions of violence, whether verbal or physical, must be appropriately limited in programmes broadcast before the watershed (in the case of television) or when children are particularly likely to be listening (in the case of radio) and must also be justified by the context. The Code reflects the fact that children are likely to be listening to the radio on their way to school and at breakfast time. There is particular focus on violence as it is considered easily imitable by children in a manner that is harmful or dangerous, and is only to be included if there is strong editorial justification. The same applies to dangerous behaviour. The most offensive language (Ofcom has conducted research as to what language is considered particularly offensive and which therefore will not be set out in this book!) is banned. Offensive language must not be used in programmes made for younger children except in the most exceptional circumstances, and any such language broadcast before the watershed needs to be justified by the context. Unsurprisingly, R18 material must not be broadcast at any time.

OFCOM AND ADULTS

Digital multi-channel television

The Communications Act 2003 made it the principal duty of Ofcom, in carrying out its functions, to further the interests of citizens in relation to communications matters and the interests of consumers in relevant markets. Ofcom is required to set and enforce standards "in the case of all television and radio services" and so regulates, and if necessary is prepared to impose sanctions upon, cable and satellite. The legislation was meant to keep pace with technological advances in television so although Ofcom deals with digital multi-channel television and digital radio it does not regulate the medium of audio-visual content through the internet.

The availability of new ways of making material available to the public, and the desire of at least a section of the public for pornographic programmes, has already caused problems and, no doubt, will do so again.

In 1992, Red Hot Dutch, a hard-core pornographic satellite service, was transmitted to the United Kingdom. It was neither a domestic satellite service nor a non-domestic satellite service; it was broadcast from the Netherlands and it used a frequency not allocated to satellite transmissions to the United Kingdom. Red Hot Television (the owners of Red Hot Dutch) was therefore able to broadcast obscene material to viewers in the United Kingdom without needing to apply for a licence.

Red Hot Television argued the United Kingdom was unable to ban the channel under the Broadcasting Act 1990 because it was prevented from doing so by the EC Directive on Transfrontier Television (89/552/EEC) (*R. v Secretary of State for National Heritage Ex p. Continental Television BV* [1993] 2 C.M.L.R. 333). The general purpose of the directive is to ensure that television programmes licensed in one Member State must enjoy freedom of reception in other Member States. A reference to the ECJ on the point was never heard because Red Hot Television ran into financial difficulties and ceased broadcasting. This important point was not resolved. Ofcom regulates films, premium subscription film services, pay-per-view services, adult-sex material on premium prescription services and digital multi-channel television and no film refused classification by BBFC (see next section) may be broadcast and BBFC 18-rated films or their equivalent must not be broadcast before 9pm on any service except on pay-per-view services, and even then they may unsuitable for broadcast at that time. Pay-per-view services may broadcast BBFC 18-rated films at any time provided the period pre 9pm and after 5.40am has a protection system such as a mandatory PIN to restrict access. Premium subscription services and pay-per-view/night services may broadcast "adult-sex" material between 10pm and 5.30am so long as the protection systems satisfactorily restrict access solely to those authorised to view and that this subscriber is an adult. BBFC R18-rated films must not be broadcast.

Cinema exhibition

Only the Director of Public Prosecutions may bring a prosecution for obscenity in a film exhibited in a cinema. Such prosecutions are rare due to the local authority's jurisdiction over cinemas. A local authority must license the showing of each film in cinemas in its area of control. It will often do so by relying on the classification produced by the British Board of Film Classification (BBFC). The following categories are available:

- U (Universal): suitable for all;

- PG (Parental guidance): some scenes may be unsuitable for young children under 8;

- 12A: suitable for persons of 12 years and over and under 12s if accompanied by an adult at all times during the performance (cinema only);

- 15: suitable only for persons of 15 years and over;

- 18: suitable only for persons of 18 years and over; and

- R18 suitable only for restricted distribution through segregated premises to which no one under 18 is admitted.

No film that contains scenes that breach the test for obscenity in the 1959 Act would be classified by the BBFC. It would be highly unlikely for a local authority to allow the screening of films that did not have a BBFC classification. For these reasons the producers of the film will commonly give extensive powers to distributors to cut and edit films to achieve classification in the desired category—a 15 certificate, for example, produces a much greater income for the movie producer because this includes the teenage market. Hollywood movies are rarely shown as originally produced in cinemas in the United Kingdom—numerous clips are edited out to obtain the most lucrative category of classification from the BBFC.

The BBFC was established in 1912 (it was then called the British Board of Film Censors) by the film industry to try to counter the widely disparate views of local authorities as to what could and could not be shown in cinemas in their own localities. By the 1920s it had become general practice for local authorities to rely on the BBFC's classifications. It should be noted, however, that the final decision on censorship rests with the local authorities who may decide to ignore a BBFC decision at any time.

Videotape and DVD recordings

Video is subject to the same restrictions in relation to obscenity as other media. The BBFC is responsible for licensing video under s.4 of the Video Recordings Act, introduced in 1984 to stop so-called "video nasties", and ensures compliance with the law. No video that deals in any respect with sex or violence may be distributed to the public unless it has BBFC approval. No video that breaches the Obscene Publications Act 1959 may be certified by the BBFC as suitable for viewing in the home. Until August 2009 the BBFC was believed to be responsible for video and video games. It was discovered in August 2009 that the BBFC's ratings of video and video games was unenforceable and as a result the Video Recordings Act 1984 was repealed in 2010 and re-enacted to cure the defect.

In addition to risking prosecution under the Obscene Publications Acts 1959 and 1964, it is generally an offence to supply or offer to supply a video recording which has not received a classification certificate (Video Recordings Act 1984, s.9). BBFC video classifications differ slightly from those for cinema. They are as follows:

- Uc (Universal): particularly suitable for children;

- U: suitable for all;

- PG (Parental Guidance): some scenes may be unsuitable for young children;

- 12: suitable only for those aged 12 and over (no-one younger than 12 can rent or buy a 12 rated VHS, DVD, blu-ray disc, UMD or game;

- 15: suitable for persons of 15 years and over with the same ban on renting or buying as above;

- 18: suitable only for adults and no one younger than 18 may see an 18 film in the cinema and they cannot rent or buy such films either; and

- R18: suitable only for restricted distribution through licensed sex shops to which no one under 18 is admitted.

A further category, E, is available for videos that the distributor believes are exempt from the provisions of the Video Recordings Act 1984. A video work is an exempted work if, taken as a whole:

- it is designed to inform, educate or instruct;

- it is concerned with sport, religion or music; or

- it is a video game.

However, a video work will not be exempted under these provisions if, to any significant extent, it depicts a human sexual activity or gross violence.

A video work will not be exempted if, to any significant extent, it depicts criminal activity which is likely stimulate or encourage the commission of offences (s.2(3)).

Certain types of supply of video recordings will be exempted from the provisions of the Act:

- supplies which are neither for reward nor which are in the course of a business;

- supplies of material which is designed to form a record of an event or occasion (where such material does not, to any significant extent, fall foul of the above provisions) to a person who took part in such event (e.g. a wedding video);

- supply to the BBFC for classification;

- supply to the BBC, Ofcom or any other broadcaster with a view only to its being broadcast.

In licensing a video, the BBFC is required to consider whether a child or young person is likely to view the video and, if so, whether such a viewer may be harmed (or though their behaviour cause harm to society) by the manner in which the video deals with any of five specific topics. The topics are criminal behaviour, illegal drugs, violent behaviour, horrific incidents or sexual activity. If a viewer may be harmed then the BBFC is required to have special regard to that fact when deciding whether to classify the video (Video Recordings Act, s.4A). This demonstrates that the BBFC has to have regard to considerations, other than whether something may be illegal, when classifying videos. In *R. v Video Appeals Committee of the British Board of Film Classification Ex p. British Board of Film Classification* [2000] E.M.L.R. 850, it was held that an unquantified risk posed to young people did not mean that a video should not be classified because there was a speculative risk. Where there was no evidence how a child view could be affected, then a video could still be classified as long as the BBFC had properly considered the unquantified risk. This decision had the effect of making erotica more likely to be licensed as R18, and therefore more widely available as "top shelf" material.

The BBFC has made it clear that it will be wrong to assume that it has a greater tolerance of sexual violence, as this is one of the areas where its position has not changed much over the years. It remains a main concern and the effect of mixing sex and violence is looked at closely. The 1971 film *Straw Dogs*, directed by Sam Peckinpah, was originally banned because of a horrific sex depiction, but in 2002 the BBFC passed a different edit of the film where the makers of *Straw Dogs* had done their own edit which removed an impression that the film female character portrayed by Susan George enjoyed the rape. A full version contained another event which gave a different context. In 2008 the BBFC issued 1,159 films with an R18 rating (to be sold only in licensed sex shops) and 27 per cent required cuts. A R18 rating is not a legal defence for a pornographer but realistically the obscene publication squad would not take action over a film passed by the BBFC.

Films given a regular 18 certificate are only supposed to contain "simulated sex" but Michael Winterbottom's controversial *9 Songs*, released in 2004, showed that there could be exceptions. Real sex was allowed to be incorporated as the BBFC judged it to be "exceptionally justified" by the context of the film.

The internet

The internet causes a multitude of problems for proponents of legal regulation. By its nature, it is not easy to regulate. Information (whether in the form of text, still pictures or video clips) on the internet may have been placed there by any person in any country and is available free of charge (unless subject to a subscription payment) to any user anywhere in the world. A degree of certainty in this respect was introduced by the Court of Appeal in *R. v Waddon* (2000) (unreported). It held that while there can be publication on a website abroad, for example when images are uploaded on to a server outside the United Kingdom, there would be an additional publication when the images were downloaded to a computer elsewhere. Where that computer was in England, that gives rise to jurisdiction for the English courts for the purposes of hearing a prosecution under the Obscene Publications Act 1959. In *R. v Perrin* (above), the defendant appealed on the grounds that his conviction under the Obscene Publications Act 1959 violated his right to freedom of expression under art.10 of the ECHR. But the court said that there was a legitimate purpose for having on the statute book an offence of publishing an obscene article and that Parliament was entitled to conclude that a law was necessary in a democratic society. Per Kennedy L.J.:

"No one has argued that the protection of minors and other vulnerable people is not an important issue to be addressed. On the other side of the balance sheet, apart from the general right to freedom of expression, there is no public interest to be served by permitting a business for profit to supply material which most people would regard as pornographic or obscene."

For further detail see Ch.9.

Children

Children often receive special treatment from the law. Indeed censorship very often has the protection of children as its stated objective. This part therefore considers obscenity and indecency vis-à-vis the younger members of society.

The above offences of obscenity apply equally to a child readership as they do to an adult one. The test of "likely audience" may result in articles being obscene where they are available for children to consume, even if the same article would not result in the commission of an offence in respect of a wholly adult audience (see above).

In addition, it may be an offence to use children in material intended for publication. Section 1(1) of the Indecency with Children Act 1960 as amended by the Sexual Offences Act 2003 provides that:

"Any person who commits an act of gross indecency with or towards a child under the age of fourteen, or who incites a child under that age to commit such an act with him or another shall [commit an offence]."

Section 1 of the Protection of Children Act 1978, which covers children under the age of 16, makes it an offence:

"(a) to take, or permit to be taken, or to make any indecent photograph or pseudo-photographs of a child; or

(b) to distribute or show such indecent photographs or pseudo-photographs; or

(c) for a person to have in his possession such indecent photographs or pseudo-photographs, with a view to them being distributed or shown by himself or others; or

(d) to publish or cause to be published any advertisement likely to be understood as conveying that the advertiser distributes or shows such indecent photographs or pseudo-photographs, or intends to do so."

Private family photographs are given in defence in s.1A.

The offence of taking an indecent photograph also includes "making" an indecent photograph, and making includes copying, where it is done with knowledge (*Atkins v DPP* [2000] 2 All E.R. 425). Thus it is an offence to download such an image on to computer or disk, and to print such an image, as this will be copying (*R. v Bowden* [2001] 2 All E.R. 418). Photographs in the context of the 1978 Act include material comprised in a film. It should be noted that there is no definition of what is "indecent". It would appear from case law that what would be shocking, disgusting and revolting to ordinary people would be indecent. Recognised standards of propriety are to be applied. It appears though that the indecency must suggest some element of lewdness or implicit sexual reference. An exhibition at the Saatchi gallery in 2001 prompted a complaint that photographs— ostensibly family photographs showing a boy urinating and a naked girl on a beach—were indecent, but the Director of Public Prosecutions (DPP) declined to prosecute saying there was no element of provocation. The proliferation of child pornography available on the internet has given added importance to this particular indecency legislation. It is regrettably of particular importance in the modern communications era.

It is a criminal offence, under the Children and Young Persons (Harmful Publications) Act 1955, to print, publish or sell certain works which are "likely to fall into the hands of children or young persons". The offence, a prosecution for which cannot be brought without the consent of the Attorney General, relates to:

> "Any book, magazine or other like work which consists wholly or mainly of stories told in pictures (with or without the addition of written matter) being stories portraying—
>
> (a) the commission of crimes; or
> (b) acts of violence or cruelty; or
> (c) incidents of a repulsive or horrible nature;
>
> in such a way that the work as a whole would tend to corrupt a child or young person into whose hands it might fall."

As with the Obscene Publications Act 1959, Video Recordings Act and Protection of Children Act 1978, there is a power of seizure conferred on the police by the Criminal Justice and Police Act 2001.

FURTHER READING

- Official website of British Board of Film Classification: *http://www.BBFC.co.uk*

- Ofcom's website: *http://www.ofcom.org*

Obscenity and Indecency

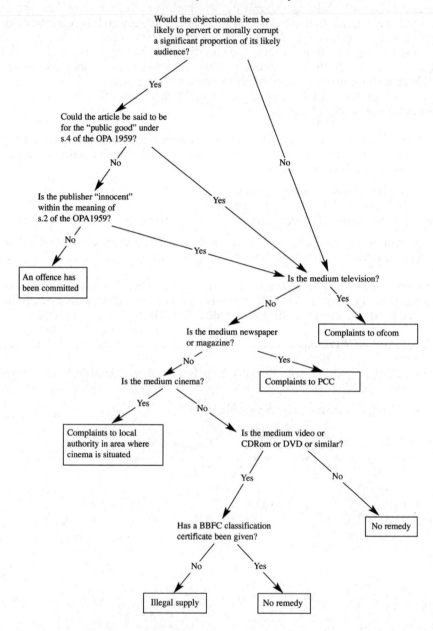

Would the objectionable item be likely to pervert or morally corrupt a significant proportion of its likely audience?

Yes

Could the article be said to be for the "public good" under s.4 of the OPA 1959?

No

No

Is the publisher "innocent" within the meaning of s.2 of the OPA1959?

Yes

No

Yes

An offence has been committed

Is the medium television?

No

Yes

Is the medium newspaper or magazine?

Complaints to ofcom

No

Yes

Is the medium cinema?

Complaints to PCC

Yes

No

Complaints to local authority in area where cinema is situated

Is the medium video or CDRom or DVD or similar?

Yes

No

Has a BBFC classification certificate been given?

No remedy

No

Yes

Illegal supply

No remedy

6. RACIAL AND RELIGIOUS HATRED

The law imposes general restrictions on the publication of certain material by the media. In some cases there will be criminal liability for such publications. The last chapter considered the criminal offence of obscenity. This chapter looks at further offences which may be committed by the media in publishing material for public consumption. They are somewhat rare in occurrence, but nevertheless worth considering in the overall aim of ensuring the publication of material with minimum legal risk.

INCITING RACIAL OR RELIGIOUS HATRED

As part of its role in maintaining the peace, the law seeks to prevent the publication of material which is likely to provoke racially motivated attacks or religious discomfort. It has done so under the Public Order Act 1986 by creating an offence of "inciting racial hatred". These provisions were extended by the Racial and Religious Hatred Act 2006 which amends the 1986 Act to create corresponding offences involving the intentional stirring up of hatred against persons on religious grounds.

Definition

Racial hatred is defined by the Public Order Act 1986, s.17 as:

"hatred against a group of persons in Great Britain defined by reference to colour, race, nationality (including citizenship) or ethnic or national origins."

Much of this definition is self-explanatory. However, some confusion arose over the meaning of the word "ethnic" in the case of *Mandela v Dowell Lee* [1983] 1 All E.R. 1062. The House of Lords, in considering whether the Sikhs are a racial group, found that the word "ethnic" was to be construed in a broad cultural and historical sense. For a group of persons to be ethnic the members had to regard themselves, and be regarded by others, as a distinct community by virtue of certain characteristics (listed below). Two of these characteristics must exist in every case:

- a long shared history, of which the group is conscious as distinguishing it from other groups, and the memory of which it kept alive; and

- a cultural tradition of its own, including family and social customs and manners, often, but not necessarily, associated with religious observance.

The other characteristics are less crucial but may have a bearing on whether a certain group would be regarded as ethnic:

- a common geographical origin, or descent from a small number of common ancestors;

- a common language, not necessarily peculiar to the group;

- a common literature peculiar to the group;

- a common religion different from that of neighbouring groups or from the general community surrounding it; and

- being a minority or being a depressed or dominant group within a larger community.

It should be noted that the House was looking at the word "ethnic" in the context of s.3 of the Race Relations Act 1976. However, there is no reason to believe that the definition should differ for the purposes of the 1986 Act.

Religious hatred is defined by s.29 A of the Public Order Act as: "hatred against a group of persons defined by reference to religious belief or lack of religious belief".

The offences

The 1986 and 2006 Acts create several offences relating to racial and religious hatred. Those of relevance to the media can be divided into those concerning non-broadcast media, for example newspapers, books, magazines and cinema, and those relevant to the broadcast media, namely radio and television.

Non-broadcast material

Section 18 of the 1986 Act makes it an offence for a person to use threatening, abusive or insulting words or behaviour, or to display any written material which is threatening, abusive or insulting if:

(a) they intend thereby to stir up racial hatred; or

(b) having regard to all the circumstances racial hatred is likely to be stirred up thereby.

For the purposes of the offence, written material includes any sign or other visible representation. It would therefore include, for example, an advertisement hoarding.

Section 19 provides that it will be an offence for a person to publish or distribute written material which is threatening, abusive or insulting if:

(a) they intend thereby to stir up racial hatred; or

(b) having regard to all the circumstances racial hatred is likely to be stirred up thereby.

Section 19 is thus of relevance to the publishing media. It may of course be difficult for the prosecution to prove that the publisher of an article intended to stir up racial hatred but the offence will also be proved where the prosecution is able to convince the court that racial hatred is likely to be stirred up by the article.

Under s.21, a person who distributes, or shows or plays, a recording of visual images or sounds which are threatening, abusive or insulting is guilty of an offence if:

(a) they intend thereby to stir up racial hatred; or

(b) having regard to all the circumstances racial hatred is likely to be stirred up thereby.

The maximum punishment for the offences in ss.18 and 19 (and s.22—see below) is seven years' imprisonment and it is not uncommon for the courts to give custodial sentences. (The maximum sentence was increased from two to seven years by the Anti-terrorism, Crime and Security Act 2001 passed in the wake of the 9/11 atrocities when there was renewed concern about racial tension.) In *R. v Relf* (1979) 1 Cr.App.R.(S.) 111, the defendant was found guilty of publishing leaflets containing derogatory remarks about West Indians, the leaflets being displayed in public places. Mr Relf spent nine months in prison. In *R. v Edwards* (1983) 5 Cr.App.R.(S.) 145, the defendant had drawn a comic strip to be published in a magazine intending to stir up racial hatred. The judge found that Mr Edwards had intended to prejudice children against Jews and Asians and sentenced him to 12 months' imprisonment.

Under s.25, the court can make an order for the forfeiture of any written material or recording to which the broadcast or non-broadcast offences relate.

Broadcast material

By virtue of s.22 of the 1986 Act, the offence can be committed as a result of the broadcast of television or radio programmes if it was intended that racial hatred be stirred up or, having regard to all the circumstances, racial hatred was likely to be stirred up by the programme. Those liable to prosecution are the person providing the programme service, the producer or director of the programme and the person who uses the offending words.

Producers, directors and broadcasters of programmes about racism should note therefore that they can be liable to prosecution even though they did not intend to stir up racial hatred. All that need be shown by the prosecution is that the material contained in the programme was likely to stir up racial hatred.

Defences

There is a general defence which applies to any media publication which is a fair and accurate report of parliamentary or court proceedings. The remaining defences depend upon whether the medium in question is by broadcast or not.

Non-broadcast material

A defence is provided to the offence in s.18 where the accused is not shown to have intended to stir up racial hatred and where they did not intend their words or behaviour to be, and was not aware that it might be, threatening, abusive or insulting. A similar defence exists in s.19 where the accused proves that they were not aware of the content of the material and had no reason to believe that it was threatening, abusive or insulting.

It is a defence under s.21 for the accused, who is not shown to have intended to stir up racial hatred, to prove that:

(a) they were not aware of the content of the recording; and

(b) did not suspect, and had no reason to suspect, that it was threatening, abusive or insulting.

Section 21 does not apply to the showing or playing of a recording solely for the purpose of enabling the recording to be included in a programme service.

Broadcast material

Where the broadcaster, producer or director is not shown to have intended to stir up racial hatred, it is a defence for them to prove that:

(a) they did not know and had no reason to suspect that the programme would involve offending material; and

(b) having regard to the circumstances in which the programme was included in a programme service, it was not reasonably practical for them to secure the removal of the material.

The producer and director have a further defence where it is not shown that there was intention to stir up racial hatred and where it is proved that the accused had no reason to suspect that:

(a) the programme would be included in a programme service; or

(b) the circumstances in which the programme would be so included would be such that racial hatred would be likely to be stirred up.

The 2006 Act augments the above provisions by new ss.29A–N of the 1986 Act which create similar offences in relation to the intentional stirring up of religious hatred.

7. CONTEMPT

INTRODUCTION

Contempt of court refers to the court's ability to punish any person who interferes, in any way, with the proper functioning of the court system. That interference may take a number of forms. For example, a person could commit contempt by swearing at a judge in court or by using a tape recorder or taking photographs using a mobile phone in court. In one amusing case (*Balogh v Crown Court at St Albans* [1974] 3 All E.R. 283), a solicitor's clerk, to relieve his boredom with court proceedings, obtained a canister of laughing gas intending to introduce the gas into the court through the ventilation system. He was sentenced to six months' imprisonment for contempt although his conviction was overturned on appeal. As Lord Donaldson said in *Att Gen v Newspaper Publishing Plc* [1988] Ch. 33:

> "The law of contempt is based on the broadest of principles, namely that the courts cannot and will not permit interference with the due administration of justice. Its application is universal."

A conviction for contempt of court, for which the punishment can be a fine or even imprisonment, is a very real danger for journalists and the media when reporting current affairs. Contempt may be committed by the media in a number of ways, for example by publishing information which is the subject of a court order forbidding its release, or by publishing material in breach of an undertaking not to publish. These examples of contempt will be looked at in Ch.8.

This chapter will consider, in the main, the form of contempt that is of most importance to the media and of which it is at most risk of committing: the publishing of information which is likely adversely to affect (or "prejudice") a fair trial. This is the means by which the legal system can ensure that information likely to affect the outcome of criminal cases is not circulated. The object is for there to be trial in the courtroom rather than trial by media.

EXAMPLE

A newspaper report states that X is due to go on trial for burglary and then goes on to say that X has served time in prison for burglary before. The trial could well be affected because the jury hearing the case against X may have read the paper and will therefore know about X's previous convictions—the general rule in criminal trials is that the jury should be unaware of the defendant's previous bad character because of the potential negative influence that this may have. The publication of X's previous convictions for burglary may mean that certain members of the jury are more likely to believe that X is guilty of the current offence and therefore more likely to convict him than if they had not seen the newspaper article.

As Lord Diplock remarked in *Att Gen v English* [1983] A.C. 116:

"Trial by newspaper or, as it should be more compendiously expressed today, trial by the media, is not to be permitted in this country."

Without the prohibition on publication that the law of contempt provides, a jury would have to be sheltered from any contamination by media release. Such is the position in the US where the Bill of Rights ensures a greater media freedom than in the United Kingdom. The Los Angeles jury members who heard the infamous OJ Simpson trial were kept separate from the community by living in a hotel for the duration of the trial. They were not permitted to read the papers or watch television or even to communicate with their families. However, the American system, unlike the British one, does allow jurors to write books about their experiences in high profile trials. On this side of the Atlantic the full force of the law was brought on the head of jury foreman Michael Seckerson who told *The Times* how a majority verdict was reached in the case of a childminder who was accused of manslaughter.

Michael Seckerson was the jury foreman in a 2007 case where childminder Kieran Henderson, from Iver Heath in Buckinghamshire, was convicted of the manslaughter of 11-month old Maeve Sheppard by a 10–2 majority. Mr Seckerson had been one of the two dissenters and *The Times* had reported that he and a fellow juror had raised concerns about the complex testimony of expert medical witnesses. The Attorney General brought a case against *The Times* and Michael Seckerson for breach of s.8 of the Contempt of Court Act 1981, which banned disclosure of "votes cast, statements made, opinions expressed or arguments advanced" by jurors in their deliberations during a trial (and incidentally this would cover a libel jury too, as unusually for civil proceedings defamation cases are still usually heard by a jury rather than by a judge alone). *The Times* argued that art.10 of the Human Rights Act meant that contempt proceedings were unjustified and that the media had a right to keep the public informed about court proceedings. The High Court disagreed—the judges said that the jury system depended on open and frank deliberations in secret, without any individual jury member feeling that their potentially unpopular views might become public later.

Inexplicable mistakes continue to be made, as a court heard in July 2008 when the Attorney General brought proceedings against ITV Central Limited. During one of its morning news reports covering the murder trial of five men due to start later that day, an ITV journalist had referred to the fact that one of the accused had been convicted of murder and was serving a sentence of imprisonment for that offence. The report was repeated a further two times the same day. As a result the trial judge postponed the start of the trial for 14 days to avoid prejudice to the defendants.

ITV pleaded guilty to contempt and argued in mitigation that the error of publishing details of previous convictions was so "blindingly obvious" that it could not have anticipated that one of its reporters would make such an error. As a result it had tightened up its procedures. ITV also voluntarily agreed to pay the third party costs incurred (over £37,000) which the court took into account when imposing a relatively modest fine of £25,000. See the Courts Act 2003 and SI 2004/2408 for consideration of whether media is responsible for "serious misconduct". The offer to pay the wasted costs was wise as the courts have the power to order third parties to pay costs if a trial has to be abandoned. There had been a real risk that members of the jury might have heard the broadcast and the "simplicity" of the error could not detract from the seriousness of the publication of such information. Journalists should know that previous convictions should not be disclosed in such circumstances. Experience has shown the courts that such mistakes have happened before and will happen again.

Much of the discussion in this chapter will centre around the provisions of the Contempt of Court Act 1981 which, following the case of *The Sunday Times v United Kingdom* (1979) 2 E.H.R.R. 245, amended and clarified the law of contempt, attempting to bring it into line with the Convention for the Protection of Human Rights and Fundamental Freedoms.

There are two offences of contempt:

(1) the statute-based offence under the 1981 Act which does not require any proof of intention to prejudice ("strict liability" contempt); and

(2) the old common law offence which requires the prosecution to prove (beyond a reasonable doubt) *intention* on the part of the defendant to prejudice a fair trial.

Contempt under the 1981 Act is a more narrowly defined offence than common law contempt. The statute has created a criminal offence of strict liability in the sense that the prosecution does not have to prove that the publisher or broadcaster intended to prejudice legal proceedings. The residual common law offence requires the proof of this intention (see below). Because of the difficulty in such proof, prosecutions of the media under the Act are far more frequent than at common law.

Under the Criminal Justice Act 2003, serious criminal cases can be tried by judge alone (rather than with a jury). The first such case was heard at the Royal Courts of Justice in early 2010 (*R. v Twomey*) and others have followed.

Applications for contempt of court are usually brought by the Attorney General before the Divisional Court of the Queen's Bench Division.

STRICT LIABILITY CONTEMPT

For a successful prosecution under the 1981 Act, the Attorney General will not need to prove that the defendant intended to prejudice a fair trial. He must simply show to the court that:

(a) there is a publication (in writing, by broadcast or in any other form of communication) addressed to the public or a section of the public which creates a substantial risk that the course of justice in particular legal proceedings will be seriously impeded or prejudiced; and

(b) that the proceedings were "active".

Substantial risk of serious prejudice

It will be necessary for the prosecution to prove first that the risk to a fair trial is substantial and, secondly, that the effect of publication would be a serious impediment or prejudice.

There must be a substantial risk that the course of justice in particular court proceedings will be seriously impeded or prejudiced. Whether or not there is such a risk will depend to a large extent on the type of court that is to hear the proceedings. Crown Court proceedings (see Ch.1) are the most common type of proceedings to be the subject of a contempt case because the jury members (who decide upon the guilt or innocence of the defendant) are far more likely to be influenced by what they see or hear in the media than is a judge. It is considered that a judge, who is greatly experienced in determining matters on the evidence before him or her alone, is impervious to material published by the media. That a newspaper could not prejudice the Supreme Court emerged from the long running row between Tiny Rowlands and Mohammed Fayed in the 1980s (the *Lonrho* case).

The risk itself must be practical, and not merely a theoretical risk. Thus each case will have to be looked at on its own facts. In *Att Gen v Guardian Newspapers Ltd* [1992] 3 All E.R. 38, the *Guardian* published an article criticising judges for their propensity to impose reporting restrictions in major fraud trials. The article, written by the city editor, mentioned in particular a trial of six defendants in Manchester in relation to which reporting restrictions had been imposed. The reason for the restriction was that one of the defendants faced a pending trial in the Isle of Man. The Court of Appeal pointed out that the publication of a statement that a defendant in criminal proceedings was awaiting trial on other charges did not necessarily create a substantial risk that the course of justice in those future proceedings would be seriously impeded. The question in each case then is whether at the time of publication the statement created a substantial risk that the course of justice would be seriously impeded—not whether it was the type of publication, such as a national newspaper, which was inherently likely to create such risk.

The offence may be committed even though there is no actual prejudice provided that the risk is substantial. The meaning of substantial was considered in the Maxwell brothers' pension fund trial (*MGN Pension Trustees Ltd v Bank of America National Trust and Saving Association* [1995] E.M.L.R. 99). The judge said that it did not have the meaning of "weighty" but rather meant "not insubstantial" or "not minimal". The House of Lords said that the words "substantial risk" should be taken as meaning a risk which, assessed at the time of publication, is not merely remote. (*Att Gen v English* [1983] A.C. 116 HL).

However, Lord Denning M.R., speaking of juries (in *R. v Horsham Justices Ex p. Farquharson* [1982] 1 Q.B. 762), said that they were generally not influenced by what they have read in the press:

> "They are good sensible people. They go by the evidence that is adduced before them not by what they may have read in the newspapers. The risk of their being influenced is so slight it can usually be regarded as insubstantial."

Lord Denning's relaxed view on the media has not always found favour with the courts since the 1980s.

Three factors that will have a particular effect on whether or not there is a substantial risk to a fair trial are the following:

(a) Type of court hearing the case

Notwithstanding Lord Denning's remarks in the *Horsham Justices* case, judges are commonly of the opinion that juries are likely to be swayed by what they hear or read in the media. Thus the most likely venue to be held to be contaminated by media publication is the Crown Court, where all criminal trials are by jury. The only other significant type of case tried by jury is defamation, although it is less likely that media publications concerning defamation proceedings will be the subject of contempt proceedings.

It should be noted, however, that prejudice is not limited to the circumstance where a jury is or might be affected. A media report which affects the conduct or plea of a defendant in a criminal court could be held to be in contempt. As Lord Bridge said in *Re Lonrho Plc* [1990] 2 A.C. 154 at 208:

> "Whether the course of justice in particular proceedings will be impeded or prejudiced by a publication must depend primarily on whether the publication will bring influence to bear which is likely to divert the proceedings in some way from the course which they would otherwise have followed."

Lord Oliver followed this line of reasoning in his judgment in *Att Gen v Times Newspapers Ltd, The Times*, February 12 1983, when he said:

> "The course of justice is not just concerned with the outcome of proceedings. It is concerned with the whole process of the law, including the freedom of a person accused of a crime to elect, so far as the law permits him to do so, the mode of trial which he prefers and to conduct his defence in the way which seems best to him and to his advisers."

(b) Circulation of the publication

The geographical location of the court and the corresponding area and prominence of the publication will often affect the chances of there being a substantial risk of serious prejudice to a fair trial. This is especially the case where the area of circulation of the publication is some distance from the trial centre. The risk would be less likely, for example, where a local (and not available online) Guildford newspaper carries a report that a man charged and to be tried in York has previous convictions for the same offence. The members of the York jury are unlikely to have read the local Guildford newspaper—it is of course possible that they did, but a mere possibility will not be enough for there to be a substantial risk. The risk of creating serious prejudice is therefore much greater where a publication is of great prominence and reaches a mass audience, for example, a national newspaper or television broadcast. In *Att Gen v (1) British Broadcasting Corporation (2) Hat Trick Productions Ltd*, unreported, June 12, 1996, contempt proceedings were brought in relation to the popular BBC comedy programme *Have I Got News For You*. The then presenter, Angus Deayton, referred to the Maxwell brothers, who at the time were awaiting trial for fraud, as "heartless scheming bastards". In deciding to fine each respondent £10,000, the court held that it was a factor in assessing the level of risk that it had been shown at peak time and had been repeated and reached a total audience of some 6.1 million people.

(c) Time delay to trial: the "fade factor"

The likely delay between the report and the trial is a further important factor in determining whether there is likely to be a substantial risk of serious prejudice. The longer the delay (criminal cases may take several months or even years to come to trial), the more likely that there will not be such a substantial risk. In *Att Gen v Independent Television News* [1995] 1 Cr.App.R. 204, ITV broadcast a news item produced for it by ITN which reported the murder of a police officer. It stated that the suspect was an IRA terrorist who had been convicted of the murder of an SAS officer. The trial of the accused took place nine months after the broadcast. The court found that memories of any potential jury members could be expected to fade during that time, and ITN was found not to have committed contempt. Of course it is possible that certain notorious stories or articles that are particularly memorable will stay in a juror's mind for many months, if not longer. In *Att Gen v Morgan* [1998] E.M.L.R. 294, an article in the *News of the World* concerned a large-scale conspiracy to distribute counterfeit money entitled, "We smash £100m fake cash ring". The defendants, Tony Hassan and Anthony Caldori, successfully applied for a stay of proceedings at trial due to the article in the *News of the World*. At the time of publication of the article, the time delay to trial was likely to be about eight months. The court held that, although this was a considerable time delay, the jury could be expected to remember aspects of the article due to the prominence given to the publication and the likely impact on the reader. References to the criminal record of one of the defendants, and the criminal background of both, permeated the entire article and were a striking feature which would not be easily forgotten. The arrests had arisen out of an investigation by a

News of the World reporter. The involvement of the media in this way highlights additional problems—here a journalist had exposed the defendants' conduct in co-operation with the police, but for the purpose of obtaining the story for publication in the newspaper. The journalist naturally wishes to publish the story in a prominent manner with as much background detail as possible and before any of his competitors learn of the story, but this practice may not sit well with the contempt laws. A similar situation arose as a result of a *News of the World* investigation in 2002, which claimed to have uncovered a plot to kidnap Victoria Beckham. Although arrests were made, the charges were eventually dropped on the grounds that some prosecution witnesses were unreliable due to their involvement in the newspaper's investigation. There is an uneasy tension between journalism and law enforcement in this area.

Publications during the course of a trial itself are at very great risk of causing substantial prejudice. The timing of the publication was a key factor in attracting a £75,000 fine for the *Sunday Mirror* in the most notorious contempt case of recent years (*Att Gen v MGN Ltd* [2002] EWHC 907). The newspaper published an interview with the father of a victim of an assault, in which those charged with offences included Leeds United footballers. The article suggested that the attack had been racially motivated—even though it had been expressly stated, to the trial jury, this was not the case. The publication took place over the weekend while the jury was out deliberating its verdict and, as a result, the trial collapsed amid enormous publicity and public complaint about the cost of the abandoned proceedings directed squarely at the newspaper. The aborted trial had cost more than £1 million.

The publishers admitted the publication constituted contempt, but the court said that even though there were some mitigating factors and the newspaper had a previously good record, the gravity of the contempt justified the significant fine. Similarly, *Att Gen v News Group Newspapers* (Unreported April 16, 1999 DC) concerned the trial of the docklands bombers. One accused was convicted of conspiracy to bomb and the jury adjourned overnight to consider the murder charge. The *Sun* meanwhile published an allegation that the man (McCartle) was under arrest as an IRA sniper. The murder charge was abandoned and the case was referred to the Attorney General for prosecution. The *Sun* was fined £35,000—a figure which would have been considerably higher if it was not for the newspaper's immediate apology to the court and the victims' families.

Once it is established that there is a substantial risk of prejudice, it falls on the prosecution to go on to prove that the effect will be serious. This is largely a question of whether the article that has been published could tip the scales of justice one way or the other. The media could try to escape liability by showing that the judge in the case could prevent the allegedly contemptuous article having any serious effect by disallowing persons who had read the article from being jury members, although this is unlikely to succeed where a national publication with mass circulation is concerned.

Ten guiding principles

The test for serious prejudice was considered in *Att Gen v MGN* [1997] E.M.L.R. 284. The background to the case was the arrest of Geoffrey Knights for alleged assault on two people, including the former *EastEnders* actress Gillian Taylforth. The eventual criminal trial was stopped by the trial judge because he felt that all the preceding media coverage *taken together* would have prejudiced the trial. Various publications made allegations such as "Knights beat me to a pulp", that the victim was "battered with an iron bar", and might be "blinded" and "scarred for life". In the action by the Attorney General against some of the newspapers concerned, the court found that the prosecution had not proved that the publications, taken individually, met the necessary test under s.2(2) of the 1981 Act. Schiemann L.J. took the opportunity to set out 10 guiding principles governing application of the strict liability rule.

(1) Each case must be decided on its own facts.

(2) The court will look at each publication separately and test matters as at the time of publication; nevertheless, the mere fact that, by reason of earlier publications, there is already some risk of prejudice does not prevent a finding that the latest publication has created a further risk.

(3) The publication in question must create some risk that the course of justice in the proceedings in question will be impeded or prejudiced by that publication.

(4) That risk must be substantial.

(5) The substantial risk must be that the course of justice in the proceedings in question will not only be impeded or prejudiced but *seriously* so.

(6) The court will not convict of contempt unless it is *sure* that the publication has created this substantial risk of that serious effect on the course of justice.

(7) In making an assessment of whether the publication in question does create this substantial risk of that serious effect on the course of justice the following, amongst other matters, arise for consideration:

    (a) the likelihood of the publication coming to the attention of a potential juror;

    (b) the likely impact of the publication on an ordinary reader at the time of publication; and

    (c) the residual impact of the publication on a notional juror at the time of trial. It is this last matter which is crucial. (One must remember that in this, as in any exercise of risk assessment, a small risk multiplied by a small risk makes an even smaller risk.)

(8) In making an assessment of the likelihood of the publication coming to the attention of a potential juror, the court will consider amongst other matters:

    (a) whether the publication circulates in the area from which the jurors are likely to be drawn; and

    (b) how many copies circulated.

(9) In making an assessment of the likely impact of the publication on an

ordinary reader at the time of publication, the court will consider amongst other matters:

(a) the prominence of the article in the publication; and
(b) the novelty of the content of the article in the context of likely readers of that publication.

(10) In making an assessment of the residual impact of the publication on a notional juror at the time of trial, the court will consider amongst other matters:

(a) the length of time between publication and the likely date of the trial;
(b) the focusing effect of listening over a prolonged period to evidence in a case; and
(c) the likely effect of a judge's direction to a jury.

Examples of contempt

There are many ways in which a newspaper or other component of the media may cross the line on contempt, but the following are common examples of ways in which it might occur.

- Publishing a defendant's previous convictions. In criminal trials, the previous convictions of a defendant can be deliberately kept from a jury so as to give the defendant a "blank sheet" at the commencement of the trial. A juror who knows a defendant has a history of committing criminal offences (or worse a history of committing the type of offence which is before the court) will more readily believe that the defendant has committed the offence which is before them. The publication by the media of previous convictions of the defendant will therefore, almost invariably, amount to a real risk of contempt. However, Parliament has considered whether to change the law to allow a defendant's previous convictions to be put before a jury in certain circumstances. The Criminal Justice Act of 2003 changed the rules relating to previous convictions from December 2004, but judges can, and do, exclude evidence of bad character if unfair or not in the interests of justice. But the decision to allow evidence of bad character, which has to be "relevant", is for the judge at trial not the editor at the time of arrest.

- Publishing details of criminal trials. Publications in good faith on matters of public interest will not generally be contemptuous. In any case the jury will have been present at the trial and will have already heard the matters published. However, parts of the proceedings in a Crown Court may be heard in the absence of the jury, for example where the judge makes a ruling on the admissibility of evidence. Media publication of such matters could well prejudice the trial. Reporters must not add opinion to court reports, so do not give views such as "the witness looked shifty" or "gave evasive answers", etc.

- Publishing a defendant's photograph. In trials where the accuracy of a witness's identification of the defendant is in issue, the publication of a photograph of the defendant may be a contempt. This is due to the fact that there is a risk that the witness will then describe what they have seen in the photograph rather than what they saw at the scene of the crime.

- Publishing details of a defendant's background. Where background facts have the effect of either blackening or lauding a defendant, or suggesting dishonesty or a motive for their behaviour, this may give rise to contempt.

Active proceedings

A substantial risk of serious prejudice is not enough of itself to constitute contempt under the 1981 Act. The proceedings (which include those taking place in any court or tribunal including the Employment Tribunal) that are the subject of the contempt must be active at the time of publication.

Times at which proceedings become active are listed in Sch.2 to the Act and depend upon the type of proceedings in question. The table below shows when proceedings become active and when they cease to be active. The greatest care must be taken with criminal proceedings as these are the most likely to be the subject of a contempt prosecution. Problems commonly arise when a subject is attending the police station "to help the police with their enquiries". As can be seen from the table below, the proceedings become active from arrest. But if a suspect has attended the police station voluntarily they may not have been arrested. Care should thus be taken by the media to check whether or not any individual suspect has been arrested at the point of actual publication or broadcast.

In *AG v Daily Star* [2005] E.M.L.R. 13 DC, Express Newspapers, publishers of the *Daily Star* was fined £60,000 for contempt. In September 2003, a 17-year-old girl had alleged that she had been raped at a Park Lane hotel in London by a number of footballers and the police arrested various suspects and released them on bail. As in the *Soham* case, the Attorney General published guidelines, requests and advice to the media stating that identification was in issue and that suspects should not be identified nor any photographs of them published. This was made somewhat bizarre by the fact that some of those footballers were playing in televised Premiership matches. The internet was full of hints of the players' identities and even names. National newspapers avoided identifying the suspects but the *Daily Star* in a "bad mistake", published on October 23, 2003, named two of the suspects and published a partly pixelated photograph of one of them whilst they were answering bail in relation to the alleged offence. The newspaper argued that it was likely that the complainant knew the relevant identities of her alleged assailants but the court was not prepared to proceed on the basis of this hearsay evidence and pointed out that the complainant may have faced cross-examination of the basis that her identification as to who was present or who did what and would be tainted by what she had read (or had been told by others) in the *Daily Star*. This created a real, substantial and more than remote practical risk that the course of justice would be seriously impeded or prejudiced. The matter was aggravated by the failure to heed the warnings issued by the Attorney General.

Media defences

The following defences may be available to media defendants.

Fair and accurate report of legal proceedings

A person will not be guilty of contempt of court under the 1981 Act in respect of a:

- fair and accurate report of legal proceedings, held in public;
- published contemporaneously; and
- in good faith.

This defence will only apply to contemporaneous reports. For daily newspapers and broadcast news programmes this will usually mean that the report must be published the same day or the following day. Publications after a longer delay may still make use of the defence in certain circumstances, for example a weekly magazine will be unable to publish daily news details.

However, the court may, where it appears to be necessary for avoiding a substantial risk of prejudice to the administration of justice in those proceedings, or in any other proceedings pending or imminent, order that the publication of any report of the proceedings be postponed for whatever period is necessary. Any publication contravening the order will be in contempt whether or not it is fair and accurate, contemporaneous and in good faith (see Ch.8). Once the postponement order expires, then publication of the information will be deemed contemporaneous as at that date.

Innocent publication or distribution

A publisher of material likely to prejudice a fair trial may have a defence under s.3 of the Act as follows:

"A person is not guilty of contempt of court under the strict liability rule as the publisher of any matter to which that rule applies if at the time of publication (having taken all reasonable care) he does not know and has no reason to suspect that relevant proceedings are active."

In order to use the defence, the publisher must show that they took all reasonable steps to ensure that the proceedings were not active. This would, in appropriate circumstances, involve contacting the police to find out whether they have arrested any suspect.

In *Her Majesty's Solicitor General v Henry and News Group Newspapers Ltd* [1990] Q.B.D., March 20, 1990, the *News of the World* published a report about the disappearance of Shirley Banks in Bristol. It concerned the arrest of a man for armed robbery who, it was discovered after the arrest, had Mrs Banks's driving licence in his possession and her car in his garage. The significant part of the report described that the suspect was a "convicted sex beast" and gave graphic details of his previous sex offence and conviction.

The Solicitor General made an application to the court for the committal

When Proceedings become Active

CRIMINAL PROCEEDINGS	CIVIL PROCEEDINGS	APPEALS
Criminal proceedings become active from the point of one of the following happening to a defendant: (a) arrest without warrant; (b) issue of a warrant for arrest; (c) issue of a summons to appear in court; (d) service of an indictment or other document specifying a charge.	Civil proceedings become active from the time when arrangements for the hearing are made or where there are no such arrangements from the time the hearing begins. They cease to be active when the proceedings are disposed of or discontinued or withdrawn.	Cases of appeal ("appellate proceedings") are active from the time when they are commenced: (a) by application for leave to appeal; (b) by notice of appeal or of application for review; (c) by other originating process, until disposed of, abandoned, discontinued or withdrawn.
Conclusion of criminal proceedings by discontinuance or operation of law occurs when: (a) the charge or summons is withdrawn; (b) in the case of proceedings commenced by arrest without warrant, the person arrested is released, otherwise than on bail, without having been charged; (c) in the case of proceedings commenced by arrest warrant, the end of the period of 12 months beginning with the date of the warrant unless they have been arrested within that period; (d) the accused is found to be unfit to be tried or unfit to plead.		
Criminal proceedings are concluded: (a) by acquittal or sentence; (b) by any other verdict or order which puts an end to the proceedings; (c) by discontinuance or by operation of law.		

to prison of Wendy Henry, the editor of the *News of the World* and to fine the proprietors, News Group Newspapers Ltd. The defendants accepted that the article could constitute contempt in that it created a substantial risk that the trial of Mr Cannan would be prejudiced and that the proceedings were, at the time of publication, active within the meaning of the 1981 Act. But the defendants initially contended that they had a defence under s.3 in that they did not know and had no reason to suspect that the proceedings were active, because Cannan had originally been arrested in relation to the robbery charge and they did not know of his rearrest (while still in police custody) on the murder charge. The defence failed and the court fined the proprietors £15,000, with no order against Ms Henry.

The defence is wider for a distributor of material, for example a bookshop or newsagent. The defence is as follows:

"A person is not guilty of contempt of court under the strict liability rule as a distributor of a publication containing any such matter if at the time of distribution (having taken all reasonable care) he does not know that it contains such matter and has no reason to suspect that it is likely to do so."

Discussion of public affairs

Where a publication is made by way of a discussion of a matter of public interest it will not be a contempt of court where the risk of prejudice to legal proceedings is merely incidental to the main discussion which was made in good faith. A discussion will be in good faith where it is produced with honesty. This defence is contained in s.5 of the Act, which provides as follows:

"A publication made as or as part of a discussion in good faith of public affairs or other matters of general public interest is not to be treated as a contempt of court under the strict liability rule if the risk of impairment or prejudice to particular legal proceedings is merely incidental to the discussion."

The purpose of this defence is to allow publication of news items which are of public interest even though a potential side-effect is that later proceedings might be prejudiced.

This defence enabled the *Mail on Sunday* to publish prejudicial details of Michael Fagan's character when he was accused of burglary following a break-in at Buckingham Palace. The court agreed with the prosecution that the article carried with it a substantial risk of serious prejudice to Fagan's trial but held that the Queen's safety was an example, *par excellence*, of an item where interest was sufficient to merit application of the defence (*Att Gen v Associated Newspapers, The Times*, February 12, 1983).

The media successfully used the defence in *Att Gen v English* [1982] 2 All E.R. 903. The *Daily Mail* published an article in support of a "pro-life" candidate for parliamentary election criticising the practice of allowing deformed babies to die of starvation. The article was published in the same week as a doctor's trial for murder. The evidence against him was that he had allowed a handicapped baby to starve. The Attorney General applied for an order that the editor and owners of the paper had committed strict liability contempt. The House of Lords held that the test of whether the risk of prejudice was merely incidental to the discussion was not whether an article could have been written as effectively without the prejudicial passages or whether some other phraseology might have been substituted for them that could have reduced the risk of prejudicing the trial. Instead it is whether the risk created by the words actually chosen by the author was no more than an incidental consequence of getting its main theme across.

The more closely the subject-matter of an article relates to particular legal proceedings, the less likely it will be that the risk of prejudice is merely incidental to the discussion. In the *David English* case, the *Daily Mail* article made no mention of the trial of the doctor. But in *Att Gen v TVS Television Ltd* (*The Times*, July 7, 1989), TVS had broadcast a programme entitled, "The New Rachmans" in January 1988. The programme concerned certain landlords in Reading who were obtaining money by deception from the Department of Health and Social Security and were using bullying tactics in the handling of tenants. The programme compared the behaviour of such landlords to that of the infamous *Rachman* case of the 1960s where the evidence was that Mr Rachman would stop at nothing to get rid of tenants he did not want.

As a result of the broadcast, the trial of one of the Reading landlords on a charge of conspiracy to defraud the DHSS had to be aborted. The judge in the case said that it would have been impossible for the trial to have continued without a real risk of prejudice to the defendant. The programme broadcast by TVS had shown several still pictures of men outside the main Reading post office. Although their faces had been blacked out it was still possible to recognise the defendant who was the subject of criminal proceedings in the Crown Court.

The Attorney General brought proceedings against TVS for contempt of court. He accepted that the broadcast was in good faith but contended that it created a substantial risk of prejudice to the Crown Court trial. TVS accepted that the broadcast created a substantial risk of prejudice to the trial, but contended that the broadcast was merely incidental to the discussion under s.5 of the Act. TVS argued that the programme covered wider issues than the harassment of Reading tenants by their landlords: it concerned the general shortage of rental accommodation in the south of England. TVS went on to argue that if it was found to be in contempt there would be an intolerable stifling of media coverage of current events. The court did not agree that this would be the result and found that the broadcast could not benefit from the protection of s.5; the prejudice created by the programme was not merely incidental to the discussion.

Note that the defence only applies to strict liability under the 1981 Act. Thus the media may still be found guilty of intentional contempt (see below) even where the risk of prejudice is merely incidental to the discussion.

Recent criticism of the law of strict liability contempt

The success—or otherwise—of the contempt laws in ensuring a fair trial for defendants has come under scrutiny recently as a result of reporting of proceedings involving celebrities or notorious crimes. The concern about the cumulative effect of immense media coverage (as in the *Knights* case) was raised following the publicity of the Soham murders of Holly Wells and Jessica Chapman. The accused, Ian Huntley, was a household name from the time of his arrest with much of his background well documented. The Attorney General voiced some concerns about the coverage but no newspaper was held to be in contempt. Some commentators believe that the current law is ineffective against the possibility of prejudicial effect caused by volume of coverage, rather than any specific prejudicial content. On the other hand, newspaper publishers point to the mass of information available on the internet—much of it from overseas—to any potential juror to peruse prior to, or even during, a trial. Further controversy was generated during the *Huntley* case as a result of the Attorney General issuing a number of detailed guidance notes to editors during the police investigation and following Huntley's arrest. Although such guidance has no force of law, it appeared to be an attempt by the Attorney General to interpret the statutory provisions and suggest a particular course of conduct to newspapers. Editors voiced concerns at the direct intervention of a government law officer in the editorial decisions of publications in this way. In May 2007 the Attorney General indicated that there needs to be a review of the 1981 Act as the public would be given more details after high-profile terrorism arrests. He said research in other countries had concluded the effects of pre-trial reporting were less significant than might be thought. The courts do allow the media to report full "backgrounders" after conviction although technically proceedings are active until sentence. Proceedings become active again if an appeal is lodged.

INTENTIONAL CONTEMPT

It is possible for a person to be convicted of contempt outside the provisions of the Act but it must be proved that they intended the prejudice to a fair trial. That the common law offence of contempt survives the 1981 Act is demonstrated by s.6(c) of the Act:

> "Nothing in the foregoing provisions of the Act restricts liability for contempt of court in respect of conduct intended to impede or prejudice the administration of justice."

The offence of contempt at common law does not require that the proceedings be active but it must be shown that the defendant intended to prejudice a fair trial.

EXAMPLE

A television news broadcast shows pictures of a bank's employees and customers being held hostage by X and then goes on to list X's previous convictions including unrelated crimes. X is on the run and has not been apprehended. Here the court may say that the broadcaster must have intended prejudice because the prejudice that would be created in the minds of the jury should and would be obvious to the broadcaster. The television station may therefore have committed contempt (even though the proceedings are not active).

In *Att Gen v News Group Newspapers Ltd* [1988] 2 All E.R. 906, the *Sun* published articles entitled "Rape Case Doc: Sun Acts" and "Doc groped me, says girl". The articles referred to the alleged rape of an eight-year-old girl by a "Dr B". The Director of Public Prosecutions decided, in the absence of any evidence corroborating the girl's story, not to proceed with the case. However, the *Sun* made an offer to the girl's mother to fund a private prosecution of the doctor. She accepted the offer and, after the doctor was acquitted, the Attorney General made an application to the court in contempt at common law. The *Sun* accepted that, for the offence to be committed, proceedings did not need to be active. But the newspaper raised two arguments in its defence. The first was that common law contempt could not be committed unless the proceedings were "pending or imminent" (there had been a nine-month delay between the publication and the trial). The second was that in any case there was no intention to prejudice the proceedings. The court did not agree with either of these assertions and fined the *Sun* £75,000.

The *Sun* case has been heavily criticised on the basis that proceedings against Dr B were not pending or imminent at the time of publication and thus a conviction for contempt should not have followed. Indeed, in *Att Gen v Sport Newspapers Ltd* [1991] 1 All E.R. 503, Hodgson L.J. went as far as to say that the *Sun* case had been wrongly decided. In that case, proceedings in common law contempt were brought against the publisher and editor of the *Sport* following a story about the rape and murder of a 15-year-old schoolgirl. At the time of the publication of the article the police had a suspect for the offence, David Evans, but he had not been apprehended. David Evans had a criminal record: in 1978 he had been sentenced to a term of 10 years for attempted rape, assault and indecent assault; in 1981 he had been sentenced to a term of 10 years for rape, to run consecutively with the previous sentence.

Five days before the publication of the article, the police held a press conference with the object of soliciting public help in the tracing of Evans. Immediately prior to the police statement being made an oral warning was given by the police to those journalists who were present: "Most of you will be aware of certain matters relating to the background of the man we're about to name. Can I warn you here and now that if anything is published or broadcast about these matters then it is likely to prejudice any future legal proceedings." There were no representatives of *The Sport* present at the press conference but the paper learned of the desire of the police to keep Evans's criminal record for rape out of the media at least two days before the publication of the article. The article read as follows:

"EVANS WAS GIVEN 10 YEARS FOR RAPE
The man police want to quiz about missing schoolgirl Anna Humphries is a vicious, evil rapist, *The Sport* can reveal exclusively today. Britain's most wanted man, farm labourer David Evans, has a horrific history of sex attacks. In November, 1980, he was sentenced to ten years' jail for brutally raping a 17-year-old girl. And at the time, Evans was on parole for previous sex attacks. At his rape trial, the judge told him: 'I suspect you can't control your own urges. It is my paramount duty to protect the public.' And the judge told the court: 'He is an extremely dangerous man who could strike again.' Evans, now 31, was released earlier this year and

went back to live with his parents in the Welsh border village of Bettis-field—three miles from where 15-year-old Anna was last seen. He was just 23 when he viciously raped the screaming 17-year-old girl in his car after driving to a quiet lane in Oswestry in November, 1980 Helicopters, more than 100 soldiers and RAF mountain rescue teams joined with police dog handlers yesterday to continue the search around the Shrop-shire market town of Much Wenlock, 40 miles from Penley where Anna's shoes were found on a grass verge. Police have already said the chances of finding her alive are slim."

Evans was arrested in France five days later and in March the following year was tried and convicted of the murder of Anna Humphries. The application by the Attorney General to have the publishers and editor of the *Sport* committed for contempt turned on the question of intent. The Court of Appeal accepted that common law contempt could be committed even where the proceedings were neither pending nor imminent but held that, in this case, the publishers of the *Sport* had not intended to prejudice the administration of justice. Bingham L.J. in the Court of Appeal said:

"Such an intent need not be expressly avowed or admitted but can be inferred from all the circumstances, including the foreseeability of the consequences of the conduct, although the probability of the consequence taken to have been foreseen must be little short of overwhelming before it will suffice to establish the necessary intent. But this need not be the sole intention of the contemnor, and intention is to be distinguished from motive or desire."

In finding that the requirement of intention was not made out the judge had regard to the fact that, at the date of publication, the editor of the *Sport* regarded the commencement of proceedings against Evans as "speculative and remote". At that point in time, it was wholly uncertain that Evans would be found at all.

An example of a publication which was held to prejudice a libel trial occurred in the case of *Att Gen v Hislop* [1991] 1 All E.R. 911 where pro-ceedings were brought against the editor of *Private Eye* magazine in respect of an article published by them shortly before the trial of Sonia Sutcliffe's libel action against the self-same magazine. The article suggested that Mrs Sutcliffe, wife of convicted Peter Sutcliffe (the Yorkshire Ripper), had known what her husband was doing at the time of the murders and either did nothing about it or was lying to the police in giving him an alibi. The court found that, in respect of prejudice to potential jurors at the trial, there was contempt only under the strict liability rule because there was no intention to influence prospective jurors. However, in respect of placing improper pressure on Mrs Sutcliffe, the defendant was guilty of both intentional contempt at common law (intention to dissuade Mrs Sutcliffe from continuing with her action was established by the court) and strict liability contempt under the 1981 Act.

CONTEMPT BY PUBLISHING JURY DELIBERATIONS

The need for the secrecy of the conversations of jurors whilst in the jury room was given statutory recognition by the Contempt of Court Act 1981. Section 8 provides that:

"It is a contempt of court to obtain, disclose or solicit any particulars of statements made, opinions expressed, arguments advanced or votes cast by members of a jury in the course of their deliberations in any legal proceedings."

Thus, a person will be in contempt where they publish or solicit any particulars of communication between jury members in the jury room. A journalist would therefore commit contempt by merely asking questions of a juror in connection with conversations that took place between them and other jury members. No proceedings for contempt under s.8 may be taken without the consent of the Attorney General.

This provision applies only to the deliberations of a jury. Thus a newspaper (or its editor) will not be in contempt where it publishes a journalist's interview with a juror in respect of that juror's opinion of the trial. Nor will it be in contempt where it discloses any particulars:

(a) in the proceedings in question for the purpose of enabling the jury to arrive at their verdict, or in connection with the delivery of that verdict; or

(b) in evidence in any subsequent proceedings for an offence alleged to have been committed in relation to the jury in the first mentioned proceedings.

In *Att Gen v Associated Newspapers* [1994] 2 W.L.R. 277, the *Mail on Sunday* published an article, headed "Common people common sense common justice", which described the nature of some of the conversations that took place between jury members in the famous "Blue Arrow" fraud trial. The article discussed various jurors' opinions of the evidence in the trial and described one jury member as only agreeing with the others because he wanted to get home. The Attorney General brought proceedings against the newspaper, the editor and the journalist. It was conceded by the newspaper that the article contained particulars of jury deliberations but it contended that the publication of the article did not amount to a disclosure of those particulars because the true construction of s.8 was that such a disclosure could only be made by a juror. The newspaper said that it had not obtained the information directly from a juror but that it had been obtained via an American researcher who had interviewed two jury members and that the researcher in question was at no time acting on behalf of the newspaper. The court did not accept this argument and all three defendants were held to be in contempt of court under s.8 and were fined £30,000, £20,000 and £10,000 respectively. The House of Lords dismissed the defendants' appeal and stated that:

"There is no conflict or contrast between publication and disclosure. The latter activity has many manifestations and publication is one of them. To disclose is to expose to view, make known or reveal and in its ordinary meaning the word aptly describes both the revelation by jurors of their deliberations and further disclosure by publication in a newspaper of the same deliberations, provided always—and this will raise a question of fact—that the publication amounts to disclosure and is not a mere republication of already known facts."

The deliberations of jurors are treated with the utmost confidence and the courts are reluctant to intervene in the discussions which take place between members of a jury. In *R. v Mirza* [2004] 2 W.L.R. 201, a woman juror raised concerns after the verdict about the conduct of one of her fellow jurors. The House of Lords held that the courts would not investigate such behaviour where the complaint was not made until after the verdict. The courts themselves are not prevented from investigating the conduct of a trial by s.8 of the Contempt of Court Act 1981, but the House of Lords held that it would seriously detract from the benefits of the jury system if evidence about what took place in the jury room could be admitted on appeal and this would not be allowed. This decision resulted in new guidance being issued to jurors in February 2004. The guidance points out that jurors must be made aware that any concerns they have about fellow jurors should be raised by them with the trial judge at the time, but that this should not lead to unwarranted criticism of jurors or inappropriate threats of contempt of court being made against jurors. The trial judge is therefore required to give the jury an appropriate warning at the outset.

The media continues to seek to report concerns of jurors in important cases, as can be seen from the *Att Gen v Michael Seckerson and The Times* case. But so long as deliberations are avoided, which means that the media must make sure that the juror does not even tell them of such things (not just that they do not publish them), some information can be published—as was shown in the broadcast of concerns of a juror regarding the conviction of the murderer of Jill Dando. Years later after a retrial, Barry George was indeed acquitted by a new jury of the murder (after spending seven years in prison). Despite that acquittal, newspapers published allegations that there were grounds to suspect him of the murder and indeed that he had become obsessed with and pestered other women. This led to Mr George bringing proceedings for libel. At the end of 2009 a Statement in Open Court was read after he won libel damages from the *News of the World* and the *Sun* which apologised to him and paid him damages and his legal costs. But for years the media had been able to report with impunity (relying on the conviction and an earlier dismissal of appeal) anything they wanted to about Mr George.

INJUNCTIONS

Usually contempt of court is an issue raised at the end of the criminal trial, sometimes because defence counsel make an application that their client's case is being or has been prejudiced by media reports, or sometimes the Attorney General takes newspapers to task for potentially prejudicial reports at the time of arrest (as was the concern in the *Soham murders* case).

The Attorney General can seek an injunction to stop material reaching the public domain (or further republication). An example of this was in July 2009 when the Attorney General was granted an injunction to restrain the further sale of *The Terrorist Hunters—The Ultimate Inside Story of Britain's Fight Against Terror* published by Random House (*Att Gen v Random House Group Limited* [2009] EWHC 1727) until verdicts were delivered in the retrial of eight men accused of conspiracy to murder. The book had been sent to booksellers for sale at the end of June and the five pages of the book which gave rise to the application described events that occurred as part of "Operation Covert", the police investigation that led to charges of conspiracy to murder. It was anticipated that the jury would be retiring at the end of July, by which time the book would have been widely available. The court had to consider whether the publication of the book would create a substantial risk that the course of justice in that particular criminal trial would be seriously impeded (Contempt of Court Act 1981, s.2(2)). Tugendhat J., an experienced media judge, took into account s.12 of the Human Rights Act 1998 (although he doubted the application of s.12(3)) and considered the wording of the Act, concluding that "substantial" described the degree of risk and "seriously" described the degree of impediment or prejudice to the course of justice. He found that there was a risk of some prejudice if any of the jurors read the book, but that this was not a risk of serious prejudice because the juror would have to display disobedience to the direction of the trial judge (not to buy the book). However, there was a substantial risk that if the book was on sale the course of justice would be impeded by applications to discharge the jury from the various defendant's counsel. Section 5 of the Act was also considered as the passages were part of a discussion of public affairs where the risk of impediment to the trial was not incidental and, of course, the book could be published once the jury had reached their verdict which was expected only a month or two later.

8. REPORTING CURRENT AFFAIRS

Since the last edition of this book there have been some positive developments facilitating the free flow of information to the public. The Supreme Court is allowing filming. The Family Court is allowing journalists in. The Crown Prosecution Service is making available film or other documentation, once seen by a jury, to the media on request, to improve court reporting. Public inquiries are more open, with some filming allowed on occasion. The civil courts are giving greater access (on request and payment of the appropriate modest fees: see CPR 5.4c) to court bundles and pleadings, and even the skeleton arguments of counsel, in civil cases including injunctions. Judges do not read out their judgments but make them available to the parties, after which they are often published on the internet, accessible not just to law students and practitioners but to the public generally. The light of public scrutiny is illuminating previously dark corners of the judicial process.

That news and current events should be reported unfettered to the public is an obvious requirement of a civilised society. Much of the content of this book shows how media law has an impact on current affairs reporting. The causes of action discussed in Ch.2, for example, potentially restrict the information that may be published where it affects a person's reputation. Chapter 4 considers the negative effect of an action for breach of confidence on the media's ability to freely publish current affairs and Ch.3 the effect of copyright. In each case, specific defences exist which prevents there being too much of a muzzle on the media. This chapter considers the reporting to the public of specific types of information and the restraints that exist for each. It goes on to consider under what provisions of law a journalist can be forced to reveal the source of their information to the courts or to others.

REPORTING THE COURTS

This part is concerned with the restrictions imposed upon journalists and others when they are relaying details of court proceedings to the public. Chapter 7 considered the law of contempt of court and the restriction it provides in the limited case of a report which has a substantial risk of seriously prejudicing a fair trial. This section considers the exceptions to the general rule that the actual proceedings in court are open and that details of them may be published. Once again, the Human Rights Act 1998 has come into play in this area. In addition to consideration to be given to art.8 (right to private life) and art.10 (right to freedom of expression), art.6(1) provides:

"In the determination of his civil rights and obligations or of any criminal charge against him, everyone is entitled to a fair and public hearing within a reasonable time by an independent and impartial tribunal established by law. Judgment shall be pronounced publicly but the press and public may be excluded from all or part of the trial in the interest of morals, public order or national security in a democratic society, where the interests of juveniles or the protection of the private life of the parties so require, or to the extent strictly necessary in the opinion of the court in special circumstances where publicity would prejudice the interests of justice."

Access to the courts

The principle that justice must be seen to be done is fundamental to the legal system in this country. The public having access to court rooms is intended to lead to a general perception of the courts as places of fairness and a greater willingness amongst the public to accept the authority of judges' decisions. This trust in the working of the law is believed to be important to stop vigilantism and the courts take a tough line with those who take the law into their own hands: in December 2009 businessman Munir Hussain, 53, who fought off knife-weilding burglars who were threatening to kill his family, was jailed for 30 months. He had discovered three masked men in his house and the burglars tied him up and threatened to kill him and his family. His teenage son managed to escape and alerted his brother Tokeer Hussain. The intruders fled the house in High Wycombe. The brothers chased and caught one of the attackers, a criminal with more than 50 previous convictions. They subjected the burglar to what was described by the judge as a "dreadful, violent attack" leaving him with a permanent brain injury. The revenge attack was self defence that went too far and the judge made it absolutely clear that "whatever the circumstances, persons cannot take the law into their own hands". The Court of Appeal subsequently reduced their sentences for grievous bodily harm (Munir Hussain's sentence was reduced to 12 months and suspended for two years). The public has to rely on the courts, and so must have faith in the courts. Thus the public should know what is going on in the courts, but unfortunately the courts sometimes hide themselves away.

The vast majority of courtrooms provide public access and incorporate special seating for members of the public to observe the proceedings. Many courts also have seating for reporters, in the knowledge that such persons are the eyes and ears of the public at large. Coroners Courts are held in public unless there are issues of national security, although the coroner can order that a witness should have anonymity (as happened during the inquest into the death of Jean Charles De Menezes, shot dead by police in 2005 as he was mistaken for a terrorist, when police firearms officers gave evidence anonymously and could not be photographed outside the Coroner's Court).

This basic rule of openness provides journalists with their ticket to the courts. Access to the courts cannot be denied to the reporter (or the general public) unless there is a provision of law which allows it. In fact, the press are allowed to attend certain hearings which are not open to the public, such as Youth Court proceedings (s.47 of the Children and Young Persons Act 1933) and the testimony of witnesses under 18 in proceedings relating to an offence against or conduct contrary to decency or morality (s.37 of the Children and Young Persons Act 1933).

Certain proceedings, including trials, are occasionally held in private, i.e. in a courtroom to which the public (including reporters) does not have access. The reason for this is usually that public access to the proceedings would be prejudicial to the administration of justice or that it would damage a certain public interest. Under the Crown Court Rules 1982, the court may hold its proceedings in private where:

- there is a possibility of disorder in the courtroom;
- the identity of a witness requires protection;
- a public hearing would be detrimental to future prosecutions; or
- the case concerns a prosecution under the Official Secrets Acts 1911 and 1989.

It should be said, however, that proceedings *in camera* are relatively rare. Where a trial is to be held in private, the media may make representations and can appeal the decision to the Court of Appeal (s.159 of the Criminal Justice Act 1988).

Reporting restrictions

At common law the circumstances in which names and addresses can be withheld from the public are restricted (*R. v Evesham Justices Ex p. McDonagh* [1988] 2 W.L.R. 227). However, the media industry should be aware that certain proceedings have restrictions on what may be disclosed to the public as a result of a plethora of statutory restrictions. The Judicial Studies Board (JSB) has published papers summarising the legal controls on reporting in both the Crown Court and Magistrates' Courts. The JSB states the general position as follows:

"The general rule is that the administration of justice must be done in public. The media is in court to report the proceedings to the public, the majority of whom will be unable to be there in person but who have the right to be informed as to what has occurred. Accordingly, unless there is good and lawful reason, nothing should be done to prevent the publication to the wider public of fair and accurate reports of proceedings by the media. The open justice principle is clearly recognised by the courts and by Parliament. The common law has been supplemented in this respect by statute. The media has been given statutory rights to attend certain proceedings from which the public is excluded. Statutory defences in libel and contempt litigation are available for fair, accurate and contemporaneous reports of proceedings. Statutory rights have been provided to make representations against the imposition of restrictions on reporting or public access to proceedings. The role of the media is recognised in the case law under the European Convention on Human Rights. There are circumstances in which the court will have to consider departing from this general principle. In some cases, statute automatically restricts the giving of certain details in reports of court proceedings. Common law powers and statutory restrictions enable the court in other circumstances to exclude the public and the media and to impose temporary or permanent restrictions on the media's reports of court proceedings by making a court order. In all such circumstances, courts are encouraged to exercise their discretion to hear the media's representations at the time any court is considering imposition of an order."

However, the courts are often too easily persuaded by counsel (usually the defendant's) to inhibit reporting and too seldom does the prosecution fight with vigour to uphold the principle that justice must be seen (and reported) to be done, as set out by the House of Lords in 1913 in *Scott v Scott* [1913] A.C. 417.

It is common to encounter reporting restrictions in several types of cases.

Children and young persons

Children enjoy a special status in law in respect of media attention and the law governing this area is fragmented and complex. The press is specifically prevented, for example, from reporting any aspect of wardship proceedings (Administration of Justice Act 1960, s.12(1)). The restrictions may go further than the proceedings themselves. In an important case, which examined the evidence required to establish that restrictions imposed on the media were necessary and sufficient to warrant overriding the basic principle of freedom of speech, the BBC sought to overturn an injunction preventing it from broadcasting an interview with a 16-year-old ward of the court (*BBC v Kelly* [2001] 1 All E.R. 323). The boy had left home to join a religious group and, out of concern, his family applied to have him made a ward of the court and steps taken for him to be traced. Some publicity of the case followed and the boy concerned subsequently telephoned the BBC's *Today* programme and was interviewed. At first the court ordered that the BBC could not broadcast the interview because its subject was a ward of court, and s.12 of the Administration of Justice Act 1960 and s.97 of the Children Act 1989 imposed reporting conditions. Munby J. held that it was too serious a restraint on the media to require that any interview with a ward of court should require the court's permission. He held that the court's permission would only be required if the media involvement represented a major step in the child's life (which this interview was not) or the media activities related directly to, or was an interference with, the child's upbringing. On the other hand, where journalists interviewed children in care for a documentary, the court held that this did constitute an interference with their upbringing under council supervision and therefore should not be broadcast (*Nottingham Council v October Films, The Times*, May 21, 1999).

There has been increasing concern amongst journalists that injunctions banning the identification of children have been used to give indirect protection to adults. In December 2003, several newspapers successfully overturned an injunction which banned the identification of the children of a woman who had previously had a relationship with the notorious Soham murderer, Ian Huntley. For the journalists this meant effectively preventing identification of the mother too. Eventually the injunction was reframed to prevent the use of pictures of the juveniles or details of their schools, but to permit publication of the mother's identity.

Children in adult courts

Where a juvenile is a defendant, victim or witness in proceedings before any court except a Youth Court (for details of the court structure see Ch.1), the court may direct, by virtue of the Children and Young Persons Act 1993, s.39, that:

(a) no newspaper or broadcast report of the proceedings shall reveal the name, address, or school, or include any particulars calculated to lead to the identification, of any child or young person concerned in the proceedings, whether the minor is the subject of those proceedings or is a witness in them; and

(b) no picture shall be published in any newspaper or on television which is of any child or young person concerned in such proceedings.

The principle behind such a power is to prevent children being adversely affected by publicity and for this reason it is common (particularly in the Magistrates' Court) for judges to make s.39 orders. In *R. v Central Criminal Court Ex p. Godwin and Crook* [1995] 1 F.L.R. 132, Mr and Mrs S were tried and convicted of the manslaughter of their son and of cruelty to three of their other children. The judge in the case made an order under s.39. On appeal against the order, the Court of Appeal said that the judge had been right to make the order and that the desirability of causing no harm to the children outweighed the interests of the public in knowing as much as possible about what happened in court.

The media may make representations to the judge who is considering making an s.39 order that it should not be made, arguing that the objective of freedom of reporting should outweigh the effect upon any children involved. Two journalists did so in the *Godwin* case but in the event they were unsuccessful.

An example of a case where the media succeeded in its application to get an s.39 order lifted is provided by *Mrs R v Central Independent Television* [1994] 2 F.L.R. 151. A man had been tried and convicted of offences involving indecency with young boys. The Crown Court judge made an order during the trial prohibiting any publication that would tend to identify the boys. Central Television wanted to broadcast a television programme which included the man's picture and details of his conviction. Mrs R, the former wife of the man, applied, on behalf of their daughter, aged five, for an injunction forcing the television company to comply with the order. The judge granted the injunction but on appeal the decision was reversed. The Court of Appeal said that the programme had nothing whatever to do with the care or upbringing of the daughter and that therefore there was nothing to put in the balance against the freedom to publish.

There is a law on the statute books which would change these long-standing reporting restrictions on children, but it is not in force and appears now as if it may never be implemented. The Youth Justice and Criminal Evidence Act 1999 would require that where young people are involved in an alleged offence then there will be a ban on reporting anything which identifies those concerned (both accused, victims and witnesses) from the moment a criminal investigation starts—which may be a significant time before anyone is charged (s.44 of the Youth Justice and Criminal Evidence Act 1999).

It also would require that where proceedings do come before the courts, there would be in place a stringent order which arises *automatically* and could only be lifted where the media shows there is a substantial and unreasonable restriction on reporting which it is in the public interest to have removed (s.45).

Jigsaw identification

It is often the case that, even where a s.39 order is made, different pieces of information published in several newspapers would lead a member of the public to draw a conclusion as to the identity of a child involved in the proceedings (s.39 does not empower a judge to direct the media on how the order should be implemented). The prevention of this "jigsaw identification" is the aim of para.7 of the Press Complaints Commission Code of Practice (see Appendix E) which is headed "Children in sex cases" and provides that:

"1. The press must not, even if legally free to do so, identify children under 16 who are victims or witnesses in cases involving sex offences.
 2. In any press report of a case involving a sexual offence against a child—

  (i) The child must not be identified.
  (ii) The adult may be identified.
  (iii) The word "incest" must not be used where a child victim might be identified.
  (iv) Care must be taken that nothing in the report implies the relationship between the accused and the child."

The Ofcom Broadcasting Code (see Appendix F) contains substantially similar provisions in respect of broadcast reports. The provisions of the codes of practice are of course not legally binding on the media. In practice, identifying the adult accused and not specifying the relationship with the child is likely to be less journalistically attractive to the media as it renders little of the "story" repeatable. This is where the danger exists that if one media organisation is tempted to specify the relationship, and another abides by the PCC Code, then the articles taken together will have revealed the identity of the child concerned. The same issue arises commonly in relation to anonymity of victims of sex offences.

Youth courts

Where the Magistrates' Court is sitting as a Youth Court in the prosecution of a juvenile offender, the Children and Young Persons Act 1933, s.49 imposes an *automatic* ban on the publication or broadcast of any of the following information:

> "(a) the name, address or school or any particulars leading to the identification of any child or young person involved in the proceedings as a defendant or witness;
> (b) any photograph of, or including, any such person."

The Youth Court may however waive such a ban, and thus lift the reporting restrictions, in order to avoid injustice to the particular youth concerned. Similarly, by virtue of the Crime (Sentences) Act 1997, the court may, after allowing the parties to make representations, lift the reporting restrictions where a ban would be against the public interest.

In *McKerry v Teesdale & Wear Valley Justices* [2001] E.M.L.R. 127, the court held that the power to dispense with the anonymity of a young person was to be exercised with care. However, where it was shown that there was a legitimate public interest then this may be paramount. Here, the magistrates felt that the public would enjoy some protection from the 15-year-old (who had pleaded guilty to taking a car without consent) if they knew his name. It was also confirmed that it was right for magistrates to hear representations from the press on such issues.

The automatic s.49 restriction should be lifted by the Youth Court where a young person reaches 18 years old during the proceedings, as the reason for the protection has come to an end (*Todd v Director of Public Prosecutions* [2004] All E.R. (D) 92).

Anti-social behaviour orders (ASBOs)

As a result of public concern about teenage "tearaways" and youth gangs, a new criminal penalty called the Anti-Social Behaviour Order was introduced in December 2002. However, from its inception there was an automatic ban preventing the naming of a youth (over 10 years old) on whom the court imposed an "ASBO". Confusingly, a young person who breached the terms of the ASBO and was sentenced for its breach could be identified (except for an express ban). Following a change in the law in January 2004, as a result of the Anti-Social Behaviour Act 2003, there is no longer an automatic ban on identifying the subject of an ASBO—but the circumstance which led to its making (i.e. the criminal conduct) is still automatically subject to the usual Youth Court non-identification rule. This area has caused a great deal of confusion for local papers, for whom the reporting of neighbourhood crime is very important. The present choice, therefore, is to report the criminal conduct without naming the individual responsible, or report in isolation from any description of the crime, that a named individual is the subject of an ASBO. Neither course is likely to be satisfactory to a journalist. The court may, of course, continue to make a specific order banning identification under s.39 of the Children and Young Persons Act 1933 in any case.

In the *McKerry* case (above), the Court of Appeal said that it would be wholly wrong for any court to dispense with a juvenile's prima facie right to anonymity as an additional punishment. The court was also critical of "naming and shaming" but this approach has become circumscribed by the importance attached in more recent decisions to the deterrent effect of publicity.

In October 2004, three teenagers from Brent in London complained that publicity of ASBOs made against them was disproportionate and breached their rights to privacy under the European Convention on Human Rights. Their anti-social behaviour included loitering around, throwing stones at each other from balconies, shouting and spitting, loud music at noisy parties, smoking drugs in communal areas, graffiti, abuse and playing football in communal areas. The police approved leaflets containing photographs of the teenagers with their ages and names for distribution in the area of the exclusion zone and Brent had details of the proceedings on its community website. Although the police had not considered (as they should) whether the publicity was necessary and proportionate, the Divisional Court found this made no difference and rejected the teenagers' complaints. To avoid the risk of defamation proceedings, the court pointed out that those responsible for the publicity must leave no room for misidentification. The Home Office guidance "Publicising Anti-Social Behaviour Orders" (2005) encourages naming on the basis that ASBOs protect local communities.

An ASBO can contain only negative prohibitions. It cannot contain a positive obligation (such as hitching up one's trousers). An application for an ASBO is within the magistrate's civil jurisdiction but a breach of an ASBO is a criminal offence (up to five years imprisonment, up to two years imprisonment for those under 18 years of age).

Adult criminal courts

Committal proceedings

Committal proceedings take place in the Magistrates' Court and occur where the defendant in a criminal case is to be tried in the Crown Court (see Ch.1). Committal proceedings do not now usually include consideration of the evidence and are done on the basis of documents alone. However, a defendant may seek to submit that there is not enough evidence against them to be transferred to the Crown Court. In this instance, unless reporting restrictions are lifted, the only information which may be published in a report of the proceedings is as follows:

- the identity of the court and the names of the examining justices;

- the names, addresses and occupations of the parties and witnesses and the ages of the accused and witnesses;
- the offence or offences, or a summary of them, with which the accused is or are charged;
- the names of counsel and solicitors engaged in the proceedings;
- where the proceedings are adjourned, the date and place to which they are adjourned;
- whether the case is transferred to the Crown Court;
- any arrangements as to bail on committal or adjournment;
- whether legal aid was granted to the accused or any of the accused; and
- whether reporting restrictions were lifted.

(See Magistrates' Court Act 1980).

Reporting restrictions may be lifted upon the application of the accused. However, where there is more than one accused in any one case and one or more of them object to the lifting of reporting restrictions, they will only be lifted where the magistrates are of the opinion that it is in the interests of justice to do so.

Sexual offences

Where a person is charged with a sexual offence and the Director of Public Prosecutions is of the opinion that the three elements below are satisfied, the normal rules on committal for trial (see above) will not apply and the defendant will be transferred to the Crown Court without any consideration by the magistrates (Criminal Justice Act 1991, s.53). The three elements are:

- the nature of the offence makes it suitable for trial in the Crown Court;
- a child who is the victim or witness of the offence will be called as a witness at the trial; and
- to avoid any prejudice to the welfare of the child the case should move to the Crown Court without delay.

The defendant in such a case has the right to apply to the Crown Court for dismissal of the transfer on the grounds of insufficient evidence. Where they do so, any report of the proceedings shall be limited to the same points as detailed above.

The judge may make an order for reporting restrictions to be lifted (Criminal Justice Act 1991, Sch.6), but if the accused objects to the lifting the judge may only do so where they consider it to be in the interest of justice.

Rape

In an attempt to encourage women to report to the police details of sexual offences committed against them, Parliament has provided anonymity for the victim. It is an offence to publish or broadcast the name, address or still or moving pictures of a woman once she or any other person has made an allegation of a rape offence against her (Sexual Offences (Amendment) Act 1976, s.4(1)(a)). This restriction remains in force for the lifetime of the alleged victim.

Once a person has been accused of rape (this will usually be the point where the defendant is charged), the restrictions on publication become more stringent: no matter or article likely to lead members of the public to identify a woman as the complainant in relation to that accusation shall be published or broadcast (s.4(1)(b)).

The media will, however, be permitted to publish such material where the judge makes a direction for the restrictions to be removed. They will do so where:

(a) upon application by the person accused of a rape offence before commencement of the trial, the direction is required for the purpose of inducing persons to come forward who are likely to be needed as witnesses at the trial and the applicant's defence is likely to be substantially prejudiced without such a direction; or

(b) at the trial, they are satisfied that the lack of such a direction would impose a substantial and unreasonable restriction upon the reporting of proceedings at the trial and that it is in the public interest to remove the restriction.

Further, a woman who is an alleged victim of a rape offence may give written consent to the publication of matter which would be likely to lead to her identification. Proof of such consent will be a defence to a criminal prosecution brought against a newspaper or broadcaster (s.4(5A)).

A rape offence for these purposes means any of the following:

- rape;

- attempted rape;

- aiding, abetting, counselling and procuring rape;

- incitement to rape;

- conspiracy to rape; and

- burglary with intent to rape.

The anonymity afforded to alleged rape victims now applies to male rape (an offence created by the Criminal Justice & Public Order Act 1994).

Complainants in almost all other sexual offences are also protected from identification by virtue of the Sexual Offences (Amendment) Act 1992. This imposes a ban for life on reporting the identity of the alleged victim once an allegation has been made and continues after charge. It applies to rape, indecent assault, indecency with children and almost all other sexual offences. Section 48 of the Youth Justice and Criminal Evidence Act 1999 streamlined the reporting restrictions on sexual offences.

Serious fraud

By virtue of the Criminal Justice Act 1987, serious fraud (the term "fraud" has no legal definition as such but includes the offences of obtaining property by deception, false accounting, fraudulent trading, theft and conspiracy to defraud) cases can be transferred to the Crown Court without any consideration by the Magistrates' Court. The normal committal procedure (see above) is thus effectively short-circuited.

Serious fraud cases will be transferred using the fast-track procedure where one of a list of designated persons (including the Director of Public Prosecutions, the Director of the Serious Fraud Office and the Commissioners of the Inland Revenue) certifies the case as being so suitable.

Despite this quick, behind-closed-doors way of processing the transfer, the defendant may apply to the Crown Court for such a transfer to be dismissed on the ground that there is insufficient evidence for a jury to properly convict. In addition, where the trial is to proceed, the Crown Court judge may order a preparatory hearing to clarify the issues to go before the jury. Media reports of the application for dismissal and the preparatory hearing must be limited to:

- the identity of the court and the name of the judge;
- the names, ages, home addresses and occupations of the accused and witnesses;
- any relevant business information (largely confined to the names and addresses of any relevant business, firm or company);
- the offence or offences, or a summary of them, with which the accused is charged;
- the names of counsel and solicitors in the proceedings;
- where the proceedings are adjourned, the date and place to which they are adjourned;
- any arrangements as to bail; and
- whether legal aid was granted to the accused.

These restrictions cease upon a successful application by the defendant for dismissal or at the end of the trial.

General

Early hearings

Before a criminal trial at the Crown Court, there will often be pre-trial hearings dealing with procedural matters and, for example, bail applications. Sections 41 and 42 of the Criminal Procedure and Investigations Act 1996 means that there are automatic restrictions preventing the reporting of such hearings and the rulings made, until the full trial is concluded.

In addition, where a trial is to be a long or complex one, ss.37 and 38 govern reporting restrictions at preparatory hearings that may be held. The media may broadcast only the following information:

- the identity of the court and the name of the judge;

- the names, ages, home addresses and occupations of the accused and witnesses;

- the offence or offences, or a summary of them, with which the accused is charged;

- the names of counsel and solicitors in the proceedings;

- where the proceedings are adjourned, the date and place to which they are adjourned;

- any arrangements as to bail; and

- whether legal aid was granted to the accused.

Witnesses

A trial judge can consider making an order under s.4(2) or s.11 of the Contempt of Court Act 1981 to protect the identity of a witness (see the section on Contempt of Court later in this chapter) or under the jurisdiction of the court. Somewhat ironically perhaps this has been used by the media to protect the identity of its own witnesses in libel cases as well as to protect the identity of witnesses from the media. Lord Northcliffe, a pioneer of tabloid journalism and Founder of the *Daily Mail*, asserted a long time ago that "news is what somebody somewhere wants to suppress", but the *Daily Mail* supported an application by a witness in a libel trial before Eady J. that her identity should be protected because of concerns that when she was describing her sex life with the claimant it might have a deleterious effect on her children. Bizarrely this led to the defendant newspaper being unable to report properly its own evidence in its defence, something the newspaper's editor may have forgotten when lambasting the leading media judge Eady J. for allowing the introduction of privacy principles of European origin into the English courts (*Ivereigh v Associated Newspapers* [2008] EWHC 339 (QB).

The court's powers have, in part, been enhanced by the Youth Justice and Criminal Evidence Act 1999. This provides that vulnerable witnesses (such as young people, disabled people and those in fear or distress) may be protected by a "special measures direction" which excludes all reporters, except one nominated representative, from court (s.25). The legislation also provides that the court may direct that nothing can be published to identify such a witness—either during the trial or in perpetuity (s.46), which came into force on October 7, 2004. Such orders are only to be made where a witness was in fear or distress to such an extent that their ability to give evidence may be affected. To grant a reporting direction, a court must determine that a witness is "eligible for protection" and that the direction is likely to improve either the quality of evidence given by their witness or the level of co-operation given by the witness. Such directions are not meant to be common place and the court must take into account the offence to which the proceedings relate; the age of the witness; the social and cultural background and ethnic origins; the domestic and employment circumstances; any religious beliefs or political opinions of the witness (if relevant); and any behaviour towards the witness on the part of the accused, members of the family or associates of the accused. The court must consider any view expressed by the witness, as well as whether it would be in the interests of justice to give a reporting direction, and the public interest in avoiding the imposition of a substantial and unreasonable restriction on the reporting of the proceedings. Section 52 requires the court to have regard to the interests of the open reporting of crime, the open reporting of matters relating to human health and safety and the prevention and exposure of miscarriages of justice.

If any publication includes any matter in contravention of an s.46 reporting direction, a summary offence is committed and the editor or publisher of a newspaper is guilty of the offence. But it is a defence to prove that the editor was not aware, and neither suspected nor had reason to suspect, that the publication included the matter or report in question; or that the witness had given written consent to the inclusion of the matter in the publication.

Contempt of court

It will be contempt of court to publish any information which could lead to a substantial risk of serious prejudice to a fair trial (see Ch.7). However, the media will not be in contempt in respect of:

- a fair and accurate report of legal proceedings;
- held in public;
- published contemporaneously; and
- in good faith (Contempt of Court Act 1981, s.4).

The type of contempt discussed in Ch.7 is usually confined to reports of future or anticipated court proceedings. There is a further aspect of contempt that must be considered in relation to media reports of the proceedings themselves. The 1981 Act gives the court the power to order the media to refrain from publishing certain details of the trial. Section 4(2) provides:

"The court may, where it appears to be necessary for avoiding a substantial risk of prejudice to the administration of justice in those proceedings, or in any other proceedings, pending or imminent, order that the publication of any report of those proceedings, or any part of those proceedings, be postponed for such period as the court thinks necessary for that purpose."

It will rarely be prejudicial to the trial to publish details of matters heard in open court and so s.4(2) orders will be rare. A s.4(2) order will often be made in relation to proceedings in the Crown Court which are heard in the absence of the jury (although note that it is contempt at common law to publish material which is stated while the jury has been sent out). Where the defence (or, less commonly, the prosecution) in a criminal trial make an application to the judge for certain evidence to be excluded, for example evidence of the defendant's confession, such an application will be heard in open court but without the jury being present. Where such an application is to be made, the advocate will indicate their intention to the judge, who will ask the jury to transfer to the jury room until the application has been heard. If the application to exclude evidence is successful then the jury will not be told of the existence of the evidence. This important safeguard for the defendant would be useless if the jury were able to read details of what occurred in court in the next morning's newspaper.

The second situation is where the defendant is being tried for a number of offences. At the conclusion of the current proceedings, the defendant will stand trial on other charges. If the media published details of the current offence there is a risk that the future proceedings would be prejudiced. If the judge thinks there to be a real risk of such prejudice he will tell reporters present in court that they are not to publish certain details of the pro-ceedings. The number of terrorism cases which have been taking place over the last few years has led to a substantial expansion in the number of orders and restrictions imposed by the criminal courts on the media, with the result that some trials cannot be reported until months after the jury's verdict due to further related trials. The courts seem to think that this is satisfactory, but it causes irritation not just to editors but to the police and prosecutors who are unable to reassure the public (who may well remember the sensational circumstances of a particular series of arrests) that justice is being done and is being seen to be done.

Further, the court may, where it considers it appropriate, make an order under s.4(2) which prevents the disclosure of a person's name in open court. An example of where this may occur is the trial of a person accused of blackmail. The victim will need to give evidence against the blackmailer and describe details of the blackmail itself. It is likely that victims of blackmail would not come forward if they anticipated the publication of their names.

Where there is such an exemption from disclosure of a person's name in open court the judge may order that there should be no media publication of the matter at all. Section 11 of the 1981 Act provides that:

"In any case where a court (having power to do so) allows a name or other matter to be withheld from the public in proceedings before the court, the court may give such directions prohibiting the publication of that name or matter in connection with the proceedings as appear to the court to be necessary for the purpose for which it was so withheld."

In order that the courts can later determine whether a contempt under these provisions has been committed, an order made by a judge under s.4(2) or s.11 must be written and should state:

(a) its precise scope;

(b) the time limit on the order; and

(c) the purpose for which the order is made.

In this way the media can be sure of the exact restrictions that apply to them.

The principal difference between s.4(2) and s.11 is that a ban on publication under the former section will commonly be for a limited duration (usually until the end of the trial). A s.11 ban will be absolute. The media may disagree with the making of a s.4(2) or s.11 order, for example where it is felt that the judge was wrong to make the order or that its terms are too restrictive and may decide to challenge it. This may be done by:

- employing counsel to make representations to the trial judge during the course of the proceedings; or

- a "person aggrieved" by such an order may appeal to the Court of Appeal under s.159 of the Criminal Justice Act 1988 (leave is required and this may be problematic as the media is not a party to the criminal proceedings).

In the Maxwell brothers case (*MGN Pension Trustees Ltd v Bank of America National Trust and Saving Association* [1995] E.M.L.R. 99) there was an application by the Serious Fraud Office to postpone the reporting of civil actions brought by trustees of the pension funds until after the criminal trial of those involved. The application was opposed by six newspapers. The judge, in refusing to grant the application, said that there were three questions to be answered as the preconditions of making such an order:

(i) was there a substantial risk of prejudice to the administration of justice in the criminal trials? If so,

(ii) did it appear necessary for avoiding that risk that there should be some order postponing publication of reports of the civil actions? If so,

(iii) ought the court in its discretion to make any, and if so what, order?

The courts and television

The broadcast of court proceedings held within the jurisdiction is prohibited (Criminal Justice Act 1925, s.41). Persons wishing to dispense with the ban have often cited, by way of argument, the benefits of publicity: better public awareness of important issues; more people being able to witness the judicial process (and thus seeing justice being done); better behaved advocates and judges. The televised trial of O.J. Simpson in California proved to be a setback for such supporters of abolition of the prohibition in the United Kingdom. Many of the criticisms levelled at the US case—the length of the trial, the extravagant behaviour of the lawyers and the obvious playing to the camera of many of those involved in the trial—were arguably the result of the televising of the proceedings. The inquiry held by Lord Hutton into the circumstances of the death of Dr David Kelly, the government weapons inspector, was a more recent test for the question of the broadcast of proceedings in this country. Broadcasters including ITN, Sky, and Channel 4 sought permission to record and broadcast the evidence, which included evidence from the then Prime

Minister Tony Blair. Lord Hutton ruled against the televised broadcast of proceedings on the grounds that it would cause additional stress for some witnesses, who included Dr Kelly's widow, and that the absence of television filming did not mean that the inquiry was not "public" as required by the principle of open justice.

The courts and the government are still considering televising proceedings. Court of Appeal hearings have been filmed and example ITV News reports presented to the judges and broadcasters in the hope that the courts will come to realise that the perception of secrecy does more harm than the possible inconvenience of television cameras. The Supreme Court has allowed the filming of its work. However, judges and politicians fear that filming will deter witnesses and risk inhibiting justice in the courts. The fact that judges and lawyers have been known to fall asleep during cases has not yet been used as an excuse to keep the prying eyes of cameras outside the courtroom. Family courts, led by Munby J., have encouraged greater transparency and there are calls for open and public debate in the media about the workings of the family justice system in the interests of public confidence (see paras 99 and 103 of the judgment of Munby J. in *Ray B (Child)* [2004] EWHC 411 (Fam). This was prompted by concerns about the reporting of family cases involving such controversial topics as cot deaths, forcible adoption and Munchausen's Syndrome by Proxy. New rules in 2009 allowed journalists into Family courts to hear most kinds of cases. But the government has not yet changed the law on what can and cannot be reported. Budgetary constraints mean that editors are not particularly keen to have reporters watching the Family courts in action but unable to write anything but the most general articles of what is going on there. Certain hearings are still excluded, including those for the purposes of judicially assisted conciliation or negotiation. Accredited media representatives may be excluded on specified grounds, which are that it is necessary:

(a) in the interests of any child concerned in, or connected with, the proceedings; or

(b) for the safety or protection of a party, a witness in the proceedings, or a person connected with such a party or witness; or

(c) for the orderly conduct of the proceedings; or

(d) where the court is satisfied that justice will otherwise be impeded or prejudiced. [FPR Rule 16A(3)].

So the onus is on the person seeking to exclude the press to satisfy the judge that it is not really desirable but necessary. It is s.12 of the Administration of Justice Act 1960 that stops journalists communicating the information that they witness in court. Journalists should be advised of the toughness of the Family courts when it comes to protecting its customers: in *X v Dempster* [1999] 1 F.L.R. 894 Wilson J. found that the *Daily Mail* had overstepped the line in publishing (about a case in the Family courts):

"Says a friend of the mother, 'She has been portrayed as a bad mother who is unfit to look after her children. Nothing could be further from the truth. She is wonderful to them and they love her. She wants custody of them and we will see what happens in court.'"

The judge was satisfied that the portrayal of the mother in proceedings as a bad mother went beyond merely a description of the nature of the dispute (a description of the dispute being something that Munby J. had felt was allowable in his decision *Kent CC v B (A Child)* [2004] EWHC 411 (Fam)) and the media should remember that s.97(2) of the Children Act 1989 makes it a criminal offence to identify to the world at large a child as being the subject of proceedings under which an order may be made under that Act. The section ceases to apply once proceedings have concluded, but the courts can make an order preventing the identification of children who have been involved in such proceedings. As there is an onus on the party seeking a restriction to inform the media of its intention to seek such an injunction, such orders are rare.

REPORTING PARLIAMENT

Proceedings in parliament should be, and are necessarily, beyond reproach in any court. MPs, during parliamentary proceedings, are free to speak on any matter without fear of legal consequence. This freedom extends to media reports of parliamentary proceedings. Thus the media can publish the comments which are made in parliament and need not be in fear of a libel writ (assuming the publication is made without malice). Contempt of court is a potential problem for the media. A Member of Parliament will not be punished (by the courts) for potentially prejudicial comments made in parliament (as a Conservative Northern Ireland Secretary once did) but if the media presented something mentioned in parliament in a sensationalist way that risked prejudice to a particular trial, then the Attorney General might consider commencing proceedings. Prosecution would be unlikely.

Such media freedom stems from, and is guaranteed by, art.9 of the Bill of Rights 1688 which provides that:

"The freedom of speech and debates or proceedings in Parliament ought not to be impeached or questioned in any court or place out of Parliament."

Proceedings in the UK parliaments (including the Scottish Parliament and the Welsh Assembly) are now televised.

Whilst matters stated by MPs during parliamentary sessions and the word for word report of it in *Hansard* are subject to absolute privilege, reports of such matters in the press or on television have merely qualified privilege. Thus the motives behind publication may be examined. However, MPs also have the possibility of waiving their parliamentary privilege where conduct in parliament becomes an issue in defamation proceedings (s.13 of the Defamation Act 1996), to allow them to put such matters in evidence (see Ch.2 for details of privilege in defamation).

The importance of free debate in Parliament, and its reporting by the media, was highlighted in 2009 by a "super injunction" (see Ch.4) obtained by lawyers acting for multinational company Trafigura. A gag on Parliamentary question was lifted and the attempt to stifle criticism failed.

OFFICIAL SECRETS

Current affairs reporting may concern matters which fall into the category of official secrets. The prohibition on publication of official secrets is set out in two statutes: the Official Secrets Acts 1911 and 1989. The 1989 Act abolishes the formerly controversial s.2 of the 1911 Act but it is still necessary to examine the provisions of both statutes.

The 1911 Act

Section 1 provides that it is an offence (punishable with up to 14 years' imprisonment) if:

"any person for any purpose prejudicial to the safety or interests of the State—

    (a) approaches, inspects, passes over or is in the neighbourhood of, or enters any prohibited place within the meaning of this Act; or

    (b) makes any sketch, plan, model or note which is calculated to be or might be or is intended to be directly or indirectly useful to an enemy; or

    (c) obtains, collects, records or publishes, or communicates to any other person any secret official code word or pass word, or any sketch, plan, model, article or note, or other document or information which is calculated to be or might be or is intended to be directly or indirectly useful to an enemy."

Paragraph (c) of this offence is most likely to be relevant to the media. However, s.1 is concerned primarily with spying and prosecutions of media defendants have been rare.

In 1978 two journalists were charged under s.1 as a result of the interview (with a view to publication in *Time Out* magazine) of a soldier who had worked at a signals intercept base in Cyprus. The charges in the "*ABC*" case (as it was known) were dropped at the insistence of the judge, who thought that they were oppressive. He stated that the section could apply to the media (as well as to spies) but ought to be reserved for cases where there was some evidence of collusion with a foreign power.

The 1989 Act

The 1989 Act abolished s.2 of the 1911 Act. Section 2 made it an offence to publish or receive any details of official business, but was such a widely defined section that it made it an offence to publish innocuous information such as the type of food served in the canteen of a government department. Section 2 was replaced with several different offences which each specifically relate to a different type of information. It is now a criminal offence for an employee of the Crown (e.g. a minister, civil servant or member of the armed forces) or a government contractor to disclose information in one of the following six classes:

- security and intelligence (s.1);

- defence (s.2);
- international relations (s.3);
- crime (s.4);
- information on government phone-tapping, interception of letters or other communications (s.5); and
- information entrusted in confidence to other states or international organisations (s.6).

Section 5 provides that is a criminal offence for any person (thus including a journalist, editor or programme producer):

(a) without lawful authority,

(b) to disclose information, which

(c) they received from a Crown employee or government contractor either

    (i) on terms requiring it to be held in confidence, or
    (ii) in circumstances in which such confidence was reasonably expected by the Crown servant or government contractor,

where,

(d) they knew or had reasonable cause to believe the information was protected from disclosure by the provisions of the 1989 Act.

The prosecution must prove that the publisher had reason to believe that the publication would be damaging to the security services or to the interests of the United Kingdom.

Additionally, in relation to information covered by ss.1 to 3 of the Act (i.e. information relating to security and intelligence, defence and international relations), the prosecution must prove that:

    (i) the disclosure is damaging; and

    (ii) the publisher had reasonable cause to believe that it would be damaging.

Prosecutions under the 1989 Act may only be commenced with the authority of the Attorney General, except in the case of information relating to crime in which case the consent of the Director of Public Prosecutions is required.

In 2000, former MI5 agent David Shayler wrote in a letter and an article for national newspapers about activities of the security services, and particularly that MI6 agents were involved in a failed plot to assassinate the Libyan leader Colonel Gaddafi. He was prosecuted under ss.1 and 4 of the 1989 Act for these disclosures. Mr Shayler argued that it was in the public interest for him to reveal information about such important matters of British defence policy to the general public. But the House of Lords held that there was no public interest defence to an official secrets prosecution and that it was in accordance with art.10 of the Human Rights Convention to place restraints on the free speech of former security officers (*R. v Shayler* [2001] 1 W.L.R. 2206).

Defence advisory notices

The media will usually comply with a notice issued by the Defence Press and Broadcasting Advisory Committee to refrain from publishing certain information (a DA notice). Such notices form the backbone of the voluntary system of self-censorship practiced by the media in matters of national security.

DA notices have no legal effect and prosecutions do not usually follow from their breach. However, editors considering publishing such information should be advised that the government regards it as sensitive and thus prosecution under the Official Secrets Acts 1911 and 1989 becomes possible.

There are currently five standing DA notices dealing with information relating to the following areas:

- military operations, plans and capabilities;

- nuclear and non-nuclear weapons and operational equipment;

- ciphers and secure communications;

- sensitive installations and home addresses; and

- UK security and intelligence services and Special Forces.

Each notice sets out precise details of the information it is seeking to protect and the reason for such protection. The full text of the notices can be obtained from the Ministry of Defence at *www.dnotice.org.uk.*

The Committee may also issue specific notices informing the media that a particular story would be likely to threaten national security. None has been issued in recent years.

PROTECTION OF JOURNALISTS' SOURCES

Much of the information that is obtained by journalists is obtained from persons who would not wish their names to be associated with the imparting of such information. Indeed, were it not for the journalist's promise to keep their identities secret, many of the people who would otherwise provide information would be unlikely to do so. There is thus a public interest in the protection of a journalist's source of information. Such a need is recognised by the National Union of Journalists' Code of Conduct, which provides in cl.14 that a journalist shall "protect confidential sources of information" (see Appendix G). The law also recognises the benefit in the anonymity of journalistic sources and there is a presumption that it will be against the public interest for such sources to be revealed except in certain circumstances where other objectives with an overriding public interest require it.

There are four principal legal provisions under which a journalist can be forced to disclose the source of information. They are contained in the following statutes:

- Contempt of Court Act 1981;

- Police and Criminal Evidence Act 1984;

- Official Secrets Act 1989;

- The Police Act 1997;

- Regulation of Investigatory Powers Act 2000;

- Serious Organised Crime and Police Act 2005; and

- Anti-terrorism legislation.

It should be noted that the requirement in the Data Protection Act 1998 to disclose the source of information comprising personal data will generally not apply to journalists (see Ch.9).

Contempt of Court Act 1981

That there is a need for the protection of journalists' "sources" in a free society is recognised by the Contempt of Court Act 1981. Section 10 provides that a court shall not require a person to disclose the source of information contained in a publication for which they are responsible unless it can be established to the satisfaction of the court that disclosure is necessary:

- in the interests of national security;

- in the interests of justice;

- for the prevention of crime; or

- for the prevention of disorder.

An important decision in this area of the law is the case of *X v Morgan-Grampian Publishers* [1991] 1 A.C. 1. In 1989 Mr William Goodwin, a trainee journalist working for *The Engineer*, was telephoned by an informant who gave him unsolicited information about a company called Tetra Ltd. It was apparent from this information that Tetra Ltd was in financial difficulties— it had an expected loss of £2.1 million for 1989 and was in the process of raising a £5 million loan. Mr Goodwin telephoned Tetra Ltd to check these facts and subsequently prepared a draft article for *The Engineer*. Tetra Ltd applied for an injunction to prevent Morgan-Grampian (the publishers of *The Engineer*) from publishing Mr Goodwin's article. It told the court that the information had come from a draft of its confidential corporate plan which had gone missing on November 1, 1989. The court granted an injunction which prevented publication of the article. Tetra Ltd did not leave the matter there. It then applied to the High Court for an order requiring Mr Goodwin to disclose the name of the person who had supplied the information to him. A third party can be required to provide such information where it is found to be involved in another's wrongful act, even if they are innocently involved. Where documents are stolen or disclosed in breach of contract or confidence, then a newspaper publishing the information will be "involved" in the wrongdoing. Tetra's lawyers said that it was necessary "in the interest of justice", within the meaning of s.10 of the Contempt of Court Act 1981, that the source of the information be disclosed to enable Tetra to bring proceedings against the source to recover the missing document. The High Court granted the order and both the Court of Appeal and the House of Lords dismissed Mr Goodwin's appeal against the decision. Lord Bridge said that:

"While no one doubts the importance of protecting journalists' sources, no one, I think, seriously advocates an absolute privilege against disclosure admitting of no exceptions. Since the enactment of section 10 of the 1981 Act both the protection of journalists' sources and the limited grounds on which it may exceptionally be necessary to override that protection have been laid down by Parliament ... The journalist cannot be left to be judge in his own cause and decide whether or not to make disclosure. This would be an abdication of the role of Parliament and the courts in the matter and in practice would be tantamount to conferring an absolute privilege. Of course the courts, like other human institutions, are fallible and a journalist ordered to disclose his source may, like other disappointed litigants, feel that the court's decision was wrong. But to contend that the individual litigant, be he a journalist or anyone else, has a right of 'conscientious objection' which entitles him to set himself above the law if he does not agree with the court's decision, is a doctrine which directly undermines the rule of law and is wholly unacceptable in a democratic society."

In respect of the provision of the Code of Conduct of the National Union of Journalists which provides that journalists must not reveal their sources, Lord Bridge went on to say:

"Any rule of professional conduct enjoining a journalist to protect his confidential sources must, impliedly if not expressly, be subject to whatever exception is necessary to enable the journalist to obey the orders of a court of competent jurisdiction. Freedom of speech is itself a right which is dependent on the rule of law for its protection and it is paradoxical that a serious challenge to the rule of law should be mounted by responsible journalists."

Despite the court order, Mr Goodwin refused to disclose his notes and identify his source and, in April 1990, was fined £5,000 by the High Court for being in contempt of court.

The unnerving position of the law as a result of this case stood largely unchallenged until March 1996 when the European Court of Human Rights (ECtHR) adjudicated upon Mr Goodwin's application for review (funded in part by the NUJ). The ECtHR found (by 11 votes to 7) that the court order to force Mr Goodwin to disclose his source breached art.10 of the ECHR (see Appendix C). On the desirability for a journalist's sources to be protected, the court said that without such protection:

"Sources could be deterred from assisting the press in informing the public on matters of public interest. As a result the vital public watchdog role of the press could be undermined and the ability of the press to

provide accurate and reliable information could be adversely affected."
(See *Goodwin v UK* (*The Times*, March 28, 1996).)

The ECtHR said that the order requiring the applicant to reveal his source
and the fine imposed upon him for having refused to do so could not be
regarded as having been "necessary in a democratic society" for the protection of Tetra's rights under English law, even considering the margin of
appreciation available to the national authorities.

Notwithstanding the decision of the ECtHR in *Goodwin*, there has continued to be decisions which have shown that a journalist's word to protect
their source may be more vulnerable than the press might like.

In *Ashworth Security Hospital v MGN Ltd* ([2002] 1 W.L.R. 2033), the *Daily
Mirror* obtained details of the medical records of Ian Brady, the notorious
Moors murderer, who at the time was detained in Ashworth Security
Hospital and was on hunger strike. The newspaper did not know the original source of the information, but had obtained it in return for payment
from an intermediary. It wished to protect the identity of the intermediary
as it was believed that he would inevitably lead to the primary source. The
hospital brought proceedings to order MGN (publishers of the *Daily Mirror*)
to disclose the identity of its source. The House of Lords eventually ruled
that MGN must identify its source. The Lords said that the disclosure was
in the interests of justice, even where the hospital was not actually taking
proceedings against the original wrongdoer. They held that it was essential
that the source should be identified and punished to deter similar future
behaviour, and in order not to jeopardise the important confidential nature
of medical records. But that was not the end of the story. The *Daily Mirror*
disclosed the intermediary as a freelance investigative journalist called
Robin Ackroyd, but Mr Ackroyd still refused to name his primary source at
the hospital. The hospital applied for judgment against Mr Ackroyd on the
grounds that he could not possibly succeed in his claim in light of the
previous action against the newspaper. But the Court of Appeal said his
case was different to the newspaper and deserved a full trial. Mr Ackroyd
had many sources at the hospital (who were unpaid for their information)
and who, according to Mr Ackroyd, acted in the public interest by revealing
some serious concerns as regards the management and care at the hospital.
If Mr Ackroyd could successfully show there was greater public interest in
protecting his sources, than the hospital could show in identifying who had
disclosed secret medical records, then he might rely on the s.10 protection.
One problem for the hospital, which needed to show an "overriding public
interest amounting to a pressing social need", was that, with the passage of
time, it was less likely that the hospital could show that the behaviour of
leaking information would be repeated or become a pattern.

The matter only came before the High Court in February 2006 and the
judge found that Robin Ackroyd was "a responsible journalist" acting "in
the public interest" in obtaining the story about how Brady was being force
fed and his treatment by the high-security hospital. The hospital appealed
and said that it was disappointed with a 2007 ruling of the Court of Appeal
against it. The first instance judge had stressed that nothing he had said
should be taken as "providing any encouragement to those who would
disclose medical records". He made his decision in the light of the passage
of time (the original publication was in December 1999 in the *Daily Mirror*)

and new evidence which indicated that the source did not act for money and that the material leaked was "limited". Also the stance of Ian Brady had changed. So, although the media might applaud the result, the legal principles (that such orders may be granted against journalists) remain unchanged. Since the *Ashworth Security Hospital* case against the *Daily Mirror* a possibly complicating factor that has arisen is privacy law (see Ch.4), in particular the protection given to medical information as highlighted in the *Naomi Campbell* case (also against the *Daily Mirror*). However, as Ian Brady appears to be almost uniquely evil there is arguably little public interest in protecting his medical history and information aboout whether he was or was not being force fed.

Another hard fought case on protection of sources was *Interbrew v Financial Times* [2002] E.M.L.R. 243 where a number of national newspapers resisted an application by the brewer Interbrew to disclose a leaked, and apparently partially-forged, document about a takeover. The Court of Appeal ordered the newspaper to hand over the copy of the document to allow Interbrew to pursue legal action against the source of the document, on the basis that the source's motive was to cause mischief. It was held that the brewer's interests of justice outweighed the public interest in protecting such a source because the fact that the document had apparently been forged suggested that the purpose was indeed to cause mischief. (Incidentally, the court also held that it made no difference whether a journalist expressly promised confidentiality to a source, or whether it was merely implied in the circumstances that a source would believe that all information confidentially provided to newspapers would give rise to anonymity.) However, the newspapers (including the *Guardian* and the *Financial Times*) still refused to hand over the document and risked being in contempt of court for defying its order. Interbrew handed its case over to be pursued by the Financial Services Authority, but it was discontinued in September 2003.

The Police and Criminal Evidence Act 1984

The police were given powers under The Police and Criminal Evidence Act 1984 to enter premises and to seize certain documents that are relevant to their investigation of a criminal offence. Before the court will issue a warrant for this purpose, a Justice of the Peace must be satisfied that the offence committed is a "Serious Arrestable Offence" (see Glossary) and that there is reason to believe that relevant evidence exists at the address to be searched. There is some protection given to certain journalistic material in s.8 of the Act, which provides that such material is excluded from this general provision. However, journalistic material may still be seized in certain circumstances. In order to understand these provisions, it is necessary to define two terms which are used in the statute: "excluded material" and "special procedure material". The above general search provisions will not apply to excluded and special procedure material. To be excluded material, the material must be:

"journalistic material which a person holds in confidence and which consists:

    (i) of documents; or
    (ii) of records other than documents."

A person holds journalistic material in confidence for this purpose if:

(a) they hold it subject to an express or implied undertaking to hold it in confidence or subject to a restriction on disclosure or an obligation of secrecy contained in any Act of Parliament; and

(b) it has been continuously held (by one or more persons) subject to such an undertaking, restriction or obligation since it was first acquired or created for the purposes of journalism.

All other journalistic material, i.e. material held for the purposes of journalism which does not fall within the above definition, is known for the purposes of the 1984 Act as "special procedure material". Special procedure material can be seized provided that the procedure in Sch.1 to the 1984 Act is complied with. This provides that an application must be made to a circuit judge. Notice of the application must be served upon the party who is requested to produce the documents and that party may make representations at the hearing. The circuit judge may make an order granting access to special procedure material if he is given reasonable grounds to believe that a Serious Arrestable Offence has been committed and that:

- the material sought is likely to be of substantial value to the investigation;

- the material sought is likely to be relevant evidence;

- other methods of obtaining the evidence have failed or have not been tried because they had no realistic prospect of success; and

- it is in the public interest that the beneficial effect on the investigation and the circumstances under which the material is held.

Access to excluded material will only be granted where the circuit judge has reasonable grounds to believe that such material exists at premises specified in the application and that:

- another statute would, were it not for the protection of such material given by the Police and Criminal Evidence Act, have allowed a police officer access to such material; and

- such access would have been appropriate.

The toughening of police powers (and greater supervision of them) heralded by the Police Act 1997, Regulation of Investigatory Powers Act 2000 and Serious Organised Crime and Police Act 2005 have provided opportunities for police to lawfully gain access to citizens' documents, and journalists can be caught up in investigations too.

The Official Secrets Act 1989

Official secrets were discussed earlier in this chapter in relation to the criminal offence of disclosing information which falls into one or more of the six categories of information in the 1989 Act. Section 8 of the Act provides that where any person possesses certain information in the form of a document or article, it is a criminal offence to fail to hand it over to a government official when requested to do so. The information to which s.8 relates is that which has been disclosed by a government employee or entrusted to another in confidence by such an employee or any information entrusted in confidence to other states or international organisations.

Terrorism

In common law there is no legal privilege between a journalist and an informant (see *British Steel Corp v Granada Television Ltd* [1981] A.C. 1096 HL), although this position was modified by the Contempt of Court Act 1981. But if a journalist receives information not from a confidential source who has been promised anonymity, but during the course of enquiries into terrorists or terrorist acts (including action outside the United Kingdom), a reporter may find themselves to be at the heart of a police investigation. Therefore, journalists should be aware that the Terrorism Act 2000 is widely drafted and offences can occur if funds are paid that end up in the possession of terrorists. Section 19 imposes a duty to disclose certain information even if this is only a suspicion. Journalists seeking to infiltrate terrorist groups could find themselves in even greater jeopardy than they might imagine. The Crown Prosecution Service is likely to be cautious in prosecuting journalists, but if information was known to a journalist and not imparted to the police before a terrorist atrocity occurred, the public interest may favour action being taken. The stance of the courts can be seen in the contempt cases where investigative journalists and their editors have been fined for exposing criminals and publishing too much detail of their criminal pasts.

9. THE INTERNET

This chapter considers the main challenges for the law created by the widespread and growing use of technology for the transfer and dissemination of information and services to ever wider audiences.

The internet has expanded dramatically in recent years and continues to grow exponentially. Due to the slower pace of the change of the law as compared with technology, it has been necessary to adapt existing law to fit new legal situations, as well as develop some new rules to deal with the particular circumstances which arise in an internet context. Although the internet was historically an anarchic and "lawless" place, the courts are increasingly called upon to enforce penalties and remedies for acts committed in cyberspace. Few would argue, for example, against the protection of children from hardcore pornography. But the very nature of the internet, being a communications system that inherently does not recognise national laws or geographical frontiers, produces challenges for the law far beyond anything it has had to cope with to date. The challenges thus created for the laws of defamation, copyright and obscenity are briefly considered here, although as the internet has so many different facets and purposes, a review of all the legal issues it raises is beyond the scope of this book.

THE NATURE OF THE INTERNET

The origins of the internet can be traced back to an experiment by the US Department of Defense in 1969 when three computers in California were connected with one in Utah. Its aim was to create a network of computers called ARPANET (Advanced Research Projects Agency Network) which would survive attack by routing information in a complex pattern between various interconnected computers in various parts of the US. The idea was that if any one part of the system were destroyed the remainder would continue to function. In 1972, 40 computers made up the network. By 1981 when the network had begun to be extended for academic use, 200 computers located all around the world (mostly in universities) were connected. Today, almost every office and business, and many homes have internet access.

Each internet connection has a unique numeric (or Internet Protocol) address (the 'IP address') consisting of four sets of numbers with a value between 0 and 255, each separated by a full stop. Digital information can thus be sent from any computer on the internet and directed specifically to any other computer. For ease of human use, the numbers forming the IP address are translated into a language version of the Internet Protocol, called "domain names". Domain names are sets of letters and/or numbers separated by full stops. For example, *www.guardian.co.uk* is the domain name for the *Guardian* newspaper online. Any user wanting to access the *Guardian*'s server (or "site") would type the above letters into the appropriate internet browser software and a specialised computer known as a domain name server will perform the task of matching the domain name to the relevant IP address. Domain names consist of a number of categories. Top level domains are the final part of an internet address and may be generic such as *.com* (for a corporation), *.net* (for a network provider) and *.org* (for an organisation), or country specific such as *.uk* or *.nl* (for the Netherlands). Second level domains refine the address further by identifying a particular server connected to the internet. An internet address may consist of one or more top level domains together with one or more second level domains. The lists of addresses used by the domain name servers are maintained by The Internet Corporation for Assigned Names and Numbers (ICANN), a non-profit making organisation set up by the American Government and based in California. ICANN assigns the task of keeping national registers of names to one organisation in each country. Nominet UK, for example, is the naming authority for Britain and its counterpart in the US is Network Solutions Inc. It should be noted that these organisations will not check to see whether an applicant for a particular domain name is "entitled" to use that name prior to assignment. However, Nominet does operate a dispute resolution service where parties have a disagreement over domain name registration. The Nominet policy is upheld by a panel of experts which determines individual cases. Where it is found that there has been "abusive registration", Nominet can award the transfer of the domain name. Under the Nominet policy, a complainant must show that:

(i) the complainant has rights in respect of a name or mark which is identical or similar to the domain name; and

(ii) the domain name, in the hands of the respondent, is an abusive registration.

An "abusive registration" refers to a domain name which either:

(i) was registered or otherwise acquired in a manner which, at the time when the registration or acquisition took place, took unfair advantage of or was unfairly detrimental to the complainant's rights; or

(ii) has been used in a manner which took unfair advantage of or was unfairly detrimental to the complainant's rights.

As can be seen from the decision below, the parties are required to submit evidence of the legitimacy of their use of the name. The need for such a dispute resolution service has arisen mainly as result of cyber squatting, where individuals commonly acquire the domain name of a celebrity or business and then offer it for sale for a substantial sum. The following is an example of a Nominet DRS decision: *F-Secure Corp Plc v Global Publications Ltd (DRS Case No. 7578)*. The decision was given on October 20, 2009, the complaint having been lodged on July 28, 2009, showing the relative rapidity of the process. The complainant was a company publicly traded on the Helsinki Stock Exchange chiefly concerned with developing anti-virus and security software for computers. It was established in 1988 and had operated an office in England (F-Secure (UK) Ltd) since 1999. The respondent was a UK company which owned a large portfolio of domain names. The respondent registered the domain name "fsecure.co.uk" on June 6, 2004. The complainant was the owner of trade marks which incorporated the word "F-SECURE". The respondent did not have any licence or authorisation from the complainant to register the domain name either on the date of registration or otherwise. It was found that the complainant owned rights and that the ownership of the domain name by the respondent amounts to an abusive registration, and so it was directed that the domain name should be transferred to the complainant.

In the United Kingdom, an action will also lie in the tort of passing off against anyone using a domain name which is similar to a trade mark (see *British Telecommunications Plc v One in a Million Ltd* [1998] 4 All E.R. 476). For example, Easygroup—well-known for its budget airline brand "easyjet" and car rental "easycar", succeeded against an individual who operated a number of websites that used the word "easy" in a similar way. The court found that the intention was to deceive the public into believing that the websites were associated with the Easygroup businesses, and ordered that the names were transferred to Easygroup (*Easygroup IP Licensing v Sermbezis* Unreported November 4, 2003 EWHC (Ch D)).

Internet Service Providers (ISPs)

ISPs are organisations which provide individuals and companies with access to the internet in return for a fee or for a free subscription. Examples are Virgin, BT Internet and AOL. The huge growth of broadband internet access (allowing much faster data transmission than the early dial-up access using a telephone line) has transformed the speed of internet browsing, downloading and all the other functions of the internet. The revenue of an ISP is generated by subscriptions, user fees and advertising.

World Wide Web (WWW)

The World Wide Web began life in 1993 and is the most user-friendly aspect of the internet. It consists of a vast number of websites (or homepages) which any user of the internet can "visit" by entering the address of the site as their destination. Individuals, partnerships and companies around the globe have set up websites for a variety of reasons—originally to publicise their activities and services, but more recently to provide a platform from which to sell products and services to the public or to other businesses (more commonly known as electronic commerce). Web pages are devised using a computer language called HyperText Mark-up Language (HTML) and are translated into words and pictures by the individual user's browser software. Links (sometimes known as "hypertext links" or "hot links") are pieces of highlighted or underlined text on a web page which provide, by virtue of a user's mouse click, a gateway to another web page.

Search engines

Once connected, a user may wish to find a particular internet site but not know the address of the site. A search engine, software which is accessible from any connection to the internet, can be used to find sites by matching chosen words and phrases with existing material on the internet. Examples are of course *Google* and most recently *Bing,* unveiled in May 2009 (branded as a 'Decision Engine') by Microsoft.

Email

One of the most widespread uses of the internet is of course email (electronic mail). Using domain names coupled with addresses of individuals within each domain, messages can be sent between users of the internet. The fact that such messages are in digital form means that they are not limited to text but may be sound, graphics, photographs and moving images.

Instant messaging and internet voice calling

As well as email, instant messaging facilities are provided by many ISPs (MSN messenger, Yahoo messenger) allowing for real-time exchange of messages (known as 'chats') like a written conversation. Further, advances in sound and video applications have allowed these to be accompanied by video link using webcams attached to the users' computers, or to take the form of voice conversations using both webcams and microphones. The best-known application allowing such contact is 'Skype'.

Forums and message boards

Taking the place of the bulletin board in the earlier history of the internet, forums and message boards are an increasingly popular feature of the web. They allow users to post content and express their views on just about every subject under the sun. Usually, registration is required via an email address which is verified, and users select a pseudonym under which they can then post material (known as UGC—'user-generated content') anonymously. This anonymity is something with which the law has recently been grappling—see **DEFAMATION** later in this chapter—because obviously there is the possibility for abuse of these facilities which allow anyone with access to a computer to engage in world-wide publication. The forums and message boards are governed by terms and conditions, and are often subject to moderation, i.e. control by a service which reviews postings and removes any which breach the terms and conditions.

Blogs

Derived from the phrase "web log", a blog is a personal website (provided by blogging services such as Blogger/Blogspot and LiveJournal) on which the user can post anything he or she chooses. Many are like personal journals, others are more akin to magazines containing serious political or cultural content; often they include photographic or video content (either original or gathered elsewhere on the internet), and a number have attained a prominent position akin to conventional publications, especially as regards political comment and analysis (e.g. *The Huffington Post*, a blog which tops many of the 'most influential blogs' rankings at the time of writing). The number of blogs obviously increases daily—statistics indicate that the global total in 2009 is not far off 200 million blogs worldwide.

Social networking sites

Sites such as Facebook, MySpace, Bebo and many others are another key phenomenon of the first decade of the 21st century, joined during the latter years of the decade by Twitter (described as a "social networking and micro-blogging site"). They are sites where each user compiles a personal profile page of data about themselves, their family, interests, and adds "friends", contacts with whom they share some common point of interest. On Twitter users "follow" other individuals using the service, and post brief comments and updates ("tweets"), many including photos—hence the term "micro-blogging". Direct private messaging facilities are available. The colossal growth in traffic is illustrated by one study which estimated that between March 2008 and March 2009, the number of Twitter users rose from around 500,000 to 14 million.

DATA PROTECTION

Data protection is dealt with in this chapter due to its close relationship with internet transactions. However, consideration of the legislation (the Data Protection Act 1998 and the Privacy and Electronic Communications (EC Directive) Regulations 2003) should not be narrowly confined. It is of immense significance to people generally and the media in particular. To take one example, an individual who finds that a newspaper has published a story about him (whether online or in paper form) may not only require the newspaper to provide him with a copy of all information the newspaper holds on him in its database but may also, in certain circumstances, require the newspaper to publish a correction where the article is inaccurate.

This section gives a brief overview of the rights of individuals to access personal information held about them by others and the legal requirements for holding and dealing with such personal data. For further detail refer to P. Carey, *Data Protection—a practical guide to UK and EU law*, 3rd edn (Oxford: Oxford University Press, 2009).

Introduction

Modern data protection legislation can be traced back to the 1970s and the threat to personal privacy posed by the advent of computers and the consequent facilitation of rapid data manipulation. The existing law at that time (which consisted of not much more than a potential action in breach of confidence—see Ch.4) was felt insufficient to meet the concern as to the amount of information held by organisations about individuals. The Younger Committee on Privacy (Cmnd. 5012, 1972) recommended the introduction of guiding principles for the use of computers which manipulated personal data.

It was more than a decade later when the Data Protection Act 1984 set up the office of the Data Protection Registrar and required all users of personal data to register their processing and to comply with a set of eight Data Protection Principles. The latest legislation, the Data Protection Act 1998 (enacted by the UK to comply with European Directive 95/46/EC), takes matters considerably further, as do the Privacy and Electronic Communications Regulations 2003, which regulate the use of cookies on websites and electronic marketing.

The individual's rights

The basic rights of the individual are contained in Pt II of the 1998 Act. In order to understand the provisions some terminology should be defined (s.1(1)).

Initial definitions

For the purposes of the legislation the person who is protected is called the *data subject*, defined as "an individual who is the subject of personal data".

The information that gives rise to the rights of the data subject is called *personal data* and is defined as:

"Data which relate to a living individual who can be identified—

    (a) from those data, or
    (b) from those data and other information which is in the possession of, or is likely to come into the possession of, the data controller."

It should be noted that personal data includes "any *expression of opinion* about the individual and any *indication of the intentions* of the data controller or any other person in respect of the individual". In one of the few considerations of the Act so far, the Court of Appeal held that the interpretation of personal data should be linked to privacy (*Durant v Financial Services Authority* [2003] EWCA Civ 1746). Thus, personal data may be information which is either biographical, i.e. going beyond merely recording the data subject's involvement in an event with no personal connotations, or which has the data subject as its focus.

A *data controller* is "a person who (either alone or jointly or in common with other persons) determines the purposes for which *and* the manner in which any personal data are, or are to be, processed".

Processing has an extremely wide definition in the Act and essentially means anything that can be done with data including downloading information from the internet, transmitting information by email and reading a piece of information on a computer screen.

The 1984 Act related only to automatically processed data. The right of access to material that forms part of a relevant filing system (and therefore to paper-based records) in the 1998 Act is likely to be the most costly and time-consuming aspect of the new regime. A *relevant filing system* is defined as:

> "Any set of information relating to individuals to the extent that, although the information is not processed by means of equipment operating automatically in response to instructions given for that purpose, the set is structured, either by reference to individuals or by reference to criteria relating to individuals, in such a way that specific information relating to a particular individual is readily accessible."

It seems that a key requirement of a relevant filing system is the structuring by reference to individuals, e.g. personnel files which each have an individual's name on the front. If manually-recorded data does not form part of a relevant filing system then it need not comply with any of the provisions in the Act. Journalists could thus be advised to keep information on others stored on a set of individual sheets of paper which are randomly sorted rather than kept alphabetically by name, so as to avoid the subject access provisions discussed below. Of course, all information stored on computer, laptop or handheld device will be subject to the Act.

EXAMPLE

Glossy Productions advertises glossy magazine subscriptions on its website. Patricia sees the information and, whilst online, responds to the company expressing her interest and requesting more details. She is requested to give her name, address, telephone number and date of birth. The information is automatically entered into the company's computer database. The above defined terms apply to this scenario as follows:

Data controller—Glossy Productions

Data subject—Patricia

Personal data—information about Patricia's name, address, telephone number and date of birth

Processing—this occurs where the personal data are: requested from Patricia; entered into the computer system; read on-screen; printed out; used to send a brochure; transferred to any other person or company

Basic rights of access

Section 7 provides that a data subject is entitled, upon written request to a data controller, to be promptly informed whether personal data of which the individual is the data subject are being processed by or on behalf of the data controller. A fee (subject to the statutory maximum—currently £10) may be charged by the data controller for this service and the data controller has 40 days from the receipt by the data controller of such a request to comply. The 40-day time limit does not start to run until the data controller has received the fee and/or has been supplied with sufficient information to enable compliance with the request.

Where personal data are being processed by or on behalf of the data controller, the data subject is entitled to be given a description of:

(i) the personal data of which that individual is the data subject;

(ii) the purposes for which they are being or are to be processed; and

(iii) the recipients or classes of recipients to whom they are or may be disclosed.

In addition, the data subject is entitled to have communicated to him or her *in a form which is capable of being understood*:

(i) the information constituting any personal data of which that individual is the data subject; and

(ii) any information available to the data controller as to the *source* of those data.

In most cases the first of these rights of the data subject will be met by the data controller forwarding a copy of the information (plus an intelligible explanation of its content where the meaning is obscure due to, for example, the use of codes or abbreviations) to the data subject.

The right to receive information as to the source of the data is a new right that did not appear in the 1984 legislation. Journalists and others who are concerned about disclosing sources must be especially careful here (although they may be able to use the "media defence" in appropriate circumstances—see below).

EXAMPLE

(This example continues from the example in the previous section.) Patricia receives the brochure from Glossy Publications but notices something odd about the address label on the packaging. Her name appears as "Mrs Patricia E. Robinson". She feels sure that she did not give information as to her middle name, nor that she was married. She sends an email to Glossy Publications asking for a copy of all the information they hold on her and details of the source of that information. The company must supply Patricia with the information she has requested and must do so within 40 days of receiving her request—a maximum of £10 may be charged by Glossy Publications for this service.

Automated decisions

Section 7(1)(d) provides that where the personal data are being processed automatically for the purpose of evaluating matters relating to the data subject and the processing has or is likely to be the sole basis of a decision significantly affecting the data subject, he or she is entitled to be informed by the data controller of the *logic* (unless such logic constitutes a trade secret—s.8(5)) behind the decision-taking. A common example of such an automated decision-making process is credit scoring. Where a computer programme, as a result of information keyed-in, reaches a decision as to whether to extend a loan to an individual then the individual concerned is entitled to a description of the decision-making process, i.e. the method by which the decision was reached.

Preventing processing (general)

Section 10 provides that where the processing of personal data is causing or is likely to cause *unwarranted and substantial damage* or *unwarranted and substantial distress* to the data subject or another, the data subject is entitled to request (upon the expiry of a reasonable period) to cease, or not to begin, processing, unless one of the following apply:

(a) the data subject has given his consent to the processing;

(b) the processing is necessary—

    (i) for the performance of a contract to which the data subject is a party, or

    (ii) for the taking of steps at the request of the data subject with a view to entering into a contract;

(c) the processing is necessary for compliance with any legal obligation to which the data controller is subject, other than an obligation imposed by contract;

(d) the processing is necessary in order to protect the vital interests of the data subject; or

(e) any other circumstance as prescribed by the Secretary of State by order.

Preventing processing (direct marketing)

The marketing strategy known as *direct marketing* (defined in s.11(3) as "communication, by whatever means, of any advertising or marketing material which is directed to particular individuals"—and therefore includes specifically targeted emails) is subject to a right by the data subject to prevent processing for this purpose. An individual may require, under s.11(1), that the data controller (within a reasonable time) cease, or not begin, processing, for the purposes of direct marketing, personal data of which he or she is the data subject. The request should be in writing. There are no exceptions to the right to prevent processing for the purposes of direct marketing. The court can order compliance with the data subject notice where it is satisfied that the data controller has failed to comply with the notice.

More recent legislation has added to the restrictions on direct marketing. The Privacy and Electronic Communications (EC Directive) Regulations 2003 mean that marketing emails can, subject to one exception, only be sent where an individual has previously agreed to receive them.

EXAMPLE
Kirsty is sent an email from Marketing International Plc inviting her to purchase a product or service. Kirsty sends an email to the company requesting them to delete her name, address and any other details from

their database. Within a reasonable time of receiving the letter the company must cease processing Kirsty's personal data for the purposes of direct marketing. Marketing International Plc may continue to hold the information for other purposes.

Rectification, blocking, erasure and destruction

Under s.14 where a court is satisfied that personal data processed by the data controller are *inaccurate* (i.e. "incorrect or misleading as to any matter of fact"—s.70(2)) it may make an order for the rectification, blocking, erasure or destruction of such data. In addition, the court may order the rectification, blocking, erasure or destruction of any personal data which contain an expression of opinion which is based on the inaccurate data.

In many cases the inaccurate data held by the data controller will have been passed on to a *third party*. Where the court orders rectification, blocking, erasure or destruction, or is satisfied by the data subject's claim that personal data which have been rectified, blocked, erased or destroyed were inaccurate, it can, where it is reasonably practicable to do so, make an order that the data controller inform the third party of the rectification, blocking, erasure or destruction. In determining whether it is reasonably practicable to make such an order the court will take into account the number of third parties to whom the inaccurate data have been disclosed.

Compensation

An individual who suffers damage as a result of the contravention by the data controller of any provision of the statute is entitled apply to the court for compensation. Compensation for distress may be claimed in all cases where the individual has suffered damage. Compensation for distress without damage may be claimed only where the contravention relates to the processing of data for the *special purposes*, i.e. for the purposes of journalism or for artistic or literary purposes (see below).

Where proceedings are brought against a data controller for compensation it is a defence for the data controller to show that such care was taken as in all the circumstances was reasonably required to comply with the provision concerned.

The Data Protection Principles

The Data Protection Principles are listed in the first Schedule to the Act. The principles form the backbone of the legislation and their importance is underlined by the extent of the powers of the Data Protection Commissioner in relation to their enforcement. The box below sets out the Eight Data Protection Principles.

The First, Seventh and Eighth Principles will be discussed in more detail as they are likely to have considerable impact on internet processing.

The Eight Principles

1. Personal data shall be processed fairly and lawfully and such processing must comply with at least one of a set of specified conditions. [Additional conditions apply to sensitive personal data].

2. Personal data shall be obtained only for one or more specified and lawful purposes, and shall not be processed in any manner incompatible with that purpose or those purposes.

3. Personal data shall be adequate, relevant and not excessive in relation to the purpose or purposes for which they are processed.

4. Personal data shall be accurate and, where necessary, kept up to date.

5. Personal data processed for any purpose or purposes shall not be kept for longer than is necessary for that purpose or those purposes.

6. Personal data shall be processed in accordance with the rights of data subjects under the Act.

7. Appropriate technical and organisational measures shall be taken against unauthorised or unlawful processing of personal data and against accidental loss or destruction of, or damage to, personal data.

8. Personal data shall not be transferred to a country or territory outside the European Economic Area unless that country or territory ensures an adequate level of protection for the rights and freedoms of data subjects in relation to the processing of personal data.

The first principle

"Personal data shall be processed fairly and lawfully and, in particular, shall not be processed unless—

(a) at least one of the conditions in Schedule 2 is met, and
(b) in the case of sensitive personal data, at least one of the conditions in Schedule 3 is also met."

Under the first principle, processing will not be lawful unless one of the conditions in Sch.2 to the 1998 Act is met. In the case of sensitive personal data, processing will not be fair unless one of the conditions in Sch.2 *and* one of the conditions in Sch.3 is met.

It should be noted that compliance with Sch.2, and where relevant Sch.3, does not guarantee that the processing will be fair and lawful. It may well be that the processing in question is unfair or unlawful (and thus not in compliance with the first principle) for another reason. Furthermore, the processing may breach another of the principles or a provision in another statute.

It is essential that data controllers obtain information correctly, i.e. in accordance with the first principle. Failure to do so puts all subsequent processing in jeopardy. Not only must data be obtained fairly but the obtaining itself must meet the relevant Sch.2 and Sch.3 conditions (see below).

The interpretation provisions in Sch.1 state that regard must be had to the method of obtaining the data in determining whether the processing is fair. It is clear that processing will be unfair where any person from whom it has been obtained is deceived or misled as to its intended purpose. Care should thus be taken when constructing websites to ensure that the user has the appropriate information.

Where data is obtained *from the data subject* it will not be treated as processed fairly, and hence will breach the first principle, unless the data controller ensures (so far as is practicable) that the data subject has, or has ready access to, the following information:

(a) the identity of the data controller;

(b) the purpose or purposes for which the data are intended to be processed; and

(c) any other information which is necessary to enable processing to be fair (Sch.1, Pt II, para.2(3)).

Where the data controller did not obtain the information from the data subject there is an exception to the obligation to notify the data subject of the matters listed in (a) to (d) above. This applies where one of the following two *primary conditions* are true—

(a) the provision of that information would involve a disproportionate effort; or

(b) that the recording of the information to be contained in the data by, or the disclosure of the data by, the data controller is necessary for compliance with any legal obligation to which the data controller is subject, other than an obligation imposed by contract (Sch.1, Pt II, para.3(2)).

Thus, where information is obtained from a third party and one of the above primary conditions applies then the obligation to inform the data subject is nullified. There is no definition of "disproportionate" in the Act. It would seem to relate to the consequences of the activity for the data subject. Where the effort needed to contact the data subject is considerable then this is likely to constitute disproportionate effort unless it is outweighed by the consequences for the data subject, for example, because it involves significant, or otherwise important, processing. The second of the two primary conditions would apply where the data controller is under a statutory duty to obtain details about the data subject from a third party.

In the case of journalistic processing, s.32 of the Data Protection Act 1998 operates to remove the requirement to supply fair collection information.

Criteria for lawful processing—Schedule 2

For processing to be lawful at least one of the conditions in Sch.2 (see box below) must be met. There are no exceptions to this rule. The first condition relates to the data subject giving his consent to the processing, and is likely to be the most important. In many cases, such as marketing list rental for example, the first condition is the only one that could possibly apply.

The Sch.2 conditions for lawful processing:

---

1. The data subject has given his consent to the processing.

2. The processing is necessary—

    (a) for the performance of a contract to which the data subject is a party, or
    (b) for the taking of steps at the request of the data subject with a view to entering into a contract.

3. The processing is necessary for compliance with any legal obligation to which the data controller is subject, other than an obligation imposed by contract.

4. The processing is necessary in order to protect the vital interests of the data subject.

5. The processing is necessary—

    (a) for the administration of justice,
    (b) for the exercise of any functions conferred on any person by or under any enactment,
    (c) for the exercise of any functions of the Crown, a Minister of the Crown or a government department, or
    (d) for the exercise of any other functions of a public nature exercised in the public interest by any person.

6. The processing is necessary for the purposes of legitimate interests pursued by the data controller or by the third party or parties to whom the data are disclosed, except where the processing is unwarranted in any particular case by reason of prejudice to the rights and freedoms or legitimate interests of the data subject.

Sensitive personal data

The Act creates a new category of sensitive personal data. A data controller who processes sensitive personal data must, in addition to satisfying one of the criteria in Sch.2, also comply with one of the conditions in Sch.3. It is thus vital for data controllers to check all sensitive processing to see that it complies with one of the provisions. *Sensitive personal data* is personal data consisting of information as to—

(a) the racial or ethnic origin of the data subject;

(b) his political opinions;

(c) his religious or other beliefs;

(d) whether he is a member of a trade union;

(e) his physical or mental health or condition;

(f) his sexual life;

(g) the commission or alleged commission by him of any offence; or

(h) any proceedings for any offence committed or alleged to have been committed by him, the disposal of such proceedings or the sentence of any court in such proceedings (s.2).

The Sch.3 conditions for the lawful processing of sensitive personal data are as follows:

---

1. The data subject has given his explicit consent to the processing of the personal data.

2. The processing is necessary for the purposes of exercising or performing any right or obligation which is conferred or imposed by law on the data controller in connection with employment.

3. The processing is necessary to protect the vital interests of the data subject or another person.

4. The processing is carried out as part of the legitimate activities of a not-for-profit body or association.

5. The information contained in the personal data has been made public as a result of steps deliberately taken by the data subject.

6. The processing is necessary in relation to legal rights.

7. The processing is necessary—

    (a) for the administration of justice,
    (b) for the exercise of any functions conferred on any person by or under an enactment, or
    (c) for the exercise of any functions of the Crown, a Minister of the Crown or a government department.

8. The processing is necessary for medical purposes.

9. The processing is necessary to trace equality of opportunity between peoples of different racial or ethnic backgrounds.

10. Any other condition made by the Secretary of State.

The Secretary of State has made such an order: Data Protection (Processing of Sensitive Personal Data) Order 2000. The third of these conditions is of particular relevance to journalists, as it permits the processing of sensitive personal data where its disclosure is in the substantial public interest; is in connection with the commission of crime or dishonesty, improper conduct or mismanagement; and is for the purpose of journalism with a view to publication.

The seventh principle

> "Appropriate technical and organisational measures shall be taken against unauthorised or unlawful processing of personal data and against accidental loss or destruction of, or damage to, personal data."

The seventh principle is of relevance to information obtained and processed over the internet and provides, in essence, that appropriate care must be taken of the personal data. The interpretation provisions in Sch.1 suggest that account must be taken of the state of technology (and its cost) available at the relevant time. The protective measures must ensure a level of security which is appropriate to the harm which might result from the events mentioned in the seventh principle and the nature of the data to be protected. All staff who handle personal data in the workplace should be given training on the main aspects of data protection law. Recent decisions by the Information Commissioner indicate that data security is of increasing importance. Media companies will wish to ensure that laptops taken out of company buildings are not only password protected but also encrypted. For further information on the requirements in this rapidly changing area, readers are directed to the periodical publication *Privacy & Data Protection Journal* (*http://www.pdpjournals.com*).

The eighth principle

> "Personal data shall not be transferred to a country or territory outside the European Economic Area unless that country or territory ensures an adequate level of protection for the rights and freedoms of data subjects in relation to the processing of personal data."

The European Economic Area consists of the 27 Member States of the European Union plus Norway, Iceland and Liechtenstein. There is no restriction on the transfer of information between those countries. A transfer of personal data to any other country is unlawful unless that country has an adequate level of protection for such data.

Exemption for journalism, literature and art

Journalists invariably hold personal data on living individuals in their computer hard drives or on disks or laptops or handheld PCs and may use the internet to transfer such data to their employers from various locations. In many cases this is sensitive personal data within the meaning of the Act, being information relating to, for example, a person's racial origin, political opinion or sex life. It is very unlikely that any of the conditions for the processing of sensitive personal data in Sch.3 apply to the media. Investigative journalism would clearly be hampered if the consent of the data subject was a requirement of processing.

The following provisions of Act will not apply to the media where the exemption operates:

- The Data Protection Principles (except the seventh).

- The subject access provisions in s.7.

- Right to prevent processing likely to cause damage or distress (s.10).

- Rights in relation to automated decision-taking (s.12).

- Right to rectification, blocking, erasure or destruction (subss.14(1) to (3)).

To benefit from the exemption personal data must be processed for the "*special purposes*" and each of the following three prerequisites must be satisfied:

(a) the processing must be undertaken with a view to the publication by any person of any journalistic, literary or artistic material;

(b) the data controller must reasonably believe that, having regard in particular to the special importance of the public interest in freedom of expression, publication would be in the public interest; and

(c) the data controller must reasonably believe that, in all the circumstances, compliance with the provision in question is incompatible with the special purposes.

The *special purposes* are defined in s.3 as meaning any one or more of the following:

- the purposes of journalism;

- artistic purposes; and

- literary purposes.

In considering whether the data controller reasonably believes the publication to be in the public interest he may have regard to his compliance with the provisions of "any relevant code of practice". In the case of newspaper journalists and editors the relevant code will be that of the Press Complaints Commission (see Appendix E) and for broadcasters, the Ofcom Broadcasting Codes (see Appendix F).

Clearly, compliance with the Act would often be impossible for journalists. Where pictures or text are stored on computer in preparation for an article, then under the Act if the data subject learnt of the proposed publication he could potentially bring an action to stop the processing on the grounds that it was likely to cause him distress and effectively kill off the story. The journalistic exemption is therefore vital, but should not be considered a blanket protection under all circumstances.

In *Campbell v MGN* [2004] UKHL 22 (see Ch.4 for further details) the model Naomi Campbell added to her claim for breach of confidence, a claim for breach of the Data Protection Act 1998 and sought compensation under s.13. At first instance, the judge decided that Ms Campbell was entitled to damages under the Act because the newspaper had not complied with the Act (for example, it had no specific condition to allow it to process sensitive personal data) and because he decided that the journalistic exemption did not apply once publication had taken place. The Court of

Appeal decided a number of important points of law concerning the journalistic exemption. It held that the Act did apply to the publication of hard copies of information which had previously been processed by computer, thus meaning that almost all forms of modern printing would be caught by the Act and need to comply. But the Court took a different view on the exemption and, crucially for journalists, held that it applied both before and after publication. On the facts, it also held that *The Mirror* could demonstrate public interest in its story and satisfy the conditions required by s.32. Accordingly, the newspaper was able to rely on the exemption and did not owe Ms Campbell damages under the Act. In the House of Lords, the question of the applicability of data protection law was largely ignored.

DEFAMATION

Defamation is discussed generally in Ch.2 and exactly the same principles apply, regardless of method of publication. It is a cause of action which has particular significance for the internet. The internet provides an extremely rapid vehicle for the dissemination of information with a potential global audience of millions, via blogs, "UGC" (user-generated content) on message boards and forums, and most recently 'tweeting' on Twitter, all of which have become a global pastime. There has also been a growing number of celebrity gossip websites and email circulars containing rumours of a frequently scandalous nature which are too risky for newspapers to carry. In Ch.2, a number of internet-based cases were discussed in the context of the general rules relating to defamation law. Some developments more specific to the demands of the internet are considered here.

Internet Service Providers (ISPs)

One issue regarding defamation on the internet is to what extent ISPs should be liable for defamatory material they unwittingly pass on. The problem is created by the nature of the function of a service provider, which is often that of a mere conduit through which electronic information passes (although some service providers maintain a house-keeping function whereby they search for and remove offensive material).

The Defamation Act 1996, s.1, gives limited protection to ISPs by providing a defence for the "operator of or provider of access to a communications system by means of which the defamatory statement is transmitted or made available, by a person over whom he has no effective control". Such an operator or provider must show that they took reasonable care in relation to the publication of defamatory statements and that they did not know, and had no reason to believe, that what they did caused or contributed to the publication of such a statement. Thus the ISP must show that they took reasonable care in relation to the publication. Precisely what this means is left to the courts but there is some guidance given in s.1(6) of the Act which provides that regard shall be had to:

(a) the extent of their responsibility for the content of the statement or the decision to publish it;

(b) the nature or circumstances of the publication; and

(c) the previous conduct or character of the author, editor or publisher of the statement complained of.

In order to be able to use the defence the defendant must be able to show that it was not the "author, editor or publisher" of the statement complained of. The first case concerning defamation on the internet in the English jurisdiction, *Laurence Godfrey v Demon Internet* (1999) I.T.C.L.R. 282, decided that an ISP should not be regarded as an author, editor or publisher for the purposes of the Act. In that case a posting to a newsgroup, which purported to have emanated from the claimant, was "squalid, obscene and defamatory" of the claimant. On January 17, 1997, the claimant sent a letter by fax to the defendant's managing director, informing him that the posting was a forgery and that he was not responsible for it and requesting him to remove the item from its Usenet news server. Although the defendant received the fax the item was not removed and remained available on its news server until its expiry on January 27. Upon proceedings being defended by the defendant, the claimant applied to strike out parts of the defence.

The argument of the ISP that it was not a common law publisher for the purposes of defamation law was rejected by the judge. However, on the meanings contained in the Defamation Act 1996 the court agreed with the defendant that the ISP was not a "publisher" for the purposes of s.1. The requirements of s.1(1)(b) (reasonable care in respect of publication) and s.1(1)(c) (no knowledge or reason to believe that that what it did caused or contributed to the publication of a defamatory statement) caused great difficulty for the defendant, as it knew of the defamatory posting after receipt of the claimant's fax but chose not to remove it. It was the opinion of the court, therefore, that the defendant could be liable for the defamatory comments contained within its newsgroups.

The decision in *Godfrey* was distinguished in 2006 in the case of *Bunt v Tilley* [2006] EWHC 407 (QB). There were in fact six defendants, and the judgment of Eady J. related to the three ISP defendants (AOL, BT and Tiscali). The action concerned defamatory postings made in internet chat rooms. The judge ruled that the act of publication must involve some element of intention—in other words, to be held liable as a publisher, the ISP must be aware at the time the relevant words were published, that it had done so. It is not necessary to be aware that the words were defamatory. "It is not enough," said Eady J., "that a person merely plays a passive instrumental role in the process." Hence he went on as follows:

"I would not, in the absence of any authority to the contrary, attribute liability at common law to a telephone company or other passive medium of communication such as an ISP. It is not analogous to someone in the position of a distributor, who might at common law be regarded as having 'published.'"

The burden is on the claimant to prove what the ISP's role was (which the claimant here had failed to do). The position would be different if the ISP in question was actually hosting the website or chatroom. As noted in Ch.2, Eady J. went on to find that s.1 would afford a complete defence in relation to a claim involving allegedly "defamatory postings of which the defendant had not been put on notice". The judgment also contained findings in relation to the Electronic Commerce (EC Directive) Regulations 2002, which also include a provision designed to protect ISPs. The Regulations (which have a wide application to all types of electronic communications and businesses) apply to "information society services" (ISSs) which are defined as any service normally provided for remuneration, at a distance, by electronic means and at the individual request of a recipient of services. This includes providing access to a communication network or the transmission of information via such a network and therefore covers the services of ISPs. Regulation 19 provides that where an ISS consists of storage of information which is provided by the third party (such as an ISP hosting a website), then the service provider will not be liable for damages, as long as: (i) it does not have "actual knowledge" that any activity was in breach of the law; (ii) once it has such knowledge it acts expeditiously to remove the offending information; and (iii) the third party was not acting under the authority or control of the ISP. As the key here is not having knowledge of the defamatory material, and acting quickly to remove it once an ISP does have knowledge, then the situation is not materially different to the s.(1) defence under the Defamation Act 1996 (although there are other detailed differences between the two defences outside the scope of this book).

In *Bunt v Tilley*, Eady J. found that the defendant ISPs clearly fell within the definition of ISSs, and also within the defences provided by the relevant regulations for "mere conduit", "caching" or "hosting" activities.

The law as it stands therefore gives some protection for ISPs. However, the requirement for them to react to being put on notice of defamatory material is difficult, as they are effectively put in the position of judge and jury over whether material in respect of which they have received notice is defamatory or not. If it is, then they are obliged to remove it immediately to avoid liability themselves, regardless of whether the author may insist on the truth of his/her statements. The ISP will not usually be in a position to test the veracity of the publication and therefore must always err on the side of caution. It is argued with some force that this is inimical to the ethos of freedom of expression for which the internet should be the prime medium. An enormous amount of defamatory material makes it way on to the internet unknown to the ISPs. The result of the current state of the law is that, as regular experience shows, a defamed person will almost always find the ISP an easier target from whom to seek redress, rather than the original author—particularly if all that is desired is that the offending wording be removed.

The important recent case of *Metropolitan International Schools Ltd (t/a Skillstrain and/or Train2game) v Designtechnica Corp (t/a Digital Trends)* [2009] EWHC 1765 (QB) reviewed and confirmed the current state of the law regarding ISPs, but focused on a crucial aspect of internet technology, the search engine. The provider of search facilities (in this case, Google Inc) could not be liable for search results containing alleged libels, Eady J. held, because Google Inc could not be regarded as the publisher of material appearing in a search result. Importantly, unlike a standard ISP, notification to Google does not operate to remove this protection, owing to the mechanical nature of search engine technology. As the judge said:

"A search engine, however, is a different kind of Internet intermediary. It is not possible to draw a complete analogy with a website host. One cannot merely press a button to ensure that the offending words will never reappear on a Google search snippet: there is no control over the search terms typed in by future users."

Online archives

The internet has made possible the creation of a vast repository of electronic information, accessible to anyone at any time. It is one of its greatest virtues, and also one of its biggest liabilities. Where an article published in a hard copy of a newspaper is in permanent form, most people do not retain and regularly access back issues. However, for publications with an online edition (now the vast majority of newspapers and journals), the archive section provides a most useful tool for readers. The question that has faced the courts is to what extent the publisher of an online publication should be held liable for defamatory material in archived stories. It is rather bizarre that the leading case here comes from the year *David Copperfield* was published: *Duke of Brunswick v Harmer* (1849) 14 QB 186. In a nutshell, the Duke heard about a libel and sent his servant to buy the relevant back-copy of the newspaper from the publisher's office many years after the original publication. The court did *not* allow the defendant to rely on the original limitation period—a new period started with the new sale.

This is known as the "multiple publication rule". It was applied in *Loutchansky v Times Newspapers Ltd* [2002] QB 783 (CA). *The Times* had published an article about a Russian businessman alleging that he was a money launderer and a smuggler of restricted weapons. *The Times* was ultimately found to have failed to reach a standard of responsible journalism (and did not seek to prove that its allegations were true), and was liable to the claimant. During lengthy proceedings, it was learned that the story was still available on *The Times*'s website and a fresh claim was brought over this internet publication. *The Times* argued that to hold it liable for each and every time a story was accessed on the internet was too great a restraint on its freedom of expression and asked the court to modify the general rule that every repetition of a defamatory statement gave rise to additional liability. The Court of Appeal held that while there was a social utility in maintaining archives, it was a comparatively insignificant restraint on freedom of expression. Archive material was stale news and it was right that a claimant should have redress against publishers who did not maintain archives responsibly. Where a story was, or might be, defamatory, an appropriate warning should be attached. *The Times* failed in an application to the European Court that this ruling breached its art.10 rights (ECHR judgment March 10, 2009) because it was held that the obligation to attach a legal warning is not a disproportionate interference with *The Times*' art.10 rights to freedom of speech. The ECHR in its judgment did indicate that libel proceedings brought against a newspaper after a significant period without exceptional circumstances to justify the delay, might infringe art.10.

English law does not feature the "single publication rule" which applies in many US states, for example, which in this context would have meant that loading a publication on *The Times*' website constituted a single publication that occurred at the time it was put on the website regardless of the period during which it remained there. Online publishers must therefore take special care that archives are responsibly managed.

On September 16, 2009, the Ministry of Justice opened a consultation called "Defamation and the internet: the multiple publication rule" including a paper considering the arguments for and against the rule and the alternative single publication rule: *http://www.justice.gov.uk/consultations/ defamation-internet-consultation-paper.htm*.

International publication

As with other aspects of defamation law, the question of international publication is not unique. Many US and UK newspapers are available in countries across the globe. But the mass globalisation of publication that is brought about by the internet has given fresh significance to this problem for the law. Where a claim may be brought against a defendant (known as jurisdiction) is a fiendishly complex topic with many different aspects. One needs to be able to effect service of the claim against the defendant outside of England and Wales, the court must decide that it is the best placed court to hear the case, it may be necessary to establish the relevant law in a number of other countries and, finally, where a defendant is in another country, it is necessary for the successful claimant to be able to enforce its judgment overseas. These issues are beyond the scope of this book, but they are questions which commonly arise in modern defamation law in the context of internet publication.

In summary, it is only possible to bring an action in England and Wales for damage caused by publication in this jurisdiction and in other countries if the claimant has a reputation in these countries and is able to recover damages for defamation there. This is known as the "double actionability" rule.

EXAMPLE

The London-based *Daily Bugle* publishes a defamatory story about a famous actor, Joey Mason, who is well known overseas and has residences in Germany, Spain, Monte Carlo and the US. As well as appearing in the hard copy of the *Daily Bugle* (which is available in England only), it puts the story on its website which is read around the world.

Joey Mason brings proceedings against the *Daily Bugle* in London for damage to his reputation in all the countries in which he lives. To succeed, he must also show that the local law in Germany, Spain, Monaco and the US would award him damages for defamation.

The situation becomes even more complex where an individual in England wants to take action over internet publication, where the author or publisher is overseas. The court must then decide whether England and Wales is the most appropriate forum to hear the case. There is a general presumption that proceedings may be brought in the jurisdiction where the harm occurred, which in defamation is the place where the publication takes place. It is clear that deciding which is an "appropriate forum" will depend very much on the facts of each case.

In the important case of *King v Lewis* [2004] EWHC 168 (QB) Eady J. said this at first instance:

"Publication is regarded as taking place where the defamatory words are heard or read: *Bata v Bata* (1948) WN 366. What is more, by analogy, the common law currently regards the publication of an Internet posting as taking place when it is down-loaded: *Godfrey v Demon Internet* [2001] QB 201; *Loutchansky v Times Newspapers Ltd* [2002] QB 783 at [58]; *Gutnick v Dow Jones Inc* [2002] HCA 56 at [44]".

Hence the tort is committed at the place where the publication occurs, i.e. where the internet page is accessed, where the computer user is situated—not at the place where the material is prepared for publication, or the place where it was uploaded to a web server.

In the *King* case on appeal ([2004] EWCA Civ132), the Court of Appeal upheld Eady J.'s refusal ([2004] EWHC 168 (QB)) to overturn the permission given to boxing promoter Don King to serve his libel claim from outside the jurisdiction. The defendants alleged that the claimant had failed to satisfy the Court that England and Wales is the proper place (*forum conveniens*) in which to bring the claim (see CPR 6.37(3)).

This country was the proper place, despite these facts: the allegations complained of were published on California-based boxing websites directed at predominantly US-based readers; the claimant was an American citizen and based in the US—his business and connections were primarily American, although there was evidence of substantial income here, where he was also well-known; the defendants were all US-based; the allegations were responses made by one of the defendants to an attack on him published by the claimant in a US publication (the *New York Daily News*); the context for the allegations was ongoing litigation between the parties in New York; and this was clear "forum-shopping"—i.e. London was an advantageous place to choose to sue because a libel claim in the USA was likely to fail, owing to the rule in the *Sullivan* case that gives public figures a very high hurdle before they can sue for libel.

The deciding elements seem to have been:

1) a substantial tort had been committed in this country (over 20,000 "hits" from the UK on one of the two websites); and

2) the claimant had a substantial reputation here and connections with this jurisdiction.

Note these words in the Court of Appeal's judgment:

"A global publisher should not be too fastidious as to the part of the globe where he is made a libel defendant. We by no means propose a free-for-all for claimants libelled on the Internet. The Court must still ascertain the most appropriate forum: the parties' connections with this or that jurisdiction will still have to be considered; there will be cases (like the present) where only two jurisdictions are really in contention. ... in an internet case the court's discretion will tend to be more open-textured than otherwise; for that is the means by which the court may give effect to the publisher's choice of a global medium. But as always, every case depends upon its own circumstances."

A recent case where this was applied is *Mardas v New York Times Co* [2008] EWHC 3135 (QB).

The claimant was resident in Greece, but was well-known in this jurisdiction and had lived here in the UK for 33 years. He also had two children who lived in England, both with British nationality. Eady J. held that "there is no artificiality about seeking to protect his reputation within this country".

The reference to "artificiality" is no doubt a recognition of the criticism levelled by commentators and lawyers at the way in which England has at the start of the 21st century become the centre of what is termed "libel tourism"—foreign claimants appearing to take advantage of the English rules and the increasingly international nature of publication thanks to the internet. Much controversy was triggered when American journalist Rachel Ehrenfeld wrote a book called *Funding Evil* (about the financing of terrorism). The book was published only in the US but was available in England via internet booksellers (23 were bought here), plus the first chapter was available online. A Saudi buinessman, Khalid bin Mahfouz, sued for libel in England and was successful. The reaction in the US has led to new legislation in several states (including New York and California) barring the enforcement of English libel judgments there on the grounds that they are inimical to free speech. Another notorious example was the litigation by the Ukrainian businessman Rinat Akhmetov (ranked in Forbes as the 241st richest man in the world), who sued two Ukrainian online journals in London and won. Commentators found it absurd that the English courts could be used by "a Ukrainian attacked in a Ukrainian newspaper in Ukrainian in the Ukraine". A key concern is that, out of fear of a libel complaint in England, responsible writers who could not afford to defend themselves may decide not to risk engaging in perfectly legitimate comment and analysis, and that free speech is being fettered by this "self-censorship" (this is sometimes referred to as "the chilling effect" of English libel law). In 2009, The Libel Reform Campaign was launched. Amongst its proposals were that no case should be heard in England unless at least 10 per cent of copies of the relevant publication have circulated here, and that interactive online services and interactive chat should be exempted from liability. Time will tell if these and other proposals find favour with the law-makers.

Even now, however, it would be wrong to think that the doors of the English courts are wide open to foreign litigants. The next section deals with a development designed to limit use of this jurisdiction to deserving cases only.

Abuse of process

Where publication of the libel is merely "technical", the courts will now stay (i.e. dismiss) proceedings, on the long-established basis that such a complaint is an abuse of process. The leading case is *Jameel v Dow Jones & Co Inc* [2005] EWCA Civ 75.

This case concerned an article implicating the claimant in funding terrorism; which appeared on the defendant's Wall Street Journal Online, available to subscribers. The evidence was that only five subscribers in England and Wales had accessed the words complained of and, of these, three were Mr Jameel's lawyers and business associates. The claim was dismissed as an abuse of the process of the English court. In the memorable words of Lord Phillips M.R.:

"If the claimant succeeds in this action and is awarded a small amount of damages, it can perhaps be said that he will have achieved vindication for the damage done to his reputation in this country, but both the damage and the vindication will be minimal. The cost of the exercise will have been out of all proportion to what has been achieved. The game will not merely not have been worth the candle, it will not have been worth the wick. ...

It would not be right to permit this action to proceed. It would be an abuse of process to continue to commit the resources of the English court, including substantial judge and possibly jury time, to an action where so little is now seen to be at stake. Normally where a small claim is brought, it will be dealt with by a proportionate small claims procedure. Such a course is not available in an action for defamation where, although the claim is small, the issues are complex and subject to special procedure under the CPR."

To conclude, a very recent case illustrates how the English courts now approach many of the above principles: *Emlick v Al Nisr Publishing LLC* (Unreported July 15, 2009 EWHC).

The claimant was a Scottish businessman with a reputation in England and Wales. He sued the publishers of *Gulf News* over an article in April 2008 (in the paper and on its website) warning that property investors in Dubai "should be on their guard" as the claimant was "misleading investors both in the UAE and abroad".

The judge, Moloney J., noted that the internet is very different from the print medium, the web can be "pernicious" in bringing allegations to the attention of those who are not even searching for them and search engines can draw attention to allegations even if they are not what the searcher is looking for. He found that there had been substantial publication, the majority of the publication in England and Wales having been via the internet. He also held that the defendants should be held responsible for third-party republications of the original article, on the basis that it is foreseeable that other websites or bloggers will take advantage of the ease with which the material can be republished.

Combatting Anonymity

It was noted above that a characteristic of UGC is that the user who posts content for world-wide publication can (and usually does) choose to be anonymous. A Facebook page or Twitter account can be opened under a false identity, or even under someone else's identity. This is of course a barrier if a libel (or for that matter, a breach of privacy or copyright) is committed which the victim wants or needs to deal with by stronger means than simply relying on a complaint to the host or ISP under the relevant terms and conditions.

ISPs will not usually volunteer identification details for those running an offending website or blog, using email services or posting UGC on message boards or forums. However, it is worth noting that s.35(2) of the Data Protection Act 1998 appears to allow voluntary disclosure:

"(2) Personal data are exempt from the non-disclosure provisions where the disclosure is necessary—

(a) for the purpose of, or in connection with, any legal proceedings (including prospective legal proceedings), or
(b) for the purpose of obtaining legal advice,

or is otherwise necessary for the purposes of establishing, exercising or defending legal rights."

To deal with the fact that, in practice, identification details are not available voluntarily, there is a growing body of cases where the jurisdiction established by *Norwich Pharmacal Co v Customs and Excise Commissioners* [1974] AC 133 has been used to obtain an order of the court for disclosure of all information (in this instance, in the possession of the ISP) which will identify or assist in the identification of the real wrongdoer.

The cases include the following:

- *Totalise Plc v Motley Fool Ltd* [2002] 1 W.L.R. 1233 (CA).

- *Sheffield Wednesday Football Club Ltd v Hargreaves* [2007] EWHC 2375 (QBD) ("*Owlstalk*").

- *Smith v ADVFN Plc* [2008] EWCA Civ 518 (CA).

- *Tycon Energy Corp v The Motley Fool Ltd* Unreported December 9, 2008 EQHC (QBD).

There are some general principles emerging from these cases: on a *Norwich Pharmacal* application, the judge will scrutinise alleged libels and weigh up any entitlement on the internet user's part to expect that their privacy would be protected (e.g. evidenced by their use of anonymous pseudonyms—although see the *Nightjack* case below) against the claimant's right to protect his or her reputation. The nature and gravity of the alleged libels is likely to be a crucial factor. Disclosure may not be allowed where allegations are "barely defamatory or little more than abusive or likely to be understood as jokes", said the judge in the *Owlstalk* case, which concerned supporters' comments on a message board relating to their football club Sheffield Wednesday ("the Owls"). Some were vulgar comments, of the sort football fans often make. But some were more serious allegations about the management of the club, and the judge ordered the identity of those posters to be revealed. It is worth noting that the party making such an application against an ISP will have to bear the costs. The same applies under the alternative procedure provided by CPR 31.17 (orders for disclosure against a person not a party): see CPR Pt 48.1(2).

The approach of the courts was further developed in an important recent decision: *Author of a Blog v Times Newspapers Ltd* [2009] EWHC 1358 (QB) (the *"Nightjack"* case). This was not a libel case, but a claim brought under the developing law of privacy by the internet user to try and stop the public revelation of his identity.

The Times discovered (by journalistic enquiry) the identity of a blogger who wrote under the pseudonym "Nightjack". Fearful for his job (in the police) he sought an injunction for breach of privacy. The judge Eady J. dismissed the claim. The mere fact that the blogger wanted to remain anonymous did not mean that he had a "reasonable expectation" of doing so or that *The Times* was under an enforceable obligation to him to maintain that anonymity. Eady J. ruled that Mr Horton had *no* "reasonable expectation" to anonymity because "blogging is essentially a public rather than a private activity" and the "blogs did not contain any information which was implicitly confidential in nature and, therefore, deserving of privacy". The judge also commented that even if there had been a right of privacy, it would have been outweighed in the context of this case by the fact that it was in the public interest for readers to know that it was a serving police officer commenting in this way.

A 2008 case involving a false social networking page is an intriguing illustration of how the law can be used to tackle reputational issues involving the internet: *Applause Stores Productions Ltd v Raphael* [2008] EWHC 1781 (QB).

This was a case of anonymity where an internet user had posed as someone else. Grant Raphael and Mathew Firsht had been friends. They fell out in a big way, and Raphael set up a Facebook profile in the name of Firsht containing a mixture of true and false personal information (e.g. about sexual, political and religious preferences). He also started a Facebook group, linked to the false profile by hyperlink, that was called "Has Mathew Firsht lied to you?", and on which defamatory words were posted about Firsht and his company Applause Stores.

Firsht was not a Facebook user, but discovered the false profile and group page by accident and immediately alerted Facebook, who removed the page.

He obtained a *Norwich Pharmacal* order against Facebook for disclosure of the registration data provided by the user responsible for creating the false material. The data included e-mail addresses and the IP addresses of all computers used to access Facebook by the owner of those e-mail addresses. A forensic study of this information led to Raphael. Libel proceedings followed and the claimants were successful.

Blogs and newspapers: regulation

In 2007 the regulatory remit of the Press Complaints Commission (PCC) was extended to include editorial audio-visual material on newspaper and magazine websites. The extension recognised that "on-line versions" of newspapers and magazines have moved on from the internet replication of material that already existed in a printed version of the publication to routinely carrying material not available in print form. The accompanying Guidance Note explains that the PCC's remit should be seen as covering editorial material on newspaper and magazine titles websites where it meets two key requirements:

1. That the editor of the newspaper or magazine is responsible for it and could reasonably have been expected both to exercise editorial control over it and apply the terms of the Code.

2. That it was not pre-edited to conform to the on-line or off-line standards of another media regulatory body.

So newspaper related blogs e.g. *http://www.blogs.telegraph.co.uk* should arguably come within the PCC's remit, especially if a letter to the editor results in a decision that material should remain on the blog.

PORNOGRAPHY

It is common knowledge that the internet contains a great deal of pornographic material. Much of this type of material falls within the definition of obscenity (see Ch.5). Child pornography is of particular concern and in many jurisdictions around the world, including the United Kingdom, the taking of pornographic photographs of children is illegal. Governments are, however, in disagreement as to what measures to adopt to counter the proliferation of child pornography and other objectionable internet content. The Protection of Children Act 1978 makes it an offence to distribute, show or publish any indecent photograph or image of a child or what appears to be a child. The Sexual Offences Act 2003 raised the age definition of a "child" to 18 years of age.

In this country, the Internet Watch Foundation (*http://www.iwf.org.uk*) plays a prominent role in attempting to control this aspect of the internet. Founded in 1996 by ISPs and other entities in the online industry, it is funded by the EU and works closely with the police and government. The IWF's remit is to monitor (and receive reports from the public about) certain categories of material found on the internet in the UK (primarily child pornography, but also criminally obscene material). Material will be reported to the police as and when required. An unusual illustration of its activites appears below in relation to the *Girls (Scream) Aloud* case in 2009.

A distinction must be made here between content which is illegal, such as child pornography (a phrase which the IWF disapproves of, preferring "child sexual abuse images"), and "adult" images which may be considered unsuitable for some viewers. The accessibility of the latter is moderated to some extent by the fact that many pornographic sites are run for profit and hence users must provide credit card details before obtaining the content they seek. Nevertheless vast amounts of "adult" material are available freely—not only by way of preview pages for pornographic sites but also uploaded by internet users in blogs and photo and video sharing sites. The risk of children obtaining pornographic material on the internet is significant; the vast increase in internet access at home (on mobile phones as well as computers) being of course the chief area of concern. Porn-blocking software and "safe search" functions are widely available for parents to install on computers at home, and education throughout society about the means available to stop access to unsuitable material would seem likely to be at least as effective as the deployment of the law in minimising the effects of online pornography. A number of entities have been created to this end, e.g. the UK Council for Child Internet Safety, created under the aegis of the

Home Office Taskforce on Child Protection on the Internet, and is made up of more than 140 organisations, including Google, Microsoft, Bebo and the NSPCC. Full details appear on their website (*http://www.dcsf.gov.uk/ukccis/*) including the launch on December 8, 2009 of the first Child Internet Safety Strategy. Reference is made to new research showing the large percentages of children who have come across inappropriate internet material, or whose parents do not monitor or limit their online activity, out of the overall 99 per cent of 8 to 17-year-olds with internet access. UKCCIS works in tandem with the Child Exploitation and Online Protection Centre (CEOP), another recently-created entity, which is a member of the Virtual Global Taskforce and affiliated to the UK law enforcement authorities, in particular the Serious Organised Crime Agency (SOCA). CEOP's website offers a help website for all aspects of internet safety: *http://www.ceop.gov.uk/*.

Returning to the law's role in this area, graphic sexual images displayed on a "preview" webpage for a subscription service were the subject of a prosecution under the Obscene Publications Act 1959 in *R. v Perrin* [2002] EWCA Crim 747. Although the evidence only showed that one police officer in the course of his investigation into the crime had seen the page, the concern was clearly the effect on children who may be likely to see it. Per Kennedy L.J.:

"The publication relied on in this case is the making available of preview material to any viewer who may choose to access it (including of course vulnerable young people) We emphasise that s.1(1) of the 1959 Act only requires the jury to be satisfied there is a likelihood of vulnerable persons seeing the material. The prosecution does not have to show that any such person actually saw it or would have seen it in the future."

In an early response to the arrival of the internet, s.168 of the Criminal Justice and Public Order Act 1994 added the transmission of electronically stored data to the Obscene Publications Act's definition of "publication" for obscene items contained in the digital information they pass on to others. As we have seen in Ch.5, whether material is obscene in the United Kingdom depends upon the likely audience. Virtually all material on the internet is available to any user with the correct hardware. Thus "obscene" material transmitted on this medium may include a much wider range of items than would be included in many other less readily available media because its audience is not restricted. In s.63 of the Criminal Justice and Immigration Act 2008, the possession of "extreme pornographic images" is criminalised. There are detailed definition sections, but in essence the section catches still or moving images intended principally for sexual arousal involving certain types of injury, life-threatening activities and animals.

In the summer of 2009, there was much comment about the CPS's abandonment, shortly before trial, of the prosecution under the Obscene Publications Act 1959 of Darryn Walker, who had been charged with publishing obscene material on a blog, namely a story entitled "Girls (Scream) Aloud". The story was a violent sexual fantasy involving the mutilation and murder of each member of the Girls Aloud pop group. The *Daily Star* newspaper drew it to the attention of the Internet Watch Foundation, which reported it to the police. The key element of the case was the fact that the matter in question was wholly written. Previous prosecutions relating to written matter under the Obscene Publications Act 1959 (*Lady Chatterley's Lover* in 1960, *Last Exit to Brooklyn* in 1966 and *Inside Linda Lovelace* in 1976) had ended in failure. After the Court of Appeal overturned a conviction in the *Linda Lovelace* case, the Metropolitan police were reported as saying that if that work was not obscene, then "nothing was". There had grown an assumption that the written word fell in effect outside the scope of the Act.

A key factor which originally prompted the "Girls (Scream) Aloud" prosecution was apparently the assumption that the fanbase of Girls Aloud was such that there was a danger of the story being read by (and highly disturbing to) young people who found the blog as a result of a search. But evidence from a computer expert was adduced on behalf of the defendant, that in fact internet searches for "Girls Aloud" would yield millions of results. Finding the story would require the addition of search terms like "rape" and "murder", which was highly unlikely on the part of the vulnerable people whom the prosecution was intended to protect. The defendant was formally found not guilty at the start of the trial when the prosecution offered no evidence.

COPYRIGHT

Copyright (discussed generally in Ch.3) subsists in most material that can be found on the internet. For example, text will attract literary copyright, and pictures and logos will attract artistic copyright. Moving images will be protected by film copyright. Computer programs are protected as literary works. Songs and music can be downloaded from the internet for use in the home and are protected as sound recordings and musical works.

Many copyright owners have seen digital technology and, in particular, its use on the internet as posing a significant, if not insurmountable, threat to the protection of copyright works—virtually anything that can be reduced into digital form can be copied and distributed in a fast and cheap manner.

There are a substantial number of free-of-charge and subscription "file-sharing" websites which have sprung up for exactly this purpose. The high-profile Swedish case involving The Pirate Bay in 2009 (the world's largest BitTorrent tracker with over 3 million registered trackers sharing thousands of files, most of them copyright works such as movies, music and software) serves to highlight the issues relating to how the law deals with file-sharing activities. In that case, the four founders of the site were found guilty of the criminal offence of contributory copyright infringement, and also jointly liable in a concurrent civil case for damages (the defendants are appealing this decision).

In the UK, the obvious primary copyright infringer in respect of infringement over a peer-to-peer (P2P) network would be the computer user who actually downloads the copyright material, frequently music or video (in *Polydor Limited v Brown* [2005] E.W.H.C. 3191 the court made it clear that unauthorised uploading of music files for use on P2P networks constitutes copyright infringement by the individual user). However, such people are almost impossible to catch and effectively halt in practice. Therefore rights holders have to turn their attentions to other parties involved in the infringement.

The music industry in particular, mindful of how much it could potentially lose because of this development of technology, has moved quickly to enforce its rights. In the last few years the BPI (now The British Recorded Music Industry) has successfully obtained judgment against a number of individuals further up the chain who have uploaded music and distributed it illegally online to other peers. In taking this action the BPI has put a marker down that file-sharers will be at risk if they continue their activities.

In *Sony Music Entertainment (UK) Ltd v Easyinternet Café Ltd* [2003] F.S.R. 882, the court held that a CD burning service offered by a chain of internet cafés was unlawful. Files were downloaded from the internet and stored on the café's server. The customer was then able to get the file burned on to CD by staff in return for payment. Sony and others brought action for copyright infringement under ss.17 and 18 of the Copyright, Design and Patents Act 1988. Easyinternet argued that it did not know it was copying copyright material as staff were not allowed to know what the files contained or, alternatively, that the copying was within the defence as being recorded for private and domestic use (i.e. the defence that permits home videoing of TV programmes). The court held that it did not matter whether the café knew whether the material was copyright material or not, as copying was a strict liability offence and it did not require any proof of intention to do so. As the copying was done in exchange for payment, it was clearly not private and domestic use. Accordingly, the CD burning service was unlawful.

Copyright owners are also keen to secure criminal convictions against infringers due to the obvious deterrent effect and the possibility of obtaining confiscation orders. However, under English law there is no equivalent to the criminal offence of contributory copyright infringement relied on in the Pirate Bay case. As such, the difficulty of proving that an operator or ISP actually authorised the copying for the purpose of securing a criminal conviction remains. It is perhaps for this reason that in a criminal prosecution against the founder of the BitTorrent-driven music-sharing website www.OiNK.cd, the defendant was charged (and subsequently acquitted in January 2010) of conspiracy to defraud as opposed to an offence relating to copyright infringement. Given the number of uploaders and downloaders, it is generally agreed amongst rights holders that it would be more cost effective and have greater impact to concentrate efforts on P2P operators and ISPs, namely those actually facilitating the copying. However, establishing that they have authorised the copying can be problematic but not impossible (see below).

The legal position of P2P operators in respect of copying has not yet been the subject of litigation before the English courts but the issue has been dealt with in other jurisdictions including the US. One of the high profile US cases on the issue of P2P operator liability (*A&M Records Inc v Napster Inc* 239 F.3d 1004 (9th Cir., 2001)) involved Napster, an internet music-sharing site which, after being outlawed for facilitating free file swapping of popular songs, now operates a legitimate download service paying copyright dues. Napster had previously argued that it was not to blame for its subscribers' use of copyright material, but the courts held that it was responsible where it knew, or ought to have known, that it was trading in such material.

As already mentioned in this chapter, the Electronic Commerce (EC Directive) Regulations 2002 provide what is known as a "mere conduit" defence (see regs 17–19) in respect of online services. ISPs would argue that they fall squarely within such a defence and therefore cannot be held liable in respect of online infringements (provided they can demonstrate that they satisfy the requirements set out in the Regulations, which was found not to be the case in respect of the defendants in *The Pirate Bay* case).

In any event, the UK Government is keen to see ISPs do more to fight unlawful P2P file-sharing. Specific proposals to tackle piracy are set out in both the Gowers Review 2006 and the Digital Britain report (published in June 2009 by the Department for Culture, Media and Sport and the Department for Business, Innovation and Skills). The Government's review of copyright law in the digital age has resulted, in part, in the Digital Economy Act 2010. Amongst other things, the Act imposes various obligations on ISPs with the object of reducing online copyright infringement. For example, ISPs will be obliged to notify subscribers if their IP addresses are reported as being used to facilitate copyright infringement. Details of these obligations will be set out in a separate code of practice.

In the publishing sector, the case of *Shetland Times v Shetland News* [1997] S.L.T. 669 demonstrates the role copyright law plays in protecting works made available online. The *Shetland Times* had a website which contained news headlines and other articles. The *Shetland News* reproduced the *Shetland Times*'s headlines on its website. When readers clicked on a headline in the *Shetland News*'s site they were transferred to the relevant article in the *Shetland Times*'s website. The objection of the *Shetland Times* to this hypertext link was on the basis that users of the internet would thereby gain access to material in the *Shetland Times*'s website without entering the site via their home page, thus reducing the value of the site for the purposes of advertising. The case eventually settled (at least partially) out of court with the *Shetland News* agreeing to put the *Shetland Times*'s logo next to each headline with the words "A *Shetland Times* story" acting as the link.

Permitted acts for computer programs

The acts in relation to copyright which are restricted by law (discussed generally in Ch.3) apply to computer programs in the same way as other literary works. Thus, to download a computer program from the internet will amount to an infringement by copying. Certain activities (in addition to those covered elsewhere in this book, e.g. the fair dealing provisions) are permitted by virtue of provisions in the Copyright, Designs and Patents Act 1988, as amended. They are the following:

- making necessary back-up copies (s.50A);

- decompilation (s.50B);

- the use of means or devices to study, test or observe the functioning of a computer program to determine the ideas and principles underlying the program if they do so while performing the acts they are allowed to do (s.50BA); and

- making copies or adaptations necessary for lawful use (S.50C).

The first three of these permitted acts cannot be prohibited or restricted by agreement (s.296A), for example a software licence. Decompilation allows a lawful user of a copy of a computer program expressed in a low level language to convert it to a higher level language or, incidentally in the course of so converting, to copy it.

However, the Copyright and Related Rights Regulations 2003 (which implemented EC Directive 2001/29/EC) have strengthened the copyright protection available in the online context. Many computer programs include technical devices which prevent copying, or otherwise interfering with the underlying program code. Section 296 of the 1988 Act contains provisions concerning such technological protection. Where a person either provides the means to circumvent a technical device which has been applied to a computer program to protect the copyright in the program, or does anything to get around such technological measures which are applied to a copyright work (not a computer program) to protect the copyright work itself, then the copyright owner will be able to bring an action for copyright infringement.

DATABASE RIGHT

In addition to the Copyright, Designs and Patents Act 1988, which gives databases copyright protection as literary works (provided certain criteria are fulfilled), the Copyright and Rights in Databases Regulations 1997 (SI 1997/3032) bestow additional legal protection upon databases as being commercially valuable, and the product of substantial investment. The database right exists irrespectively of the subsistence of copyright in the database. In appropriate circumstances both a database right and copyright will exist in a database.

A database is defined as "a collection of independent works, data or other materials which (a) are arranged in a systematic or methodical way, and (b) are individually accessible by electronic or other means" (the Regulations take the definition from s.3A(1) of the 1988 Act).

The database right is a property right which subsists in a database "if there has been substantial investment in obtaining, verifying or presenting the contents of the database" (para.13(1)). The "maker" (defined in para.12(1) as "the person who takes the initiative in obtaining, verifying or presenting the contents of a database and assumes the risk of investing in that obtaining, verification or presentation") of the database is the first owner of the database right unless they are employed to do so, in which case the employer is the first owner (para.14). *Pennwell Publishing (UK) Limited v Onstein* [2007] E.W.H.C. 1570 (QB) concerned a departing employee from Pennwell who had added his various non-work related contact details to Pennwell's email system. The court held that where an address list is maintained on a program which is part of an employer's email system, the rights in question will usually belong to the employer even though the database might contain personal contacts of the employee. Database right exists for a period of 15 years from the end of the calendar year during which the making of the database is completed (para.17).

Infringing acts include "extraction" or "re-utilisation" of all or a substantial part of the contents of the database without the consent of the owner (para.16). Extraction means (in relation to any contents of a database) the permanent or temporary transfer of those contents to another medium by any means or in any form. Re-utilisation means making those contents available to the public by any means. Fair dealing of a database will not amount to infringement.

In the first case brought under the database right (*British Horseracing Board Ltd v William Hill Organisation Ltd* [2005] E.W.C.A. Civ 863), the court was asked to consider whether the bookmaker William Hill was infringing the rights of the British Horseracing Board (BHB). The BHB compiled a database of all information connected to racing, including information on horses, owners, trainers and jockeys which was said to cost in the region of £4 million per year to maintain. While William Hill had certain licences to reproduce certain race information in its betting shops, it had not licensed other information which appeared on its website which was derived from the BHB database. At first instance, the court held that William Hill was liable for extraction and re-utilisation of a substantial part of the BHB database, which amounted to "pre-race" information of the identity of horses in a race, date and time of the race, and identity of the racecourse. The BHB database was protected by the database right and William Hill's use of it in extracting the information and then using it on its own website was unlawful. The decision was fundamental to a number of different sporting situations where bookmakers needed to make available details of sporting events scheduled to take place, such as greyhound racing, football and cricket. In each situation, the bookmaker (or any other party) would therefore require a licence to use such event information. In this case, William Hill obtained such a licence from the BHB to make its activities lawful, but it went on to appeal the decision because of its general importance to the industry and a reference was made to the ECJ to consider the scope of the database right in light of European legislation. The ECJ placed a restrictive interpretation on the scope of database right. Amongst other things it ruled that investment in:

   (a) "obtaining" referred to the resources used to seek out *existing* independent materials and collect them in a database. It did not cover the resources used to *create* the data in the first place; and

   (b) "verification" of the contents referred to the resources used to *ensure the reliability* of the information in the database and to *monitor* the accuracy of the materials collected when the database was created. It did not cover the resources used for verification during the stage when the data was *created*.

The BHB submitted that the ECJ had proceeded on a misunderstanding of the facts about the investment that had been made in the database. However, the Court of Appeal held that the ECJ had not misunderstood the primary facts and allowed William Hill's appeal against the finding that it had infringed the BHB's database right.

Following the *William Hill* case, it is clear that in order to protect a database under the Regulations, organisations will need to demonstrate a clear division between resources used to create data in the first place and resources used to obtain, verify and/or present that data (perhaps at a later date) in a database.

The case of *Football Dataco Ltd v Brittens Pools Ltd* [2010] EWHC 841 (Ch) illustrates the difficulties in demonstrating a clear division between resources used to create data and resources used to obtain, verify and/or present data. It was held that selection decisions in the course of creating the data which made up English and Scottish football fixture lists were indivisibly linked to the creation of such data, and therefore could not be regarded as part of the selection or arrangement of the content for the purposes of database right protection. The Court went on to say that the extra effort in obtaining, verifying and presenting the contents of the football lists (post-creation) was not sufficient to amount to a substantial investment and therefore the fixture lists did not attract database right protection.

However, it was held that the process of selection and arrangement performed while data is being created could be taken into account when assessing whether copyright subsists in a database (as a literary work) under the 1988 Act (see Ch.3). In this case, there were numerous stages in the process of selecting fixture dates which involved the use of skill, labour and judgment. The Court held that this effort was quantitatively sufficient to attract database copyright under s.3A of the 1988 Act.

FURTHER READING

- P. Carey, *Data Protection—a practical guide to UK and EU law*, 3rd edn (Oxford: Oxford University Press, 2009)

10. TELEVISION

Television merits its own chapter as being the most powerful and widely accessible mass medium. It has taken on a new significance as an interactive platform for the provision of electronic and other broadcasting services, and it jostles with the computer and mobile telephone for pride of place as the human interface for the internet. The advent of digital television at the end of 1998 ushered in a new era of broadcasting for which the United Kingdom remains a world leader. New technologies such as huge flat screens and high definition 3D programmes in real time (such as live sports) are likely to mean that "the box" will keep its place in the living room for years to come. That should bolster arguments for keeping the licence fee to pay for the BBC. But competing technologies such as the latest mobile phones and laptops at one end, and live sports in pubs and even cinemas at the other, suggests that the future may involve people pulling out content when they want it and where they want it, rather than having it pushed out by broadcasters to suit the agendas of editors and advertisers. These are exciting times. The law sometimes struggles to keep pace with new uses for content, one example being copyright material being uploaded for free on YouTube.

Previous chapters have considered television wherever it was relevant to matters being discussed in those chapters. The law of defamation, for example, applies in the same way to television as it does to all other media. Similarly, the laws of malicious falsehood, obscenity, inciting racial hatred, blasphemy and current affairs reporting apply to television as much as any other medium; particular aspects of the law relevant to broadcasting were looked at in the chapters dealing with these topics.

This chapter considers the nature of the television industry in the United Kingdom, the regulation of that industry (principally by virtue of the powers of the Office of Communications (Ofcom)) and the challenges that lie ahead for broadcasters. Regulation of television in the United Kingdom underwent a seismic change with the coming into force of the Communications Act 2003. This saw an overhaul of the law in almost every area of the industry, from media ownership to technical advances, licensing and standards. It also heralded the formation of Ofcom, which absorbed the former broadcasting regulators, including the Independent Television Commission (ITC), the Broadcasting Standards Commission (BSC) and the Radio Authority.

THE PROVISION OF TELEVISION

This section sets out the current position on the provision of television in the United Kingdom by terrestrial, cable and satellite means. Terrestrial television is dominated by the five major television channels (BBC1, BBC2, ITV, Channel 4 and Five) which are all public service broadcasters. "PSB" basically adds a need sometimes to inform and educate as well as simply entertain viewers. In order to receive such broadcast transmissions a licence fee is payable by the consumer (although in fact, the licence fee is payable only in respect of the BBC). As the analogue service winds down and replacement by digital services is completed, arguments for and against the licence fee will continue to gather momentum..

ITV, Channel 4, Five, and GMTV require a licence to broadcast, obtainable from Ofcom. The type of licence depends on the service provided (see below) and is subject to potentially severe sanctions by Ofcom for its breach.

BBC

The British Broadcasting Corporation (BBC) is given authority to broadcast by virtue of a Royal Charter (originally established in 1927) (see below). The Charter, which is renewed periodically, confirms the BBC's status as a public corporation. The newest BBC Charter marked a radical overhaul of how the BBC is governed. On January 1, 2007 the BBC Trust replaced the Board of Governors as the independent body responsible for governing the BBC. The objectives of the corporation are to provide sound and television broadcasting services, and sound and television programmes of information, education and entertainment for general reception in the United Kingdom.

The activities of the BBC are uniquely funded by a licence fee levied on all homes in the United Kingdom that use a television set. In return, the BBC is bound to provide two national television services (BBC1 and BBC2, although it also broadcasts BBC3 and BBC4) and a variety of national and local radio services. All services must provide a wide range of programmes of a high general standard, must treat controversial issues with impartiality and must ensure that programmes do not cause harm and offence. The BBC is subject to the regulatory control of Ofcom in relation to the former BSC codes only. However, Ofcom cannot impose sanctions against the BBC in the way it can against licensed broadcasters.

ITV (Channel 3)

Channel 3 services (largely ITV) are a number of regional television services operated by companies licensed by Ofcom (previously licensed by the ITC).

Each of the regional Channel 3 service providers is licensed to provide a television service for a particular region of the United Kingdom for a specified number of years (all current Channel 3 licences exist for a period of 10 years and may be renewed for one or more periods of 10 years). In 2003, two of the broadcasters owning major shares of the Channel 3 audience, Granada and Carlton, merged to form one entity: ITV Plc. The merger generated debate concerning competition and plurality of ownership of television licences because, as a result of the corporate consolidation, ITV Plc now controls all of the regional Channel 3 licences in England and Wales. The merger was allowed to proceed after conditions were imposed. Those conditions are designed to protect fair competition in negotiations with advertisers. Each licence provides that a sufficient amount of time must be given over to news and current affairs programmes that deal with both national and international matters and a suitable range of programmes must be broadcast that are of particular interest to people living in the area for which the service is provided. Additionally, at least 25 per cent of broadcasting time must consist of "independent programmes", i.e. programmes produced by companies or organisations that have little or no connection with the Channel 3 broadcasters. There are 15 regional Channel 3 licence fees and one licence fee (GMTV) providing the national breakfast time service. The interest that Ofcom takes in ITV reflects its statutory duty to take into account the views and interests of those who live in different parts of the UK (the Nations and Regions). Ofcom has senior directors in Glasgow, Cardiff and Belfast, as well as London.

Channel 4

The Channel Four Television Corporation was established by the Broadcasting Act 1990 and is licensed by Ofcom (previously licensed by the ITC) to provide a television service to so much of England, Scotland and Northern Ireland as may be reasonably practicable. The licence must include conditions that ensure that:

- Channel 4 programmes contain a suitable proportion of matter calculated to appeal to tastes and interests not generally catered for by Channel 3; and

- there is appropriate innovation and experimentation in the form and content of programmes that give Channel 4 a distinctive character.

As with Channel 3 companies, it must abide by Ofcom codes on technical, programme and advertising standards.

Five (Channel 5)

Five is a national television service licensed by Ofcom (previously licensed by the ITC) to provide television programming to a certain minimum specified proportion of the United Kingdom. It was originally envisaged that Five would be rather like ITV and provide competition for that channel. However, there are no equivalent regional programming requirements for Five.

Satellite television

There is a multitude of satellite transmissions to the United Kingdom. The best known is Sky (BskyB Ltd) which uses satellites in geostationary orbit above North Africa to broadcast television signals, both analogue and digital, to Europe. Sky is required to carry (known as the "must carry" rules) all the public service broadcasters (BBC, C3, C4, S4C and C5). There are various other satellite transmissions that may be received in the United Kingdom, many of which are encrypted thus requiring decoding devices for viewing.

Certain satellite transmissions are regulated by Ofcom. Whether or not such regulation applies to a particular satellite service depends on the nature of the service itself. A satellite service may be "domestic", "non-domestic" or "foreign".

A domestic satellite service is one where the television programmes included in the service are transmitted by satellite from a place in the United Kingdom on an allocated frequency for general reception in the United Kingdom.

Non-domestic satellite services are divided into two categories:

(a) a service that consists in the transmission of television programmes by satellite:

    (i) otherwise than on an allocated frequency; and
    (ii) for general reception in the United Kingdom or in any pre-scribed country (or both), where the programmes are transmitted from a place in the United Kingdom; or

(b) a service that consists in the transmission of television programmes by satellite:

    (i) from a place that is neither in the United Kingdom nor in any prescribed country, but
    (ii) for reception in the United Kingdom.

A service that falls within the first category (e.g. Sky) which transmits from one of the prescribed countries (Belgium, Denmark, Germany, France, Greece, Luxembourg, Ireland, Italy, Portugal, Spain and the Netherlands) requires a licence to broadcast from Ofcom. A service falling within the second category will only require a licence to the extent that material is contained within the service which is provided by a person within the United Kingdom who determines the content of such programming.

A foreign satellite service is a service that is capable of being received in the United Kingdom but that is not transmitted from within the United Kingdom and does not fall within the definition of a non-domestic satellite service. There is generally no restriction nor licence requirement for such services. However, the Secretary of State may make an order "proscribing" a foreign satellite service where it offends against good taste or decency, is likely to encourage or incite crime, or is likely to lead to disorder or be offensive to public feeling (s.329 of the Communications Act 2003).

Cable television

Both the terrestrial and satellite channels are available to certain areas in the United Kingdom via a fixed line or cable network. The cable companies receive broadcast transmissions from the other sources and retransmit them to consumer households in exchange for a monthly fee. In order to operate a cable television service a licence may be required from Ofcom. The terms of the licence may impose an obligation on a cable company to transmit certain specified channels (known as a "must carry" requirement).

Digital television

Digital transmission involves the conversion of television sound and pictures into binary digits and their re-conversion by the consumer's decoding equipment, usually referred to as a "set-top box". Digital television signals are more accurate and use less power than their analogue counterparts. This latter factor, together with the use of the technique known as "video compression", means that a considerable number of channels can be broadcast using a limited frequency range. Digital television provided not only an explosion in the number of television channels available to the consumer but also heralds a massive change in the way people live their lives, making possible home shopping and home working as well as revolutionising the entertainment industry.

The Communications Act 2003 provides for the eventual phasing out of analogue broadcasts and anticipates that all television will be by digital means. All new broadcast licences must provide for digital services. This is the case for ITV, Channel 4, Five and teletext providers as their licences are renewed. The government proposes to "switch off" analogue broadcasting (which started in 2008 and ends in 2012) but until that date it is likely that the public service broadcasters will be available in both analogue and digital form.

THE REGULATION OF TELEVISION

In addition to the general laws of the United Kingdom that regulate the activities of the media generally, the medium of television is heavily regulated by an industry regulator. This section considers television regulation by Ofcom.

Ofcom

Formally launched on December 29, 2003, Ofcom is the United Kingdom's "super regulator" and was established by the Communications Act 2003 to oversee all regulation in the media and communications sectors. It takes over the role and functions of the Independent Television Commission, Broadcasting Standards Commission, Oftel, the Radio Authority and the Radiocommunications Agency (the so-called "legacy regulators"). Its creation has radically changed the structure of television regulation in the United Kingdom.

Ofcom is charged, by virtue of s.319 of the Communications Act 2003, with setting and revising a code for the standards of contents of radio and television programmes. Its 2005 broadcasting code was replaced on December 16, 2009 with a new Ofcom Broadcasting Code, which covers all programmes broadcast on or after December 16, 2009. In addition to UK statutes, the Ofcom Code also has to take into account a number of requirements relating to television in EC Directive 89/552/EEC, as amended by Directive 97/36/EC and by Directive 2007/65/EC (the "Audio Visual Media Services Directive"). The Code has also taken into account the Human Rights Act 1998. A consolidating directive is expected in 2010. However, as before, the standards objectives to be met are:

(a) that persons under the age of 18 are protected;

(b) that material likely to encourage or to incite the commission of a crime or to lead to disorder is not included in television and radio services;

(c) that news included in television and radio is presented with due impartiality;

(d) that news included in television and radio services is reported with due accuracy;

(e) that the proper degree of responsibility is exercised with respect to the content of programmes which are religious programmes;

(f) that generally accepted standards are applied to the contents of television and radio services so as to provide adequate protection for members of the public from the inclusion in such services of offensive and harmful material;

(g) that advertising that contravenes the prohibition on political advertising is not included in television or radio services;

(h) that the inclusion of advertising that may be misleading, harmful or offensive in television and radio services is prevented;

(i) that the international obligations of the United Kingdom with respect to advertising included in television and radio services are complied with;

(j) that the unsuitable sponsorship of programmes included in television and radio services is prevented;

(k) that there is no undue discrimination between advertisers who seek to have advertisements included in television and radio services; and

(l) that there is no use of techniques that exploit the possibility of conveying a message to viewers or listeners, or of otherwise influencing their minds, without their being aware, or fully aware, of what has occurred.

This standards code is enforced by Ofcom by means of a condition in every licence requiring that the code is observed and adhered to. Breaches of the code may be penalised in fines and, in the most extreme cases, forfeit of the licence. Ofcom does not, however, have the power to impose such sanctions on the BBC. Ofcom does not preview programmes, nor does it require advance schedule information. It is the responsibility of the broadcasters to ensure that the material broadcast does not offend against Code provisions. Decisions on breaches of the Code are taken by Ofcom after the broadcast.

THE LEGACY CODES

Until the old Ofcom Code took effect in 2005, the codes of the legacy regulators were, rather confusingly, still in force. They were:

1. **Code on Standards**
    Broadcasting Standards Commission

2. **Code on Fairness and Privacy**
    Broadcasting Standards Commission

3. **Programme Code**
    ITC (Independent Television Commission)

4. **Code of Programme Sponsorship**
    ITC

All these codes have now been replaced by the Ofcom Broadcasting Code of December 2009.

THE OFCOM CODE

This Code for television and radio, covering standards in programmes, sponsorship, and fairness and privacy sets out the standards Ofcom must secure. The Code was drafted in the light of the Human Rights Act 1998 and the European Convention on Human Rights. The right to freedom of expression (art.10) encompasses the audiences' right to receive creative material, information and ideas without interference but subject to restrictions prescribed by law and necessary in a democratic society (plus consideration of art.8, the right to a person's private and family life, home and correspondence). Ofcom has also taken into account art.9 (freedom of thought, conscience and religion) and art.14 (the right to enjoyment of human rights without discrimination on grounds such as sex, race and religion).

When Ofcom has found that its code has been breached, it will normally publish a finding and explain why a broadcaster has breached the Code (these findings are available in Ofcom's Broadcast Bulletins and at *http:// www.ofcom.org.uk*).

However, where a broadcaster, in Ofcom's opinion, has deliberately, seriously or repeatedly breached the Code, it may impose statutory sanctions and broadcasters are inevitably very wary of substantial fines or losing the licence to broadcast.

The Ofcom Broadcasting Code is set out at Appendix F.

When applying the Code to content, broadcasters are to be aware that the context in which the material appears is key.

As previously set out (s.319(h) of the Communications Act 2003) and the degree of "harm and offence" is the key. The likely expectation of the audience of that particular programme is to be taken into account but

Ofcom is very aware of the desirability of maintaining the independence of editorial control over programme content.

The Code does not seek to address each and every case that could arise. Individual broadcasters are likely to have their own compliance manuals to assist programme makers in maintaining the necessary standards. Broadcasters should be familiar with their audiences and ensure that programme content can always be justified by the context and the editorial needs of the programme.

Duty is on the programme maker (by contract) and broadcaster (by statute) to comply with the Code and broadcasters have compliance officers to review content. Ofcom is prepared to offer general guidance on the interpretation of the Code but broadcasters must seek their own legal advice on any compliance issues arising. Ofcom only gives informal guidance. It is not a censor and does not vet programmes prior to broadcast.

Section 1

Protecting the under eighteens

Ofcom's principle is that people under 18 years of age should be protected and, accordingly, there are rules on scheduling and content information. For example, material that might seriously impair the physical, mental or moral development of people under 18 must not be broadcast. Television broadcasters must observe the 21.00 watershed and also should take into account when school holidays occur and children are more likely to be watching programmes. The watershed does not apply to radio broadcasts but these also have to have particular regard to times when children are particularly likely to be listening (which includes the school run and breakfast time).

The use of illegal drugs, the abuse of drugs, smoking, solvent abuse and the misuse of alcohol must not be featured in programmes made primarily for children unless there is strong editorial justification. If included, it must not be condoned, encouraged or glamorised before the watershed unless there is editorial justification. There are also curbs on violence and dangerous behaviour, offensive language, sex, nudity, exorcism, the occult and the paranormal appearing before the watershed or in an inappropriate context. So language acceptable in a sitcom broadcast after 21.00 might have to be cut if subsequently broadcast at 18.00.

Unsurprisingly, Ofcom insists that due care must be taken over the physical and emotional welfare and the dignity of people under 18 who take part or are otherwise involved in programmes. This is irrespective of any consent given by the participant or their parents.

Section 2

Harm and offence

Ofcom's principle is to ensure that generally accepted standards are applied to the contents of television and radio services so as to provide adequate protection for members of the public from the inclusion in such services of harmful and/or offensive material. OFCOM highlights that s.2 should be read in conjunction with s.1 as its rules are assigned not only to provide adequate protection for adults but also to protect people under 18.

Factual programmes, such as documentaries, must not materially mislead the audience. Transgressions can result in huge fines: Ofcom's predecessor, the ITC, fined Carlton Communications £2 million (1998) for *The Connection*, a faked documentary about Colombian drug cartels. In 1999, Channel 4 was fined £150,000 because of faked scenes in a documentary about rent boys in Glasgow. The channel had not known that the scenes were not real and would have been happy to label them as "reconstructions". The rent boys were real but some of the clients were later identified as members of the documentary's production team. Broadcasters can unwittingly fall into error—the BBC faced complaints that fake guests were interviewed on the confessional talk show *The Vanessa Show*.

Programmes must not include material which, taking into account the context, condones or glamorises violent, dangerous or seriously anti-social behaviour and is likely to encourage others to copy such behaviour.

Competitions should be conducted fairly, prizes should be described accurately and rules should be clear and appropriately made known. When broadcasters are made aware of lapses in competition rules, they tend to be quick to offer to repay call charges etc. as this has been a controversial area—as the programme makers of Big Brother have found as some contestants in the reality show do what no rule-maker would expect them to do, such as walk out or use wholly unacceptable language.

TV fakery allegations were something addressed by Ofcom in 2007–08. In 2008 the BBC was fined £495,000 for misleading its audiences by "faking" phone-ins. Serious deceptions of the audience emerged on television and radio shows including high profile ones such as Comic Relief (in March 2007, a member of the production team posed as the winning caller after a problem with the phone lines (fined £45,000) and Sport Relief (a member of the production team posed as a winner on air in July 2006 (fined £45,000)). Live competitions turned out to be pre-recorded and even children's television was tarnished—in September 2007 viewers of the children's show TMi were led to believe that a member of the audience had won a competition, but it turned out to be a member of the production crew (fined £50,000).

2008 saw ITV being fined a record £5.68 million by Ofcom for abusing premium rate phone services in viewer competitions. Other broadcasters such as GMTV and Five were given huge fines too. Again, big shows were in the spotlight such as X-Factor, Dancing on Ice, Richard and Judy, Gordon Ramsay's The F-Word, and Five's Brainteaser quiz show (where a crew member had posed as a "winning contestant", resulting in a fine of £300,000). Even the Queen became involved, as a BBC documentary about her was edited out of sequence in a trailer which made it look like she was walking out of a photo session "in a huff". Television responded to the calamity by the removal of executives and a substantial tightening up of procedures to regain the public's trust. What had been heralded as the "light touch" regulator was shown to have a real bite. Ofcom's adjudications can be accessed on its website.

Section 3

Crime

The principle is to ensure that material likely to encourage or incite the commission of crime or lead to disorder is not included in television or radio services. Broadcasters should not make payments to criminals (save in the public interest) and witnesses should not be offered payment either when proceedings are active (i.e. before the end of the trial).

Section 4

Religion

Broadcasters must exercise the proper degree of responsibility with respect to the content of religious programmes. The religious views and beliefs of those belonging to a particular religion must not be subject to abusive treatment. Religious programmes must not seek to promote religious views or beliefs by stealth, must not seek recruits or improperly exploit any susceptibilities of the audience.

Section 5

Due impartiality and due accuracy and undue prominence of views and opinions

The Press Complaints Commission Code of Conduct allows the press to be partisan although it requires that the print media distinguish clearly between comment, conjecture and fact. Ofcom is tougher on news and current affairs. The principle is to ensure that news, in whatever form, is reported with due accuracy and presented with due impartiality. Relaxations in the previously very onerous statutory and regulatory requirements covering the reporting of elections and matters of political or industrial controversy have given broadcasters greater flexibility (no longer do they need to have a stopwatch to ensure that all the major political parties get approximately equal airtime) so broadcasters can have a "cluster" or "season" of programmes on the same subject but expressing different viewpoints. So one could have, as an example, a news report considering the pro-fox hunting arguments, so long as a contributors' personal views were made clear, without a detailed right of reply from the anti-fox hunting side so long as there was a time given in a near contemporaneous news programme for the opposite personal views. So long as taken as a whole there is due impartiality the fact that a particular report might focus on one side of the debate is acceptable.

But the viewers must be made aware of what they are seeing. If a presenter gives a "personal" view or makes an "authored" programme, this should be made clear and alternative viewpoints adequately represented, either in the programme or in a series of programmes taken as a whole.

Reporting matters of major political or industrial controversy and major matters relating to current public policy is often difficult bearing in mind the modest amount of time granted by schedulers for such topical debate and often requires that due impartiality must be observed. So no news broadcasts will take sides with either strikers or management nor be expected slavishly to follow the government's line in the build-up to a foreign war. An appropriately wide range of significant views must be included and given due weight in each programme or series of programmes.

Section 6

Elections and referendums

For election reporting, see the Representation of the People Act 1983 (as amended). Ofcom provides definitions for "election", "referendum", "major party", "election period", "candidate", "designated organisation" and "permitted participants" and so on. The rules insist upon true impartiality being strictly maintained in constituency reports, but the regulator has made it plain that broadcasters should not be slaves to the code (which might otherwise restrict freedom of expression as the political parties seek to pressurise editorial teams) and will look at election coverage in the round rather than focusing (as once was the case) on individual reports which could distort political coverage. Political parties reputedly would time reports with a stop watch and demand more coverage for their policies and candidates. The rise of prominent independent candidates (such as ex-journalist, the white-suited Martin Bell or presenter Esther Rantzen) made such stopwatch watching unsustainable and editors taking great care to ensure overall due impartiality.

Section 7

Fairness

Ofcom's principle is to ensure that broadcasters avoid unjust or unfair treatment of individuals or organisations in programmes. Ofcom sets out "practices to be followed" by broadcasters dealing with individuals or organisation participating in or otherwise directly affected by programmes as broadcast.

Ofcom warns that following the practices will not necessarily avoid a breach of the section but, more helpfully, also that a failure to follow all the practices does not automatically result in a finding of unfairness. Broadcasters tend to send a "right to reply" letter to those who are going to find themselves appearing on screen. Contributors to programmes should:

- be told the nature of purpose of the programme, what the programme is about and be given a clear explanation of why they were asked to contribute and when (if known) and where it is likely to be first broadcast;

- be told what kind of contribution they are expected to make;

- be informed about the areas of questioning and, wherever possible, the nature of other likely contributors;

- be told of significant changes to the programme that might reasonably affect their original consent to participate and that might cause material unfairness;

- be told the nature of their contractual rights and obligations; and

- be given clear information, if offered an opportunity to preview the programme (which is quite unusual) about whether they would be able to affect any changes to it.

However, it may be fair to withhold all or some of this information where it is justified in the public interest or under other provisions of the Fairness section of the Code.

If a programme alleges wrong-doing or incompetence and makes other significant allegations, those concerned should normally be given an appropriate and timely opportunity to respond.

As we are all familiar from watching news and current affairs programmes on television, if a person approached to contribute to a programme chooses to make no comment, the broadcast should make clear that the individual concerned has chosen not to appear and should give their explanation if it would be unfair not to do so. Where it is appropriate to represent the views of the person or organisation that is not participating in the programme, this must be done in a fair manner.

As would be expected, Ofcom requires special treatment for children. They should not be encouraged to express controversial opinions. Consent from parents or guardians should normally be obtained. Approval of a teacher may be sufficient for uncontroversial material but broadcasters always need to take into account obligations of privacy. In the last few years it has become rare for children to be identifiable in any controversial context in news and current affairs. Even politicians' children are pixilated if filmed other than at a public event.

There are special rules for entertainment style "set-ups" and wind-up calls. The usual prohibitions on deception or misrepresentation do not apply if consent is subsequently given. Celebrities get a little less protection in that consent to set-ups may not be necessary if there was a public interest justification or their inclusion is not likely to result in unjustified public ridicule or personal distress. But broadcasters need to be very wary when putting individuals on screen without their consent. Not all celebrities see the funny side of pranks.

Section 8

Privacy

This is an area that can be even more problematical than fairness. Ofcom acknowledges this and recognises that there may be difficult, on-the-spot judgments about whether privacy is unwarrantably infringed by filming or recording, especially when reporting on emergency situations such as terrorist atrocities or train crashes. With 24-hour news, there can be a very strong public interest in reporting on an emergency situation as it occurs, which makes it very difficult for broadcasters to edit out material that they might normally not broadcast or assess whether they should be filming at a particular place at all.

The principle is that broadcasters should avoid any unwarranted infringement of privacy in programmes and in connection with obtaining material included in programmes.

Any infringement of privacy must be warranted, for example, by the public interest in revealing or detecting crime, protecting public health or safety, exposing misleading claims made by individuals or organisations or disclosing incompetence that affects the public.

Legitimate expectations of privacy will vary according to the place and nature of the information, activity or condition in question, the extent to which it is in the public domain (if at all) and whether the individual concerned is already in the public eye.

Privacy may need to be respected even in public places or where the subject is under investigation.

The location of a person's home should not be revealed unless it is warranted.

Any infringement of privacy in the making of a programme should be with the person's consent or be otherwise warranted.

On privacy, the Code is pretty tough, to the point of choosing to make it clear that callers to phone-in shows are deemed to have given their consent to the broadcaster of the contribution even if some would have thought that this was pretty obvious.

Broadcasters have to exercise particular care when filming in sensitive places such as hospitals, schools or joining police operations. Surreptitious filming or recordings should only be used where it is warranted.

Surreptitious filming or recording, doorstepping or recorded "wind-up" calls to obtain material for entertainment purposes may be warranted if it is intrinsic to the entertainment and does not amount to a significant infringement of privacy such as to cause significant annoyance, distress or embarrassment. The resulting material should not be broadcast without the consent of those involved. However, if the individual and/or organisation is not identifiable in the programme, then consent for broadcast will not be required.

When journalists are involved in surreptitious filming, they would normally obtain the approval of the programme editor. Surreptitious filming may provide the evidence to justify defamatory allegations contained in a programme but the film should not be used gratuitously but only if the story justified it in the public interest and it is necessary to the credibility or authenticity of the programme.

Broadcasters must take particular care when dealing with people involved in suffering and distress. Events such as bombs going off in a city causing death and injury pose very real issues for editors because the need to inform the public has to be balanced with the potentially damaging effect on the lives of those caught up in tragedy.

The Ofcom Code also deals with sponsorship, commercial references and other matters. Viewers must never be misled. There has to be transparency and editorial independence. Advertising products has to be kept separate from the content of programmes. Appendices set out the statutory background and the Directives as well as dealing with financial promotions and investment recommendations.

Decisions on a contributor's right to privacy can be delicate but important: the broadcast of a private conversation of then Prime Minister Gordon

Brown in a car (private but still wearing a microphone) accusing a voter of being a "bigot" created a row in the 2010 General Election.

EXAMPLES OF OFCOM DECISIONS

Consideration of Sanction against: Channel Four Television Corporation

For: Programme Code breaches in giving undue prominence to a commercial product in breach of s.8.4 of Ofcom's Programme Code (ex-ITC).

On: July 19, 2004.

Decision to fine: £5,000 and Direction to transmit Ofcom's statement of finding.

Summary of decision

For the reasons set out in full in the decision, the Ofcom Content Sanctions Committee found as follows:

1. Channel Four Television Corporation (licensed by Ofcom to run the service known as "Channel 4").

2. On May 18, 2004, the *Richard and Judy Show*, on Channel 4, broadcast a videotape item and discussion on the dangers of excessive caffeine intake. On July 19, 2004, an apology and corrective was given in the *Richard and Judy Show* by Richard Madeley stating that there had been factual inaccuracies in the May 18, 2004 item. This was followed by a videotape item in which the benefits of caffeine were examined, with particular emphasis on the "caffeine energy drink" Red Bull.

3. Four viewers complained that the apology given on July 19, 2004 was followed by "what seemed like an advertisement for Red Bull with celebrity endorsements". One viewer described this as a "sponsored advert for the coffee and Red Bull industry". Another "was left wondering whether the item had been produced by makers of Red Bull and whether the broadcast was made to avoid legal action". Channel 4 Television had admitted and Ofcom had recorded that the material broadcast on July 19, 2004 breached the Programme Code ("the Code"): s.8.4 (undue prominence). The matter was also referred to the Content Sanctions Committee ("the Committee") for consideration of a statutory sanction. The Committee invited Channel 4 Television to attend the Committee meeting to give oral representations if it wished but Channel 4 Television considered, having already given written representations, that this was not necessary. The Committee considered all the relevant material including the matters that Ofcom raised in correspondence with Channel 4 Television and its written representations in response before deciding whether to impose a sanction and, if so, what level of sanction was appropriate.

4. Ofcom has a statutory duty to require compliance with its Code and

consider the imposition of a statutory sanction, where a broadcaster has "repeatedly, deliberately or seriously" breached the Code. The Committee viewed the Code breach as sufficiently serious to merit the imposition of a statutory sanction. The material very clearly breached the Code and Channel 4 Television had admitted it was in breach of s.8.4 of the Code.

5. In this case, the Committee considered whilst the broadcast of July 19, 2004 was clearly intended to make amends for the errors contained in the earlier broadcast, Channel 4 Television had demonstrated uncharacteristically poor judgement resulting in what appeared to be, at the very least, a loss of editorial control. This culminated in the distinct impression that the programme had come under external commercial influence, giving Red Bull undue prominence, both in the number of direct references to that product and also in the use of an "expert" and sporting personalities linked to the product and extolling the benefits of caffeine and Red Bull.

6. Whilst the Committee took into account Channel 4 Television's overall good compliance record (particularly given its statutory remit to innovate), it also noted that it had been found in breach in 2003 in relation to material broadcast on the Richard and Judy programme (which had been found to be misleading). On that occasion, Channel 4 Television had not been subject to any sanction.

7. The Committee also took into account Channel 4 Television's admission that on this occasion, it had breached the Code albeit that it did not consider the breach serious enough to merit any sanction.

8. Taking all relevant factors into account, the Committee determined that the Code breach was sufficiently serious that a sanction by way of a financial penalty was necessary together with a direction to broadcast a statement of Ofcom's finding. The applicable statutory maximum is a fine of five per cent of Channel 4 Television's qualifying revenue, payable to Ofcom for forwarding to the Treasury. The Committee considered that, in view of the seriousness of the infringement and taking into account all the circumstances, an appropriate fine was £5,000.

Consideration of: Playboy TV/UK Benelux Limited

For: Programme Code breaches in showing R18 version material in breach of ss.1.1 and 1.4(d) of Ofcom's Programme Code (and taking into account breaches of s.1.4(c) of the Programme Code in relation to encrypted and unencrypted material transmitted before 21:00 on April 30 and May 2, 2004 respectively).

On: May 1, 2004

Decision to fine: £25,000.

Summary of decision

For the reasons given in full in the decision set out below, Ofcom found as follows:

1. Playboy TV/UK Benelux Limited ("Playboy TV UK") is licensed by Ofcom to run the satellite service Playboy TV. It transmits adult material, encrypted and available only to subscribers. It also transmits promotional material, free to air.

2. On May 1, 2004 at 00:08, Playboy TV UK broadcast encrypted material of an R18 version film in breach of the absolute prohibition in Ofcom's (ex-ITC) Programme Code ("the Code"). Section 1.4 (d) of the Code states, in relation to feature films and other acquired material, that "No 'R18' version should be transmitted at any time". Section 1.1 is the general requirement for broadcasters not to offend. Playboy TK UK admitted that the material transmitted was an "R18" version and that the breaches were serious. Ofcom had recorded the breaches of the Programme Code. The matter was also referred to Ofcom's Content Sanctions Committee ("the Committee") for consideration of a statutory sanction. The Committee heard representations from Playboy TK UK before deciding whether to impose a sanction.

3. Ofcom viewed the Code breaches as serious. The rule prohibiting the broadcast of "R18" version material is an absolute. The material was not borderline, but very clearly breached the Code. Playboy TV UK admitted it was of a standard that is prohibited under the Code for transmission at any time, whether encrypted or not. According to Playboy TV UK, the compliance failure was the result of human error. However, the Committee believed it also indicated a failure in Playboy TV UK's management to institute adequate training and operational procedures necessary to avoid such breaches of the Code.

4. The Committee took into account as aggravating the seriousness of the Code breaches relating to the R18 material, the fact that these breaches occurred on just one of several separate occasions over a period of three days (from April 30 to May 2, 2004) when Playboy TV UK committed other breaches of the Code. On April 30, it had broadcast images in pre-watershed promotional and other material, which though encrypted, were of an 18 standard (equivalent to BBFC 18 certificate standard), in breach of s.1.4(c) of the Code, which provides that this material should only be broadcast after 22:00. On May 2, Playboy TV UK also broadcast promotional material on a free-to-air (unencrypted) basis at 20.21, which was more explicit than would be acceptable under the Code, also in breach of s.1.4(c).

5. The free-to-air material was, in particular, insufficiently protective of the interests of children. Any broadcaster licensed to transmit adult encrypted material that is restricted to subscribers but had free-to-air promotions, has an obligation to ensure that no sexually explicit material is shown even inadvertently in free-to-air promotions. For

the avoidance of doubt, Ofcom wishes to make it clear that any such infringement is not to be tolerated.

6. Ofcom took into account as mitigating the breaches Playboy TV UK's frank admission that it had breached the Code and the contrition it expressed, and the fact that all but one of the breaches occurred under encryption. The Committee also noted Playboy TV UK's acceptance that it was appropriate to consider a financial penalty in respect of these breaches.

7. Taking all these matters into account, the Committee determined that the Code breaches in respect of the R18 material were so serious that a sanction by way of a financial penalty was necessary. It concluded that in view of the seriousness of the infringement and taking into account all the circumstances, an appropriate fine was £25,000 payable to Ofcom for forwarding to the Treasury.

Quiz Call

Five, 2 July 2006, 02:00

Introduction

In a competition called *Piggy Bank*, a photograph of loose change was shown. A number of the coins overlapped. Viewers were invited to "add the pence". None of the callers who reached the studio gave the correct answer, which was revealed at the end of the competition as 425 pence. Two viewers questioned the validity of the competition. They did not believe 425 was a possible solution.

Rule 2.11 of the Broadcasting Code ("the Code") requires that "Competitions should be conducted fairly, prizes should be described accurately and rules should be clear and appropriately made known".

Response

Five said that the answer announced (425 pence) was incorrect and the correct answer was 626 pence. However, the broadcaster confirmed that no caller who had reached the studio had given the correct answer and, if they had, the programme's production company would have been able to trace the caller and award the prize in retrospect.

Five added that all competitions on *Quiz Call* were subject to assessment by the show's approvals team and that *Piggy Bank* was categorised as a "difficult mathematics" game. The broadcaster provided details of the methodology it applied to reach the programme's *Piggy Bank* competition answers. It also detailed how the methodology had been applied in this particular case.

The broadcaster said that *Quiz Call* validated the methodology of every new game. At least two members of its approvals team analysed all draft methodologies, to ensure that they were "not inconsistent with methodologies applied on similar games, that the rules cover every eventuality, that there are no grey areas and that the rules are exhaustive". After preliminary approval, the producer then created a draft game and attempted to solve it in accordance with the methodology. At least two members of the approvals team also attempted to solve it and at least one of them must not have been involved in the earlier approval process. A methodology was given final approval only if each individual reached the same answer independently.

To verify the application of a methodology for a specific competition prior to broadcast, Five confirmed that the producer and an approvals team member must solve the set problem in accordance with the methodology. In this case, both reached the same incorrect answer independently. The broadcaster assured us that this was a rare instance of individuals making the same error when applying the approved methodology.

Five said that it had met *Quiz Call's* producers, to ensure that there would be no recurrence. In future the verification process for "difficult mathematics" games of this type must be solved independently by two approvals team members and the producer, one of whom must not have been involved in the original methodology approval process.

Decision

To be run fairly, Ofcom believes that cryptic or difficult competitions in which the presenter appears to seek one specific answer must have only one pre-determined solution. Ofcom also believes that this solution should be arrived at by applying a pre-determined methodology (i.e. set of criteria and/or instructions) that can produce only this solution. Ofcom recognises that a methodology could be commercially sensitive, as a broadcaster may wish to run subsequent similar competitions. However, when necessary, they will request that the broadcaster provide them with the methodology of the competition to ensure that it has been run fairly.

The methodology provided by Five confirmed the correct answers (626 pence), when applied in this case. It appeared to Ofcom capable of producing only the correct answer and was therefore fair to viewers who had decided to participate.

However, as set out in current Ofcom guidance, for a Call TV Quiz to be run fairly, "an audience should normally be able to expect the correct solution to be provided on air, with or without its associated methodology, when a competitions ends". In this case, an apparent weakness in the game's verification process resulted in viewers not knowing the correct answer to the competition when it had ended.

Ofcom therefore welcomed the action concerning the future verification process agreed by Five with *Quiz Call's* producers, to avoid recurrence. In particular, when applying a pre-determined methodology for final approval of a specific game, Ofcom welcomed the inclusion of at least one person who had not been involved in the preliminary approval process of the methodology itself. Given the above and noting that the error had not, in this instance, resulted in any financial harm to viewers, Ofcom concluded that the matter was resolved.

Complaint by Ms V on behalf of her daughter (a minor)

Dispatches, Channel 4, July 7, 2005

Summary

Ofcom has not upheld this complaint of unfair treatment in the broadcast of the programme.

Ms V complained that her daughter was treated unfairly in an edition of the Channel 4 current affairs programme *Dispatches*. The programme examined failing standards in British secondary schools. The reporter, a qualified teacher, worked undercover as a supply teacher in a number of schools and covertly recorded her work and observations. Covertly recorded footage of Ms V's daughter throwing a pencil and responding "No" to a question from the teacher was included in the programme with her face pixelated.

Ms V complained that her daughter was treated unfairly by the programme in that she was secretly filmed in her classroom and the material broadcast without Ms V's consent; and Ms V was not given an opportunity to respond to the material prior to broadcast. Ms V further complained that her daughter's privacy was unwarrantably infringed in both the making and broadcast of the programme in that: she was filmed without Ms V's consent while at school; she was recognised in spite of pixilation by friends, family and others; the method used to obtain the material was disproportionate; and, the programme makers did not pay particular attention to her age and other vulnerabilities.

Channel 4 responded that the programme revealed important issues of such overriding public interest that, given a number of steps taken in the conduct of the filming and in concealing Ms V's daughter's identity, it was not incumbent on the programme makers to see Ms V's consent or offer her a right of reply. Furthermore, any infringement of Ms V's daughter's privacy in the making or broadcast of the programme was warranted by the public interest in the failures within the education system revealed by the programme.

Ofcom found that the programme was of significant public interest in exposing failures in the secondary education system. In part it relied on the evidence of cumulative, persistent low-level misbehaviour in the classroom, which resulted in serious disruption in order to expose how the education system was failing the children. In light of this, and of the appropriate measures taken to obscure Ms V's daughter's identity, and having taken account of the particular vulnerabilities of children, Ofcom did not find that inclusion of the footage of Ms V's daughter resulted in unfairness to her, nor that her privacy was unwarrantably infringed in either the making or broadcast of the programme.

Complaint by Mr Michael Gore

Rock School 2, Channel 4, February 5 and 12, 2006

Summary

Ofcom has not upheld this complaint by Mr Michael Gore of unwarranted infringement of privacy.

This edition of *Rock School* featured a band tour coach. Mr Gore was the driver of the coach and images of him taken from outside the coach were included in the programme as broadcast.

Mr Gore complained that his privacy was unwarrantably infringed in both the making of the programme and in the programme as broadcast because: the programme makers filmed and broadcast images of him despite his refusal to sign a release form and his request not to be filmed; and, the programme makers knowingly accepted a forged release form from his employers for his participation in the programme.

Ofcom found as follows:

a) The filming of Mr Gore did not infringe his privacy. The footage captured by the programme makers was not of a personal or private nature and the actions of the programme makers in capturing the footage did not materially disturb or interfere with Mr Gore's right to a private life.

The broadcast of footage showing Mr Gore driving the tour coach did not infringe his privacy. Ofcom found Mr Gore was not readily identifiable from the footage and the footage did not reveal particularly personal or private information about him.

b) Having found that Mr Gore's privacy was not infringed in either the making of the programme or in the programme as broadcast, Ofcom was not required to establish whether appropriate consent had been obtained by the programme makers. This is because Ofcom found that in the circumstances of this case, a consent form from Mr Gore was not required for either the filming of him or the broadcast of images of him.

News

ITV1, BBC, Sky News and GMTV, various times, June 23, 2006

Introduction

Six viewers complained about the use in various television news bulletins of CCTV images depicting an unprovoked knife attack on two students. The assault caused the death of one of the victims, Daniel Pollen, and the serious injury of the other.

Response

ITV responded to a specific complaint about use of the images in the ITV News at 12.30.

The broadcaster pointed out that the pictures formed a central part of a murder case, which had ended that day with the sentencing of the attackers. The CCTV images had already been shown on a number of channels, and had generated considerable public interest. The issue of knife crime was high on the public agenda at the time.

Additionally, both the police and the families of the two victims had made it clear that they wanted the images to be shown to illustrate the inherent danger of young men carrying knives.

The available footage had been carefully edited to ensure that the actual fatal blow delivered to the murder victim was not shown.

However, ITV accepted that greater caution should have been exercised in the use of the images, and that violence of this nature can rarely be justified before the watershed. In any event, a clear warning about the content should have been given in the introduction.

As a result, ITV News has introduced a policy making it clear that violent scenes should not be shown in future before the watershed, without the express permission of the editorial management. Additionally, a seminar has been organised for all programme editors to reinforce editorial guidelines.

The BBC responded to a complaint about the use of the images in a bulletin transmitted at 18.00. As with ITV, the BBC also stressed the public interest justification in showing the nature of such a violent crime, and pointed to the support of the victims' families.

Additionally, the BBC pointed out that the images had been placed in a proper context with a clear introduction, which warned viewers of the "appalling" and "chilling" nature of pictures to come. Finally, it pointed out that the images were not run in their entirety, but "frozen" some time before the fatal blow to the murder victim.

Sky News responded to a specific complaint that the images had been run in a news bulletin at 16.00 without any warning to viewers about the content. The channel accepted that this was the case, but said it was a mistake that occurred in the 16.00 bulletin alone. All the other bulletins carried by Sky News that day carried a clear and specific warning.

Sky, too, said that showing the images was in the public interest in the light of growing concern about "knife culture" and that the release of the images had been supported by the families and the police. The broadcaster acknowledged that this did not absolve the journalists from deciding the suitability for themselves, but suggested that viewers could better understand the use of the images in those circumstances.

Finally, Sky pointed out that the actual murderous blow cannot be seen on the released images. Instead, Daniel Pollen is seen backing away from his attacker and is out of frame when the knife strikes. This fact is made clear in the commentary.

GMTV defended the use of the images within a regional news bulletin "opt-out" for the London area. It pointed out that only a very small proportion of its viewers are children, and that its output is designated as "news". However, it accepted that it was wrong for the pictures to have been transmitted without a clear warning to viewers.

The actual stabbing of the murder victim was not shown and—within the context of coverage of the court case—it considered that the use of the images was appropriate. However, the broadcaster accepted that, with hindsight, they "needed different treatment", given the breakfast-time transmission.

GMTV has reminded all the suppliers of its regional bulletins (including ITN, who supplied this bulletin) that footage should be carefully vetted in future, and suitable warnings inserted where appropriate. As with ITV

News, new guidelines have been issued to the particular programme editors.

Decision

The images depicting the attack on Daniel Pollen and his friend were particularly graphic and disturbing. The two students are seen quite clearly waiting innocently for a taxi outside a shopping centre. They are then viciously assaulted by three men with fists and knives in an obviously unprovoked attack.

The original court case had ended a month earlier, in May, and the CCTV images had been released at that time to press and broadcasters. They were run in late evening bulletins on at least two channels, and two complaints were received by Ofcom about the graphic nature of the footage. At the time, Ofcom did not uphold the complaints because the images had been presented well after the watershed; in a proper news context; and with appropriate warnings to viewers.

These further complaints relate to the re-use of the images some four weeks later, on the day that the victim's murderer was jailed for life. It is clear that the further use of the pictures was supported by both the parents of the victims and by the police and public prosecutors.

Nevertheless, it was stated that it is important that broadcasters exercise their own judgment on whether material is suitable for transmission and, if so, how it should be handled. Ofcom noted that the further uses of these images were in bulletins transmitted before the 21.00 watershed, and that special care is required when handling particularly violent material.

Broadcasting images of a death within any factual television programme requires a very cautious approach—not least consideration of the time of broadcast—as well as clear editorial justification. However, it is important to note that the CCTV pictures—even where shown in full—did not capture either the fatal blow to the murder victim (which occurred out of frame) or the moment of his death, which happened some time later.

In the exceptional circumstances of this case, Ofcom accepted that there may be a public interest justification in showing these images in some form, even before the watershed. However, such extreme material must be handled in an appropriate manner.

Each complaint has been considered separately on its own individual merits.

ITV's use of the images within a lunchtime news bulletin raised few issues regarding the potential exposure to children. This transmission was on a weekday within normal school hours, and it is unlikely that significant numbers of children would have been watching.

Even so, viewers should have been given a clear warning about the nature of the images about to be shown, and Ofcom welcomed ITV's acknowledgement of this point. Ofcom also welcomed the assurances that tighter editorial control has been introduced over the use of violent images in pre-watershed news bulletins. For these reasons Ofcom concluded that the complaint is resolved.

The BBC's use of the pictures occurred in an early evening news bulletin. On this occasion, the context was clearly established; an indication of the nature of the images was conveyed to the audience; and the pictures were "frozen" before any of the stabbing incidents were seen. For these reasons, the complaint was not upheld.

Sky News is a dedicated news channel with a very small child audience. The CCTV images of the assault were used in a properly established context and not in a gratuitous way, such as in headline sequences or trailers. Ofcom accepted that clear warnings were given to viewers before all transmissions, except the bulletin at 16.00.

The failure to transmit a warning at 16.00 was unfortunate, but Ofcom welcomed Sky News' acknowledgement of the error. For this reason, the complaint is resolved.

GMTV's use of the images within a breakfast-time programme raised particular issues, given the potential for children to catch sight of the images, even if they are not specifically viewing the programme. Even so, Ofcom accepted that this was a news bulletin, and that some parts of the footage could be run, if handled with care.

Unlike the other reports, the item ran *before* the sentencing of the victim's murderer—scheduled for later that day—and harked back to the previous court case.

Unfortunately, the short nature of GMTV's "opted out" regional bulletin did not allow time for a proper context to be established. The violent CCTV images of the attack were already being seen on screen by the time the newsreader completed an introductory sentence ("the random knife attack which cost Daniel Pollen's life was captured on CCTV"). The problem was compounded because the tone of the introduction did not convey any sense of warning about the shocking images being shown.

Further, there was no attempt to explain to viewers precisely what was being shown. The wording itself left the *impression* that viewers were watching the actual murder of the victim when, in fact, the images ended just before the fatal blow. This casual use of exceptionally violent material added to the potential for causing offence to viewers.

Ofcom welcomed GMTV's assurance that lessons have been learned, and that procedures have been changed. Nevertheless, the particular handling of this story, within the regional news opt-out, was especially inappropriate and unsuitable and therefore in breach of Ofcom's Broadcasting Code.

"**Trail**: Although the images selected for the trail were not of the actual fatal stabbing, the accompanying script may well have left the impression it was. ('Coming up—knife crime Britain. Shocking pictures of the mindless murder that was caught on camera.')

Viewers watching the Soccer Aid charity programme would have been unprepared for such a violent interlude. There was no time for a proper context to be established, and there was no information transmitted prior to the images being broadcast.

Nevertheless, it is clear from ITV's response that the complaints have been considered seriously. We welcome the acknowledgement that greater care should have been taken, and that new guidelines have now been issued. In view of this, and the fact that, as the trail was shown at 22:15 it was not likely to be seen by children, we consider the matter resolved."

GMTV News—Breach of 2.3.

ITV News, Sky News, Trail for ITV News—Resolved.

BBC News—Not in breach.

Funniest Ever You've Been Framed

ITV1, November 1, 2008, 18.00

Introduction

Funniest Ever You've Been Framed featured a selection of humorous home video clips, including unseen material and clips shown in previous series of *You've Been Framed*.

This programme broadcast a clip in which a teenage boy microwaved an egg in its shell. The boy was filmed as he removed the heated egg (with its shell intact) from the microwave and held it up to the camera. Moments after this the egg exploded with a loud "bang", spraying its content over the camera lens.

During the clip the voice over said:

Voice over (at the beginning of the clip): "Rule one of many, here's why you should never, ever put whole eggs in the microwave".

Voice over (at end of the clip): "For pity sake don't try it yourself."

A viewer felt that the broadcast of this clip was inappropriate and would encourage children to imitate dangerous behaviour.

Ofcom asked ITV to comment with reference to r.1.13 of the Code, which includes:

"Dangerous behaviour, or the portrayal of dangerous behaviour, that is likely to be easily imitable by children in a manner that is harmful, must not be broadcast before the watershed, or when children are particularly likely to be listening, unless there is editorial justification."

Response

ITV stated that *You've Been Framed* is a "very long running and popular family entertainment show, familiar to most viewers". It said that where clips show any potentially dangerous behaviour ITV always takes care to consider whether the behaviour is likely to be easily imitable by children in a manner that might be harmful.

The broadcaster considered the clip to show an unwise but not seriously dangerous prank. It stated that the clip in question was broadcast in at least three previous *You've Been Framed* series, without raising any viewer concerns.

ITV highlighted the warning given by the voice over at the beginning and end of the clip, which said it "makes it clear that this is not an activity that should be imitated by viewers". ITV stated that, in the context of the repeated warnings and the overall tone of the programme mocking this sort of prank, it considered that the behaviour was not likely to be imitated in a harmful way by children. It also considered that, given the nature of the programme, there was editorial justification for including the clip.

However, in response to the complaint, ITV said it removed the clip from the programme (and from all the previous programmes in which it has featured) in order to prevent any further repeat broadcast. The broadcaster apologised for any distress caused to the complainant.

Decision

Ofcom noted *You've Been Framed* is an established programme that has a familiar style of ridiculous and irreverent humour.

However, the clip in question featured everyday household items: a microwave and an egg. Both items are regularly used and are of easy access. The clip itself clearly showed viewers how to make an egg explode—a potentially dangerous activity which, given its visual impact, may appeal to children. In light of these factors, Ofcom had concerns about the broadcast of this material at a time when a significant number of children were watching; audience data shows that 15.9 per cent of the audience consisted of children under the age of 15 (a total of approximately 864,000 individual children).

Ofcom noted the warnings provided at the beginning and end of the clip. However, given the clip presented laughter from the studio audience after the egg exploded and showed no negative consequences (e.g. any physical harm or pain to the individuals involved), Ofcom considered that this would have weakened the impact of these warnings. As a result, the clip could have been interpreted as both humorous and harmless, therefore encouraging children to imitate such behaviour.

While Ofcom had concerns about the broadcast of this material, it noted ITV's apology and its assurance not to repeat the material. In light of this, Ofcom considers the matter resolved.

Emmerdale

ITV1, December 16, 2008, 19.00

Introduction

Emmerdale is a weekly peak-time drama serial generically referred to as a "soap". The King family, including brothers Jimmy, Mathew and Carl, arrived in Emmerdale in 2004. Since arriving they have been portrayed as ruthless and successful businessmen involved in numerous scandals in the village. In this one-hour special Mathew King was to marry local business woman, Anna. However, his brother Carl had other ideas, informing the bride that Mathew had been responsible for her father's recent death (which was partly true). Anna cancelled the wedding and a fist fight developed between Mathew and Carl as a number of wedding guests and their brother Jimmy tried to intervene.

Seventeen viewers complained to Ofcom that the fight which developed between the King brothers was too graphic and violent for the time of transmission in the early evening at 19.00. Ofcom asked the broadcaster to comment with regard to r.1.11 which states that "Violence, its after effects and descriptions of violence...must be appropriately limited in programmes broadcast before the watershed".

Response

ITV1 said that this episode was very carefully considered in relation to rr.1.11 and 2.3 (generally accepted standards). It said that like other TV "soaps" *Emmerdale* regularly includes family conflicts. It continued that the scenes in question were a dramatic and emotionally charged climax to a long-running storyline of deceit and betrayal between family members and, given the nature of the established characters, regular viewers would have expected a confrontation between them to be explosive and potentially physical.

The broadcaster said that it was not its intention to cause viewers concern or distress, and it was aware that emotional and confrontational scenes are not to the taste of all its viewers. As a result it preceded the programme with information that the episode included a "violent encounter for the King brothers". It also edited the scenes in an attempt to moderate the explicit violence of the confrontation to a level that it judged would be acceptable for the editorial context in which it was portrayed, and that the scene in question consisted primarily of pushing, shoving and raised voices interspersed by dialogue. It said that it was filmed carefully to minimise detailed shots of violent blows seen by the viewer and, whilst a lamp stand was picked up and used in a threatening manner, care was taken to ensure that the subsequent blow from the lamp stand was not explicitly shown.

ITV1 continued that in considering the script and during editing of the sequence in question it took into account previous adjudications by Ofcom in relation to violence in "soap" dramas, for example in Bulletin 103. It concluded that the degree of threat and of actual violence was appropriately limited and, whilst it regretted that some viewers were concerned by the scenes, it considered most viewers' expectations of programming of this nature, for this time in the evening, were met.

Decision

Ofcom noted that the fight between Carl and Mathew King was sustained and at times vicious. Where ITV1 had described the action as "potentially physical", the programme did in fact feature blows and kicks (delivered and sustained by both men to the body and head) and the use of a large metal lamp stand as a weapon (which was pushed into Mathew's face with corresponding sound effect). The level of violence was further heightened by blood flowing from wounds, the smashing of household objects and a number of people shouting and screaming. This tense and violent scene lasted for two minutes. The next and final part of the programme featured a sequence showing a bloodied Mathew King behind the wheel of a van, crashing into a wall at speed. He flew through the windscreen landing with a loud thud on the floor. He died in close-up with his face covered in blood.

Emmerdale starts at 19.00, some two hours before the 21.00 watershed. It is firmly positioned and established in peak family viewing time as a "soap". It is therefore always likely that some children will be in the audience watching with adults in the home. Audience figures for this episode indicate that 482,000 children between the ages of 4 and 15, representing an 18.8 per cent share of all children viewing the television at the time, were watching the programme. This figure is not insignificant and brings with it a responsibility on the part of the broadcaster to ensure that any violence it portrays as part of the storyline is appropriately limited for the time of transmission. The broadcaster must therefore strike a balance between providing quality and engaging drama in a peak time slot and complying with the requirements of the Code as regards protecting members of the public in general and in particular children.

Ofcom noted the broadcaster regretted that some of its viewers were concerned by the scenes of violence in this episode although it considered that overall audience expectations were met. In addition, Ofcom noted that the broadcaster referred to Broadcast Bulletin 103 to which it looked for guidance regarding this particular episode. However, Ofcom considered that the In Breach Finding published against ITV1 (for another episode of *Emmerdale*) in Broadcast Bulletin 83 and a corresponding Note to Broadcasters in the same publication was more pertinent in this case. In the Note to Broadcasters Ofcom stated that:

> "Ofcom has considered that a number of cases it has dealt with recently have contained violence that goes to the limits of what is acceptable in terms of the Broadcasting Code. Therefore, it would like to remind broadcasters to take particular notice of Rule 1.11 of the Code...when portraying violence in pre-watershed programmes".

In Ofcom's view this programme contained an unacceptable level of violence for broadcast in a programme which began at 19.00 when children were likely to be watching, and indeed were, in considerable numbers. Ofcom therefore judged that the fight scene between Mathew and Karl King was in breach of r.1.11 of the Code.

Celebrity Big Brother

Channel 4, January 2 to 23, 2009

Introduction

Celebrity Big Brother is a reality based television show (based on the well-established *Big Brother* format) where 11 celebrity contestants are confined together in a controlled environment ("the House"). It is filmed 24 hours a day for three weeks. Whilst in the House, contestants "nominate" which of their fellow housemates they consider should be "evicted" from the House, with the ultimate decision as to who should leave being made by the public by means of voting via telephone. The last housemate left at the end of the series is the winner of the show. The winner of *Celebrity Big Brother 2009* was Ulrika Jonsson.

Ofcom received 527 complaints about *Celebrity Big Brother 2009*. The majority of the complainants considered that housemates were bullied or were responsible for bullying other housemates. In particular, American rap artist Coolio was the focus of many complaints for the manner in which he behaved towards some female housemates, most notably singer Michelle Heaton. Complainants were concerned that he made "misogynistic" and "sexist" comments and subjected them to "bullying" and "boorish" behaviour. However, Ofcom also received complaints that Coolio was negatively stereotyped as an aggressive black man.

Decision

Under the Communications Act 2003, Ofcom has a statutory duty to set standards for the content of broadcast television programmes in a Code with which broadcasters must comply. Ofcom must ensure broadcasters comply with the Code and perform their duties in light of the European Convention of Human Rights which provides for the right to freedom of expression.

Under the Code, broadcasters are required to apply generally accepted standards so as to ensure adequate protection to the audience from offensive or harmful material. In applying generally accepted standards the Code requires that material which may cause offence is justified by the context. Context includes such factors as the editorial content of the programme, the service on which it is broadcast and the likely expectations of the audience. Ofcom recognised that *Big Brother* is the type of programme that will almost inevitably contain controversial material and that emotional and potentially offensive exchanges will at times occur between housemates. As a series of *Celebrity Big Brother* continues, some language and behaviour capable of causing offence to some viewers will almost inevitably be broadcast. When such potentially offensive material is to be shown, it is the broadcaster's duty to ensure that it is at all times editorially justified and complies with the requirements of the Code by being placed in context. This means there is always the potential for material, which some viewers might find personally offensive, to be transmitted.

Big Brother is an entertainment programme and viewers therefore perceive that although what happens in the House is "entertainment", they also view it as "reality" i.e. they view the events as real events happening to real people. This means that the audience can genuinely become concerned for the welfare of housemates, but in the knowledge and expectation that any serious problematic or anti-social behaviour will be appropriately dealt with. This has become one of the generally accepted features of *Big Brother*.

Channel Four, in the *Big Brother* programme format, has established various editorial mechanisms through which inappropriate behaviour in the House can be challenged. For instance, through discussion in the diary room, *Big Brother* can confront and reprimand housemates about their behaviour, thereby acting as an important arbiter of what the public may perceive to be offensive language or behaviour. Reactions by housemates, *Big Brother* interventions and the diary room are all part of the well understood architecture of the programme and the context within which Channel Four is able to appropriately broadcast potentially offensive material.

In the case of *Celebrity Big Brother*, each participant is paid a fee for taking part. For them therefore, their presence in the House is a form of paid work. The contestants are free, at any time, to remove themselves from the programme, if they feel they are, or have been, unfairly treated. In addition, should any participant upon leaving the programme feel they were treated unfairly they can make a complaint to Ofcom about any alleged unfairness. Ofcom did not receive any complaints from any of the participants in *Celebrity Big Brother 2009.*

This series of *Celebrity Big Brother* featured, like previous series, a deliberately disparate group of celebrities. They included American rapper Coolio, singer LaToya Jackson, TV presenters Terry Christian and Ulrika Jonsson, glamour model Lucy Pinder and singer Michelle Heaton. Ofcom noted that, in particular, the relationship between Coolio and Michelle Heaton became fractious. It appeared clear to viewers that Coolio enjoyed baiting and teasing female housemates. However, when Coolio teased Michelle for allegedly having feelings for another housemate (Ben) she became very upset. Sensing he had hit a nerve, Coolio continued to tease her about it. It was at this point that Channel 4, through Big Brother, talked to both Coolio and Michelle separately in the diary room about what had developed between them. Michelle appeared comforted by her conversations with Big Brother and some of the other housemates, and Coolio, when told that his behaviour could be seen as intimidating, appeared to be genuinely disconcerted that this could be the case. Ofcom noted that Big Brother and fellow housemates managed to get Coolio and Michelle to resolve their issues, and their "feud" was amicably resolved when Coolio and Michelle apologised to each other for their behaviour.

Ofcom recognised that arguments, disagreements and name calling between housemates is anticipated by many viewers of *Celebrity Big Brother* who understand that a varied group of people who have willingly confined themselves in the House are competing for attention in a potentially volatile environment. In Ofcom's view Coolio was a "larger than life" character in the House, playing the role for many viewers of the "villain of the piece", where such a role, after 10 years of Big Brother, is generally expected by the audience. He exhibited an acerbic wit; was clearly at times quite bored; baited female housemates; and, was at times, generally unpleasant, making statements and references that appeared calculated to be potentially offensive and provoke a reaction. However, Ofcom accepted that it is important that Channel 4 accurately reflects what has happened in the House so that viewers are adequately informed regarding the characters and conduct of individual housemates. This is especially important given that it is viewers' understanding of this combination of factors that informs their voting decisions. Were Channel 4 significantly to "sanitise" events which have occurred in the House it could be seen by viewers as an attempt to manipulate voting.

Ofcom acknowledged that *Celebrity Big Brother* is the type of programme in which controversial matters will inevitably be raised and emotional and offensive exchanges occur, as the characters of the participants are revealed. Given this, what is broadcast may contain language and behaviour which is capable of causing offence to viewers. Viewers therefore expect the broadcaster, through Big Brother, to challenge such behaviour appropriately and for it to be in context. When Ofcom viewed this series it noted that there was indeed friction between a number of celebrity housemates: tempers frayed, emotions at times ran high, personalities clashed and name-calling abounded. The housemates did however work towards defusing tense situations themselves and, where necessary, Channel 4, through Big Brother, intervened. Big Brother, for example, called housemates to the diary room to talk through their behaviour to resolve more highly charged situations and to discuss how behaviour could be improved. As a consequence Ofcom did not consider that compliance with the Code had been brought into question by Channel 4's handling of the conduct exhibited in this particular series.

It concluded therefore that this series complied with the Code because any potentially offensive content that was shown and the manner in which the friction and the arguments were handled and presented by Big Brother on behalf of Channel 4, were adequately justified by the context.

Dispatches: The Trouble With Boris

Channel 4, March 30, 2009, 20.00

Introduction

This edition of the *Dispatches* investigative current affairs programme examined Boris Johnson's record since becoming Mayor of London in May 2008, and questioned his performance during his first year in office. It referred to the Mayor's policies on issues such as transport and the environment and questioned whether the Mayor had a coherent plan for London. The programme also looked at various high level resignations by senior members of the Mayor's team and questioned the Mayor's relationship with certain business figures, including the owners of *The Telegraph* newspaper for which the Mayor writes a weekly column. The programme included the views of a number of contributors and also included extracts from interviews with Boris Johnson and speeches made by him.

Ofcom received 18 complaints about the programme. Viewers considered that the programme made allegations about Boris Johnson which were unfair and that it was not presented with due impartiality.

In relation to fairness, Ofcom can only consider and adjudicate on complaints of unfairness when they have been brought by the "person affected" (or someone on their behalf). Ofcom had received no complaint from Boris Johnson (or from anyone authorised by him).

In relation to the concerns about impartiality, there is a requirement for broadcasters to maintain "due impartiality" when dealing with matters of political or industrial controversy or relating to current public policy. Ofcom considered that this edition of *Dispatches* did, on several occasions, deal with matters of political controversy and/or matters relating to current public policy. For example, there was discussion of London's transport policy, including reference to the Congestion Charging Zone. The programme also included sequences on Olympic funding, London's Low Emission Zone, housing policy, planning policy, the management of the Metropolitan Police and the proposed expansion of Heathrow.

Therefore, in relation to these controversial matters, Channel 4 was required to ensure that they were treated with due impartiality in accordance with s.5 of the Code. In particular:

- r.5.5, which states that "due impartiality on matters of political or industrial controversy and matters relating to current public policy must be preserved"; and

- r.5.9, which states that "presenters and reporters...may express their own views on matters of political or industrial controversy or matters relating to current public policy. However, alternative viewpoints must be adequately represented either in the programme, or in a series of programmes taken as a whole".

Decision

In considering whether a programme such as *Dispatches: The Trouble With Boris* breaches the Code, Ofcom must exercise its duties in a way which is compatible with art.10 of the European Convention of Human Rights. This protects the right to freedom of expression. This right encompasses the right to hold opinions and to receive and impart information and ideas without interference by public authority. Applied to broadcasting, art.10 therefore protects the broadcaster's right to transmit material as well as the audience's right to receive it, as long as the broadcaster ensures compliance with the rules of the Code as well as the law.

In addition, when reaching its decision in this case, Ofcom bore in mind that investigative journalism plays an essential role in public service broadcasting and is in the public interest. It is of paramount importance that broadcasters such as Channel 4 continue to explore controversial subject matter even where the broadcast of such material polarises opinion and results in complaints to Ofcom. In making investigative programmes, broadcasters must take care however to ensure that the material broadcast is in accordance with the Code. For instance matters of political controversy and matters of current public policy must be treated with due impartiality. The Code explains that "due" is an important qualification to the concept of impartiality. While impartiality itself means not favouring one side over another, "due" means adequate or appropriate to the subject and nature of the programme. The result is that an equal division of time does not have to be given to every view, nor does every argument have to be represented.

Having considered the programme's treatment of those matters to which the requirement of due impartiality applied, Ofcom concluded that overall due impartiality was maintained. There were a number of reasons for this.

The programme began with footage of Boris Johnson addressing a crowd shortly after becoming mayor. He says:

"That's my pledge to London folks, a safer, greener, fairer city".

The presenter then makes the editorial thrust of the programme clear with the following:

"He's funny, charming and unconventional but, with the nation's capital in the grip of a financial crisis, has Mayor Boris got the vision to bring London forward?"

While the programme certainly goes on to level criticisms at Boris Johnson, the alternative viewpoints required by the Code were also apparent. Within the opening five minutes of the programme there is an interview with Mr Johnson in which he outlines what he hopes to achieve by the end of his first term in office. In respect of the other controversial issues discussed in the programme, the views of the Mayor are also demonstrated.

These views are set out by means of footage from Boris Johnson's speeches both before and after his election and by extracts of his appearances at Mayor's Question Time at the London Assembly. At times too, the presenter explains the Mayor's position. For example, we are told that the Mayor is scrapping the Western extension to the London Congestion Charge Zone. On the one hand the presenter notes this will result in 30,000 more cars entering the area, but he then goes on to explain that the Mayor is adopting this policy in order to "help traders and small business" and goes on to state that the Mayor "is committed to cutting carbon emissions in other ways".

Viewers were also informed that the Mayor is suspending the latest phase in the Low Emission Zone. Although one interviewee tells the presenter that such a zone is the best policy for tackling air pollution from vehicles, the viewer is then informed by the presenter that the Mayor's reason for this suspension is because of the Low Emission Zone's "detrimental impact on small businesses". The presenter adds that the Mayor has a range of other strategies "to improve London's air, including opposing the expansion of Heathrow".

Footage is also shown of the Mayor defending his housing policy. The programme explains that this policy has seen the Mayor accused of moulding his housing strategy for political advantage. The Mayor however is seen telling the Assembly that his team has been "extremely successful in our negotiations with boroughs across London in producing a fantastic commitment to affordable housing in incredibly difficult circumstances". The presenter also states "Boris told us at no time was consideration given to the political leadership of a borough" (in the context of the Mayor's housing policy).

In conclusion, Ofcom found that the nature of this programme was clearly signalled by its title *The Trouble With Boris* and there is no doubt that it included a number of critical observations about Boris Johnson's performance as Mayor of London and his policies. However, to comply with the Code's requirement of "due impartiality" in making these observations, the programme makers were not obliged to present every facet of every argument. In the circumstances of this programme in Ofcom's opinion sufficient "alternative views" were presented in such a way that the programme was not in breach of the Code.

Not in Breach of Rules 5.5 and 5.9.

Five News at 7

Five, February 5, 2009, 19.00

Introduction

A viewer complained about an item during this edition of *Five News at 7*, in which a Garmin GPS running watch was reviewed. The complainant considered the tone and nature of the review to be promotional for the watch, that it made unflattering comments about a competitive brand and that

Garmin might have had paid for the coverage. Generally, the complainant questioned the appropriateness of a news programme including an item of this nature.

Ofcom sought Five's comments under the following Code rules:

- r.10.3: Products and services must not be promoted in programmes;

- r.10.4: No undue prominence may be given in any programme to a product or service; and

- r.10.5: Product placement is prohibited.

Ofcom also requested background information about how the watch came to be reviewed and what arrangements to feature it might have been made with the manufacturer or supplier.

<u>Response</u>

Overall, Five denied that the item was in breach of rr.10.3 and 10.5 of the Code, but accepted that "on balance" the watch may have been unduly prominent and therefore in breach of r.10.4.

Five explained that *Five News at 7* had been relaunched at the beginning of 2009, targeting a young male audience. As part of the revamp an ad hoc gadget review feature was introduced. This feature included reviews of netbooks, video goggles and a mini cinema projector. The format of the review offered a pre-recorded piece followed by a live studio "chat'" with a "gadget expert".

The broadcaster confirmed that no product is ever featured through agreement with manufacturers and that no "valuable consideration" was received by Five in return for including the Garmin watch in the programme.

After a decision to review runners' watches, the production staff selected five possible models, but could obtain only the Garmin and the Timex watches. The Timex was received only after the pre-recorded report had been completed. Also, no expert could be found to discuss the watch in the live studio segment and the reviewing reporter therefore had to fill that role.

In respect of the pre-recorded report, Five pointed out that references were made to the watch being "chunky" and "oversized on girly wrists", and that it is complicated to use, "the simple functions seem anything but simple".

Further, the broadcaster commented, during the live interview it was said that the Garmin watch comes with a substantial price tag: "but all of this comes at a price, £279 to be precise"; "comes at a price, it's quite expensive"; "they are expensive, they are a luxury"; "there are other brands that are cheaper"; "you get what you pay for with these [GPS watches generally]". Five also drew attention to the Timex watch being referred to by name and shown in close-up on a Timex branded stand.

As to editorial justification, Five argued that GPS watches are no longer limited to elite athletes and that, bearing in mind the new target audience of the programme—young males—it considered a feature on running watches was editorially justified.

Taking into account all these points, Five did not accept that the item was in breach of rr.10.3 or 10.5. In Five's view, it was neither promotional, nor did it amount to product placement.

However, the broadcaster did "accept that some of the references and information may have gone too far when considering this [the undue prominence] rule". Further, Five accepted that the item could have given the impression of external commercial influence on the programme, although there was in fact no influence. Five acknowledged that making the report only when all of the watches intended for review were available would have been preferable.

Five said that the requirements of the Code had been discussed in detail with the production staff to avoid any further problems of this sort.

Decision

Ofcom noted that Five stated that there was no commercial arrangement in place and saw no evidence that product placement took place.

However, Five did recognise that the item may have, on balance, breached the rules on "undue prominence" (r.10.4 of the Code).

In Ofcom's view the item clearly gave undue prominence to the Garmin watch. Particularly important in this respect was the manner of the listing of the product's features combined with the positive comparison with the only other watch featured, and the nature of the shot in which the Garmin watch and attachments were set out in sequence on a table, teleshopping-style.

Ofcom's guidance to r.10.4 states that:

"Undue prominence" may result from:

- the presence of, or reference to, a product or service (including company names, brand names, logos) in a programme where there is no editorial justification; or
- the manner in which a product or service (including company names, brand names, logos) appears or is referred to in a programme.

The item comprised a pre-recorded report and a live studio discussion about the Garmin watch. Within the report, a number of close-ups of the watch were shown, the watch's on-screen functions were focused on, a heart monitor accessory was shown separately, the watch was shown being used with a wireless laptop link (including a screen shot), and a table-top shot showed the watch surrounded by all its accessories (which appeared one after another).

The audio included the following comments in reference to the watch:

- "small but genius invention";
- "as easy to charge as a mobile phone";
- "this watch gives you the best of both worlds—I say this watch, generally running watches";
- "you get what you pay for with these";

- "there are other brands that are cheaper—there are other models of Garmin that are cheaper—but you got a lot less functions";

- "with that you're getting GPS, you're getting a speedometer, you're getting a pedometer; but you go for something more basic, like the Timex one you have there in your right hand and you're getting little more than a stopwatch and a light"; and

- "And is it worth it though?"

- "I think it's pretty good—you can actually buy them online cheaper than that £279. They are expensive, they are a luxury, but I think they're quite good."

In Ofcom's view, the manner in which the watch was described and shown in the programme resulted in undue prominence.

Further, the way the watch was demonstrated and the editorial nature of the report appeared to have some features in common with a teleshopping promotion. For instance, the watch and its accessories were displayed on a table-top in a stop-frame sequence in the pre-recorded report.

A further factor in judging the context of undue prominence is the nature of the programme in which a report or sequence appears. In this case the review appeared as part of a news programme, part of the discussion provided by the show's news presenter. In such a context viewers would expect more balanced reporting and perceive the content as carrying particular authority. In such circumstances, the audience is likely to expect a more exacting test of undue prominence.

As to r.10.3 (that prohibits the promotion of products and services in programmes), in Ofcom's view the position of the item was very much more doubtful than argued by Five.

Rule 10.3 states that: "Products and services must not be promoted in programmes". Broadly, Ofcom determines whether a product or service has been promoted within programmes by assessing both the degree of prominence given and the manner in which the products or services are discussed or referred to. Either can lead to "promotion" on its own, depending on the extent and emphasis given to the coverage. Although promotion will frequently be active promotion—calls to action to purchase and the like—that is not, in itself, a necessary condition for breach of the rule.

In Ofcom's view this was not only a particularly egregious example of undue prominence, especially as it appeared in a news programme, but the product was featured so heavily and in terms that were essentially uncritical, that the report also breached r.10.3.

XXX Channel AKA—Playtime Two, Giggs Featuring Kyze

Channel AKA, June 25, 2009, approximately 22.45

Introduction

Channel AKA is an urban music channel whose licence is held by Mushroom TV Limited ("Mushroom TV"). The channel is available without any access restrictions. *XXX Channel AKA* is part of the channel's late night programming, broadcast between 22.00 and 05.30. The programme features music videos of a more adult nature containing stronger images.

A viewer complained about the broadcast of the music video "Playtime Two" by Giggs Featuring Kyze, which featured material of a sexual nature. The complainant considered the sexual material broadcast in this video too strong to be available at approximately 22.45 and on this channel. Ofcom noted that the video included: frequent shots of naked breasts; women wearing revealing thongs and pulling at their underwear to expose genital detail; women touching their breasts and genital area in a sexual manner; women squirting water and licking whipped cream off each other's naked breasts; frequent shots between women's legs (while wearing thongs); frequent close up shots of female buttocks (while wearing thongs); a brief shot of a woman pulling her buttocks apart to show anal detail; and a man simulating sexual stimulation between a woman's legs.

Ofcom asked Mushroom TV for its comments in relation to rr.2.1 (generally accepted standards) and 2.3 (material which may cause offence must be justified by the context).

Response

The broadcaster said that it did not consider the content of the music video to exceed generally accepted standards. It stated that *XXX Channel AKA* is broadcast post-watershed, between 22.00 and 05.30, and includes adult-oriented music videos primarily from the urban music genre. It highlighted that the music video complained of was broadcast at 22.45. Mushroom TV continued that the programme title *XXX Channel AKA* was clearly labelled both onscreen during the broadcast and on the Electronic Programme Guide. It also said that the channel is aimed at an adult audience and has low child audience figures.

However, in response to the complaint, Mushroom TV stated that it had withdrawn the video broadcast on June 25, 2009 from the late-night playlist and replaced it with an edited version.

Decision

Rule 2.3 makes clear that "in applying generally accepted standards broadcasters must ensure that material which may cause offence is justified by the context." "Context" in turn includes a variety of different potential factors such as the editorial content of the programme, the service on which the material is broadcast, the time of broadcast and the effect of the material on viewers who may come across it unawares. In this case Ofcom considered that, given the nature and strength of the sexual imagery broadcast in this particular music video, it had the clear potential to cause offence. Therefore the broadcaster was required to ensure that the material was justified by the context in order to provide adequate protection for viewers and compliance with the Code.

Ofcom appreciated that music videos are an artistic and creative medium, which can and do sometimes contain challenging content which some may find offensive. It recognised that the music video in this case was transmitted after the watershed during Channel AKA's late night programming, which is aimed at an adult audience and features material of a more adult nature. In addition Ofcom recognised that the programme title (*XXX Channel AKA*) would have provided some indication to viewers regarding the type of content included in the programme. Given these factors, Ofcom considered that there would have been a certain amount of audience expectation for the broadcast of more challenging material during this particular programme. In taking its decision Ofcom also had regard to the broadcaster's and the audience's right to freedom of expression under art.10 of the European Convention on Human Rights.

Ofcom was concerned by the strong sexual imagery included in the "Playtime Two" video and in particular the time of broadcast. This video contained frequent shots of naked breasts; women touching their breasts and genital area in a sexual manner; women licking whipped cream off each other's breasts; and a man simulating sexual stimulation on a woman. Given the strength of the material and the time of broadcast, Ofcom did not consider that the broadcaster had applied generally accepted standards. Despite the title of the programme and the later evening scheduling, Ofcom considered that this particular material would have exceeded audience expectations for a music programme of this nature broadcast at 22.45 without any access restrictions on a music channel.

While taking into account the name of the programme and that it does include music videos of a more adult nature, it was Ofcom's view that, on balance, the broadcaster did not apply generally accepted standards to this content and the material was not justified by the context. Therefore the material breached rr.2.1 and 2.3 of the Code.

Top Gear

BBC2, August 2, 2009, 20.00

Introduction

Top Gear is the BBC's long running entertainment series about cars, presented by Jeremy Clarkson and two co-presenters, James May and Richard Hammond. This edition, the final show of the programme's thirteenth series, featured a spoof remake of an advertisement for a Volkswagen car, which showed a man committing suicide with a gunshot to the head, followed by blood splattering out after the impact. The scene also included a depiction of the dead man lying in a pool of blood.

Fifty viewers contacted Ofcom to complain about this scene which they felt was too graphic and unsuitable for the time of broadcast (20.00) because children were watching. Ofcom noted that a subsequent repeat of the programme on August 3, 2009, in a 19.00 timeslot, removed the scene in which the man was seen shooting himself in the head. This mock advertisement was one of six or seven such advertisements in this segment of the programme which employed exaggerated and absurd themes to draw attention to the Volkswagen Sirocco's perceived lack of speed. Other "advertisements" contained references to the Bible, mothers-in-law, funerals and explosions. One advertisement included a scene in a hospital waiting room. An actor who had supposedly been in a car accident was seen holding what appeared to be his own severed arm from which blood spurted in large quantities for approximately two minutes.

Ofcom asked the BBC to comment on the complaints in light of the Code r.1.11 (violence to be appropriately limited before the watershed). We also asked it to explain the reasoning for editing out the image of the man shooting himself from the 19.00 repeat of the programme.

Response

The BBC pointed out that the Code does not preclude the depiction of all violence before the watershed, even when children are likely to be watching a programme. Rule 1.11 requires that violence should be appropriately limited and in this case, the BBC said, it believed that it was limited by what it described as "the ludicrous and obviously comic depiction of the suicide."

The BBC continued that the reason for the man committing suicide was preposterous—that he had failed to buy the diesel variant of a particular car and that the loss of blood following the shooting was absurdly and deliberately exaggerated. This comic exaggeration and distancing from reality, which characterised the whole segment, were such as to limit the actual depiction of violence in the same way as a violent sequence from a children's cartoon. The fact that the original Volkswagen advertisement was also shown in its entirety highlighted to viewers that this was a witty, if slightly grotesque, send up of a classic advertisement.

In relation to the removal of the image of the man shooting himself from the repeat of the programme, shown at 19.00, the BBC acknowledged that there would have been a certain number of children amongst the programme's audience. However, it said it believed that the depiction of the suicide was appropriately limited so as to make it suitable for transmission in the programme's usual slot. The programme was broadcast at 20.00 and the sequence in question was shown at just after 20.30. The programme-makers were conscious, however, that the repeat, transmitted at 19.00, might attract a significant number of younger children so the decision was taken to re-edit the sequence and remove the images of the gun shot. The BBC emphasised that it was not done because it was felt that there an editorial misjudgement in relation to the original transmission but because they were sensitive to the fact that there may be a "sliding scale of bedtimes" in many family homes.

Decision

When applying the Code, Ofcom must carry out its duties in light of art.10 of the European Convention of Human Rights, which provides for the right to freedom of expression. Ofcom must regulate potentially harmful or offensive material in a manner that respects freedom of expression—the broadcasters' right to transmit information and the audience's right to receive it. Ofcom must therefore seek an appropriate balance between protecting members of the public from harm and offence on the one hand and the broadcaster's right to freedom of expression on the other, taking into account context.

Ofcom recognised that *Top Gear* is a series with an established audience, some of whom are children. It is known, however, for its adult-orientated content and humour, which some viewers on occasions may find challenging. Viewers have, in general, come to expect these features of the programme. In the scene complained of, in a send-up of a well known Volkswagen advertisement, an actor is seen, at close quarters, apparently killing himself by shooting himself in the head. The aftermath of the shooting is also shown as described above.

Rule 1.11 is designed to protect children from depictions of violence and its after effects in programmes broadcast before the watershed. Therefore Ofcom considered whether children were likely to be viewing the programme. Audience data indicated that a significant number—204,000— younger viewers (those aged between 4 and 9 years) were watching the original broadcast at 20.00. Ofcom noted the BBC's decision to remove the image of the gunshot to the head from the programme broadcast in the earlier timeslot of 19.00, because they considered that a greater number of younger children may have been watching at this time. In fact, the audience figures showed that substantially less—36,000 fewer younger viewers— watched the repeat. Therefore it was the case that, whilst the programme of August 2, 2009 was not aimed specifically at children, the programme regularly attracts a strong child audience and the broadcaster should have taken this into consideration when including the scene in the later broadcast.

The rule states that violence before the watershed must be appropriately limited and must also be justified by the context. Firstly, Ofcom considered whether the violence was appropriately limited. Whilst the shooting scene was only a few seconds in duration, it was Ofcom's view that the spoof suicide was graphically depicted on screen with the man holding the gun to his temple and firing and blood splattering into the air after the bloody impact of the gunshot. Its realistic depiction meant that the violent imagery was not appropriately limited.

Ofcom then considered whether the scene was contextually justified. Context includes, but is not limited to: the editorial content of the programme; the service on which the material is broadcast; the degree of harm or offence likely to be caused; and the likely expectation of the audience.

Firstly, in terms of the editorial content of the programme Ofcom took into account the established nature of *Top Gear* as described above. It also considered the BBC's argument that the comic exaggeration inherent in the spoof advertisement overall, and in this scene in particular, rendered it inoffensive and, in context, justifiable. While scenes such as the hospital patient with the severed arm, described above, were so comically exaggerated and preposterous that they could be said to be justified by the overall context of the *Top Gear* series as described above, the depiction of suicide was of a distinct nature from this and so not justified by the context.

In Ofcom's view, it was precisely because *Top Gear* is an established entertainment programme which features a typical sort of humour that many viewers, including some adults watching with children, would not have expected such a violent scene to appear. Ofcom noted there was no information before the spoof advertisement was shown which would have prepared viewers for its potentially disturbing nature and alerted adult viewers to the fact that it may be unsuitable for younger viewers. These factors taken together meant that the scene exceeded audience expectations for the programme and led Ofcom, on balance, to conclude that there was no editorial justification for its inclusion.

MTV Live: Isle of MTV music festival, featuring Lady Gaga

MTV One, November 2, 2009, 16.00

Introduction

MTV is a music channel available on satellite and cable platforms. The Isle of MTV music festival took place in July 2009 and featured a number of pop musicians. This programme included a 30 minute performance by Lady Gaga which was recorded at the festival and transmitted on November 2, 2009. During her performance, Lady Gaga addressed the audience and said "put your hands up in the air and dance, you motherfuckers". One viewer complained about the broadcast of the word "motherfuckers" at 16.00 on a weekday at a time when children could be watching.

Ofcom asked MTV Networks Europe ("MTVNE"), which complies the channel, for its comments under r.1.14 (the most offensive language must not be broadcast before the watershed) of the Code.

Response

MTVNE unreservedly apologised for the transmission of the language and explained that the programme was broadcast in error.

MTVNE explained that the programme was originally produced and edited by its sister company in Italy, and then viewed and complied by its compliance team at MTV in London with all the offensive language removed. After the material was complied, MTV in London requested the Italian office to make technical alterations to the programme's sound track. The Italian office mistakenly used the original, unedited audio of the concert to make the changes however, and this error resulted in the offensive language being made intelligible again on the soundtrack.

MTVNE outlined the extensive steps it took when it became aware of the broadcast of this offensive language. These included writing to the complainant and transmitting an apology to viewers the following week, and introducing further compliance checks on all material delivered from Italy.

Decision

Ofcom research on offensive language identified that the word "fuck" and its derivatives were considered by viewers to be very offensive. Ofcom noted MTVNE's apology for the broadcast of this offensive language and the action MTVNE took since it became aware of its transmission, including an on-air apology and the introduction of further compliance checks.

However, r.1.14 of the Code states unequivocally that "the most offensive language must not be broadcast before the watershed". Therefore the broadcast of this language before the watershed in this instance is a breach of r.1.14.

GLOSSARY

Absolute privilege—a defence to an action in defamation which attaches to fair, accurate and contemporaneous reports of court proceedings as well as publication of official reports of parliamentary proceedings.

Acquittal—the setting free of a defendant to criminal proceedings, often as a result of him being found not guilty.

Act of Parliament—a law or group of laws made by Parliament; another term for a statute.

Advocate—a person who speaks on behalf of another in court. An advocate will usually need to be legally qualified in order to have rights of audience in the courts.

Affidavit—a document sworn by a witness which gives account of that witness's evidence. Affidavits are commonly used in interim proceedings.

Appeal—an application by a party to litigation to a superior court to have the merits of the decision of an inferior court looked into by that higher court. In some cases leave of the superior court will be needed in order to be able to bring an appeal.

Arrestable offence—defined by s.24 of the Police and Criminal Evidence Act 1984 as:

(i) an offence for which the sentence is fixed by law (e.g. murder);

(ii) an offence for which the maximum punishment for a person over the age of 21 is at least five years' imprisonment; or

(iii) certain other specified offences. These are a group of miscellaneous offences set out in the Act which were arrestable before the Act was passed but which do not fit into the above categories.

A police officer is empowered to arrest without warrant a suspect upon reasonable suspicion that the suspect has committed, is in the process of committing, or is about to commit an arrestable offence. See also "Serious Arrestable Offence".

Attorney-General—the principal law officer of the Crown. One of his duties is to bring important prosecutions on behalf of the Crown. Some prosecutions (e.g. for the offence of publishing certain harmful works likely to fall into the hands of children) may not be brought without his consent. He will also conduct civil proceedings on behalf of the Crown.

Bail—the freeing of a person accused of a criminal offence on the basis of an obligation to return to the court or police station at a specific date and time in the future. There is a right to bail in every case but the police and the court may withhold bail from a suspect where there is reason to believe one or more of a list of grounds in the Bail Act 1976, the most common being that:

(i) the defendant will fail to surrender to custody;

(ii) the defendant will commit further offences whilst on bail;

(iii) the defendant will interfere with witnesses or otherwise obstruct the administration of justice.

Balance of probabilities—the standard of proof which must be achieved in a civil trial. This standard is met where one party shows that his version of events is more probable than not.

Bill—a document submitted to Parliament with a view to its being passed into law. Once a Bill has been passed it becomes an Act of Parliament.

Beyond reasonable doubt—the standard of proof of the prosecution in a criminal trial. The prosecution must show (to the magistrates in the magistrates' court and to the jury in the Crown Court) that there is no reasonable doubt that the defendant committed the offence for which he is charged.

Blasphemy—the offence which is committed when a person publishes material which amounts to indecency or ridicule concerning the Anglican faith.

British Board of Film Classification—A body set up to provide a classification certificate to each film and video based on the suitability of the film for a particular age group.

British Broadcasting Corporation—a body created by Royal Charter in 1926 which makes and broadcasts radio and television programmes.

Broadcast—the transmission of visual images, sounds or other information by wireless telegraphy which:

(a) is capable of being lawfully received by members of the public; or

(b) is transmitted for presentation to members of the public (Copyright, Designs and Patents Act 1988, s.6).

Broadcasting in the UK is regulated by Ofcom.

Burden of proof—the duty of proving a case, imposed by the court on the party trying to show that a certain issue is true. In criminal cases the general rule is that the prosecution has the burden of proving every fact in issue including disproving any defence raised by the defendant. In civil cases the party asserting a fact has the burden of proving it. The claimant must therefore prove that he has a cause of action and the defendant will have the burden of proving any defence raised. See also "Standard of Proof".

Claimant—the person who commences an action in a civil case.

Common law—a term relating to the law of England. It is a variable term dependent on context and may mean any of the following:

(a) that law which results from the system of binding precedent operated by the judiciary (as distinct from statute-based law);

(b) the original and proper law of England as administered by the common law courts (as distinct from equity);

(c) the entire law of England (as distinct from the Continental system of law known as civil law).

Contempt—any of a number of criminal offences relating to interference with the proper administration of courts of justice (see the Contempt of Court Act 1981).

Copyright—a property right which exists in:

(a) original literary, dramatic, musical or artistic works;

(b) sound recordings, films or broadcasts; and

(c) the typographical arrangement of published editions (Copyright, Designs and Patents Act 1988, s.1).

Damages—the term given to an award of money in the civil courts, paid by the defendant to the claimant by way of compensation for loss to the claimant. The claimant may request either liquidated or unliquidated damages. An application for a fixed sum of money (e.g. as a result of an action for an unpaid debt) is a request for liquidated damages. Unliquidated damages refers to a general request for compensation, the exact amount to be assessed by the judge or, in the case of a defamation action, by the jury. In addition, damages may fall into one of the following categories:

- *compensatory*—the damages awarded represent the sum of money that the claimant has lost;

- *contemptuous*—an extremely low award, usually reserved for cases where the claimant has technically won his case but the court has a low opinion of his claim;

- *exemplary*—usually a large award of damages which has, as its aim, the punishment of the defendant rather than the compensation of the claimant. A common example of such a case is where a defendant has calculated that the profit he will make from a libel will exceed any amount of damages he will be required to pay;

- *nominal*—a low award of damages used where the claimant has won his case but has suffered no loss and no moral blame can be said to attach to either party. A sum of less than £5 is common for this type of award;

- *substantial*—a potentially confusing term which refers to any award of damages in excess of nominal damages.

Data—

"information which—
- (a) is being processed by means of equipment operating automatically in response to instructions given for that purpose,
- (b) is recorded with the intention that it should be processed by means of such equipment,
- (c) is recorded as part of a relevant filing system or with the intention that it should form part of a relevant filing system, or
- (d) does not fall within paragraph (a), (b) or (c) but forms part of an accessible record an educational record or an accessible public record."

See the Data Protection Act 1998, s.1.

Defamation—a cause of action which is sub-divided into two categories (libel and slander) and which concerns a person's reputation.

Defendant—the person who is prosecuted in a criminal case and against whom an action is brought by the claimant in a civil case.

Delegated legislation—subordinate legislation created by a body other than Parliament under parliamentary authority. Such legislation may take the form of Orders in Council, Statutory Instruments or Bye-laws.

Director of Public Prosecutions—a legal officer of the government who brings certain important prosecutions; the head of the Crown Prosecution Service.

Distribution Right—a property right of a performer preventing the issuing to the public of a recording of a performance without the performer's consent.

European Commission of Human Rights—a commission which is empowered by international treaty to receive a petition from a state or individual who claims that there has been a violation of a right set out in the European Convention on Human Rights. The Commission acts as a filter in relation to applications that are made to the European Court of Human Rights: in order to get to the court, an applicant must first go through the Commission. The first filter results from the Commission's ability to reject unworthy complaints; the second results from its remit to attempt to effect a settlement of the matter between the parties concerned. A failure to do so may result in the matter being passed to the European Court of Human Rights. See also "European Court of Human Rights" and "European Convention on Human Rights".

European Convention on Human Rights—a short name for the European Convention for the Protection of Human Rights and Fundamental Freedoms, an international treaty which sets out various rights and freedoms of the individual. See also "European Commission of Human Rights" and "European Court of Human Rights".

European Court of Human Rights—a court which sits in Strasbourg to hear disputes as to the proper interpretation of the European Convention on Human Rights. See also "European Commission of Human Rights" and "European Convention on Human Rights".

European Union—the organisation formally known as the European Economic Community and created by The Treaty of Rome 1957. The original purpose of creating a free trade area among its Members has since been expanded by The Treaty on European Union (the Maastricht Treaty) to include goals of political and monetary union as well as a common defence policy.

There are various institutions with responsibility for administration of the Union, notably the Commission in Brussels, the Parliament in Strasbourg and the European Court of Justice in Luxembourg.

Ex parte injunction—an interim injunction obtained from the court, usually as a matter of urgency, without notification to the party against whom the injunction is sought.

Fair comment—a defence to an action for defamation based on a comment, made honestly, on a matter of public interest.

Indictment—a written accusation that a person has committed a crime; the document which commences proceedings in the Crown Court.

Injunction—an order of the court prohibiting a person from doing something.

An *interim* injunction is an injunction granted before, and expressed to last until, the trial of the matter at issue.

Innuendo—a meaning attached to words (in a libel action) which is other than their plain and obvious meaning.

Inter alia—"amongst other things".

Judicial review—an application to the Administrative Court pertaining to the legality of the action of a certain body.

Justification—a defence to an action in defamation based on the factual accuracy of the words used by the defendant.

Legal Aid—the system of financial assistance that can be obtained by the bringer or defender of proceedings in civil cases and by the defendant in criminal cases. Generally the applicant must show that he has a meritorious case and that his disposable income and capital are below certain limits. See the Legal Aid Act 1988.

Lending right—see "Rental Right".

Libel—a defamatory publication in a form capable of permanence.

Malice—to publish a statement knowing it to be false or being reckless as to its truth or falsity. Malice will defeat the defences of fair comment and qualified privilege in a defamation action. Malice is an essential ingredient in the tort of malicious falsehood.

Mitigation—an address to the court made by the defendant or his advocate in a criminal case. Such a speech is made after conviction and before sentence.

Moral rights—any of the set of rights created by the Copyright, Designs and Patents Act 1988, namely the right to be identified as the author or director of a work, the right to object to derogatory treatment of one's work and the right not to be falsely attributed as the author of a work.

Obscenity—an offence which a person commits by publishing obscene material, i.e. material that tends to deprave and corrupt persons who are likely to see, hear or read it.

Ofcom—the Office of Communications. The regulatory body for the media industries, which deals with regulations of both content and licensing. Set up in 2003, it has taken over the roles of the previous regulators, including the Broadcasting Standards Commission and the Independent Television Commission.

Official Secret—any information which is protected under the Official Secrets Acts. Under the Official Secrets Act 1989 such information will fall into one of six categories: security and intelligence; defence; international relations; crime; information on government phone-tapping, interception of letters or other communications; information entrusted in confidence to other states or international organisations.

Parliament—the body comprising the House of Commons, House of Lords and The Queen.

Performers' rights—one of a set of property and non-property rights which outlaw the exploitation of performances without the performers' consent.

Prosecution—the person or persons bringing proceedings against a defendant in a criminal case.

Play—

(a) any dramatic piece, whether involving improvisation or not, which is given wholly or in part by one or more persons actually present and performing and in which the whole or a major proportion of what is done by the person or persons performing, whether by way of speech, singing or acting, involves playing a role; and

(b) any ballet given wholly or in part by one or more persons actually present and performing, whether or not it falls within (a) (Theatres Act 1968).

Press Complaints Commission—a body set up by the newspaper industry to adjudicate upon complaints made in respect of newspaper articles. The PCC has drawn up a code of practice (see Appendix C), largely following the recommendations of the Calcutt Committee Report on Privacy.

Programme service—any of the following:

(a) any television service or other television programme service;

(b) any sound broadcasting service or licensable sound programme service;

(c) any other service which consists in the sending, by means of a tele-communication, of sounds or visual images or both either:

(i) for reception at two or more places in the United Kingdom (whether they are sent for simultaneous reception or at different times in response to requests made by different users of the service) or

(ii) for reception at a place in the United Kingdom for the purpose of being presented there to members of the public or to any group of persons. (Broadcasting Act 1990, s.201)

Qualified privilege—a defence to an action in defamation.

Racial hatred—a criminal offence where it is incited by any person.

Reproduction right—a property right of a performer which prevents the copying of a recording of a performance without the performer's consent.

Rental right—the property right of performers, authors and directors to authorise or prohibit the rental or lending of works containing their performances or including their works.

Satellite television—television broadcasts transmitted by satellite. These fall into one of two main groups for the purposes of regulation: *domestic* and *non-domestic* satellite service.

Serious arrestable offence—any arrestable offence (see above) which has, or is intended to have had, one of the following consequences:

(i) the death to or serious injury of any person;

(ii) substantial financial gain to any person;

(iii) serious financial loss to any person (Police and Criminal Evidence Act 1984, Sch.5).

The significance of a serious arrestable offence is that it gives the police greater powers in relation to the treatment of the suspect at a police station, e.g. a longer period of detention without charge.

Slander—defamation in a transient form; any defamation which is not libel.

Standard of proof—the measure of evidence which the court will require from a party in order to find in favour of that party. In criminal cases the standard of proof on the prosecution is "beyond reasonable doubt"; where a burden of proof rests on the defence the standard may be "on the balance of probabilities" or may be merely to produce "some evidence". The standard of proof in civil cases is "on the balance of probabilities".

Undertaking—A promise (especially in the course of legal   proceedings by a party or his legal representative) which may be enforced in the same manner as an injunction.

Video on Demand—a system which allows users to select and watch video content over a network as part of an interactive television system. VOD systems are either "streaming", in which viewing can start as the video streams over the Internet (or other network), or "download", in which the program is brought in its entirety to a set-top box before viewing starts.

Young Offender—An offender aged between 14 years and 18 years.

Youth Courts—Specialised form of magistrates' courts composed of persons whose names are on a special youth court panel which deal with the trial of children (10–13 years) and young persons.

Appendix A
DEFAMATION ACT 1952
(15 & 16 Geo. 6 & 1 Eliz. 2, c.66)

(1) Broadcast statements

Repealed by Broadcasting Act 1990 (c.42), s.203(3), Sch.21

(2) Slander affecting official, professional or business reputation

In an action for slander in respect of words calculated to disparage the plaintiff in any office, profession, calling, trade or business held or carried on by him at the time of the publication, it shall not be necessary to allege or prove special damage, whether or not the words are spoken of the plaintiff in the way of his office, profession, calling, trade or business.

(3) Slander of title, etc.

(1) In an action for slander of title, slander of goods or other malicious falsehood, it shall not be necessary to allege or prove special damage—

(a) if the words upon which the action is founded are calculated to cause pecuniary damage to the plaintiff and are published in writing or other permanent form; or

(b) if the said words are calculated to cause pecuniary damage to the plaintiff in respect of any office, profession, calling, trade or business held or carried on by him at the time of the publication.

(2) Section one of this Act shall apply for the purposes of this section as it applies for the purposes of the law of libel and slander.

Notes:

Section 3 amended by Theatres Act 1968 (c. 54), s.4(2); amended (England, Wales) by Cable and Broadcasting Act 1984 (c.46), s.28(2); amended (England, Wales) by Broadcasting Act 1990 (c.42), s.166(2)

(4) Unintentional defamation

Repealed by Defamation Act (1996 c.31), Sch.2, para.1

(5) Justification

In an action for libel or slander in respect of words containing two or more distinct charges against the plaintiff, a defence of justification shall not fail by reason only that the truth of every charge is not proved if the words not proved to be true do not materially injure the plaintiff's reputation having regard to the truth of the remaining charges.

(6) Fair comment

In an action for libel or slander in respect of words consisting partly of allegations of fact and partly of expression of opinion, a defence of fair comment shall not fail by reason only that the truth of every allegation of fact is not proved if the expression of opinion is fair comment having regard to such of the facts alleged or referred to in the words complained of as are proved.

(7) Qualified privilege of newspapers

Repealed by Defamation Act (1996 c.31), Sch.2, para.1

(8) Extent of Law of Libel Amendment Act 1888, s.3

Repealed by Defamation Act (1996 c.31), Sch.2, para.1

(9) Extension of certain defences to broadcasting

(1) Section three of the Parliamentary Papers Act 1840 (which confers protection in respect of proceedings for printing extracts from or abstracts of parliamentary papers) shall have effect as if the reference to printing included a reference to broadcasting by means of wireless telegraphy.

Repealed by Defamation Act (1996 c.31), Sch.2, para.1

(10) Limitation on privilege at elections

A defamatory statement published by or on behalf of a candidate in any election to a local government authority [to the Scottish Parliament] or to Parliament shall not be deemed to be published on a privileged occasion on the ground that it is material to a question in issue in the election, whether or not the person by whom it is published is qualified to vote at the election.

(11) Agreements for indemnity

An agreement for indemnifying any person against civil liability for libel in respect of the publication of any matter shall not be unlawful unless at the time of the publication that person knows that the matter is defamatory, and does not reasonably believe there is a good defence to any action brought upon it.

(12) Evidence of other damages recovered by plaintiff

In any action for libel or slander the defendant may give evidence in mitigation of damages that the plaintiff has recovered damages, or has brought actions for damages, for libel or slander in respect of the publication of words to the same effect as the words on which the action is founded, or has received or agreed to receive compensation in respect of any such publication.

(13) Consolidation of actions for slander, etc.

Section five of the Law of Libel Amendment Act 1888 (which provides for the consolidation, on the application of the defendants, of two or more actions for libel by the same plaintiff) shall apply to actions for slander and to actions for slander of title, slander of goods or other malicious falsehood as it applies to actions for libel; and references in that section to the same, or substantially the same, libel shall be construed accordingly.

(14) Application of Act to Scotland

This Act shall apply to Scotland subject to the following modifications, that is to say:—

(a) sections one, two, eight and thirteen shall be omitted;

(b) for section three there shall be substituted the following section—

"3. Actions for verbal injury.

In any action for verbal injury it shall not be necessary for the pursuer to aver or prove special damage if the words on which the action is founded are calculated to cause pecuniary damage to the pursuer.";

(c) subsection (2) of section four shall have effect as if at the end thereof there were added the words "Nothing in this subsection shall be held to entitle a defender to lead evidence of any fact specified in the declaration unless notice of his intention so to do has been given in the defences."; and

(d) for any reference to libel, or to libel or slander, there shall be substituted a reference to defamation; the expression "plaintiff" means pursuer; the expression "defendant" means defender; for any reference to an affidavit made by any person there shall be substituted a reference to a written declaration signed by that person; for any reference to the High Court there shall be substituted a reference to the Court of Session or, if an action of defamation is depending in the sheriff court in respect of the publication in question, the sheriff; the expression "costs" means expenses; and for any reference to a defence of justification there shall be substituted a reference to a defence of veritas.

(15)

Repealed by Northern Ireland Constitution Act 1973 (c. 36), Sch.6, Pt I

(16) Interpretation

(1) Any reference in this Act to words shall be construed as including a reference to pictures, visual images, gestures and other methods of signifying meaning.

Repealed by Defamation Act (1996 c.31), Sch.2, para.1

(17) Proceedings affected and saving

(1) This Act applies for the purposes of any proceedings begun after the commencement of this Act, whenever the cause of action arose, but does not affect any proceedings begun before the commencement of this Act.

(2) Nothing in this Act affects the law relating to criminal libel.

(18) Short title, commencement, extent and repeals

(1) This Act may be cited as the Defamation Act 1952, and shall come into operation one month after the passing of this Act.

(2) This Act [...] shall not extend to Northern Ireland.

(3)

Notes:

Subsection (2) Words repealed by Northern Ireland Constitution Act 1973 (c. 36) Sch.6 Pt I
Subsection (3) Repealed by Statute Law (Repeals) Act 1974 (c. 22), Sch. Pt XI

SCHEDULE

Repealed by Defamation Act (1996 c.31), Sch.2, para.1

Appendix B
DEFAMATION ACT 1996 (c. 31)

Responsibility for publication

1.—(1) In defamation proceedings a person has a defence if he shows that—

(a) he was not the author, editor or publisher of the statement complained of,

(b) he took reasonable care in relation to its publication, and

(c) he did not know, and had no reason to believe, that what he did caused or contributed to the publication of a defamatory statement.

(2) For this purpose "author", "editor" and "publisher" have the following meanings, which are further explained in subsection (3)—

"author" means the originator of the statement, but does not include a person who did not intend that his statement be published at all;
"editor" means a person having editorial or equivalent responsibility for the content of the statement or the decision to publish it; and
"publisher" means a commercial publisher, that is, a person whose business is issuing material to the public, or a section of the public, who issues material containing the statement in the course of that business.

(3) A person shall not be considered the author, editor or publisher of a statement if he is only involved—

(a) in printing, producing, distributing or selling printed material containing the statement;

(b) in processing, making copies of, distributing, exhibiting or selling a film or sound recording (as defined in Part I of the Copyright, Designs and Patents Act 1988) containing the statement;

(c) in processing, making copies of, distributing or selling any electronic medium in or on which the statement is recorded, or in operating or providing any equipment, system or service by means of which the statement is retrieved, copied, distributed or made available in electronic form;

(d) as the broadcaster of a live programme containing the statement in circumstances in which he has no effective control over the maker of the statement;

(e) as the operator of or provider of access to a communications system by means of which the statement is transmitted, or made available, by a person over whom he has no effective control.

In a case not within paragraphs (a) to (e) the court may have regard to those provisions by way of analogy in deciding whether a person is to be considered the author, editor or publisher of a statement.

(4) Employees or agents of an author, editor or publisher are in the same position as their employer or principal to the extent that they are responsible for the content of the statement or the decision to publish it.

(5) In determining for the purposes of this section whether a person took reasonable care, or had reason to believe that what he did caused or contributed to the publication of a defamatory statement, regard shall be had to—

(a) the extent of his responsibility for the content of the statement or the decision to publish it,

(b) the nature or circumstances of the publication, and

(c) the previous conduct or character of the author, editor or publisher.

(6) This section does not apply to any cause of action which arose before the section came into force.

Offer to make amends

2.—(1) A person who has published a statement alleged to be defamatory of another may offer to make amends under this section.

(2) The offer may be in relation to the statement generally or in relation to a specific defamatory meaning which the person making the offer accepts that the statement conveys ("a qualified offer").

(3) An offer to make amends—

(a) must be in writing,

(b) must be expressed to be an offer to make amends under section 2 of the Defamation Act 1996, and

(c) must state whether it is a qualified offer and, if so, set out the defamatory meaning in relation to which it is made.

(4) An offer to make amends under this section is an offer—

(a) to make a suitable correction of the statement complained of and a sufficient apology to the aggrieved party,

(b) to publish the correction and apology in a manner that is reasonable and practicable in the circumstances, and

(c) to pay to the aggrieved party such compensation (if any), and such costs, as may be agreed or determined to be payable.

The fact that the offer is accompanied by an offer to take specific steps does not affect the fact that an offer to make amends under this section is an offer to do all the things mentioned in paragraphs (a) to (c).

(5) An offer to make amends under this section may not be made by a person after serving a defence in defamation proceedings brought against him by the aggrieved party in respect of the publication in question.

(6) An offer to make amends under this section may be withdrawn before it is accepted; and a renewal of an offer which has been withdrawn shall be treated as a new offer.

Accepting an offer to make amends

3.—(1) If an offer to make amends under section 2 is accepted by the aggrieved party, the following provisions apply.

(2) The party accepting the offer may not bring or continue defamation proceedings in respect of the publication concerned against the person making the offer, but he is entitled to enforce the offer to make amends, as follows.

(3) If the parties agree on the steps to be taken in fulfilment of the offer, the aggrieved party may apply to the court for an order that the other party fulfil his offer by taking the steps agreed.

(4) If the parties do not agree on the steps to be taken by way of correction, apology and publication, the party who made the offer may take such steps as he thinks appropriate, and may in particular—

(a) make the correction and apology by a statement in open court in terms approved by the court, and

(b) give an undertaking to the court as to the manner of their publication.

(5) If the parties do not agree on the amount to be paid by way of compensation, it shall be determined by the court on the same principles as damages in defamation proceedings.

The court shall take account of any steps taken in fulfilment of the offer and (so far as not agreed between the parties) of the suitability of the correction, the sufficiency of the apology and whether the manner of their publication was reasonable in the circumstances, and may reduce or increase the amount of compensation accordingly.

(6) If the parties do not agree on the amount to be paid by way of costs, it shall be determined by the court on the same principles as costs awarded in court proceedings.

(7) The acceptance of an offer by one person to make amends does not affect any cause of action against another person in respect of the same publication, subject as follows.

(8) In England and Wales or Northern Ireland, for the purposes of the Civil Liability (Contribution) Act 1978—

(a) the amount of compensation paid under the offer shall be treated as paid in bona fide settlement or compromise of the claim; and

(b) where another person is liable in respect of the same damage (whether jointly or otherwise), the person whose offer to make amends was accepted is not required to pay by virtue of any contribution under section 1 of that Act a greater amount than the amount of the compensation payable in pursuance of the offer.

(9) In Scotland—

(a) subsection (2) of section 3 of the Law Reform (Miscellaneous Provisions)

(Scotland) Act 1940 (right of one joint wrongdoer as respects another to recover contribution towards damages) applies in relation to compensation paid under an offer to make amends as it applies in relation to damages in an action to which that section applies; and

(b) where another person is liable in respect of the same damage (whether jointly or otherwise), the person whose offer to make amends was accepted is not required to pay by virtue of any contribution under section 3(2) of that Act a greater amount than the amount of compensation payable in pursuance of the offer.

(10) Proceedings under this section shall be heard and determined without a jury.

Failure to accept offer to make amends

4.—(1) If an offer to make amends under section 2, duly made and not withdrawn, is not accepted by the aggrieved party, the following provisions apply.

(2) The fact that the offer was made is a defence (subject to subsection (3)) to defamation proceedings in respect of the publication in question by that party against the person making the offer.

A qualified offer is only a defence in respect of the meaning to which the offer related.

(3) There is no such defence if the person by whom the offer was made knew or had reason to believe that the statement complained of—

(a) referred to the aggrieved party or was likely to be understood as referring to him, and

(b) was both false and defamatory of that party.

but it shall be presumed until the contrary is shown that he did not know and had no reason to believe that was the case.

(4) The person who made the offer need not rely on it by way of defence, but if he does he may not rely on any other defence.

If the offer was a qualified offer, this applies only in respect of the meaning to which the offer related.

(5) The offer may be relied on in mitigation of damages whether or not it was relied on as a defence.

Limitation of actions: England and Wales

5.—(1) The Limitation Act 1980 is amended as follows.

(2) For section 4A (time limit for action for libel or slander) substitute—

"4A. Time limit for actions for defamation or malicious falsehood.

The time limit under section 2 of this Act shall not apply to an action for—

(a) libel or slander, or

(b) slander of title, slander of goods or other malicious falsehood.

but no such action shall be brought after the expiration of one year from the date on which the cause of action accrued.".

(3) In section 28 (extension of limitation period in case of disability), for subsection (4A) substitute—

"(4A) If the action is one to which section 4A of this Act applies, subsection (1) above shall have effect—

    (a) in the case of an action for libel or slander, as if for the words from "at any time" to "occurred" there were substituted the words "by him at any time before the expiration of one year from the date on which he ceased to be under a disability"; and

    (b) in the case of an action for slander of title, slander of goods or other malicious falsehood, as if for the words "six years" there were substituted the words "one year".

(4) For section 32A substitute—

"Discretionary exclusion of time limit for actions for defamation or malicious falsehood

    32A.—Discretionary exclusion of time limit for actions for defamation or malicious falsehood.

(1) If it appears to the court that it would be equitable to allow an action to proceed having regard to the degree to which—

    (a) the operation of section 4A of this Act prejudices the plaintiff or any person whom he represents, and

    (b) any decision of the court under this subsection would prejudice the defendant or any person whom he represents,

the court may direct that that section shall not apply to the action or shall not apply to any specified cause of, action to which the action relates.

(2) In acting under this section the court shall have regard to all the circumstances of the case and in particular to—

    (a) the length of, and the reasons for, the delay on the part of the plaintiff;

    (b) where the reason or one of the reasons for the delay was that all or any of the facts relevant to the cause of action did not become known to the plaintiff until after the end of the period mentioned in section 4A—

        (i) the date on which any such facts did become known to him, and
        (ii) the extent to which he acted promptly and reasonably once he knew whether or not the facts in question might be capable of giving rise to an action; and

    (c) the extent to which, having regard to the delay, relevant evidence is likely—

        (i) to be unavailable, or
        (ii) to be less cogent than if the action had been brought within the period mentioned in section 4A.

(3) In the case of an action for slander of title, slander of goods, or other malicious falsehood brought by a personal representative—

    (a) the references in subsection (2) above to the plaintiff shall be construed as including the deceased person to whom the cause of action accrued and any previous personal representative of that person; and

    (b) nothing in section 28(3) of this Act shall be construed as affecting the court's discretion under this section.

(4) In this section "the court" means the court in which the action has been brought".

(5) In section 36(1) (expiry of time limit no bar to equitable relief), for paragraph (aa) substitute—

"(a) the time limit under section 4A for actions for libel or slander, or for slander of title, slander of goods or other malicious falsehood;"

(6) The amendments made by this section apply only to causes of action arising after the section comes into force.

Limitation of actions: Northern Ireland

6.—(1) The Limitation (Northern Ireland) Order 1989 is amended as follows.
(2) In Article 6 (time limit: certain actions founded on tort) for paragraph (2) substitute—

"(2) Subject to Article 51, an action for damages for—

(a) libel or slander, or

(b) slander of title, slander of goods or other malicious falsehood,

may not be brought after the expiration of one year from the date on which the cause of action accrued.".

(3) In Article 48 (extension of time limit), for paragraph (7) substitute—

"(7) Where the action is one to which Article 6(2) applies, paragraph (1) has effect—

(a) in the case of an action for libel and slander, as if for the words from "at any time" to "occurred" there were substituted the words "by him at any time before the expiration of one year from the date on which he ceased to be under a disability"; and

(b) in the case of an action for slander of title, slander of goods or other malicious falsehood, as if for the words "six years" there were substituted the words "one year".

(4) For Article 51 substitute—

"Court's power to override time limit: actions for defamation or malicious falsehood.

51.—
(1) If it appears to the court that it would be equitable to allow an action to proceed having regard to the degree to which—

(a) the provisions of Article 6(2) prejudice the plaintiff or any person whom he represents; and

(b) any decision of the court under this paragraph would prejudice the defendant or any person whom he represents,

the court may direct that those provisions are not to apply to the action, or are not to apply to any specified cause of action to which the action relates.

(2) In acting under this Article the court is to have regard to all the circumstances of the case and in particular to—

(a) the length of, and the reasons for, the delay on the part of the plaintiff;

(b) in a case where the reason, or one of the reasons, for the delay was that all or any of the facts relevant to the cause of action did not become known to the plaintiff until after the expiration of the period mentioned in Article 6(2)—

    (i) the date on which any such facts did become known to him, and
    (ii) the extent to which he acted promptly and reasonably once he knew whether or not the facts in question might be capable of giving rise to an action; and

(c) the extent to which, having regard to the delay, relevant evidence is likely—

    (i) to be unavailable, or
    (ii) to be less cogent than if the action had been brought within the time allowed by Article 6(2).

(3) In the case of an action for slander of title, slander of goods or other malicious falsehood brought by a personal representative—

(a) the references in paragraph (2) to the plaintiff shall be construed as including the deceased person to whom the cause of action accrued and any previous personal representative of that person; and

(b) nothing in Article 48(3) shall be construed as affecting the court's discretion under this Article.

(4) In this Article "the court" means the court in which the action has been brought.

(5) The amendments made by this section apply only to causes of action arising after the section comes into force.

Ruling on the meaning of a statement

7.—In defamation proceedings the court shall not be asked to rule whether a statement is arguably capable, as opposed to capable, of bearing a particular meaning or meanings attributed to it.

Summary disposal of claim

8.—(1) In defamation proceedings the court may dispose summarily of the plaintiff's claim in accordance with the following provisions.

(2) The court may dismiss the plaintiff's claim if it appears to the court that it has no realistic prospect of success and there is no reason why it should be tried.

(3) The court may give judgment for the plaintiff and grant him summary relief (see section 9) if it appears to the court that there is no defence to the claim which has a realistic prospect of success, and that there is no other reason why the claim should be tried.

Unless the plaintiff asks for summary relief, the court shall not act under this subsection unless it is satisfied that summary relief will adequately compensate him for the wrong he has suffered.

(4) In considering whether a claim should be tried the court shall have regard to—

(a) whether all the persons who are or might be defendants in respect of the publication complained of are before the court;

(b) whether summary disposal of the claim against another defendant would be inappropriate;

(c) the extent to which there is a conflict of evidence;

(d) the seriousness of the alleged wrong (as regards the content of the statement and the extent of publication); and

(e) whether it is justifiable in the circumstances to proceed to a full trial.

(5) Proceedings under this section shall be heard and determined without a jury.

Meaning of summary relief

9.—(1) For the purposes of section 8 (summary disposal of claim) "summary relief" means such of the following as may be appropriate—

(a) a declaration that the statement was false and defamatory of the plaintiff;

(b) an order that the defendant publish or cause to be published a suitable correction and apology;

(c) damages not exceeding £10,000 or such other amount as may be prescribed by order of the Lord Chancellor;

(d) an order restraining the defendant from publishing or further publishing the matter complained of.

(2) The content of any correction and apology, and the time, manner, form and place of publication, shall be for the parties to agree.

If they cannot agree on the content, the court may direct the defendant to publish or cause to be published a summary of the court's judgment agreed by the parties or settled by the court in accordance with rules of court.

If they cannot agree on the time, manner, form or place of publication, the court may direct the defendant to take such reasonable and practicable steps as the court considers appropriate.

(3) Any order under subsection (1)(c) shall be made by statutory instrument which shall be subject to annulment in pursuance of a resolution of either House of Parliament.

Summary disposal: rules of court

10.—(1) Provision may be made by rules of court as to the summary disposal of the plaintiff's claim in defamation proceedings.

(2) Without prejudice to the generality of that power, provision may be made—

(a) authorising a party to apply for summary disposal at any stage of the proceedings;

(b) authorising the court at any stage of the proceedings—

    (i) to treat any application, pleading or other step in the proceedings as an application for summary disposal, or

    (ii) to make an order for summary disposal without any such application;

(c) as to the time for serving pleadings or taking any other step in the proceedings in a case where there are proceedings for summary disposal;

(d) requiring the parties to identify any question of law or construction which the court is to be asked to determine in the proceedings;

(e) as to the nature of any hearing on the question of summary disposal, and in particular—

    (i) authorising the court to order affidavits or witness statements to be prepared for use as evidence at the hearing, and

    (ii) requiring the leave of the court for the calling of oral evidence, or the introduction of new evidence, at the hearing;

(f) authorising the court to require a defendant to elect, at or before the hearing, whether or not to make an offer to make amends under section 2.

Summary disposal: application to Northern Ireland

11.—In their application to Northern Ireland the provisions of sections 8 to 10 (summary disposal of claim) apply only to proceedings in the High Court.

Evidence of convictions

12.—(1) In section 13 of the Civil Evidence Act 1968 (conclusiveness of convictions for purposes of defamation actions), in subsections (1) and (2) for "a person" substitute "the plaintiff" and for "that person" substitute "he"; and after subsection (2) insert—

"(2A) In the case of an action for libel or slander in which there is more than one plaintiff—

(a) the references in subsections (1) and (2) above to the plaintiff shall be construed as references to any of the plaintiffs, and

(b) proof that any of the plaintiffs stands convicted of an offence shall be conclusive evidence that he committed that offence so far as that fact is relevant to any issue arising in relation to his cause of action or that of any other plaintiff".

The amendments made by this subsection apply only where the trial of the action begins after this section comes into force.

(2) In section 12 of the Law Reform (Miscellaneous Provisions) (Scotland) Act 1968 (conclusiveness of convictions for purposes of defamation actions), in subsections (1) and (2) for "a person" substitute "the pursuer" and for "that person" substitute "he"; and after subsection (2) insert—

"(2A) In the case of an action for defamation in which there is more than one pursuer—

(a) the references in subsections (1) and (2) above to the pursuer shall be construed as references to any of the pursuers, and

(b) proof that any of the pursuers stands convicted of an offence shall be conclusive evidence that he committed that offence so far as that fact is relevant to any issue arising in relation to his cause of action or that of any other pursuer".

The amendments made by this subsection apply only for the purposes of an action begun after this section comes into force, whenever the cause of action arose.

(3) In section 9 of the Civil Evidence Act (Northern Ireland) 1971 (conclusiveness of convictions for purposes of defamation actions), in subsections (1) and (2) for "a person" substitute "the plaintiff" and for "that person" substitute "he"; and after subsection (2) insert—

"(2A) In the case of an action for libel or slander in which there is more than one plaintiff—

(a) the references in subsections (1) and (2) to the plaintiff shall be construed as references to any of the plaintiffs, and

(b) proof that any of the plaintiffs stands convicted of an offence shall be conclusive evidence that he committed that offence so far as that fact is relevant to any issue arising in relation to his cause of action or that of any other plaintiff.".

The amendments made by this subsection apply only where the trial of the action begins after this section comes into force.

Evidence concerning proceedings in Parliament

13.—(1) Where the conduct of a person in or in relation to proceedings in Parliament is in issue in defamation proceedings, he may waive for the purposes of those proceedings, so far as concerns him, the protection of any enactment or rule of law which prevents proceedings in Parliament being impeached or questioned in any court or place out of Parliament.

(2) Where a person waives that protection—

(a) any such enactment or rule of law shall not apply to prevent evidence being given, questions being asked or statements, submissions, comments or findings being made about his conduct, and

(b) none of those things shall be regarded as infringing the privilege of either House of Parliament.

(3) The waiver by one person of that protection does not affect its operation in relation to another person who has not waived it.

(4) Nothing in this section affects any enactment or rule of law so far as it protects a person (including a person who has waived the protection referred to above) from legal liability for words spoken or things done in the course of, or for the purposes of or incidental to, any proceedings in Parliament.

(5) Without prejudice to the generality of subsection (4), that subsection applies to—

(a) the giving of evidence before either House or a committee;

(b) the presentation or submission of a document to either House or a committee;

(c) the preparation of a document for the purposes of or incidental to the transacting of any such business;

(d) the formulation, making or publication of a document, including a report, by or pursuant to an order to either House or a committee; and

(e) any communication with the Parliamentary Commissioner for Standards or any person having functions in connection with the registration of members' interests.

In this subsection "a committee" means a committee of either House or a joint committee of both House of Parliament.

Reports of court proceedings absolutely privileged

14.—(1) A fair and accurate report of proceedings in public before a court to which this section applies, if published contemporaneously with the proceedings, is absolutely privileged.

(2) A report of proceedings which by an order of the court, or as a consequence of any statutory provision, is required to be postponed shall be treated as published contemporaneously if it is published as soon as practicable after publication is permitted.

(3) This section applies to—

(a) any court in the United Kingdom,

(b) the European Court of Justice or any court attached to that court,

(c) the European Court of Human Rights, and

(d) any international criminal tribunal established by the Security Council of the United Nations or by an international agreement to which the United Kingdom is a party.

In paragraph (a) "court" includes any tribunal or body exercising the judicial power of the State.

(4) In section 8(6) of the Rehabilitation of Offenders Act 1974 and in Article 9(6) of the Rehabilitation of Offenders (Northern Ireland) Order 1978 (defamation actions: reports of court proceedings), for "section 3 of the Law of Libel Amendment Act 1888" substitute "section 14 of the Defamation Act 1996".

Reports, etc. protected by qualified privilege

15.—(1) The publication of any report or other statement mentioned in Schedule 1 to this Act is privileged unless the publication is shown to be made with malice, subject as follows.

(2) In defamation proceedings in respect of the publication of a report or other statement mentioned in Part IIof that Schedule, there is no defence under this section if the plaintiff shows that the defendant—

(a) was requested by him to publish in a suitable manner a reasonable letter or statement by way of explanation or contradiction, and

(b) refused or neglected to do so.

For this purpose "in a suitable manner" means in the same manner as the publication complained of or in a manner that is adequate and reasonable in the circumstances.

(3) This section does not apply to the publication to the public, or a section of the public, of matter which is not of public concern and the publication of which is not for the public benefit.

(4) Nothing in this section shall be construed—

(a) as protecting the publication of matter the publication of which is prohibited by law, or

(b) as limiting or abridging any privilege subsisting apart from this section.

Repeals

16.—The enactments specified in Schedule 2 are repealed to the extent specified.

Interpretation

17.—(1) In this Act—

"publication" and "publish", in relation to a statement, have the meaning they have for the purposes of the law of defamation generally, but "publisher" is specially defined for the purposes of section 1;
"statement" means words, pictures, visual images, gestures or any other method of signifying meaning; and
"statutory provision" means—

  (a) a provision contained in an Act or in subordinate legislation within the meaning of the Interpretation Act 1978, [...]

  [(aa) a provision contained in an Act of the Scottish Parliament or in an instrument made under such an Act,] or

  (b) a statutory provision within the meaning given by section 1(f) of the Interpretation Act (Northern Ireland) 1954.

(2) In this Act as it applies to proceedings in Scotland—

"costs" means expenses; and
"plaintiff" and "defendant" mean pursuer and defender.

General provisions

18.—(1) The following provisions of this Act extend to England and Wales—

section 1 (responsibility for publication),
sections 2 to 4 (offer to make amends), except section 3(9),
section 5 (time limit for actions for defamation or malicious falsehood).
section 7 (ruling on the meaning of a statement),
sections 8 to 10 (summary disposal of claim),
section 12(1) (evidence of convictions),
section 13 (evidence concerning proceedings in Parliament),
sections 14 and 15 and Schedule 1 (statutory privilege).
section 16 and Schedule 2 (repeals) so far as relating to enactments extending to England and Wales,
section 17(1) (interpretation),
this subsection,
section 19 (commencement) so far as relating to provisions which extend to England and Wales, and
section 20 (short title and saving).

(2) The following provisions of this Act extend to Scotland—

section 1 (responsibility for publication),
sections 2 to 4 (offer to make amends), except section 3(8),
section 12(2) (evidence of convictions),
section 13 (evidence concerning proceedings in Parliament),
section 14 and 15 and Schedule 1 (statutory privilege).
section 16 and Schedule 2 (repeals) so far as relating to enactments extending to Scotland,
section 17 (interpretation),
this subsection,

section 19 (commencement) so far as relating to provisions which extend to Scotland, and

section 20 (short title and saving).

(3) The following provisions of this Act extend to Northern Ireland—

section 1 (responsibility for publication).

sections 2 to 4 (offer to make amends), except section 3(9),

section 6 (time limit for actions for defamation or malicious falsehood),

section 7 (ruling on the meaning of a statement),

sections 8 to 11 (summary disposal of claim),

section 12(3) (evidence of convictions),

section 13 (evidence concerning proceedings in Parliament),

sections 14 and 15 and Schedule 1 (statutory privilege),

section 16 and Schedule 2 (repeals) so far as relating to enactments extending to Northern Ireland,

section 17(1) (interpretation), this subsection,

section 19 (commencement) so far as relating to provisions which extend to Northern Ireland, and

section 20 (short title and saving).

Commencement

19.—(1) Sections 18 to 20 (extent, commencement and other general provisions) come into force on Royal Assent.

(2) The following provisions of this Act come into force at the end of the period of two months beginning with the day on which this Act is passed—

section 1 (responsibility for publication),

sections 5 and 6 (time limit for actions for defamation or malicious falsehood),

section 12 (evidence of convictions),

section 13 (evidence concerning proceedings in Parliament),

section 16 and the repeals in Schedule 2, so far as consequential on the above provisions, and

section 17 (interpretation), so far as relating to the above provisions.

(3) The provisions of this Act otherwise come into force on such day as may be appointed—

(a) for England and Wales or Northern Ireland, by order of the Lord Chancellor, or

(b) for Scotland, by order of the Secretary of State,

and different days may be appointed for different purposes.

(4) Any such order shall be made by statutory instrument and may contain such transitional provisions as appear to the Lord Chancellor or Secretary of State to be appropriate.

Short title and saving

20.—(1) This Act may be cited as the Defamation Act 1996.

(2) Nothing in this Act affects the law relating to criminal libel.

SCHEDULES

QUALIFIED PRIVILEGE

PART I

STATEMENTS HAVING QUALIFIED PRIVILEGE WITHOUT EXPLANATION OR CONTRADICTION

1. A fair and accurate report of proceedings in public of a legislature anywhere in the world.

2. A fair and accurate report of proceedings in public before a court anywhere in the world.

3. A fair and accurate report of proceedings in public of a person appointed to hold a public inquiry by a government or legislature anywhere in the world.

4. A fair and accurate report of proceedings in public anywhere in the world of an international organisation or an international conference.

5. A fair and accurate copy of or extract from any register or other document required by law to be open to public inspection.

6. A notice or advertisement published by or on the authority of a court, or of a judge or officer of a court, anywhere in the world.

7. A fair and accurate copy of or extract from matter published by or on the authority of a government or legislature anywhere in the world.

8. A fair and accurate copy of or extract from matter published anywhere in the world by an international organisation or an international conference.

PART II

STATEMENTS PRIVILEGED SUBJECT TO EXPLANATION OR CONTRADICTION

9.—(1) A fair and accurate copy of or extract from a notice or other matter issued for the information of the public by or on behalf of—

(a) a legislature in any member State or the European Parliament;

(b) the government of any member State, or any authority performing governmental functions in any member State or part of a member State, or the European Commission;

(c) an international organisation or international conference.

(2) In this paragraph "governmental functions" includes police functions,

10. A fair and accurate copy of or extract from a document made available by a court in any member State or the European Court of Justice (or any court attached to that court), or by a judge or officer of any such court.

11.—(1) A fair and accurate report of proceedings at any public meeting or sitting in the United Kingdom of—

(a) a local authority, local authority committee or in the case of a local authority which are operating executive arrangements the executive of that authority or a committee of that executive;

(b) a justice or justices of the peace acting otherwise than as a court exercising judicial authority;

(c) a commission, tribunal, committee or person appointed for the purposes of any inquiry by any statutory provision, by Her Majesty or by a Minister of the Crown, a member of the Scottish Executive or a Northern Ireland Department;

(d) a person appointed by a local authority to hold a local inquiry in pursuance of any statutory provision;

(e) any other tribunal, board, committee or body constituted by or under, and exercising functions under, any statutory provision.

(1A) In the case of a local authority which are operating executive arrangements, a fair and accurate record of any decision made by any member of the executive where that record is required to be made and available for public inspection by virtue of section 22 of the Local Government Act 2000 or of any provision in regulations made under that section.

(2) In sub-paragraphs (1)(a) and (1A)—

"executive" and "executive arrangements" have the same meaning as in Part II of the Local Government Act 2000;
"local authority" means—

(a) in relation to England and Wales, a principal council within the meaning of the Local Government Act 1972, any body falling within any paragraph of section 100J(1) of that Act or an authority or body to which the Public Bodies (Admission to Meetings) Act 1960 applies,

(b) in relation to Scotland, a council constituted under section 2 of the Local Government etc. (Scotland) Act 1994 or an authority or body to which the Public Bodies (Admission to Meetings) Act 1960 applies,

(c) in relation to Northern Ireland, any authority or body to which sections 23 to 27 of the Local Government Act (Northern Ireland) 1972 apply; and

"local authority committee" means any committee of a local authority or of local authorities, and includes—

(a) any committee or sub-committee in relation to which sections 100A to 100D of the Local Government Act 1972 apply by virtue of section 100E of that Act (whether or not also by virtue of section 100J of that Act), and

(b) any committee or sub-committee in relation to which sections 50A to 50D of the Local Government (Scotland) Act 1973 apply by virtue of section 50E of that Act.

(3) A fair and accurate report of any corresponding proceedings in any of the Channel Islands or the Isle of Man or in another member State.

12.—(1) A fair and accurate report of proceedings at any public meeting held in a member State.

(2) In this paragraph a "public meeting" means a meeting bona fide and lawfully held for a lawful purpose and for the furtherance or discussion of a matter of public concern, whether admission to the meeting is general or restricted.

13.—(1) A fair and accurate report of proceedings at a general meeting of a UK public company.

(2) A fair and accurate copy of or extract from any document circulated to members of a UK public company—

(a) by or with the authority of the board of directors of the company,

(b) by the auditors of the company, or

(c) by any member of the company in pursuance of a right conferred by any statutory provision.

(3) A fair and accurate copy of or extract from any document circulated to members of a UK public company which relates to the appointment, resignation, retirement or dismissal of directors of the company.

(4) In this paragraph "UK public company" means—

(a) a public company within the meaning of section 1(3) of the Companies Act 1985 or Article 12(3) of the Companies (Northern Ireland) Order 1986 or

(b) a body corporate incorporated by or registered under any other statutory provision, or by Royal Charter, or formed in pursuance of letters patent.

(5) A fair and accurate report of proceedings at any corresponding meeting of, or copy of or extract from any corresponding document circulated to members of, a public company formed under the law of any of the Channel Islands or the Isle of Man or of another member State.

14.—A fair and accurate report of any finding or decision of any of the following descriptions of association, formed in the United Kingdom or another member State, or of any committee or governing body of such an association—

(a) an association formed for the purpose of promoting or encouraging the exercise of or interest in any art, science, religion or learning, and empowered by its constitution to exercise control over or adjudicate on matters of interest or concern to the association, or the actions or conduct of any person subject to such control or adjudication;

(b) an association formed for the purpose of promoting or safeguarding the interests of any trade, business, industry or profession, or of the persons carrying on or engaged in any trade, business, industry or profession, and empowered by its constitution to exercise control over or adjudicate upon matters connected with that trade, business, industry or profession, or the actions or conduct of those persons;

(c) an association formed for the purpose of promoting or safeguarding the interests of a game, sport or pastime to the playing or exercise of which members of the public are invited or admitted, and empowered by its constitution to exercise control over or adjudicate upon persons connected with or taking part in the game, sport or pastime;

(d) an association formed for the purpose of promoting charitable objects or other objects beneficial to the community and empowered by its constitution to exercise control over or to adjudicate on matters of interest or concern to the association, or the actions or conduct of any person subject to such control or adjudication.

15.—(1) A fair and accurate report of, or copy of or extract from, any adjudication, report, statement or notice issued by a body, officer or other person designated for the purposes of this paragraph—

(a) for England and Wales or Northern Ireland, by order of the Lord Chancellor, and

(b) for Scotland, by order of the Secretary of State.

(2) An order under this paragraph shall be made by statutory instrument which shall be subject to annulment in pursuance of a resolution of either House of Parliament.

PART III

SUPPLEMENTARY PROVISIONS

16.—(1) In this Schedule—

"court" includes any tribunal or body exercising the judicial power of the State;
"international conference" means a conference attended by representatives of two or more governments;
"international organisation" means an organisation of which two or more governments are members, and includes any committee or other subordinate body of such an organisation; and
"legislature" includes a local legislature.

(2) References in this Schedule to a member State include any European dependent territory of a member State.

(3) In paragraphs 2 and 6 "court" includes—

(a) the European Court of Justice (or any court attached to that court) and the Court of Auditors of the European Communities,

(b) the European Court of Human Rights,

(c) any international criminal tribunal established by the Security Council of the United Nations or by an international agreement to which the United Kingdom is a party, and

(d) the International Court of Justice and any other judicial or arbitral tribunal deciding matters in dispute between States.

(4) In paragraphs 1, 3 and 7 "legislature" includes the European Parliament.

17.—(1) Provision may be made by order identifying—

(a) for the purposes of paragraph 11, the corresponding proceedings referred to in sub-paragraph (3);

(b) for the purposes of paragraph 13, the corresponding meetings and documents referred to in sub-paragraph (5).

(2) An order under this paragraph may be made—

(a) for England and Wales or Northern Ireland, by the Lord Chancellor, and

(b) for Scotland, by the Secretary of State.

(3) An order under this paragraph shall be made by statutory instrument which shall be subject to annulment in pursuance of a resolution of either House of Parliament.

Appendix B

SCHEDULE 2

Repeals

Chapter	Short title	Extent of repeal
1888 c. 64	Law of Libel Amendment Act 1888.	Section 3.
1952 c. 66	Defamation Act 1952.	Section 4. Sections 7, 8 and 9(2) and (3). Section 16(2) and (3). The Schedule.
1955 c. 20	Revision of the Army and Air Force Acts (Transitional Provisions) Act 1955.	In Schedule 2, the entry relating to the Defamation Act 1952.
1955 c. 11 (N.I.).	Defamation Act (Northern Ireland) 1955.	Section 4. Section 7, 8 and 9(2) and (3). Section 14(2). The Schedule.
1972 c. 9 (N.I.).	Local Government Act (Northern Ireland) 1972.	In Schedule 8, paragraph 12.
1981 c. 49	Contempt of Court Act 1981.	In section 4(3), the words "and of section 3 of the Law of Libel Amendment Act 1888 (privilege)".
1981 c. 61	British Nationality Act 1981.	In Schedule 7, the entries relating to the Defamation Act 1952 and the Defamation Act (Northern Ireland) 1955.
1985 c. 43	Local Government (Access to Information) Act 1985.	In Schedule, paragraphs 2 and 3.
1985 c. 61	Administration of Justice Act 1985.	Section 57.
S.I. 1986/ 594 (N.I. 3).	Education and Libraries (Northern Ireland) Order 1986.	Article 97(2).
1990 c. 42	Broadcasting Act 1990.	Section 166(3). In Schedule 20, paragraphs 2 and 3.

Appendix C
HUMAN RIGHTS ACT 1998 (c.42)

INTRODUCTION

The Convention Rights.
1.—(1) In this Act "the Convention rights" means the rights and fundamental freedoms set out in—

(a) Articles 2 to 12 and 14 of the Convention,

(b) Articles 1 to 3 of the First Protocol, and

(c) Articles 1 and 2 of the Sixth Protocol,

as read with Articles 16 to 18 of the Convention.
(2) Those Articles are to have effect for the purposes of this Act subject to any designated derogation or reservation (as to which see sections 14 and 15).
(3) The Articles are set out in Schedule 1.
(4) The Secretary of State may by order make such amendments to this Act as he considers appropriate to reflect the effect, in relation to the United Kingdom, of a protocol.
(5) In subsection (4) "protocol" means a protocol to the Convention—

(a) which the United Kingdom has ratified; or

(b) which the United Kingdom has signed with a view to ratification.

(6) No amendment may be made by an order under subsection (4) so as to come into force before the protocol concerned is in force in relation to the United Kingdom.

2.—(1) A court or tribunal determining a question which has arisen in connection with a Convention right must take into account any—

(a) judgment, decision, declaration or advisory opinion of the European Court of Human Rights,

(b) opinion of the Commission given in a report adopted under Article 31 of the Convention,

(c) decision of the Commission in connection with Article 26 or 27(2) of the Convention, or

(d) decision of the Committee of Ministers taken under Article 46 of the Convention,

whenever made or given, so far as, in the opinion of the court or tribunal, it is relevant to the proceedings in which that question has arisen.

(2) Evidence of any judgment, decision, declaration or opinion of which account may have to be taken under this section is to be given in proceedings before any court or tribunal in such manner as may be provided by rules.

(3) In this section "rules" means rules of court or, in the case of proceedings before a tribunal, rules made for the purposes of this section—

(a) by the Lord Chancellor or the Secretary of State, in relation to any proceedings outside Scotland;

(b) by the Secretary of State, in relation to proceedings in Scotland; or

(c) by a Northern Ireland department, in relation to proceedings before a tribunal in Northern Ireland—

    (i) which deals with transferred matters; and

    (ii) for which no rules made under paragraph (a) are in force.

3.—(1) So far as it is possible to do so, primary legislation and subordinate legislation must be read and given effect in a way which is compatible with the Convention rights.

(2) This section—

(a) applies to primary legislation and subordinate legislation whenever enacted;

(b) does not affect the validity, continuing operation or enforcement of any incompatible primary legislation; and

(c) does not affect the validity, continuing operation or enforcement of any incompatible subordinate legislation if (disregarding any possibility of revocation) primary legislation prevents removal of the incompatibility.

4.—(1) Subsection (2) applies in any proceedings in which a court determines whether a provision of primary legislation is compatible with a Convention right.

(2) If the court is satisfied that the provision is incompatible with a Convention right, it may make a declaration of that incompatibility.

(3) Subsection (4) applies in any proceedings in which a court determines whether a provision of subordinate legislation, made in the exercise of a power conferred by primary legislation, is compatible with a Convention right.

(4) If the court is satisfied—

(a) that the provision is incompatible with a Convention right, and

(b) that (disregarding any possibility of revocation) the primary legislation concerned prevents removal of the incompatibility,

it may make a declaration of that incompatibility.

(5) In this section "court" means—

(a) the House of Lords;

(b) the Judicial Committee of the Privy Council;

(c) the Courts-Martial Appeal Court;

(d) in Scotland, the High Court of Justiciary sitting otherwise than as a trial court or the Court of Session;

(e) in England and Wales or Northern Ireland, the High Court or the Court of Appeal.

(6) A declaration under this section ("a declaration of incompatibility")—

(a) does not affect the validity, continuing operation or enforcement of the provision in respect of which it is given; and

(b) is not binding on the parties to the proceedings in which it is made.

5.—(1) Where a court is considering whether to make a declaration of incompatibility, the Crown is entitled to notice in accordance with rules of court.

(2) In any case to which subsection (1) applies—

(a) a Minister of the Crown (or a person nominated by him),

(b) a member of the Scottish Executive,

(c) a Northern Ireland Minister,

(d) a Northern Ireland department,

is entitled, on giving notice in accordance with rules of court, to be joined as a party to the proceedings.

(3) Notice under subsection (2) may be given at any time during the proceedings.

(4) A person who has been made a party to criminal proceedings (other than in Scotland) as the result of a notice under subsection (2) may, with leave, appeal to the House of Lords against any declaration of incompatibility made in the proceedings.

(5) In subsection (4)—

"criminal proceedings" includes all proceedings before the Courts-Martial Appeal Court; and

"leave" means leave granted by the court making the declaration of incompatibility or by the House of Lords.

6.—(1) It is unlawful for a public authority to act in a way which is incompatible with a Convention right.

(2) Subsection (1) does not apply to an act if—

(a) as the result of one or more provisions of primary legislation, the authority could not have acted differently; or

(b) in the case of one or more provisions of, or made under, primary legislation which cannot be read or given effect in a way which is compatible with the Convention rights, the authority was acting so as to give effect to or enforce those provisions.

(3) In this section "public authority" includes—

(a) a court or tribunal, and

(b) any person certain of whose functions are functions of a public nature,

but does not include either House of Parliament or a person exercising functions in connection with proceedings in Parliament.

(4) In subsection (3) "Parliament" does not include the House of Lords in its judicial capacity.

(5) In relation to a particular act, a person is not a public authority by virtue only of subsection (3)(b) if the nature of the act is private.

(6) "An act" includes a failure to act but does not include a failure to—

(a) introduce in, or lay before, Parliament a proposal for legislation; or

(b) make any primary legislation or remedial order.

7.—(1) A person who claims that a public authority has acted (or proposes to act) in a way which is made unlawful by section 6(1) may—

(a) bring proceedings against the authority under this Act in the appropriate court or tribunal, or

(b) rely on the Convention right or rights concerned in any legal proceedings,

but only if he is (or would be) a victim of the unlawful act.

(2) In subsection (1)(a) "appropriate court or tribunal" means such court or tribunal as may be determined in accordance with rules; and proceedings against an authority include a counterclaim or similar proceeding.

(3) If the proceedings are brought on an application for judicial review, the applicant is to be taken to have a sufficient interest in relation to the unlawful act only if he is, or would be, a victim of that act.

(4) If the proceedings are made by way of a petition for judicial review in Scotland, the applicant shall be taken to have title and interest to sue in relation to the unlawful act only if he is, or would be, a victim of that act.

(5) Proceedings under subsection (1)(a) must be brought before the end of—

(a) the period of one year beginning with the date on which the act complained of took place; or

(b) such longer period as the court or tribunal considers equitable having regard to all the circumstances,

but that is subject to any rule imposing a stricter time limit in relation to the procedure in question.

(6) In subsection (1)(b) "legal proceedings" includes—

(a) proceedings brought by or at the instigation of a public authority; and

(b) an appeal against the decision of a court or tribunal.

(7) For the purposes of this section, a person is a victim of an unlawful act only if he would be a victim for the purposes of Article 34 of the Convention if proceedings were brought in the European Court of Human Rights in respect of that act.

(8) Nothing in this Act creates a criminal offence.

(9) In this section "rules" means—

(a) in relation to proceedings before a court or tribunal outside Scotland, rules made by the Lord Chancellor or the Secretary of State for the purposes of this section or rules of court,

   (b) in relation to proceedings before a court or tribunal in Scotland, rules made by the Secretary of State for those purposes,

   (c) in relation to proceedings before a tribunal in Northern Ireland-

      (i) which deals with transferred matters; and

     (ii) for which no rules made under paragraph (a) are in force,

   rules made by a Northern Ireland department for those purposes,

and includes provision made by order under section 1 of the Courts and Legal Services Act 1990.

(10) In making rules, regard must be had to section 9.

(11) The Minister who has power to make rules in relation to a particular tribunal may, to the extent he considers it necessary to ensure that the tribunal can provide an appropriate remedy in relation to an act (or proposed act) of a public authority which is (or would be) unlawful as a result of section 6(1), by order add to—

   (a) the relief or remedies which the tribunal may grant; or

   (b) the grounds on which it may grant any of them.

(12) An order made under subsection (11) may contain such incidental, supplemental, consequential or transitional provision as the Minister making it considers appropriate.

(13) "The Minister" includes the Northern Ireland department concerned.

8.—(1) In relation to any act (or proposed act) of a public authority which the court finds is (or would be) unlawful, it may grant such relief or remedy, or make such order, within its powers as it considers just and appropriate.

(2) But damages may be awarded only by a court which has power to award damages, or to order the payment of compensation, in civil proceedings.

(3) No award of damages is to be made unless, taking account of all the circumstances of the case, including—

   (a) any other relief or remedy granted, or order made, in relation to the act in question (by that or any other court), and

   (b) the consequences of any decision (of that or any other court) in respect of that act,

the court is satisfied that the award is necessary to afford just satisfaction to the person in whose favour it is made.

(4) In determining—

   (a) whether to award damages, or

   (b) the amount of an award,

the court must take into account the principles applied by the European Court of Human Rights in relation to the award of compensation under Article 41 of the Convention.

(5) A public authority against which damages are awarded is to be treated—

   (a) in Scotland, for the purposes of section 3 of the Law Reform (Miscellaneous Provisions) (Scotland) Act 1940 as if the award were made in an action of damages in which the authority has been found liable in respect of loss or damage to the person to whom the award is made;

(b) for the purposes of the Civil Liability (Contribution) Act 1978 as liable in respect of damage suffered by the person to whom the award is made.

(6) In this section—

"court" includes a tribunal;
"damages" means damages for an unlawful act of a public authority; and
"unlawful" means unlawful under section 6(1).

9.—(1) Proceedings under section 7(1)(a) in respect of a judicial act may be brought only—

(a) by exercising a right of appeal;

(b) on an application (in Scotland a petition) for judicial review; or

(c) in such other forum as may be prescribed by rules.

(2) That does not affect any rule of law which prevents a court from being the subject of judicial review.

(3) In proceedings under this Act in respect of a judicial act done in good faith, damages may not be awarded otherwise than to compensate a person to the extent required by Article 5(5) of the Convention.

(4) An award of damages permitted by subsection (3) is to be made against the Crown; but no award may be made unless the appropriate person, if not a party to the proceedings, is joined.

(5) In this section—

"appropriate person" means the Minister responsible for the court concerned, or a person or government department nominated by him;
"court" includes a tribunal;
"judge" includes a member of a tribunal, a justice of the peace and a clerk or other officer entitled to exercise the jurisdiction of a court;
"judicial act" means a judicial act of a court and includes an act done on the instructions, or on behalf, of a judge; and
"rules" has the same meaning as in section 7(9).

10.—(1) This section applies if—

(a) a provision of legislation has been declared under section 4 to be incompatible with a Convention right and, if an appeal lies—

   (i) all persons who may appeal have stated in writing that they do not intend to do so;

  (ii) the time for bringing an appeal has expired and no appeal has been brought within that time; or

 (iii) an appeal brought within that time has been determined or abandoned; or

(b) it appears to a Minister of the Crown or Her Majesty in Council that, having regard to a finding of the European Court of Human Rights made after the coming into force of this section in proceedings against the United Kingdom, a provision of legislation is incompatible with an obligation of the United Kingdom arising from the Convention.

(2) If a Minister of the Crown considers that there are compelling reasons for proceeding under this section, he may by order make such amendments to the legislation as he considers necessary to remove the incompatibility.

(3) If, in the case of subordinate legislation, a Minister of the Crown considers—

(a) that it is necessary to amend the primary legislation under which the sub-ordinate legislation in question was made, in order to enable the incompatibility to be removed, and

(b) that there are compelling reasons for proceeding under this section,

he may by order make such amendments to the primary legislation as he considers necessary.

(4) This section also applies where the provision in question is in subordinate legislation and has been quashed, or declared invalid, by reason of incompatibility with a Convention right and the Minister proposes to proceed under paragraph 2(b) of Schedule 2.

(5) If the legislation is an Order in Council, the power conferred by subsection (2) or (3) is exercisable by Her Majesty in Council.

(6) In this section "legislation" does not include a Measure of the Church Assembly or of the General Synod of the Church of England.

(7) Schedule 2 makes further provision about remedial orders.

11. A person's reliance on a Convention right does not restrict—

(a) any other right or freedom conferred on him by or under any law having effect in any part of the United Kingdom; or

(b) his right to make any claim or bring any proceedings which he could make or bring apart from sections 7 to 9.

12.—(1) This section applies if a court is considering whether to grant any relief which, if granted, might affect the exercise of the Convention right to freedom of expression.

(2) If the person against whom the application for relief is made ("the respondent") is neither present nor represented, no such relief is to be granted unless the court is satisfied—

(a) that the applicant has taken all practicable steps to notify the respondent; or

(b) that there are compelling reasons why the respondent should not be notified.

(3) No such relief is to be granted so as to restrain publication before trial unless the court is satisfied that the applicant is likely to establish that publication should not be allowed.

(4) The court must have particular regard to the importance of the Convention right to freedom of expression and, where the proceedings relate to material which the respondent claims, or which appears to the court, to be journalistic, literary or artistic material (or to conduct connected with such material), to—

(a) the extent to which—

(i) the material has, or is about to, become available to the public; or
(ii) it is, or would be, in the public interest for the material to be published;

(b) any relevant privacy code.

(5) In this section—

"court" includes a tribunal; and
"relief" includes any remedy or order (other than in criminal proceedings).

13.—(1) If a court's determination of any question arising under this Act might affect the exercise by a religious organisation (itself or its members collectively) of the Convention right to freedom of thought, conscience and religion, it must have particular regard to the importance of that right.

(2) In this section "court" includes a tribunal.

14.—(1) In this Act "designated derogation" means—

(a) the United Kingdom's derogation from Article 5(3) of the Convention; and

(b) any derogation by the United Kingdom from an Article of the Convention, or of any protocol to the Convention, which is designated for the purposes of this Act in an order made by the Secretary of State.

(2) The derogation referred to in subsection (1)(a) is set out in Part I of Schedule 3.

(3) If a designated derogation is amended or replaced it ceases to be a designated derogation.

(4) But subsection (3) does not prevent the Secretary of State from exercising his power under subsection (1)(b) to make a fresh designation order in respect of the Article concerned.

(5) The Secretary of State must by order make such amendments to Schedule 3 as he considers appropriate to reflect—

(a) any designation order; or

(b) the effect of subsection (3).

(6) A designation order may be made in anticipation of the making by the United Kingdom of a proposed derogation.

15.—(1) In this Act "designated reservation" means—

(a) the United Kingdom's reservation to Article 2 of the First Protocol to the Convention; and

(b) any other reservation by the United Kingdom to an Article of the Convention, or of any protocol to the Convention, which is designated for the purposes of this Act in an order made by the Secretary of State.

(2) The text of the reservation referred to in subsection (1)(a) is set out in Part II of Schedule 3.

(3) If a designated reservation is withdrawn wholly or in part it ceases to be a designated reservation.

(4) But subsection (3) does not prevent the Secretary of State from exercising his power under subsection (1)(b) to make a fresh designation order in respect of the Article concerned.

(5) The Secretary of State must by order make such amendments to this Act as he considers appropriate to reflect—

(a) any designation order; or

(b) the effect of subsection (3).

16.—(1) If it has not already been withdrawn by the United Kingdom, a designated derogation ceases to have effect for the purposes of this Act—

(a) in the case of the derogation referred to in section 14(1)(a), at the end of the period of five years beginning with the date on which section 1(2) came into force;

(b) in the case of any other derogation, at the end of the period of five years beginning with the date on which the order designating it was made.

(2) At any time before the period—

(a) fixed by subsection (1)(a) or (b), or

(b) extended by an order under this subsection,

comes to an end, the Secretary of State may by order extend it by a further period of five years.

(3) An order under section 14(1)(b) ceases to have effect at the end of the period for consideration, unless a resolution has been passed by each House approving the order.

(4) Subsection (3) does not affect—

(a) anything done in reliance on the order; or

(b) the power to make a fresh order under section 14(1)(b).

(5) In subsection (3) "period for consideration" means the period of forty days beginning with the day on which the order was made.

(6) In calculating the period for consideration, no account is to be taken of any time during which—

(a) Parliament is dissolved or prorogued; or

(b) both Houses are adjourned for more than four days.

(7) If a designated derogation is withdrawn by the United Kingdom, the Secretary of State must by order make such amendments to this Act as he considers are required to reflect that withdrawal.

17.—(1) The appropriate Minister must review the designated reservation referred to in section 15(1)(a)—

(a) before the end of the period of five years beginning with the date on which section 1(2) came into force; and

(b) if that designation is still in force, before the end of the period of five years beginning with the date on which the last report relating to it was laid under subsection (3).

(2) The appropriate Minister must review each of the other designated reservations (if any)—

(a) before the end of the period of five years beginning with the date on which the order designating the reservation first came into force; and

(b) if the designation is still in force, before the end of the period of five years beginning with the date on which the last report relating to it was laid under subsection (3).

(3) The Minister conducting a review under this section must prepare a report on the result of the review and lay a copy of it before each House of Parliament.

18.—(1) In this section "judicial office" means the office of—

(a) Lord Justice of Appeal, Justice of the High Court or Circuit judge, in England and Wales;

(b) judge of the Court of Session or sheriff, in Scotland;

(c) Lord Justice of Appeal, judge of the High Court or county court judge, in Northern Ireland.

(2) The holder of a judicial office may become a judge of the European Court of Human Rights ("the Court") without being required to relinquish his office.

(3) But he is not required to perform the duties of his judicial office while he is a judge of the Court.

(4) In respect of any period during which he is a judge of the Court—

(a) a Lord Justice of Appeal or Justice of the High Court is not to count as a judge of the relevant court for the purposes of section 2(1) or 4(1) of the Supreme Court Act 1981 (maximum number of judges) nor as a judge of the Supreme Court for the purposes of section 12(1) to (6) of that Act (salaries etc.);

(b) a judge of the Court of Session is not to count as a judge of that court for the purposes of section 1(1) of the Court of Session Act 1988 (maximum number of judges) or of section 9(1)(c) of the Administration of Justice Act 1973 ("the 1973 Act") (salaries etc.);

(c) a Lord Justice of Appeal or judge of the High Court in Northern Ireland is not to count as a judge of the relevant court for the purposes of section 2(1) or 3(1) of the Judicature (Northern Ireland) Act 1978 (maximum number of judges) nor as a judge of the Supreme Court of Northern Ireland for the purposes of section 9(1)(d) of the 1973 Act (salaries etc.);

(d) a Circuit judge is not to count as such for the purposes of section 18 of the Courts Act 1971 (salaries etc.);

(e) a sheriff is not to count as such for the purposes of section 14 of the Sheriff Courts (Scotland) Act 1907 (salaries etc.);

(f) a county court judge of Northern Ireland is not to count as such for the purposes of section 106 of the County Courts Act Northern Ireland) 1959 (salaries etc.).

(5) If a sheriff principal is appointed a judge of the Court, section 11(1) of the Sheriff Courts (Scotland) Act 1971 (temporary appointment of sheriff principal) applies, while he holds that appointment, as if his office is vacant.

(6) Schedule 4 makes provision about judicial pensions in relation to the holder of a judicial office who serves as a judge of the Court.

(7) The Lord Chancellor or the Secretary of State may by order make such transitional provision (including, in particular, provision for a temporary increase in the maximum number of judges) as he considers appropriate in relation to any holder of a judicial office who has completed his service as a judge of the Court.

19.—(1) A Minister of the Crown in charge of a Bill in either House of Parliament must, before Second Reading of the Bill—

(a) make a statement to the effect that in his view the provisions of the Bill are compatible with the Convention rights ("a statement of compatibility"); or

(b) make a statement to the effect that although he is unable to make a statement of compatibility the government nevertheless wishes the House to proceed with the Bill.

(2) The statement must be in writing and be published in such manner as the Minister making it considers appropriate.

20.—(1) Any power of a Minister of the Crown to make an order under this Act is exercisable by statutory instrument.

(2) The power of the Lord Chancellor or the Secretary of State to make rules (other than rules of court) under section 2(3) or 7(9) is exercisable by statutory instrument.

(3) Any statutory instrument made under section 14, 15 or 16(7) must be laid before Parliament.

(4) No order may be made by the Lord Chancellor or the Secretary of State under section 1(4), 7(11) or 16(2) unless a draft of the order has been laid before, and approved by, each House of Parliament.

(5) Any statutory instrument made under section 18(7) or Schedule 4, or to which subsection (2) applies, shall be subject to annulment in pursuance of a resolution of either House of Parliament.

(6) The power of a Northern Ireland department to make—

(a) rules under section 2(3)(c) or 7(9)(c), or

(b) an order under section 7(11),

is exercisable by statutory rule for the purposes of the Statutory Rules (Northern Ireland) Order 1979.

(7) Any rules made under section 2(3)(c) or 7(9)(c) shall be subject to negative resolution; and section 41(6) of the Interpretation Act Northern Ireland) 1954 (meaning of "subject to negative resolution") shall apply as if the power to make the rules were conferred by an Act of the Northern Ireland Assembly.

(8) No order may be made by a Northern Ireland department under section 7(11) unless a draft of the order has been laid before, and approved by, the Northern Ireland Assembly.

21.—(1) In this Act—

"amend" includes repeal and apply (with or without modifications);
"the appropriate Minister" means the Minister of the Crown having charge of the appropriate authorised government department (within the meaning of the Crown Proceedings Act 1947);
"the Commission" means the European Commission of Human Rights;
"the Convention" means the Convention for the Protection of Human Rights and Fundamental Freedoms, agreed by the Council of Europe at Rome on 4th November 1950 as it has effect for the time being in relation to the United Kingdom;
"declaration of incompatibility" means a declaration under section 4;
"Minister of the Crown" has the same meaning as in the Ministers of the Crown Act 1975;
"Northern Ireland Minister" includes the First Minister and the deputy First Minister in Northern Ireland;
"primary legislation" means any—

(a) public general Act;

(b) local and personal Act;

(c) private Act;

(d) Measure of the Church Assembly;

(e) Measure of the General Synod of the Church of England;

(f) Order in Council—

    (i)   made in exercise of Her Majesty's Royal Prerogative;

    (ii) made under section 38(1)(a) of the Northern Ireland Constitution Act 1973 or the corresponding provision of the Northern Ireland Act 1998; or

    (iii) amending an Act of a kind mentioned in paragraph (a), (b) or (c);

and includes an order or other instrument made under primary legislation (otherwise than by the National Assembly for Wales, a member of the Scottish Executive, a Northern Ireland Minister or a Northern Ireland department) to the extent to which it operates to bring one or more provisions of that legislation into force or amends any primary legislation;

"the First Protocol" means the protocol to the Convention agreed at Paris on 20th March 1952;

"the Sixth Protocol" means the protocol to the Convention agreed at Strasbourg on 28th April 1983;

"the Eleventh Protocol" means the protocol to the Convention (restructuring the control machinery established by the Convention) agreed at Strasbourg on 11th May 1994;

"remedial order" means an order under section 10;

"subordinate legislation" means any—

  (a) Order in Council other than one—

      (i)   made in exercise of Her Majesty's Royal Prerogative;

      (ii) made under section 38(1)(a) of the Northern Ireland Constitution Act 1973 or the corresponding provision of the Northern Ireland Act 1998; or

      (iii) amending an Act of a kind mentioned in the definition of primary legislation;

  (b) Act of the Scottish Parliament;

  (c) Act of the Parliament of Northern Ireland;

  (d) Measure of the Assembly established under section 1 of the Northern Ireland Assembly Act 1973;

  (e) Act of the Northern Ireland Assembly;

  (f) order, rules, regulations, scheme, warrant, byelaw or other instrument made under primary legislation (except to the extent to which it operates to bring one or more provisions of that legislation into force or amends any primary legislation);

  (g) order, rules, regulations, scheme, warrant, byelaw or other instrument made under legislation mentioned in paragraph (b), (c), (d) or (e) or made under an Order in Council applying only to Northern Ireland;

  (h) order, rules, regulations, scheme, warrant, byelaw or other instrument made by a member of the Scottish Executive, a Northern Ireland Minister or a Northern Ireland department in exercise of prerogative or other executive functions of Her Majesty which are exercisable by such a person on behalf of Her Majesty;

"transferred matters" has the same meaning as in the Northern Ireland Act 1998; and

"tribunal" means any tribunal in which legal proceedings may be brought.

(2) The references in paragraphs (b) and (c) of section 2(1) to Articles are to

Articles of the Convention as they had effect immediately before the coming into force of the Eleventh Protocol.

(3) The reference in paragraph (d) of section 2(1) to Article 46 includes a reference to Articles 32 and 54 of the Convention as they had effect immediately before the coming into force of the Eleventh Protocol.

(4) The references in section 2(1) to a report or decision of the Commission or a decision of the Committee of Ministers include references to a report or decision made as provided by paragraphs 3, 4 and 6 of Article 5 of the Eleventh Protocol (transitional provisions).

(5) Any liability under the Army Act 1955, the Air Force Act 1955 or the Naval Discipline Act 1957 to suffer death for an offence is replaced by a liability to imprisonment for life or any less punishment authorised by those Acts; and those Acts shall accordingly have effect with the necessary modifications.

22.—(1) This Act may be cited as the Human Rights Act 1998.

(2) Sections 18, 20 and 21(5) and this section come into force on the passing of this Act.

(3) The other provisions of this Act come into force on such day as the Secretary of State may by order appoint; and different days may be appointed for different purposes.

(4) Paragraph (b) of subsection (1) of section 7 applies to proceedings brought by or at the instigation of a public authority whenever the act in question took place; but otherwise that subsection does not apply to an act taking place before the coming into force of that section.

(5) This Act binds the Crown.

(6) This Act extends to Northern Ireland.

(7) Section 21(5), so far as it relates to any provision contained in the Army Act 1955, the Air Force Act 1955 or the Naval Discipline Act 1957, extends to any place to which that provision extends.

SCHEDULE 1

THE ARTICLES

PART I

THE CONVENTION

RIGHTS AND FREEDOMS

ARTICLE 2

RIGHT TO LIFE

1. Everyone's right to life shall be protected by law. No one shall be deprived of his life intentionally save in the execution of a sentence of a court following his conviction of a crime for which this penalty is provided by law.

2. Deprivation of life shall not be regarded as inflicted in contra-vention of this Article when it results from the use of force which is no more than absolutely necessary:

(a) in defence of any person from unlawful violence;

(b) in order to effect a lawful arrest or to prevent the escape of a person lawfully detained;

(c) in action lawfully taken for the purpose of quelling a riot or insurrection.

ARTICLE 3

PROHIBITION OF TORTURE

No one shall be subjected to torture or to inhuman or degrading treatment or punishment.

ARTICLE 4

PROHIBITION OF SLAVERY AND FORCED LABOUR

1. No one shall be held in slavery or servitude.
2. No one shall be required to perform forced or compulsory labour.
3. For the purpose of this Article the term "forced or compulsory labour" shall not include:

(a) any work required to be done in the ordinary course of detention imposed according to the provisions of Article 5 of this Convention or during conditional release from such detention;

(b) any service of a military character or, in case of conscientious objectors in countries where they are recognised, service exacted instead of compulsory military service;

(c) any service exacted in case of an emergency or calamity threatening the life or well-being of the community;

(d) any work or service which forms part of normal civic obligations.

ARTICLE 5

RIGHT TO LIBERTY AND SECURITY

1. Everyone has the right to liberty and security of person. No one shall be deprived of his liberty save in the following cases and in accordance with a procedure prescribed by law:

(a) the lawful detention of a person after conviction by a competent court;

(b) the lawful arrest or detention of a person for non-compliance with the lawful order of a court or in order to secure the fulfilment of any obligation prescribed by law;

(c) the lawful arrest or detention of a person effected for the purpose of bringing him before the competent legal authority on reasonable suspicion of having committed an offence or when it is reasonably considered necessary to prevent his committing an offence or fleeing after having done so;

(d) the detention of a minor by lawful order for the purpose of educational supervision or his lawful detention for the purpose of bringing him before the competent legal authority;

(e) the lawful detention of persons for the prevention of the spreading of infectious diseases, of persons of unsound mind, alcoholics or drug addicts or vagrants;

(f) the lawful arrest or detention of a person to prevent his effecting an unauthorised entry into the country or of a person against whom action is being taken with a view to deportation or extradition.

2. Everyone who is arrested shall be informed promptly, in a language which he understands, of the reasons for his arrest and of any charge against him.

3. Everyone arrested or detained in accordance with the provisions of paragraph 1(c) of this Article shall be brought promptly before a judge or other officer authorised by law to exercise judicial power and shall be entitled to trial within a reasonable time or to release pending trial. Release may be conditioned by guarantees to appear for trial.

4. Everyone who is deprived of his liberty by arrest or detention shall be entitled to take proceedings by which the lawfulness of his detention shall be decided speedily by a court and his release ordered if the detention is not lawful.

5. Everyone who has been the victim of arrest or detention in contravention of the provisions of this Article shall have an enforceable right to compensation.

ARTICLE 6

RIGHT TO A FAIR TRIAL

1. In the determination of his civil rights and obligations or of any criminal charge against him, everyone is entitled to a fair and public hearing within a reasonable time by an independent and impartial tribunal established by law. Judgment shall be pronounced publicly but the press and public may be excluded from all or part of the trial in the interest of morals, public order or national security in a democratic society, where the interests of juveniles or the protection of the private life of the parties so require, or to the extent strictly necessary in the opinion of the court in special circumstances where publicity would prejudice the interests of justice.

2. Everyone charged with a criminal offence shall be presumed innocent until proved guilty according to law.

3. Everyone charged with a criminal offence has the following minimum rights:

(a) to be informed promptly, in a language which he understands and in detail, of the nature and cause of the accusation against him;

(b) to have adequate time and facilities for the preparation of his defence;

(c) to defend himself in person or through legal assistance of his own choosing or, if he has not sufficient means to pay for legal assistance, to be given it free when the interests of justice so require;

(d) to examine or have examined witnesses against him and to obtain the attendance and examination of witnesses on his behalf under the same conditions as witnesses against him;

(e) to have the free assistance of an interpreter if he cannot understand or speak the language used in court.

ARTICLE 7

NO PUNISHMENT WITHOUT LAW

1. No one shall be held guilty of any criminal offence on account of any act or omission which did not constitute a criminal offence under national or international law at the time when it was committed. Nor shall a heavier penalty be imposed than the one that was applicable at the time the criminal offence was committed.

2. This Article shall not prejudice the trial and punishment of any person for any act or omission which, at the time when it was committed, was criminal according to the general principles of law recognised by civilised nations.

Article 8

Right to Respect for Private and Family Life

1. Everyone has the right to respect for his private and family life, his home and his correspondence.

2. There shall be no interference by a public authority with the exercise of this right except such as is in accordance with the law and is necessary in a democratic society in the interests of national security, public safety or the economic well-being of the country, for the prevention of disorder or crime, for the protection of health or morals, or for the protection of the rights and freedoms of others.

Article 9

Freedom of Thought, Conscience and Religion

1. Everyone has the right to freedom of thought, conscience and religion; this right includes freedom to change his religion or belief and freedom, either alone or in community with others and in public or private, to manifest his religion or belief, in worship, teaching, practice and observance.

2. Freedom to manifest one's religion or beliefs shall be subject only to such limitations as are prescribed by law and are necessary in a democratic society in the interests of public safety, for the protection of public order, health or morals, or for the protection of the rights and freedoms of others.

Article 10

Freedom of Expression

1. Everyone has the right to freedom of expression. This right shall include freedom to hold opinions and to receive and impart information and ideas without interference by public authority and regardless of frontiers. This Article shall not prevent States from requiring the licensing of broadcasting, television or cinema enterprises.

2. The exercise of these freedoms, since it carries with it duties and responsibilities, may be subject to such formalities, conditions, restrictions or penalties as are prescribed by law and are necessary in a democratic society, in the interests of national security, territorial integrity or public safety, for the prevention of disorder or crime, for the protection of health or morals, for the protection of the reputation or rights of others, for preventing the disclosure of information received in confidence, or for maintaining the authority and impartiality of the judiciary.

Article 11

Freedom of Assembly and Association

1. Everyone has the right to freedom of peaceful assembly and to freedom of association with others, including the right to form and to join trade unions for the protection of his interests.

2. No restrictions shall be placed on the exercise of these rights other than such as are prescribed by law and are necessary in a democratic society in the interests of national security or public safety, for the prevention of disorder or crime, for the protection of health or morals or for the protection of the rights and freedoms of others. This Article shall not prevent the imposition of lawful restrictions on the exercise of these rights by members of the armed forces, of the police or of the administration of the State.

Article 12

Right to marry

Men and women of marriageable age have the right to marry and to found a family, according to the national laws governing the exercise of this right.

Article 14

Prohibition of discrimination

The enjoyment of the rights and freedoms set forth in this Convention shall be secured without discrimination on any ground such as sex, race, colour, language, religion, political or other opinion, national or social origin, association with a national minority, property, birth or other status.

Article 16

Restrictions on Political Activity of Aliens

Nothing in Articles 10, 11 and 14 shall be regarded as preventing the High Contracting Parties from imposing restrictions on the political activity of aliens.

Article 17

Prohibition of Abuse of Rights

Nothing in this Convention may be interpreted as implying for any State, group or person any right to engage in any activity or perform any act aimed at the destruction of any of the rights and freedoms set forth herein or at their limitation to a greater extent than is provided for in the Convention.

Article 18

Limitation on Use of Restrictions on Rights

The restrictions permitted under this Convention to the said rights and freedoms shall not be applied for any purpose other than those for which they have been prescribed.

Part II

The First Protocol

Article 1

Protection of Property

Every natural or legal person is entitled to the peaceful enjoyment of his possessions. No one shall be deprived of his possessions except in the public interest and subject to the conditions provided for by law and by the general principles of international law.

The preceding provisions shall not, however, in any way impair the right of a State to enforce such laws as it deems necessary to control the use of property in accordance with the general interest or to secure the payment of taxes or other contributions or penalties.

ARTICLE 2

RIGHT TO EDUCATION

No person shall be denied the right to education. In the exercise of any functions which it assumes in relation to education and to teaching, the State shall respect the right of parents to ensure such education and teaching in conformity with their own religious and philosophical convictions.

ARTICLE 3

RIGHT TO FREE ELECTIONS

The High Contracting Parties undertake to hold free elections at reasonable intervals by secret ballot, under conditions which will ensure the free expression of the opinion of the people in the choice of the legislature.

PART III

THE SIXTH PROTOCOL

ARTICLE 1

ABOLITION OF THE DEATH PENALTY

The death penalty shall be abolished. No one shall be condemned to such penalty or executed.

ARTICLE 2

DEATH PENALTY IN TIME OF WAR

A State may make provision in its law for the death penalty in respect of acts committed in time of war or of imminent threat of war; such penalty shall be applied only in the instances laid down in the law and in accordance with its provisions. The State shall communicate to the Secretary General of the Council of Europe the relevant provisions of that law.

SCHEDULE 2

REMEDIAL ORDERS

1.—(1) A remedial order may—

(a) contain such incidental, supplemental, consequential or transitional provision as the person making it considers appropriate;

(b) be made so as to have effect from a date earlier than that on which it is made;

(c) make provision for the delegation of specific functions;

(d) make different provision for different cases.

(2) The power conferred by sub-paragraph (1)(a) includes—

(a) power to amend primary legislation (including primary legislation other than that which contains the incompatible provision); and

(b) power to amend or revoke subordinate legislation (including subordinate legislation other than that which contains the incompatible provision).

(3) A remedial order may be made so as to have the same extent as the legislation which it affects.

(4) No person is to be guilty of an offence solely as a result of the retrospective effect of a remedial order.

2. No remedial order may be made unless—

(a) a draft of the order has been approved by a resolution of each House of Parliament made after the end of the period of 60 days beginning with the day on which the draft was laid; or

(b) it is declared in the order that it appears to the person making it that, because of the urgency of the matter, it is necessary to make the order without a draft being so approved.

3.—(1) No draft may be laid under paragraph 2(a) unless—

(a) the person proposing to make the order has laid before Parliament a document which contains a draft of the proposed order and the required information; and

(b) the period of 60 days, beginning with the day on which the document required by this sub-paragraph was laid, has ended.

(2) If representations have been made during that period, the draft laid under paragraph 2(a) must be accompanied by a statement containing—

(a) a summary of the representations; and

(b) if, as a result of the representations, the proposed order has been changed, details of the changes.

4.—(1) If a remedial order ("the original order") is made without being approved in draft, the person making it must lay it before Parliament, accompanied by the required information, after it is made.

(2) If representations have been made during the period of 60 days beginning with the day on which the original order was made, the person making it must (after the end of that period) lay before Parliament a statement containing—

(a) a summary of the representations; and

(b) if, as a result of the representations, he considers it appropriate to make changes to the original order, details of the changes.

(3) If sub-paragraph (2)(b) applies, the person making the statement must—

(a) make a further remedial order replacing the original order; and

(b) lay the replacement order before Parliament.

(4) If, at the end of the period of 120 days beginning with the day on which the original order was made, a resolution has not been passed by each House approving the original or replacement order, the order ceases to have effect (but without that affecting anything previously done under either order or the power to make a fresh remedial order).

5. In this Schedule—

"representations" means representations about a remedial order (or proposed remedial order) made to the person making (or proposing to make) it and includes any relevant Parliamentary report or resolution; and
"required information" means—

    (a)   an explanation of the incompatibility which the order (or proposed order) seeks to remove, including particulars of the relevant declaration, finding or order; and

    (b)   a statement of the reasons for proceeding under section 10 and for making an order in those terms.

6. In calculating any period for the purposes of this Schedule, no account is to be taken of any time during which—

    (a)   Parliament is dissolved or prorogued; or

    (b)   both Houses are adjourned for more than four days.

SCHEDULE 3

DEROGATION AND RESERVATION

PART I

DEROGATION

The 1988 notification
The United Kingdom Permanent Representative to the Council of Europe presents his compliments to the Secretary General of the Council, and has the honour to convey the following information in order to ensure compliance with the obligations of Her Majesty's Government in the United Kingdom under Article 15(3) of the Convention for the Protection of Human Rights and Fundamental Freedoms signed at Rome on 4 November 1950.

There have been in the United Kingdom in recent years campaigns of organised terrorism connected with the affairs of Northern Ireland which have manifested themselves in activities which have included repeated murder, attempted murder, maiming, intimidation and violent civil disturbance and in bombing and fire raising which have resulted in death, injury and widespread destruction of property. As a result, a public emergency within the meaning of Article 15(1) of the Convention exists in the United Kingdom.

The Government found it necessary in 1974 to introduce and since then, in cases concerning persons reasonably suspected of involvement in terrorism connected with the affairs of Northern Ireland, or of certain offences under the legislation, who have been detained for 48 hours, to exercise powers enabling further detention without charge, for periods of up to five days, on the authority of the Secretary of State. These powers are at present to be found in Section 12 of the Prevention of Terrorism (Temporary Provisions) Act 1984, Article 9 of the Prevention of Terrorism (Supplemental Temporary Provisions) Order 1984 and Article 10 of the Prevention of Terrorism (Supplemental Temporary Provisions) (Northern Ireland) Order 1984.

Section 12 of the Prevention of Terrorism (Temporary Provisions) Act 1984 provides for a person whom a constable has arrested on reasonable grounds of suspecting him to be guilty of an offence under Section 1, 9 or 10 of the Act, or to be or to have been involved in terrorism connected with the affairs of Northern Ireland, to be detained in right of the arrest for up to 48 hours and thereafter, where the

Secretary of State extends the detention period, for up to a further five days. Section 12 substantially re-enacted Section 12 of the Prevention of Terrorism (Temporary Provisions) Act 1976 which, in turn, substantially re-enacted Section 7 of the Prevention of Terrorism (Temporary Provisions) Act 1974.

Article 10 of the Prevention of Terrorism (Supplemental Temporary Provisions) (Northern Ireland) Order 1984 (SI 1984/417) and Article 9 of the Prevention of Terrorism (Supplemental Temporary Provisions) Order 1984 (SI 1984/418) were both made under Sections 13 and 14 of and Schedule 3 to the 1984 Act and substantially re-enacted powers of detention in Orders made under the 1974 and 1976 Acts. A person who is being examined under Article 4 of either Order on his arrival in, or on seeking to leave, Northern Ireland or Great Britain for the purpose of determining whether he is or has been involved in terrorism connected with the affairs of Northern Ireland, or whether there are grounds for suspecting that he has committed an offence under Section 9 of the 1984 Act, may be detained under Article 9 or 10, as appropriate, pending the conclusion of his examination. The period of this examination may exceed 12 hours if an examining officer has reasonable grounds for suspecting him to be or to have been involved in acts of terrorism connected with the affairs of Northern Ireland.

Where such a person is detained under the said Article 9 or 10 he may be detained for up to 48 hours on the authority of an examining officer and thereafter, where the Secretary of State extends the detention period, for up to a further five days.

In its judgment of 29 November 1988 in the Case of *Brogan and Others*, the European Court of Human Rights held that there had been a violation of Article 5(3) in respect of each of the applicants, all of whom had been detained under Section 12 of the 1984 Act. The Court held that even the shortest of the four periods of detention concerned, namely four days and six hours, fell outside the constraints as to time permitted by the first part of Article 5(3). In addition, the Court held that there had been a violation of Article 5(5) in the case of each applicant.

Following this judgment, the Secretary of State for the Home Department informed Parliament on 6 December 1988 that, against the background of the terrorist campaign, and the over-riding need to bring terrorists to justice, the Government did not believe that the maximum period of detention should be reduced. He informed Parliament that the Government were examining the matter with a view to responding to the judgment. On 22 December 1988, the Secretary of State further informed Parliament that it remained the Government's wish, if it could be achieved, to find a judicial process under which extended detention might be reviewed and where appropriate authorised by a judge or other judicial officer. But a further period of reflection and consultation was necessary before the Government could bring forward a firm and final view.

Since the judgment of 29 November 1988 as well as previously, the Government have found it necessary to continue to exercise, in relation to terrorism connected with the affairs of Northern Ireland, the powers described above enabling further detention without charge for periods of up to 5 days, on the authority of the Secretary of State, to the extent strictly required by the exigencies of the situation to enable necessary enquiries and investigations properly to be completed in order to decide whether criminal proceedings should be instituted. To the extent that the exercise of these powers may be inconsistent with the obligations imposed by the Convention the Government has availed itself of the right of derogation conferred by Article 15(1) of the Convention and will continue to do so until further notice.

Dated 23 December 1988.

The 1989 notification
The United Kingdom Permanent Representative to the Council of Europe presents

his compliments to the Secretary General of the Council, and has the honour to convey the following information.

In his communication to the Secretary General of 23 December 1988, reference was made to the introduction and exercise of certain powers under section 12 of the Prevention of Terrorism (Temporary Provisions) Act 1984, Article 9 of the Prevention of Terrorism (Supplemental Temporary Provisions) Order 1984 and Article 10 of the Prevention of Terrorism (Supplemental Temporary Provisions) (Northern Ireland) Order 1984.

These provisions have been replaced by section 14 of and paragraph 6 of Schedule 5 to the Prevention of Terrorism (Temporary Provisions) Act 1989, which make comparable provision. They came into force on 22 March 1989. A copy of these provisions is enclosed.

The United Kingdom Permanent Representative avails himself of this opportunity to renew to the Secretary General the assurance of his highest consideration.

23 March 1989.

PART II

RESERVATION

At the time of signing the present (First) Protocol, I declare that, in view of certain provisions of the Education Acts in the United Kingdom, the principle affirmed in the second sentence of Article 2 is accepted by the United Kingdom only so far as it is compatible with the provision of efficient instruction and training, and the avoidance of unreasonable public expenditure.

Dated 20 March 1952

Made by the United Kingdom Permanent Representative to the Council of Europe.

SCHEDULE 4

JUDICIAL PENSIONS

1.—(1) The appropriate Minister must by order make provision with respect to pensions payable to or in respect of any holder of a judicial office who serves as an ECHR judge.

(2) A pensions order must include such provision as the Minister making it considers is necessary to secure that—

(a) an ECHR judge who was, immediately before his appointment as an ECHR judge, a member of a judicial pension scheme is entitled to remain as a member of that scheme;

(b) the terms on which he remains a member of the scheme are those which would have been applicable had he not been appointed as an ECHR judge; and

(c) entitlement to benefits payable in accordance with the scheme continues to be determined as if, while serving as an ECHR judge, his salary was that which would (but for section 18(4)) have been payable to him in respect of his continuing service as the holder of his judicial office.

2. A pensions order may, in particular, make provision—

(a) for any contributions which are payable by a person who remains a member of a scheme as a result of the order, and which would otherwise be payable by deduction from his salary, to be made otherwise than by deduction from his salary as an ECHR judge; and

(b) for such contributions to be collected in such manner as may be determined by the administrators of the scheme.

3. A pensions order may amend any provision of, or made under, a pensions Act in such manner and to such extent as the Minister making the order considers necessary or expedient to ensure the proper administration of any scheme to which it relates.

4. In this Schedule—

"appropriate Minister" means—

(a) in relation to any judicial office whose jurisdiction is exercisable exclusively in relation to Scotland, the Secretary of State; and

(b) otherwise, the Lord Chancellor;

"ECHR judge" means the holder of a judicial office who is serving as a judge of the Court;
"judicial pension scheme" means a scheme established by and in accordance with a pensions Act;
"pensions Act" means—

(a) the County Courts Act Northern Ireland) 1959;

(b) the Sheriffs' Pensions (Scotland) Act 1961;

(c) the Judicial Pensions Act 1981; or

(d) the Judicial Pensions and Retirement Act 1993; and

"pensions order" means an order made under paragraph 1.

Appendix D
THE ELECTRONIC COMMERCE
(EC DIRECTIVE) REGULATIONS 2002
(SI 2002/2013)

Citation and commencement

1.—(1) These Regulations may be cited as the Electronic Commerce (EC Directive) Regulations 2002 and except for regulation 16 shall come into force on 21st August 2002.

(2) Regulation 16 shall come into force on 23rd October 2002.

Interpretation

2.—(1) In these Regulations and in the Schedule—

"commercial communication" means a communication, in any form, designed to promote, directly or indirectly, the goods, services or image of any person pursuing a commercial, industrial or craft activity or exercising a regulated profession, other than a communication—

    (a) consisting only of information allowing direct access to the activity of that person including a geographic address, a domain name or an electronic mail address; or

    (b) relating to the goods, services or image of that person provided that the communication has been prepared independently of the person making it (and for this purpose, a communication prepared without financial consideration is to be taken to have been prepared independently unless the contrary is shown);

"the Commission" means the Commission of the European Communities;
"consumer" means any natural person who is acting for purposes other than those of his trade, business or profession;

"coordinated field" means requirements applicable to information society service providers or information society services, regardless of whether they are of a general nature or specifically designed for them, and covers requirements with which the service provider has to comply in respect of—

(a) the taking up of the activity of an information society service, such as requirements concerning qualifications, authorisation or notification, and

(b) the pursuit of the activity of an information society service, such as requirements concerning the behaviour of the service provider, requirements regarding the quality or content of the service including those applicable to advertising and contracts, or requirements concerning the liability of the service provider,

but does not cover requirements such as those applicable to goods as such, to the delivery of goods or to services not provided by electronic means;

"the Directive" means Directive 2000/31/EC of the European Parliament and of the Council of 8 June 2000 on certain legal aspects of information society services, in particular electronic commerce, in the Internal Market (Directive on electronic commerce);

"EEA Agreement" means the Agreement on the European Economic Area signed at Oporto on 2 May 1992 as adjusted by the Protocol signed at Brussels on 17 March 1993;

"enactment" includes an enactment comprised in Northern Ireland legislation and comprised in, or an instrument made under, an Act of the Scottish Parliament;

"enforcement action" means any form of enforcement action including, in particular—

(a) in relation to any legal requirement imposed by or under any enactment, any action taken with a view to or in connection with imposing any sanction (whether criminal or otherwise) for failure to observe or comply with it; and

(b) in relation to a permission or authorisation, anything done with a view to removing or restricting that permission or authorisation;

"enforcement authority" does not include courts but, subject to that, means any person who is authorised, whether by or under an enactment or otherwise, to take enforcement action;

"established service provider" means a service provider who is a national of a member State or a company or firm as mentioned in Article 48 of the Treaty and who effectively pursues an economic activity by virtue of which he is a service provider using a fixed establishment in a member State for an indefinite period, but the presence and use of the technical means and technologies required to provide the information society service do not, in themselves, constitute an establishment of the provider; in cases where it cannot be determined from which of a number of places of establishment a given service is provided, that service is to be regarded as provided from the place of establishment where the provider has the centre of his activities relating to that service; references to a service provider being established or to the establishment of a service provider shall be construed accordingly;

"information society services" (which is summarised in recital 17 of the Directive as covering "any service normally provided for remuneration, at a distance, by means of electronic equipment for the processing (including digital compression) and storage of data, and at the individual request of a recipient of a service") has the meaning set out in Article 2(a) of the Directive, (which refers to Article 1(2) of Directive 98/34/EC of the European Parliament and of the Council of 22 June

1998 laying down a procedure for the provision of information in the field of technical standards and regulations, as amended by Directive 98/48/EC of 20 July 1998);

"member State" includes a State which is a contracting party to the EEA Agreement;

"recipient of the service" means any person who, for professional ends or otherwise, uses an information society service, in particular for the purposes of seeking information or making it accessible;

"regulated profession" means any profession within the meaning of either Article 1(d) of Council Directive 89/48/EEC of 21 December 1988 on a general system for the recognition of higher-education diplomas awarded on completion of professional education and training of at least three years' duration or of Article 1(f) of Council Directive 92/51/EEC of 18 June 1992 on a second general system for the recognition of professional education and training to supplement Directive 89/48/EEC;

"service provider" means any person providing an information society service;

"the Treaty" means the treaty establishing the European Community.

(2) In regulation 4 and 5, "requirement" means any legal requirement under the law of the United Kingdom, or any part of it, imposed by or under any enactment or otherwise.

(3) Terms used in the Directive other than those in paragraph (1) above shall have the same meaning as in the Directive.

Exclusions

3.—(1) Nothing in these Regulations shall apply in respect of—

(a) the field of taxation;

(b) questions relating to information society services covered by the Data Protection Directive and the Telecommunications Data Protection Directive and Directive 2002/58/EC of the European Parliament and of the Council of 12th July 2002 concerning the processing of personal data and the protection of privacy in the electronic communications sector (Directive on privacy and electronic communications);

(c) questions relating to agreements or practices governed by cartel law; and

(d) the following activities of information society services—

    (i) the activities of a public notary or equivalent professions to the extent that they involve a direct and specific connection with the exercise of public authority,

    (ii) the representation of a client and defence of his interests before the courts, and

    (iii) betting, gaming or lotteries which involve wagering a stake with monetary value.

(2) These Regulations shall not apply in relation to any Act passed on or after the date these Regulations are made or in exercise of a power to legislate after that date.

(3) In this regulation—

"cartel law" means so much of the law relating to agreements between undertakings, decisions by associations of undertakings or concerted practices as relates to agreements to divide the market or fix prices;

"Data Protection Directive" means Directive 95/46/EC of the European Parliament and of the Council of 24 October 1995 on the protection of individuals with regard to the processing of personal data and on the free movement of such data; and

"Telecommunications Data Protection Directive" means Directive 97/66/EC of the European Parliament and of the Council of 15 December 1997 concerning the processing of personal data and the protection of privacy in the tele-communications sector.

Internal market

4.—(1) Subject to paragraph (4) below, any requirement which falls within the coordinated field shall apply to the provision of an information society service by a service provider established in the United Kingdom irrespective of whether that information society service is provided in the United Kingdom or another member State.

(2) Subject to paragraph (4) below, an enforcement authority with responsibility in relation to any requirement in paragraph (1) shall ensure that the provision of an information society service by a service provider established in the United Kingdom complies with that requirement irrespective of whether that service is provided in the United Kingdom or another member State and any power, remedy or procedure for taking enforcement action shall be available to secure compliance.

(3) Subject to paragraphs (4), (5) and (6) below, any requirement shall not be applied to the provision of an information society service by a service provider established in a member State other than the United Kingdom for reasons which fall within the coordinated field where its application would restrict the freedom to provide information society services to a person in the United Kingdom from that member State.

(4) Paragraphs (1), (2) and (3) shall not apply to those fields in the annex to the Directive set out in the Schedule.

(5) The reference to any requirements the application of which would restrict the freedom to provide information society services from another member State in paragraph (3) above does not include any requirement maintaining the level of protection for public health and consumer interests established by Community acts.

(6) To the extent that anything in these Regulations creates any new criminal offence, it shall not be punishable with imprisonment for more than two years or punishable on summary conviction with imprisonment for more than three months or with a fine of more than level 5 on the standard scale (if not calculated on a daily basis) or with a fine of more than £100 a day.

Derogations from Regulation 4

5.—(1) Notwithstanding regulation 4(3), an enforcement authority may take measures, including applying any requirement which would otherwise not apply by virtue of regulation 4(3) in respect of a given information society service, where those measures are necessary for reasons of—

(a) public policy, in particular the prevention, investigation, detection and pro-secution of criminal offences, including the protection of minors and the fight against any incitement to hatred on grounds of race, sex, religion or nationality, and violations of human dignity concerning individual persons;

(b) the protection of public health;

(c) public security, including the safeguarding of national security and defence, or

(d) the protection of consumers, including investors,

and proportionate to those objectives.

(2) Notwithstanding regulation 4(3), in any case where an enforcement authority with responsibility in relation to the requirement in question is not party to the proceedings, a court may, on the application of any person or of its own motion, apply any requirement which would otherwise not apply by virtue of regulation 4(3) in respect of a given information society service, if the application of that enactment or requirement is necessary for and proportionate to any of the objectives set out in paragraph (1) above.

(3) Paragraphs (1) and (2) shall only apply where the information society service prejudices or presents a serious and grave risk of prejudice to an objective in paragraph (1)(a) to (d).

(4) Subject to paragraphs (5) and (6), an enforcement authority shall not take the measures in paragraph (1) above, unless it—

(a) asks the member State in which the service provider is established to take measures and the member State does not take such measures or they are inadequate; and

(b) notifies the Commission and the member State in which the service provider is established of its intention to take such measures.

(5) Paragraph (4) shall not apply to court proceedings, including preliminary proceedings and acts carried out in the course of a criminal investigation.

(6) If it appears to the enforcement authority that the matter is one of urgency, it may take the measures under paragraph (1) without first asking the member State in which the service provider is established to take measures and notifying the Commission and the member State in derogation from paragraph (4).

(7) In a case where a measure is taken pursuant to paragraph (6) above, the enforcement authority shall notify the measures taken to the Commission and to the member State concerned in the shortest possible time thereafter and indicate the reasons for urgency.

(8) In paragraph (2), "court" means any court or tribunal.

General information to be provided by a person providing an information society service

6.—(1) A person providing an information society service shall make available to the recipient of the service and any relevant enforcement authority, in a form and manner which is easily, directly and permanently accessible, the following information—

(a) the name of the service provider;

(b) the geographic address at which the service provider is established;

(c) the details of the service provider, including his electronic mail address, which make it possible to contact him rapidly and communicate with him in a direct and effective manner;

(d) where the service provider is registered in a trade or similar register available to the public, details of the register in which the service provider is entered and his registration number, or equivalent means of identification in that register;

(e) where the provision of the service is subject to an authorisation scheme, the particulars of the relevant supervisory authority;

(f) where the service provider exercises a regulated profession—

> (i) the details of any professional body or similar institution with which the service provider is registered;
>
> (ii) his professional title and the member State where that title has been granted;
>
> (iii) a reference to the professional rules applicable to the service provider in the member State of establishment and the means to access them; and

(g) where the service provider undertakes an activity that is subject to value added tax, the identification number referred to in Article 22(1) of the sixth Council Directive 77/388/EEC of 17 May 1977 on the harmonisation of the laws of the member States relating to turnover taxes—Common system of value added tax: uniform basis of assessment.

(2) Where a person providing an information society service refers to prices, these shall be indicated clearly and unambiguously and, in particular, shall indicate whether they are inclusive of tax and delivery costs.

Commercial communications

7.—A service provider shall ensure that any commercial communication provided by him and which constitutes or forms part of an information society service shall—

(a) be clearly identifiable as a commercial communication;

(b) clearly identify the person on whose behalf the commercial communication is made;

(c) clearly identify as such any promotional offer (including any discount, premium or gift) and ensure that any conditions which must be met to qualify for it are easily accessible, and presented clearly and unambiguously; and

(d) clearly identify as such any promotional competition or game and ensure that any conditions for participation are easily accessible and presented clearly and unambiguously.

Unsolicited commercial communications

8.—A service provider shall ensure that any unsolicited commercial communication sent by him by electronic mail is clearly and unambiguously identifiable as such as soon as it is received.

Information to be provided where contracts are concluded by electronic means

9.—(1) Unless parties who are not consumers have agreed otherwise, where a contract is to be concluded by electronic means a service provider shall, prior to an order being placed by the recipient of a service, provide to that recipient in a clear, comprehensible and unambiguous manner the information set out in (a) to (d) below—

(a) the different technical steps to follow to conclude the contract;

(b) whether or not the concluded contract will be filed by the service provider and whether it will be accessible;

(c) the technical means for identifying and correcting input errors prior to the placing of the order; and

(d) the languages offered for the conclusion of the contract.

(2) Unless parties who are not consumers have agreed otherwise, a service provider shall indicate which relevant codes of conduct he subscribes to and give information on how those codes can be consulted electronically.

(3) Where the service provider provides terms and conditions applicable to the contract to the recipient, the service provider shall make them available to him in a way that allows him to store and reproduce them.

(4) The requirements of paragraphs (1) and (2) above shall not apply to contracts concluded exclusively by exchange of electronic mail or by equivalent individual communications.

Other information requirements

10.—Regulations 6, 7, 8 and 9(1) have effect in addition to any other information requirements in legislation giving effect to Community law.

Placing of the order

11.—(1) Unless parties who are not consumers have agreed otherwise, where the recipient of the service places his order through technological means, a service provider shall—

(a) acknowledge receipt of the order to the recipient of the service without undue delay and by electronic means; and

(b) make available to the recipient of the service appropriate, effective and accessible technical means allowing him to identify and correct input errors prior to the placing of the order.

(2) For the purposes of paragraph (1)(a) above—

(a) the order and the acknowledgement of receipt will be deemed to be received when the parties to whom they are addressed are able to access them; and

(b) the acknowledgement of receipt may take the form of the provision of the service paid for where that service is an information society service.

(3) The requirements of paragraph (1) above shall not apply to contracts concluded exclusively by exchange of electronic mail or by equivalent individual communications.

Meaning of the term "order"

12.—Except in relation to regulation 9(1)(c) and regulation 11(1)(b) where "order" shall be the contractual offer, "order" may be but need not be the contractual offer for the purposes of regulations 9 and 11.

Liability of the service provider

13.—The duties imposed by regulations 6, 7, 8, 9(1) and 11(1)(a) shall be enforceable, at the suit of any recipient of a service, by an action against the service provider for damages for breach of statutory duty.

Compliance with Regulation 9(3)

14.—Where on request a service provider has failed to comply with the requirement in regulation 9(3), the recipient may seek an order from any court having jurisdiction in relation to the contract requiring that service provider to comply with that requirement.

Right to rescind contract

15. Where a person—

(a) has entered into a contract to which these Regulations apply, and

(b) the service provider has not made available means of allowing him to identify and correct input errors in compliance with regulation 11(1)(b),

he shall be entitled to rescind the contract unless any court having jurisdiction in relation to the contract in question orders otherwise on the application of the service provider.

Amendments to the Stop Now Orders (EC Directive) Regulations 2001

16.—(1) The Stop Now Orders (EC Directive) Regulations 2001 are amended as follows.

(2) In regulation 2(3), at the end there shall be added—

"(k) regulations 6, 7, 8, 9, and 11 of the Electronic Commerce (E.C. Directive) Regulations 2002.".

(3) In Schedule 1, at the end there shall be added—

"11. Directive 2000/31/EC of the European Parliament and of the Council of 8th June 2000 on certain legal aspects of information society services, in particular electronic commerce, in the Internal Market (Directive on Electronic Commerce)."

Mere conduit

17.—(1) Where an information society service is provided which consists of the transmission in a communication network of information provided by a recipient of the service or the provision of access to a communication network, the service provider (if he otherwise would) shall not be liable for damages or for any other pecuniary remedy or for any criminal sanction as a result of that transmission where the service provider—

(a) did not initiate the transmission;

(b) did not select the receiver of the transmission; and

(c) did not select or modify the information contained in the transmission.

(2) The acts of transmission and of provision of access referred to in paragraph (1) include the automatic, intermediate and transient storage of the information transmitted where:

(a) this takes place for the sole purpose of carrying out the transmission in the communication network, and

(b) the information is not stored for any period longer than is reasonably necessary for the transmission.

Caching

18.—Where an information society service is provided which consists of the transmission in a communication network of information provided by a recipient of the service, the service provider (if he otherwise would) shall not be liable for damages or for any other pecuniary remedy or for any criminal sanction as a result of that transmission where—

(a) the information is the subject of automatic, intermediate and temporary storage where that storage is for the sole purpose of making more efficient onward transmission of the information to other recipients of the service upon their request, and

(b) the service provider—

    (i) does not modify the information;

    (ii) complies with conditions on access to the information;

    (iii) complies with any rules regarding the updating of the information, specified in a manner widely recognised and used by industry;

    (iv) does not interfere with the lawful use of technology, widely recognised and used by industry, to obtain data on the use of the information; and

    (v) acts expeditiously to remove or to disable access to the information he has stored upon obtaining actual knowledge of the fact that the information at the initial source of the transmission has been removed from the network, or access to it has been disabled, or that a court or an administrative authority has ordered such removal or disablement.

Hosting

19.—Where an information society service is provided which consists of the storage of information provided by a recipient of the service, the service provider (if he otherwise would) shall not be liable for damages or for any other pecuniary remedy or for any criminal sanction as a result of that storage where—

(a) the service provider—

    (i) does not have actual knowledge of unlawful activity or information and, where a claim for damages is made, is not aware of facts or circumstances from which it would have been apparent to the service provider that the activity or information was unlawful; or

    (ii) upon obtaining such knowledge or awareness, acts expeditiously to remove or to disable access to the information, and

(b) the recipient of the service was not acting under the authority or the control of the service provider.

Protection of rights

20.—(1) Nothing in regulations 17, 18 and 19 shall—

(a) prevent a person agreeing different contractual terms; or

(b) affect the rights of any party to apply to a court for relief to prevent or stop infringement of any rights.

(2) Any power of an administrative authority to prevent or stop infringement of any rights shall continue to apply notwithstanding regulations 17, 18 and 19.

Defence in Criminal Proceedings: burden of proof

21.—(1) This regulation applies where a service provider charged with an offence in criminal proceedings arising out of any transmission, provision of access or storage falling within regulation 17, 18 or 19 relies on a defence under any of regulations 17, 18 and 19.

(2) Where evidence is adduced which is sufficient to raise an issue with respect to that defence, the court or jury shall assume that the defence is satisfied unless the prosecution proves beyond reasonable doubt that it is not.

Notice for the purposes of actual knowledge

22.—In determining whether a service provider has actual knowledge for the purposes of regulations 18(b)(v) and 19(a)(i), a court shall take into account all matters which appear to it in the particular circumstances to be relevant and, among other things, shall have regard to—

   (a) whether a service provider has received a notice through a means of contact made available in accordance with regulation 6(1)(c), and

   (b) the extent to which any notice includes—

      (i) the full name and address of the sender of the notice;
      (ii) details of the location of the information in question; and
      (iii) details of the unlawful nature of the activity or information in question.

Alan Johnson,
Minister of State for Employment Relations Industry and the Regions, Department of Trade and Industry

30th July 2002

SCHEDULE

Regulation 4(4)

1. Copyright, neighbouring rights, rights referred to in Directive 87/54/EEC and Directive 96/9/EC and industrial property rights.

2. The freedom of the parties to a contract to choose the applicable law.

3. Contractual obligations concerning consumer contracts.

4. Formal validity of contracts creating or transferring rights in real estate where such contracts are subject to mandatory formal requirements of the law of the member State where the real estate is situated.

5. The permissibility of unsolicited commercial communications by electronic mail.

Appendix E
EDITORS' CODE OF PRACTICE

This is the newspaper and periodical industry's Code of Practice. It is framed and revised by the Editors' Code Committee made up of independent editors of national, regional and local newspapers and magazines. The Press Complaints Commission, which has a majority of lay members is charged with enforcing the Code, using it to adjudicate complaints. It was ratified by the PCC in September 2009. Clauses marked * are covered by exceptions relating to the public interest.

THE EDITORS' CODE

All members of the press have a duty to maintain the highest professional standards. The Code, which includes this preamble and the public interest exceptions below, sets the benchmark for those ethical standards, protecting both the rights of the individual and the public's right to know. It is the cornerstone of the system of self-regulation to which the industry has made a binding commitment.

It is essential that an agreed code be honoured not only to the letter but in the full spirit. It should not be interpreted so narrowly as to compromise its commitment to respect the rights of the individual, nor so broadly that it constitutes an unnecessary interference with freedom of expression or prevents publication in the public interest.

It is the responsibility of editors and publishers to apply the Code to editorial material in both printed and online versions of publications. They should take care to ensure it is observed rigorously by all editorial staff and external contributors, including non-journalists, in printed and online versions of publications.

Editors should co-operate swiftly with the PCC in the resolution of complaints. Any publication judged to have breached the Code must print the adjudication in full and with due prominence, including headline reference to the PCC.

1 Accuracy

i) The press must take care not to publish inaccurate, misleading or distorted information, including pictures.

ii) A significant inaccuracy, misleading statement or distortion once recognised must be corrected, promptly and with due prominence, and—where appropriate—an apology published.

iii) the Press, whilst free to be partisan, must distinguish clearly between comment, conjecture and fact.

iv) A publication must report fairly and accurately the outcome of an action for defamation to which it has been a party, unless an agreed settlement states otherwise, or an agreed statement is published.

2 Opportunity to reply

A fair opportunity for reply to inaccuracies must be given when reasonably called for.

3 * Privacy

i) Everyone is entitled to respect for his or her private and family life, home, health and correspondence, including digital communications.

ii) Editors will be expected to justify intrusions into any individual's private life without consent. Account will be taken of the complainant's own public disclosures of information.

iii) It is unacceptable to photograph individuals in private places without their consent.

Note—Private places are public or private property where there is a reasonable expectation of privacy.

4 * Harassment

i) Journalists must not engage in intimidation, harassment or persistent pursuit.

ii) They must not persist in questioning, telephoning, pursuing or photographing individuals once asked to desist; nor remain on their property when asked to leave and must not follow them. If requested, they must identify themselves and whom they represent.

iii) Editors must ensure these principles are observed by those working for them and take care not to use non-compliant material from other sources.

5 Intrusion into grief or shock

i) In cases involving personal grief or shock, enquiries and approaches must be made with sympathy and discretion and publication handled sensitively. This should not restrict the right to report legal proceedings, such as inquests.

*ii) When reporting suicide, care should be taken to avoid excessive detail about the method used.

6 * Children

i) Young people should be free to complete their time at school without unnecessary intrusion.

ii) A child under 16 must not be interviewed or photographed on issues involving their own or another child's welfare unless a custodial parent or similarly responsible adult consents.

iii) Pupils must not be approached or photographed at school without the permission of the school authorities.

iv) Minors must not be paid for material involving children's welfare, nor parents or guardians for material about their children or wards, unless it is clearly in the child's interest.

v) Editors must not use the fame, notoriety or position of a parent or guardian as sole justification for publishing details of a child's private life.

7 * Children in sex cases

1. The press must not, even if legally free to do so, identify children under 16 who are victims or witnesses in cases involving sex offences.
2. In any press report of a case involving a sexual offence against a child—

i) The child must not be identified.

ii) The adult may be identified.

iii) The word "incest" must not be used where a child victim might be identified.

iv) Care must be taken that nothing in the report implies the relationship between the accused and the child.

8 * Hospitals

i) Journalists must identify themselves and obtain permission from a responsible executive before entering non-public areas of hospitals or similar institutions to pursue enquiries.

ii) The restrictions on intruding into privacy are particularly relevant to enquiries about individuals in hospitals or similar institutions.

9 * Reporting of Crime

i) Relatives or friends of persons convicted or accused of crime should not generally be identified without their consent, unless they are genuinely relevant to the story.

ii) Particular regard should be paid to the potentially vulnerable position of children who witness, or are victims of, crime. This should not restrict the right to report legal proceedings.

10 * Clandestine devices and subterfuge

i) The press must not seek to obtain or publish material acquired by using hidden cameras or clandestine listening devices; or by intercepting private or mobile telephone calls, messages or emails; or by the unauthorised removal of documents or photographs; or by accessing digitally-held private information without consent.

ii) Engaging in misrepresentation or subterfuge, including by agents or intermediaries, can generally be justified only in the public interest and then only when the material cannot be obtained by other means.

11 Victims of sexual assault

The press must not identify victims of sexual assault or publish material likely to contribute to such identification unless there is adequate justification and they are legally free to do so.

12 Discrimination

i) The press must avoid prejudicial or pejorative reference to an individual's race, colour, religion, gender, sexual orientation or to any physical or mental illness or disability.

ii) Details of an individual's race, colour, religion, sexual orientation, physical or mental illness or disability must be avoided unless genuinely relevant to the story.

13 Financial journalism

i) Even where the law does not prohibit it, journalists must not use for their own profit financial information they receive in advance of its general publication, nor should they pass such information to others.

ii) They must not write about shares or securities in whose performance they know that they or their close families have a significant financial interest without disclosing the interest to the editor or financial editor.

iii) They must not buy or sell, either directly or through nominees or agents, shares or securities about which they have written recently or about which they intend to write in the near future.

14 Confidential sources

Journalists have a moral obligation to protect confidential sources of information.

15 Witness payments in criminal trials

i) No payment or offer of payment to a witness—or any person who may reasonably be expected to be called as a witness—should be made in any case once proceedings are active as defined by the Contempt of Court Act 1981. This prohibition lasts until the suspect has been freed unconditionally by police without charge or bail or the proceedings are otherwise discontinued; or has entered a guilty plea to the court; or, in the event of a not guilty plea, the court has announced its verdict.

*ii) Where proceedings are not yet active but are likely and foreseeable, editors must not make or offer payment to any person who may reasonably be expected to be called as a witness, unless the information concerned ought demonstrably to be published in the public interest and there is an over-riding need to make or promise payment for this to be done; and all reasonable steps have been taken to ensure no financial dealings influence the evidence those witnesses give. In no circumstances should such payment be conditional on the outcome of a trial.

*iii) Any payment or offer of payment made to a person later cited to give evidence in proceedings must be disclosed to the prosecution and defence. The witness must be advised of this requirement.

16 * Payment to criminals

i)   Payment or offers of payment for stories, pictures or information, which seek to exploit a particular crime or to glorify or glamorise crime in general, must not be made directly or via agents to convicted or confessed criminals or to their associates—who may include family, friends and colleagues.

ii) Editors invoking the public interest to justify payment or offers would need to demonstrate that there was good reason to believe the public interest would be served. If, despite payment, no public interest emerged, then the material should not be published.

THE PUBLIC INTEREST

There may be exceptions to the clauses marked * where they can be demonstrated to be in the public interest.
   1. The public interest includes, but is not confined to:

i)   Detecting or exposing crime or serious impropriety.

ii) Protecting public health and safety.

iii) Preventing the public from being misled by an action or statement of an individual or organisation.

   2. There is a public interest in freedom of expression itself.
   3. Whenever the public interest is invoked, the PCC will require editors to demonstrate fully that they reasonably believed that publication, or journalistic activity undertaken with a view to publication, would be in the public interest.
   4. The PCC will consider the extent to which material is already in the public domain, or will become so.
   5. In cases involving children under 16, editors must demonstrate an exceptional public interest to over-ride the normally paramount interest of the child.

PCC GUIDANCE NOTES

Court Reporting (1994)
Reporting of international sporting events (1998)
Prince William and privacy (1999)
On the reporting cases involving paedophiles (2000)
The Judiciary and harassment (2003)
Refugees and Asylum Seekers (2003)
Lottery Guidance Note (2004)
On the reporting of people accused of crime (2004)
Data Protection Act, Journalism and the PCC Code (2005)
Editorial co-operation (2005)
Financial Journalism: Best Practice Note (2005)
On the reporting of mental health issues (2006)

Copies of the above can be obtained online at www.pcc.org.uk

Press Complaints Commission
Halton House, 20/23 Holborn, London EC1N 2JD
Telephone: 020 7831 0022 **Fax:** 020 7831 0025
Textphone: 020 7831 0123 (for deaf or hard of hearing people)
Helpline: 0845 600 2757

Appendix F
OFCOM BROADCASTING CODE

How to Use the Code

The Code is set out in terms of principles, meanings and rules and, for Sections Seven (Fairness) and Eight (Privacy) also includes a set of "practices to be followed" by broadcasters. The principles are there to help readers understand the standards objectives and to apply the rules. Broadcasters must ensure that they comply with the rules as set out in the Code. The meanings help explain what Ofcom intends by some of the words and phrases used in the Code. The most relevant broadcasting legislation is noted under each section heading so readers can turn to the legislation if they wish.

When applying the Code to content, broadcasters should be aware that the context in which the material appears is key. In setting this Code, Ofcom has taken into account (as required by section 319(4) of the Act) the following:

a. the degree of harm and offence likely to be caused by the inclusion of any particular sort of material in programmes generally or in programmes of a particular description;

b. the likely size and composition of the potential audience for programmes included in television and radio services generally or in television and radio services of a particular description;

c. the likely expectation of the audience as to the nature of a programme's content and the extent to which the nature of a programme's content can be brought to the attention of potential members of the audience;

d. the likelihood of persons who are unaware of the nature of a programme's content being unintentionally exposed, by their own actions, to that content;

e. the desirability of securing that the content of services identifies when there is a change affecting the nature of a service that is being watched or listened to and, in particular, a change that is relevant to the application of the standards set under this section;

f. the desirability of maintaining the independence of editorial control over programme content.

These criteria have informed Ofcom's approach to setting the Code and therefore must be taken into account by broadcasters when interpreting the rules.

The Code does not seek to address each and every case that could arise. Broadcasters may face a number of individual situations which are not specifically referred to in this Code. Examples included in the Code are not exhaustive. However, the principles, as outlined in the following sections, should make clear what the Code is designed to achieve and help broadcasters make the necessary judgements.

To assist further those who work in broadcasting, as well as viewers and listeners who wish to understand broadcasting standards, non-binding guidance to accompany the Code will also be issued by Ofcom on the Ofcom website and will be reviewed regularly.

Broadcasters should be familiar with their audiences and ensure that programme content can always be justified by the context and the editorial needs of the programme. (In the Code, the word "programmes" is taken to mean both television programmes and radio programmes/programming.)

Broadcasters may make programmes about any issue they choose, but it is expected that broadcasters will ensure at all times that their programmes comply with the general law, as well as the Code.

General guidance on the Code

It is the responsibility of the broadcaster to comply with the Code. Programme makers who require further advice on applying this Code should, in the first instance, talk to those editorially responsible for the programme and to the broadcaster's compliance and legal officers.

Ofcom can offer general guidance on the interpretation of the Code. However, any such advice is given on the strict understanding that it will not affect Ofcom's discretion to judge cases and complaints after transmission and will not affect the exercise of Ofcom's regulatory responsibilities. Broadcasters should seek their own legal advice on any compliance issues arising. Ofcom will not be liable for any loss or damage arising from reliance on informal guidance.

SECTION ONE:

PROTECTING THE UNDER-EIGHTEENS

(Relevant legislation includes, in particular, sections 3(4)(h) and 319(2)(a) and (f) of the Communications Act 2003, Article 22 of the Audiovisual Media Services Directive, and Article 10 of the European Convention on Human Rights.)

This section must be read in conjunction with Section Two: Harm and Offence.

Principle

To ensure that people under eighteen are protected.

Rules

Scheduling and content information

1.1 Material that might seriously impair the physical, mental or moral development of people under eighteen must not be broadcast.

1.2 In the provision of services, broadcasters must take all reasonable steps to protect people under eighteen. For television services, this is in addition to their obligations resulting from the Audiovisual Media Services Directive (in particular, Article 22, see Appendix 2).

1.3 Children must also be protected by appropriate scheduling from material that is unsuitable for them.

Meaning of "children":

Children are people under the age of fifteen years.

Meaning of "appropriate scheduling":

Appropriate scheduling should be judged according to:

- the nature of the content;
- the likely number and age range of children in the audience, taking into account school time, weekends and holidays;
- the start time and finish time of the programme;
- the nature of the channel or station and the particular programme; and
- the likely expectations of the audience for a particular channel or station at a particular time and on a particular day.

1.4 Television broadcasters must observe the watershed.

Meaning of "the watershed":

The watershed only applies to television. The watershed is at 2100. Material unsuitable for children should not, in general, be shown before 2100 or after 0530.

On premium subscription film services which are not protected as set out in Rule 1.24, the watershed is at 2000. There is no watershed on premium subscription film services or pay per view services which are protected as set out in Rule 1.24 and 1.25 respectively.

1.5 Radio broadcasters must have particular regard to times when children are particularly likely to be listening.

Meaning of "when children are particularly likely to be listening":

This phrase particularly refers to the school run and breakfast time, but might include other times.

1.6 The transition to more adult material must not be unduly abrupt at the watershed (in the case of television) or after the time when children are particularly likely to be listening (in the case of radio). For television, the strongest material should appear later in the schedule.

1.7 For television programmes broadcast before the watershed, or for radio programmes broadcast when children are particularly likely to be listening, clear information about content that may distress some children should be given, if appropriate, to the audience (taking into account the context).

(For the meaning of "context" see Section Two: Harm and Offence.)

The coverage of sexual and other offences in the UK involving under-eighteens

1.8 Where statutory or other legal restrictions apply preventing personal identification, broadcasters should also be particularly careful not to provide clues which may lead to the identification of those who are not yet adult (the defining age may differ in different parts of the UK) and who are, or might be, involved as a victim, witness, defendant or other perpetrator in the case of sexual offences featured in criminal, civil or family court proceedings:

- by reporting limited information which may be pieced together with other information available elsewhere, for example in newspaper reports (the "jigsaw effect");

- inadvertently, for example by describing an offence as "incest"; or

- in any other indirect way.

(Note: Broadcasters should be aware that there may be statutory reporting restrictions that apply even if a court has not specifically made an order to that effect.)

1.9 When covering any pre-trial investigation into an alleged criminal offence in the UK, broadcasters should pay particular regard to the potentially vulnerable position of any person who is not yet adult who is involved as a witness or victim, before broadcasting their name, address, identity of school or other educational establishment, place of work, or any still or moving picture of them. Particular justification is also required for the broadcast of such material relating to the identity of any person who is not yet adult who is involved in the defence as a defendant or potential defendant.

Drugs, smoking, solvents and alcohol

1.10 The use of illegal drugs, the abuse of drugs, smoking, solvent abuse and the misuse of alcohol:

- must not be featured in programmes made primarily for children unless there is strong editorial justification;

- must generally be avoided and in any case must not be condoned,

- encouraged or glamorised in other programmes broadcast before the watershed (in the case of television), or when children are particularly likely to be listening (in the case of radio), unless there is editorial justification;

- must not be condoned, encouraged or glamorised in other programmes likely to be widely seen or heard by under-eighteens unless there is editorial justification.

Violence and dangerous behaviour

1.11 Violence, its after-effects and descriptions of violence, whether verbal or physical, must be appropriately limited in programmes broadcast before the watershed (in the case of television) or when children are particularly likely to be listening (in the case of radio) and must also be justified by the context.

1.12 Violence, whether verbal or physical, that is easily imitable by children in a manner that is harmful or dangerous:

- must not be featured in programmes made primarily for children unless there is strong editorial justification;

- must not be broadcast before the watershed (in the case of television) or when children are particularly likely to be listening (in the case of radio), unless there is editorial justification.

1.13 Dangerous behaviour, or the portrayal of dangerous behaviour, that is likely to be easily imitable by children in a manner that is harmful:

- must not be featured in programmes made primarily for children unless there is strong editorial justification;

- must not be broadcast before the watershed (in the case of television) or when children are particularly likely to be listening (in the case of radio), unless there is editorial justification.

(Regarding Rules 1.11 to 1.13 see Rules 2.4 and 2.5 in Section Two: Harm and Offence.)

Offensive language

1.14 The most offensive language must not be broadcast before the watershed (in the case of television) or when children are particularly likely to be listening (in the case of radio).

1.15 Offensive language must not be used in programmes made for younger children except in the most exceptional circumstances.

1.16 Offensive language must not be broadcast before the watershed (in the case of television) or when children are particularly likely to be listening (in the case of radio), unless it is justified by the context. In any event, frequent use of such language must be avoided before the watershed.

(Regarding Rules 1.14 to 1.16 see Rule 2.3 in Section Two: Harm and Offence.)

Sexual material

1.17 Material equivalent to the British Board of Film Classification (BBFC) R18rating must not be broadcast at any time.

1.18 "Adult sex material"—material that contains images and/or language of a strong, sexual nature which is broadcast for the primary purpose of sexual arousal or stimulation—must not be broadcast at any time other than between 2200 and 0530 on premium subscription services and pay per view/night services which operate with mandatory restricted access.

In addition, measures must be in place to ensure that the subscriber is an adult.

Meaning of "mandatory restricted access":

Mandatory restricted access means there is a PIN protected system (or other equivalent protection) which cannot be removed by the user, that restricts access solely to those authorised to view.

1.19 Broadcasters must ensure that material broadcast after the watershed which contains images and/or language of a strong or explicit sexual nature, but is not 'adult sex material' as defined in Rule 1.18 above, is justified by the context.

(See Rules 1.6 and 1.18 and Rule 2.3 in Section Two: Harm and Offence which includes meaning of "context".)

1.20 Representations of sexual intercourse must not occur before the watershed (in the case of television) or when children are particularly likely to be listening (in the case of radio), unless there is a serious educational purpose. Any discussion on, or portrayal of, sexual behaviour must be editorially justified if included before the watershed, or when children are particularly likely to be listening, and must be appropriately limited.

Nudity

1.21 Nudity before the watershed must be justified by the context.

Films, premium subscription film services, pay per view services

1.22 No film refused classification by the British Board of Film Classification (BBFC) may be broadcast unless it has subsequently been classified or the BBFC has confirmed that it would not be rejected according to the standards currently operating. Also, no film cut as a condition of classification by the BBFC may be transmitted in a version which includes the cut material unless:

- the BBFC has confirmed that the material was cut to allow the film to pass at a lower category; or
- the BBFC has confirmed that the film would not be subject to compulsory cuts according to the standards currently operating.

1.23 BBFC 18-rated films or their equivalent must not be broadcast before 2100 on any service (except for pay per view services), and even then they may be unsuitable for broadcast at that time.
1.24 Premium subscription film services may broadcast up to BBFC 15-rated films or their equivalent, at any time of day provided that mandatory restricted access is in place pre-2000 and post-0530.
In addition, those security systems which are in place to protect children must be clearly explained to all subscribers.
(See meaning of "mandatory restricted access" under Rule 1.18 above.)
1.25 Pay per view services may broadcast up to BBFC 18-rated films or their equivalent, at any time of day provided that mandatory restricted access is in place pre-2100 and post-0530.

In addition:

- information must be provided about programme content that will assist adults to assess its suitability for children;
- there must be a detailed billing system for subscribers which clearly itemises all viewing including viewing times and dates; and
- those security systems which are in place to protect children must be clearly explained to all subscribers.

(See meaning of "mandatory restricted access" under Rule 1.18 above.)
1.26 BBFC R18-rated films must not be broadcast.

Exorcism, the occult and the paranormal

1.27 Demonstrations of exorcisms, occult practices and the paranormal (which purport to be real), must not be shown before the watershed (in the case of television) or when children are particularly likely to be listening (in the case of radio). Paranormal practices which are for entertainment purposes must not be broadcast when significant numbers of children may be expected to be watching, or are particularly likely to be listening. (This rule does not apply to drama, film or comedy.)

(See Rules 2.6 to 2.8 in Section Two: Harm and Offence and Rule 4.7 in Section Four: Religion.)

The involvement of people under eighteen in programmes

1.28 Due care must be taken over the physical and emotional welfare and the dignity of people under eighteen who take part or are otherwise involved in programmes. This is irrespective of any consent given by the participant or by a parent, guardian or other person over the age of eighteen *in loco parentis*.

1.29 People under eighteen must not be caused unnecessary distress or anxiety by their involvement in programmes or by the broadcast of those programmes.

1.30 Prizes aimed at children must be appropriate to the age range of both the target audience and the participants.

(See Rule 2.16 in Section Two: Harm and Offence.)

SECTION TWO:

HARM AND OFFENCE

(Relevant legislation includes, in particular, sections 3(4)(g) and (l) and 319(2)(a), (f) and (l) of the Communications Act 2003, and Articles 10 and 14 of the European Convention on Human Rights.)

This section must be read in conjunction with Section One: Protecting the Under-Eighteens. The rules in this section are designed not only to provide adequate protection for adults but also to protect people under-eighteen.

Principle

To ensure that generally accepted standards are applied to the content of television and radio services so as to provide adequate protection for members of the public from the inclusion in such services of harmful and/or offensive material.

Rules

Generally Accepted Standards

2.1 Generally accepted standards must be applied to the contents of television and radio services so as to provide adequate protection for members of the public from the inclusion in such services of harmful and/or offensive material.

2.2 Factual programmes or items or portrayals of factual matters must not materially mislead the audience.

(Note to Rule 2.2: News is regulated under Section Five of the Code.)

2.3 In applying generally accepted standards broadcasters must ensure that material which may cause offence is justified by the context (see meaning of "context" below). Such material may include, but is not limited to, offensive language, violence, sex, sexual violence, humiliation, distress, violation of human dignity, discriminatory treatment or language (for example on the grounds of age, disability, gender, race, religion, beliefs and sexual orientation). Appropriate information should also be broadcast where it would assist in avoiding or minimising offence.

Meaning of "context":

Context includes (but is not limited to):

- the editorial content of the programme, programmes or series;
- the service on which the material is broadcast;
- the time of broadcast;
- what other programmes are scheduled before and after the programme or programmes concerned;
- the degree of harm or offence likely to be caused by the inclusion of any particular sort of material in programmes generally or programmes of a particular description;
- the likely size and composition of the potential audience and likely expectation of the audience;
- the extent to which the nature of the content can be brought to the attention of the potential audience for example by giving information; and
- the effect of the material on viewers or listeners who may come across it unawares.

Violence, dangerous behaviour and suicide

2.4 Programmes must not include material (whether in individual programmes or in programmes taken together) which, taking into account the context, condones or glamorises violent, dangerous or seriously antisocial behaviour and is likely to encourage others to copy such behaviour.

(See Rules 1.11 to 1.13 in Section One: Protecting the Under-Eighteens.)

2.5 Methods of suicide and self-harm must not be included in programmes except where they are editorially justified and are also justified by the context.

(See Rule 1.13 in Section One: Protecting the Under-Eighteens.)

Exorcism, the occult and the paranormal

2.6 Demonstrations of exorcism, the occult, the paranormal, divination, or practices related to any of these that purport to be real (as opposed to entertainment) must be treated with due objectivity.

(See Rule 1.27 in Section One: Protecting the Under-Eighteens, concerning scheduling restrictions.)

2.7 If a demonstration of exorcism, the occult, the paranormal, divination, or practices related to any of these is for entertainment purposes, this must be made clear to viewers and listeners.

2.8 Demonstrations of exorcism, the occult, the paranormal, divination, or practices related to any of these (whether such demonstrations purport to be real or are for entertainment purposes) must not contain life-changing advice directed at individuals.

(Religious programmes are exempt from this rule but must, in any event, comply with the provisions in Section Four: Religion. Films, dramas and fiction generally are not bound by this rule.)

Meaning of "life-changing":

Life-changing advice includes direct advice for individuals upon which they could reasonably act or rely about health, finance, employment or relationships.

Hypnotic and other techniques, simulated news and photosensitive epilepsy

2.9 When broadcasting material featuring demonstrations of hypnotic techniques, broadcasters must exercise a proper degree of responsibility in order to prevent hypnosis and/or adverse reactions in viewers and listeners. The hypnotist must not broadcast his/her full verbal routine or be shown performing straight to camera.

2.10 Simulated news (for example in drama or in documentaries) must be broadcast in such a way that there is no reasonable possibility of the audience being misled into believing that they are listening to, or watching, actual news.

2.11 Broadcasters must not use techniques which exploit the possibility of conveying a message to viewers or listeners, or of otherwise influencing their minds without their being aware, or fully aware, of what has occurred.

2.12 Television broadcasters must take precautions to maintain a low level of risk to viewers who have photosensitive epilepsy. Where it is not reasonably practicable to follow the Ofcom guidance (see the Ofcom website), and where broadcasters can demonstrate that the broadcasting of flashing lights and/or patterns is editorially justified, viewers should be given an adequate verbal and also, if appropriate, text warning at the start of the programme or programme item.

Broadcast competitions and voting

2.13 Broadcast competitions and voting must be conducted fairly.

2.14 Broadcasters must ensure that viewers and listeners are not materially misled about any broadcast competition or voting.

2.15 Broadcasters must draw up rules for a broadcast competition or vote. These must be clear and appropriately made known. In particular, significant conditions that may affect a viewer's or listener's decision to participate must be stated at the time an invitation to participate is broadcast.

2.16 Broadcast competition prizes must be described accurately.

(See also Rule 1.30 in Section One: Protecting the Under-Eighteens, which concerns the provision of appropriate prizes for children.)

Note:
For broadcast competitions and voting that involve the use of premium rate services (PRS), broadcasters should also refer to Rules 10.9 and 10.10.

Meaning of "broadcast competition":

A competition or free prize draw featured in a programme in which viewers or listeners are invited to enter by any means for the opportunity to win a prize.

Meaning of "voting":
Features in a programme in which viewers or listeners are invited to register a vote by any means to decide or influence, at any stage, the outcome of a contest.

SECTION THREE:

CRIME

(Relevant legislation includes, in particular, sections 3(4)(j) and 319(2)(b) of the Communications Act 2003, Article 3(b) of the Audiovisual Media Services Directive, and Article 10 of the European Convention on Human Rights.)

Principle

To ensure that material likely to encourage or incite the commission of crime or to lead to disorder is not included in television or radio services.

Rules

3.1 Material likely to encourage or incite the commission of crime or to lead to disorder must not be included in television or radio services.

3.2 Descriptions or demonstrations of criminal techniques which contain essential details which could enable the commission of crime must not be broadcast unless editorially justified.

3.3 No payment, promise of payment, or payment in kind, may be made to convicted or confessed criminals whether directly or indirectly for a programme contribution by the criminal (or any other person) relating to his/her crime/s. The only exception is where it is in the public interest.

3.4 While criminal proceedings are active, no payment or promise of payment may be made, directly or indirectly, to any witness or any person who may reasonably be expected to be called as a witness. Nor should any payment be suggested or made dependent on the outcome of the trial. Only actual expenditure or loss of earnings necessarily incurred during the making of a programme contribution may be reimbursed.

3.5 Where criminal proceedings are likely and foreseeable, payments should not be made to people who might reasonably be expected to be witnesses unless there is a clear public interest, such as investigating crime or serious wrongdoing, and the payment is necessary to elicit the information. Where such a payment is made it will be appropriate to disclose the payment to both defence and prosecution if the person becomes a witness in any subsequent trial.

3.6 Broadcasters must use their best endeavours so as not to broadcast material that could endanger lives or prejudice the success of attempts to deal with a hijack or kidnapping.

SECTION FOUR:

RELIGION

(Relevant legislation includes, in particular, sections 319(2)(e) and 319(6) of the Communications Act 2003, and Articles 9, 10 and 14 of the European Convention on Human Rights.)

The rules in this section apply to religious programmes.

Principles

To ensure that broadcasters exercise the proper degree of responsibility with respect to the content of programmes which are religious programmes.

To ensure that religious programmes do not involve any improper exploitation of any susceptibilities of the audience for such a programme.

To ensure that religious programmes do not involve any abusive treatment of

the religious views and beliefs of those belonging to a particular religion or religious denomination.

Rules

4.1 Broadcasters must exercise the proper degree of responsibility with respect to the content of programmes which are religious programmes.

> Meaning of a "religious programme":
>
> A religious programme is a programme which deals with matters of religion as the central subject, or as a significant part, of the programme.

4.2 The religious views and beliefs of those belonging to a particular religion or religious denomination must not be subject to abusive treatment.

4.3 Where a religion or religious denomination is the subject, or one of the subjects, of a religious programme, then the identity of the religion and/or denomination must be clear to the audience.

4.4 Religious programmes must not seek to promote religious views or beliefs by stealth.

4.5 Religious programmes on television services must not seek recruits. This does not apply to specialist religious television services. Religious programmes on radio services may seek recruits.

> Meaning of "seek recruits":
>
> Seek recruits means directly appealing to audience members to join a religion or religious denomination.

4.6 Religious programmes must not improperly exploit any susceptibilities of the audience.

(See Rules 10.13 to 10.16 in Section 10: Commercial References and Other Matters, regarding appeals.)

4.7 Religious programmes that contain claims that a living person (or group) has special powers or abilities must treat such claims with due objectivity and must not broadcast such claims when significant numbers of children may be expected to be watching (in the case of television), or when children are particularly likely to be listening (in the case of radio).

SECTION FIVE:

DUE IMPARTIALITY AND DUE ACCURACY AND UNDUE PROMINENCE OF VIEWS AND OPINIONS

(Relevant legislation includes, in particular, sections 319(2)(c) and (d), 319(8) and section 320 of the Communications Act 2003, and Article 10 of the European Convention on Human Rights.)

This section of the Code does not apply to BBC services funded by the licence fee, which are regulated on these matters by the BBC Trust.

Principles

To ensure that news, in whatever form, is reported with due accuracy and presented with due impartiality.

To ensure that the special impartiality requirements of the Act are complied with.

Rules

> Meaning of "due impartiality":
>
> "Due" is an important qualification to the concept of impartiality. Impartiality itself means not favouring one side over another. "Due" means adequate or appropriate to the subject and nature of the programme. So "due impartiality" does not mean an equal division of time has to be given to every view, or that every argument and every facet of every argument has to be represented. The approach to due impartiality may vary according to the nature of the subject, the type of programme and channel, the likely expectation of the audience as to content, and the extent to which the content and approach is signalled to the audience. Context, as defined in Section Two: Harm and Offence of the Code, is important.

Due impartiality and due accuracy in news

5.1 News, in whatever form, must be reported with due accuracy and presented with due impartiality.

5.2 Significant mistakes in news should normally be acknowledged and corrected on air quickly. Corrections should be appropriately scheduled.

5.3 No politician may be used as a newsreader, interviewer or reporter in any news programmes unless, exceptionally, it is editorially justified. In that case, the political allegiance of that person must be made clear to the audience.

Special impartiality requirements: news and other programmes

Matters of political or industrial controversy and matters relating to current public policy

> Meaning of "matters of political or industrial controversy and matters relating to current public policy":
>
> Matters of political or industrial controversy are political or industrial issues on which politicians, industry and/or the media are in debate. Matters relating to current public policy need not be the subject of debate but relate to a policy under discussion or already decided by a local, regional or national government or by bodies mandated by those public bodies to make policy on their behalf, for example non-governmental organisations, relevant European institutions, etc.

The exclusion of views or opinions

(Rule 5.4 applies to television and radio services except restricted services.)

5.4 Programmes in the services (listed above) must exclude all expressions of the views and opinions of the person providing the service on matters of political and industrial controversy and matters relating to current public policy (unless that person is speaking in a legislative forum or in a court of law). Views and opinions relating to the provision of programme services are also excluded from this requirement.

The preservation of due impartiality

(Rules 5.5 to 5.12 apply to television programme services, teletext services, national radio and national digital sound programme services.)

5.5 Due impartiality on matters of political or industrial controversy and matters relating to current public policy must be preserved on the part of any person providing a service (listed above). This may be achieved within a programme or over a series of programmes taken as a whole.

Meaning of "series of programmes taken as a whole":

This means more than one programme in the same service, editorially linked, dealing with the same or related issues within an appropriate period and aimed at a like audience. A series can include, for example, a strand, or two programmes (such as a drama and a debate about the drama) or a "cluster" or "season" of programmes on the same subject.

5.6 The broadcast of editorially linked programmes dealing with the same subject matter (as part of a series in which the broadcaster aims to achieve due impartiality) should normally be made clear to the audience on air.

5.7 Views and facts must not be misrepresented. Views must also be presented with due weight over appropriate timeframes.

5.8 Any personal interest of a reporter or presenter, which would call into question the due impartiality of the programme, must be made clear to the audience.

5.9 Presenters and reporters (with the exception of news presenters and reporters in news programmes), presenters of "personal view" or "authored" programmes or items, and chairs of discussion programmes may express their own views on matters of political or industrial controversy or matters relating to current public policy. However, alternative viewpoints must be adequately represented either in the programme, or in a series of programmes taken as a whole. Additionally, presenters must not use the advantage of regular appearances to promote their views in a way that compromises the requirement for due impartiality. Presenter phone-ins must encourage and must not exclude alternative views.

5.10 A personal view or authored programme or item must be clearly signalled to the audience at the outset. This is a minimum requirement and may not be sufficient in all circumstances. (Personality phone-in hosts on radio are exempted from this provision unless their personal view status is unclear.)

Meaning of "personal view" and "authored":

"Personal view" programmes are programmes presenting a particular view or perspective. Personal view programmes can range from the outright expression of highly partial views, for example by a person who is a member of a lobby group and is campaigning on the subject, to the considered "authored" opinion of a journalist, commentator or academic, with professional expertise or a specialism in an area which enables her or him to express opinions which are not necessarily mainstream.

Matters of major political or industrial controversy and major matters relating to current public policy

5.11 In addition to the rules above, due impartiality must be preserved on matters of major political and industrial controversy and major matters relating to current public policy by the person providing a service (listed above) in each programme or in clearly linked and timely programmes.

> Meaning of "matters of major political or industrial controversy and major matters relating to current public policy":
>
> These will vary according to events but are generally matters of political or industrial controversy or matters of current public policy which are of national, and often international, importance, or are of similar significance within a smaller broadcast area.

5.12 In dealing with matters of major political and industrial controversy and major matters relating to current public policy an appropriately wide range of significant views must be included and given due weight in each programme or in clearly linked and timely programmes. Views and facts must not be misrepresented.

The prevention of undue prominence of views and opinions on matters of political or industrial controversy and matters relating to current public policy

(Rule 5.13 applies to local radio services (including community radio services), local digital sound programme services (including community digital sound programme services) and radio licensable content services.)

5.13 Broadcasters should not give undue prominence to the views and opinions of particular persons or bodies on matters of political or industrial controversy and matters relating to current public policy in all the programmes included in any service (listed above) taken as a whole.

> Meaning of "undue prominence of views and opinions":
>
> Undue prominence is a significant imbalance of views aired within coverage of matters of political or industrial controversy or matters relating to current public policy.
>
> Meaning of "programmes included in any service ... Taken as a whole":
>
> Programmes included in any service taken as a whole means all programming on a service dealing with the same or related issues within an appropriate period.

SECTION SIX:

ELECTIONS AND REFERENDUMS

(Relevant legislation includes, in particular, sections 319(2)(c) and 320 of the Communications Act 2003, and Article 10 of the European Convention on Human Rights. Broadcasters should also have regard to relevant sections of the Representation of the People Act 1983 (as amended) ("RPA")—see in particular sections 66A, 92 and 93 (which is amended by section 144 of the Political Parties, Elections and Referendums Act 2000).)

This section of the Code does not apply to BBC services funded by the licence fee, which are regulated on these matters by the BBC Trust.

Rules made under section 333 of the Communications Act 2003 (regarding party election broadcasts, party political broadcasts and referendum campaign broadcasts) and paragraph 18 of Schedule 12 are contained in *Ofcom Rules on Party Political and Referendum Broadcasts* on the Ofcom website. However, such broadcasts are also required to comply with the relevant provisions of this Code, for example the provisions regarding harm and offence—notwithstanding that the content is normally the responsibility of the relevant political parties.

Principle

To ensure that the special impartiality requirements in the Communications Act 2003 and other legislation relating to broadcasting on elections and referendums, are applied at the time of elections and referendums.

Rules

Programmes at the time of elections and referendums

6.1 The rules in Section Five, in particular the rules relating to matters of major political or industrial controversy and major matters relating to current public policy, apply to the coverage of elections and referendums.

Programmes at the time of elections and referendums in the UK

The remainder of this section only applies during the actual election or referendum period which is defined below.

Meaning of "election":

For the purpose of this section elections include a parliamentary general election, parliamentary by-election, local government election, mayoral election, Scottish Parliament election, Welsh, Northern Ireland and London Assembly elections, and European parliamentary election.

Meaning of "referendum":

For the purpose of this section a referendum (to which the Political Parties, Elections and Referendums Act 2000 applies) includes a UK-wide, national or regional referendum but does not extend to a local referendum.

6.2 Due weight must be given to the coverage of major parties during the election period. Broadcasters must also consider giving appropriate coverage to other parties and independent candidates with significant views and perspectives.

Meaning of "major party":

At present in the UK major parties are the Conservative Party, the Labour Party and the Liberal Democrats. In addition, major parties in Scotland and Wales respectively are the Scottish National Party and Plaid Cymru. The major parties in Northern Ireland are the Democratic Unionist Party, Sinn Fein, Social Democratic and Labour Party, and the Ulster Unionist Party.

Meaning of "election period":

For a parliamentary general election, this period begins with the announcement of the dissolution of Parliament. For a parliamentary by-election, this period begins with the issuing of a writ or on such earlier date as is notified in the London Gazette. For the Scottish Parliament elections, the period begins with the dissolution of the Scottish Parliament or, in the case of a by-election, with the date of the occurrence of a vacancy. For the National Assembly for Wales, the Northern Ireland Assembly, the London Assembly and for local government elections, it is the last date for publication of notices of the election. For European parliamentary elections, it is the last date for publication of the notice of election, which is 25 days before the election. In all cases the period ends with the close of the poll.

Meaning of "candidate":

Candidate has the meaning given to it in section 93 of the Representation of the People Act 1983 (as amended) and means a candidate standing nominated at the election or included in a list of candidates submitted in connection with it.

6.3 Due weight must be given to designated organisations in coverage during the referendum period. Broadcasters must also consider giving appropriate coverage to other permitted participants with significant views and perspectives.

Meaning of "designated organisation" and "permitted participants":

Designated organisations and permitted participants are those that are designated by the Electoral Commission.

Meaning of "referendum period":

For referendums different periods may apply. A referendum held under the Northern Ireland Act 1998 (as amended) begins when the draft of an Order is laid before Parliament for approval by each House. In the case of a referendum held under other Acts, the time at which a referendum period commences is given in the individual Acts. In the case of an Order before Parliament, the time will be given in that Order. In all cases the period ends with the close of the poll.

6.4 Discussion and analysis of election and referendum issues must finish when the poll opens. (This refers to the opening of actual polling stations. This rule does not apply to any poll conducted entirely by post.)

6.5 Broadcasters may not publish the results of any opinion poll on polling day itself until the election or referendum poll closes. (For European Parliamentary elections, this applies until all polls throughout the European Union have closed.)

6.6 Candidates in UK elections, and representatives of permitted participants in UK referendums, must not act as news presenters, interviewers or presenters of any type of programme during the election period.

6.7 Appearances by candidates (in UK elections) or representatives (of permitted participants in UK referendums) in non-political programmes that were planned or scheduled before the election or referendum period may continue, but no new appearances should be arranged and broadcast during the period.

Constituency coverage and electoral area coverage in elections

(Rules 6.8 to 6.13 will only apply to S4C if S4C has adopted them under the RPA as its Code of Practice.)

6.8 Due impartiality must be strictly maintained in a constituency report or discussion and in an electoral area report or discussion.

> Meaning of "electoral area":
>
> Electoral area (for example electoral division, borough ward or other area) is the local government equivalent to the parliamentary term "constituency".

6.9 If a candidate takes part in an item about his/her particular constituency, or electoral area, then candidates of each of the major parties must be offered the opportunity to take part. (However, if they refuse or are unable to participate, the item may nevertheless go ahead.)

6.10 In addition to Rule 6.9, broadcasters must offer the opportunity to take part in constituency or electoral area reports and discussions, to all candidates within the constituency or electoral area representing parties with previous significant electoral support or where there is evidence of significant current support. This also applies to independent candidates. (However, if a candidate refuses or is unable to participate, the item may nevertheless go ahead.)

6.11 Any constituency or electoral area report or discussion after the close of nominations must include a list of all candidates standing, giving first names, surnames and the name of the party they represent or, if they are standing independently, the fact that they are an independent candidate. This must be conveyed in sound and/or vision. Where a constituency report on a radio service is repeated on several occasions in the same day, the full list need only be broadcast on one occasion. If, in subsequent repeats on that day, the constituency report does not give the full list of candidates, the audience should be directed to an appropriate website or other information source listing all candidates and giving the information set out above.

6.12 Where a candidate is taking part in a programme on any matter, after the election has been called, s/he must not be given the opportunity to make constituency points, or electoral area points about the constituency or electoral area in which s/he is standing, when no other candidates will be given a similar opportunity.

6.13 If coverage is given to wider election regions, for example in elections to the Scottish Parliament, Welsh Assembly, Northern Ireland Assembly, London Assembly or European Parliament, then Rules 6.8 to 6.12 apply in offering participation to candidates. In these instances, all parties who have a candidate in the appropriate region should be listed in sound and/or vision, but it is not necessary to list candidates individually. However, any independent candidate who is not standing on a party list must be named. Where a report on a radio service is repeated on several occasions in the same day, the full list need only be broadcast on one occasion. If, in subsequent repeats on that day, the constituency report does not give the full list of candidates, the audience should be directed to an appropriate website or other information source listing all candidates and giving the information set out above.

SECTION SEVEN:

FAIRNESS

(Relevant legislation includes, in particular, sections 3(2)(f) and 326 of the Communications Act 2003 and sections 107(1) and 130 of the Broadcasting Act 1996 (as amended), Article 23 of the Audiovisual Media Services Directive and Article 10 of the European Convention on Human Rights.)

Foreword

This section and the following section on privacy are different from other sections of the Code. They apply to how broadcasters treat the individuals or organisations directly affected by programmes, rather than to what the general public sees and/or hears as viewers and listeners.

As well as containing a principle and a rule this section contains "practices to be followed" by broadcasters when dealing with individuals or organisations participating in or otherwise directly affected by programmes as broadcast. Following these practices will not necessarily avoid a breach of this section of the code (Rule 7.1).

However, failure to follow these practises will only constitute a breach where it results in unfairness to an individual or organisation in the programme. Importantly, the Code does not and cannot seek to set out all the "practices to be followed" in order to avoid unfair treatment.

The following provisions in the next section on privacy are also relevant to this section:

- the explanation of public interest that appears in the meaning of "warranted" under Rule 8.1 in Section Eight: Privacy;

- the meaning of surreptitious filming or recording that appears under "practices to be followed" 8.13 in Section Eight: Privacy.

Principle

To ensure that broadcasters avoid unjust or unfair treatment of individuals or organisations in programmes.

Rule

7.1 Broadcasters must avoid unjust or unfair treatment of individuals or organisations in programmes.

Practices to be followed (7.2 to 7.14 below)

Dealing fairly with contributors and obtaining informed consent

7.2 Broadcasters and programme makers should normally be fair in their dealings with potential contributors to programmes unless, exceptionally, it is justified to do otherwise.

7.3 Where a person is invited to make a contribution to a programme (except when the subject matter is trivial or their participation minor) they should normally, at an appropriate stage:

- be told the nature and purpose of the programme, what the programme is about and be given a clear explanation of why they were asked to contribute and when (if known) and where it is likely to be first broadcast;

- be told what kind of contribution they are expected to make, for example live, pre-recorded, interview, discussion, edited, unedited, etc.;

- be informed about the areas of questioning and, wherever possible, the nature of other likely contributions;

- be made aware of any significant changes to the programme as it develops which might reasonably affect their original consent to participate, and which might cause material unfairness;

- be told the nature of their contractual rights and obligations and those of the programme maker and broadcaster in relation to their contribution; and be given clear information, if offered an opportunity to preview the programme, about whether they will be able to effect any changes to it.

Taking these measures is likely to result in the consent that is given being "informed consent" (referred to in this section and the rest of the Code as "consent").

It may be fair to withhold all or some of this information where it is justified in the public interest or under other provisions of this section of the Code.

7.4 If a contributor is under sixteen, consent should normally be obtained from a parent or guardian, or other person of eighteen or over *in loco parentis*. In particular, persons under sixteen should not be asked for views on matters likely to be beyond their capacity to answer properly without such consent.

7.5 In the case of persons over sixteen who are not in a position to give consent, a person of eighteen or over with primary responsibility for their care should normally give it on their behalf. In particular, persons not in a position to give consent should not be asked for views on matters likely to be beyond their capacity to answer properly without such consent.

7.6 When a programme is edited, contributions should be represented fairly.

7.7 Guarantees given to contributors, for example relating to the content of a programme, confidentiality or anonymity, should normally be honoured.

7.8 Broadcasters should ensure that the re-use of material, i.e. use of material originally filmed or recorded for one purpose and then used in a programme for another purpose or used in a later or different programme, does not create unfairness. This applies both to material obtained from others and the broadcaster's own material.

Opportunity to contribute and proper consideration of facts

7.9 Before broadcasting a factual programme, including programmes examining past events, broadcasters should take reasonable care to satisfy themselves that:

- material facts have not been presented, disregarded or omitted in a way that is unfair to an individual or organisation; and

- anyone whose omission could be unfair to an individual or organisation has been offered an opportunity to contribute.

7.10 Programmes—such as dramas and factually-based dramas—should not portray facts, events, individuals or organisations in a way which is unfair to an individual or organisation.

7.11 If a programme alleges wrongdoing or incompetence or makes other significant allegations, those concerned should normally be given an appropriate and timely opportunity to respond.

7.12 Where a person approached to contribute to a programme chooses to make no comment or refuses to appear in a broadcast, the broadcast should make clear that the individual concerned has chosen not to appear and should give their explanation if it would be unfair not to do so.

7.13 Where it is appropriate to represent the views of a person or organisation that is not participating in the programme, this must be done in a fair manner.

Deception, set-ups and 'wind-up' calls

7.14 Broadcasters or programme makers should not normally obtain or seek information, audio, pictures or an agreement to contribute through misrepresentation or deception. (Deception includes surreptitious filming or recording.) However:

- it may be warranted to use material obtained through misrepresentation or deception without consent if it is in the public interest and cannot reasonably be obtained by other means;

- where there is no adequate public interest justification, for example some unsolicited wind-up calls or entertainment set-ups, consent should be obtained from the individual and/or organisation concerned before the material is broadcast;

- if the individual and/or organisation is/are not identifiable in the programme then consent for broadcast will not be required;

- material involving celebrities and those in the public eye can be used without consent for broadcast, but it should not be used without a public interest justification if it is likely to result in unjustified public ridicule or personal distress. (Normally, therefore such contributions should be pre-recorded.)

(See "practices to be followed" 8.11 to 8.15 in Section Eight: Privacy.)

SECTION EIGHT:

PRIVACY

(Relevant legislation includes, in particular, sections 3(2)(f) and 326 of the Communications Act 2003, sections 107(1) and 130 of the Broadcasting Act 1996 (as amended), and Articles 8 and 10 of the European Convention on Human Rights.)

Foreword

This section and the preceding section on fairness are different from other sections of the Code. They apply to how broadcasters treat the individuals or organisations directly affected by programmes, rather than to what the general public sees and/or hears as viewers and listeners.

As well as containing a principle and a rule this section contains "practices to be followed" by broadcasters when dealing with individuals or organisations participating or otherwise directly affected by programmes, or in the making of programmes. Following these practices will not necessarily avoid a breach of this section of the Code (Rule 8.1). *However, failure to follow these practises will only constitute a breach where results in an unwarranted infringement of privacy.* Importantly, the Code does not and cannot seek to set out all the "practices to be followed" in order to avoid an unwarranted infringement of privacy.

The Broadcasting Act 1996 (as amended) requires Ofcom to consider complaints about unwarranted infringement of privacy in a programme or in connection with the obtaining of material included in a programme. This may call for some difficult on-the-spot judgments about whether privacy is unwarrantably infringed by filming or recording, especially when reporting on emergency situations ("practices to be followed" 8.5 to 8.8 and 8.16 to 8.19). We recognise there may be a strong public interest in reporting on an emergency situation as it occurs and we understand there may be pressures on broadcasters at the scene of a disaster or emergency that may make it difficult to judge at the time whether filming or recording is an unwarrantable infringement of privacy. These are factors Ofcom will take into account when adjudicating on complaints.

Where consent is referred to in Section Eight it refers to informed consent. Please see "practice to be followed" 7.3 in Section Seven: Fairness.

Principle

To ensure that broadcasters avoid any unwarranted infringement of privacy in programmes and in connection with obtaining material included in programmes.

Rule

8.1 Any infringement of privacy in programmes, or in connection with obtaining material included in programmes, must be warranted.

Meaning of "warranted":

In this section "warranted" has a particular meaning. It means that where broadcasters wish to justify an infringement of privacy as warranted, they should be able to demonstrate why in the particular circumstances of the case, it is warranted. If the reason is that it is in the public interest, then the broadcaster should be able to demonstrate that the public interest outweighs the right to privacy. Examples of public interest would include revealing or detecting crime, protecting public health or safety, exposing misleading claims made by individuals or organisations or disclosing incompetence that affects the public.

Practices to be followed (8.2 to 8.22)

Private lives, public places and legitimate expectation of privacy

---

Meaning of "legitimate expectation of privacy":

Legitimate expectations of privacy will vary according to the place and nature of the information, activity or condition in question, the extent to which it is in the public domain (if at all) and whether the individual concerned is already in the public eye. There may be circumstances where people can reasonably expect privacy even in a public place. Some activities and conditions may be of such a private nature that filming or recording, even in a public place, could involve an infringement of privacy. People under investigation or in the public eye, and their immediate family and friends, retain the right to a private life, although private behaviour can raise issues of legitimate public interest.

8.2 Information which discloses the location of a person's home or family should not be revealed without permission, unless it is warranted.

8.3 When people are caught up in events which are covered by the news they still have a right to privacy in both the making and the broadcast of a programme, unless it is warranted to infringe it. This applies both to the time when these events are taking place and to any later programmes that revisit those events.

8.4 Broadcasters should ensure that words, images or actions filmed or recorded in, or broadcast from, a public place, are not so private that prior consent is required before broadcast from the individual or organisation concerned, unless broadcasting without their consent is warranted.

Consent

8.5 Any infringement of privacy in the making of a programme should be with the person's and/or organisation's consent or be otherwise warranted.

8.6 If the broadcast of a programme would infringe the privacy of a person or organisation, consent should be obtained before the relevant material is broadcast, unless the infringement of privacy is warranted. (Callers to phone-in shows are deemed to have given consent to the broadcast of their contribution.)

8.7 If an individual or organisation's privacy is being infringed, and they ask that the filming, recording or live broadcast be stopped, the broadcaster should do so, unless it is warranted to continue.

8.8 When filming or recording in institutions, organisations or other agencies, permission should be obtained from the relevant authority or management, unless it is warranted to film or record without permission. Individual consent of employees or others whose appearance is incidental or where they are essentially anonymous members of the general public will not normally be required.

- However, in potentially sensitive places such as ambulances, hospitals, schools, prisons or police stations, separate consent should normally be obtained before filming or recording and for broadcast from those in sensitive situations (unless not obtaining consent is warranted). If the individual will not be identifiable in the programme then separate consent for broadcast will not be required.

Gathering information, sound or images and the re-use of material

8.9 The means of obtaining material must be proportionate in all the circumstances and in particular to the subject matter of the programme.

8.10 Broadcasters should ensure that the re-use of material, i.e. use of material originally filmed or recorded for one purpose and then used in a programme for another purpose or used in a later or different programme, does not create an unwarranted infringement of privacy. This applies both to material obtained from others and the broadcaster's own material.

8.11 Doorstepping for factual programmes should not take place unless a request for an interview has been refused or it has not been possible to request an interview, or there is good reason to believe that an investigation will be frustrated if the subject is approached openly, and it is warranted to doorstep. However, normally broadcasters may, without prior warning interview, film or record people in the news when in public places.

(See "practice to be followed" 8.15.)

Meaning of "doorstepping":

Doorstepping is the filming or recording of an interview or attempted interview with someone, or announcing that a call is being filmed or recorded for broadcast purposes, without any prior warning. It does not, however, include vox-pops (sampling the views of random members of the public).

8.12 Broadcasters can record telephone calls between the broadcaster and the other party if they have, from the outset of the call, identified themselves, explained the purpose of the call and that the call is being recorded for possible broadcast (if that is the case) unless it is warranted not to do one or more of these practices. If at a later stage it becomes clear that a call that has been recorded will be broadcast (but this was not explained to the other party at the time of the call) then the broadcaster must obtain consent before broadcast from the other party, unless it is warranted not to do so. (See "practices to be followed" 7.14 and 8.13 to 8.15.)

8.13 Surreptitious filming or recording should only be used where it is warranted. Normally, it will only be warranted if:

- there is *prima facie* evidence of a story in the public interest; and
- there are reasonable grounds to suspect that further material evidence could be obtained; and
- it is necessary to the credibility and authenticity of the programme.

See "practices to be followed" 7.14, 8.12, 8.14 and 8.15.)

> Meaning of "surreptitious filming or recording":
>
> Surreptitious filming or recording includes the use of long lenses or recording devices, as well as leaving an unattended camera or recording device on private property without the full and informed consent of the occupiers or their agent. It may also include recording telephone conversations without the knowledge of the other party, or deliberately continuing a recording when the other party thinks that it has come to an end.

8.14 Material gained by surreptitious filming and recording should only be broadcast when it is warranted.
(See also "practices to be followed" 7.14 and 8.12 to 8.13 and 8.15.)

8.15 Surreptitious filming or recording, doorstepping or recorded 'wind-up' calls to obtain material for entertainment purposes may be warranted if it is intrinsic to the entertainment and does not amount to a significant infringement of privacy such as to cause significant annoyance, distress or embarrassment. The resulting material should not be broadcast without the consent of those involved. However if the individual and/or organisation is not identifiable in the programme then consent for broadcast will not be required.
(See "practices to be followed" 7.14 and 8.11 to 8.14.)

Suffering and distress

8.16 Broadcasters should not take or broadcast footage or audio of people caught up in emergencies, victims of accidents or those suffering a personal tragedy, even in a public place, where that results in an infringement of privacy, unless it is warranted or the people concerned have given consent.

8.17 People in a state of distress should not be put under pressure to take part in a programme or provide interviews, unless it is warranted.

8.18 Broadcasters should take care not to reveal the identity of a person who has died or of victims of accidents or violent crimes, unless and until it is clear that the next of kin have been informed of the event or unless it is warranted.

8.19 Broadcasters should try to reduce the potential distress to victims and/or relatives when making or broadcasting programmes intended to examine past events that involve trauma to individuals (including crime) unless it is warranted to do otherwise. This applies to dramatic reconstructions and factual dramas, as well as factual programmes.

- In particular, so far as is reasonably practicable, surviving victims and/or the immediate families of those whose experience is to feature in a programme, should be informed of the plans for the programme and its intended broadcast, even if the events or material to be broadcast have been in the public domain in the past.

People under sixteen and vulnerable people

8.20 Broadcasters should pay particular attention to the privacy of people under sixteen. They do not lose their rights to privacy because, for example, of the fame or notoriety of their parents or because of events in their schools.

8.21 Where a programme features an individual under sixteen or a vulnerable person in a way that infringes privacy, consent must be obtained from:

- a parent, guardian or other person of eighteen or over *in loco parentis*; and

- wherever possible, the individual concerned;

- unless the subject matter is trivial or uncontroversial and the participation minor, or it is warranted to proceed without consent.

8.22 Persons under sixteen and vulnerable people should not be questioned about private matters without the consent of a parent, guardian or other person of eighteen or over *in loco parentis* (in the case of persons under sixteen), or a person with primary responsibility for their care (in the case of a vulnerable person), unless it is warranted to proceed without consent.

> Meaning of "vulnerable people":
>
> This varies, but may include those with learning difficulties, those with mental health problems, the bereaved, people with brain damage or forms of dementia, people who have been traumatised or who are sick or terminally ill.

SECTION NINE:

SPONSORSHIP

(Relevant legislation includes, in particular, sections 319(2)(i) and (j) and 319(4)(e) and (f) of the Communications Act 2003, Articles 1, 3(e), 3(f) and 10(1), of the Audiovisual Media Services Directive, and Article 10 of the European Convention on Human Rights.)

This section of the Code does not apply to BBC services funded by the licence fee.

Principle

To ensure that the unsuitable sponsorship of programmes on radio and television is prevented, with particular reference to:

- **transparency—to ensure sponsorship arrangements are transparent;**

- **separation—to ensure that sponsorship messages are separate from programmes and to maintain a distinction between advertising and sponsorship; and**

- **editorial independence—to ensure that the broadcaster maintains editorial control over sponsored content and that programmes are not distorted for commercial purposes.**

In this Principle, programmes include "channels" as defined below.

Rules

Meaning of "sponsored programme", "sponsored channel" and "sponsor":

A sponsored programme, which includes an advertiser-funded programme, is a programme that has had some or all of its costs met by a sponsor with a view to promoting its own or another's name, trademark, image, activities, services, products or any other direct or indirect interest.

A channel is a television or radio service. A sponsored channel is a channel that has had some or all of its costs met by a sponsor with a view to promoting its own or another's name, trademark, image, activities, services, products or any other direct or indirect interest.

Costs include any part of the costs connected to the production or broadcast of the programme or channel.

A sponsor is any public or private undertaking (other than the broadcaster or programme producer), who is sponsoring the programme, programming or channel in question with a view to promoting their or another's name, trademark, image, activities, services, products or any other direct or indirect interest. This meaning extends to those who are otherwise supplying or funding the programme or channel.

Content that may not be sponsored

9.1 The following may not be sponsored:

- news bulletins and news desk presentations on radio; and
- news and current affairs programmes on television.

Meaning of "current affairs programme(s)":

A current affairs programme is one that contains explanation and analysis of current events and issues, including material dealing with political or industrial controversy or with current public policy.

Prohibited and restricted sponsors

9.2 No channel or programme may be sponsored by a sponsor that is not allowed to advertise on the relevant medium.

9.3 Sponsorship on radio and television must comply with both the advertising content and scheduling rules that apply to that medium.

The content of sponsored output

9.4 A sponsor must not influence the content and/or scheduling of a channel or programme in such a way as to impair the responsibility and editorial independence of the broadcaster.

9.5 There must be no promotional reference to the sponsor, its name, trademark, image, activities, services or products or to any of its other direct or indirect interests. There must be no promotional generic references. Non-promotional references are permitted only where they are editorially justified and incidental.

> Meaning of "promotional reference":
>
> This includes, but is not limited to, references that encourage, or are intended to encourage, the purchase or rental of a product or service.

Sponsorship credits

Television and radio

9.6 Sponsorship must be clearly identified as such by reference to the name and/or logo of the sponsor. For programmes, credits must be broadcast at the beginning and/or end of the programme.

9.7 The relationship between the sponsor and the sponsored channel or programme must be transparent.

Radio

9.8 During longer sponsored output, credits must be broadcast as appropriate to create the degree of transparency required.

9.9 Credits must be short branding statements. However, credits may contain legitimate advertising messages.

9.10 Credits must be cleared for broadcast in the same way as advertisements.

9.11 Programme trails are treated as programmes and the same sponsorship rules apply.

Television

9.12 Sponsorship credits must be clearly separated from programmes by temporal or spatial means.

9.13 Sponsorship must be clearly separated from advertising. Sponsor credits must not contain advertising messages or calls to action. In particular, credits must not encourage the purchase or rental of the products or services of the sponsor or a third party.

9.14 Where a programme trail contains a reference to the sponsor of the programme, the sponsor reference must remain brief and secondary.

SECTION TEN:

COMMERCIAL REFERENCES AND OTHER MATTERS

Relevant legislation includes, in particular, sections 319(2)(f) and (i) and 319(4)(e) and (f) of the Communications Act 2003, Articles 1, 3(e), 10(1), and 18 of the Audiovisual Media Services Directive, section 21(1) of the Financial Services and Markets Act 2000, paragraph 3 of the Investment Recommendation (Media) Regulations Act 2005, and Article 10 of the European Convention on Human Rights.)

This section of the Code does not apply to BBC services funded by the licence fee, which are regulated on these matters by the BBC Trust.

The rules in this section are subject to, and supplemented by, Ofcom's Cross-promotion Code.

Principles

To ensure that the independence of editorial control over programme content is maintained and that programmes are not distorted for commercial purposes.

To ensure that the advertising and programme elements of a service are clearly separated.

Rules

10.1 Broadcasters must maintain the independence of editorial control over programme content.

10.2 Broadcasters must ensure that the advertising and programme elements of a service are kept separate.

Products or services in programmes

10.3 Products and services must not be promoted in programmes. This rule does not apply to programme-related material.
(See Rule 10.6.)

10.4 No undue prominence may be given in any programme to a product or service.

> Note:
>
> "Undue prominence" may result from:
>
> - the presence of, or reference to, a product or service (including company names, brand names, logos) in a programme where there is no editorial justification; or
>
> - the manner in which a product or service (including company names, brand names, logos) appears or is referred to in a programme.

10.5 Product placement is prohibited.

> Meaning of "product placement":
>
> Product placement is the inclusion of, or a reference to, a product or service within a programme in return for payment or other valuable consideration to the programme maker or broadcaster (or any representative or associate of either).
>
> - Prop placement: For the purpose of this rule, references to products or services acquired at no, or less than full, cost, where their inclusion within the programme is justified editorially, will not be considered to be product placement. On television, a brief, basic text acknowledgement of the provider of these products or services may be included within the end credits of the programme. This is permitted only where the identity of the product is not otherwise apparent from the programme itself.
>
> - Acquired programmes: With the exception of children's programmes produced after 19 December 2009, Rule 10.5 does not apply to arrangements covering the inclusion of products or services in a programme acquired from outside the UK and films made for cinema provided that no broadcaster regulated by Ofcom and involved in the broadcast of that programme or film directly benefits from the arrangement.
>
> Children's programmes in this context are programmes commissioned for, or specifically directed at, audiences below the age of 16.

Broadcasters should note that all acquired programmes or films must nevertheless comply with all other relevant rules in this Code. In relation to references to products and services in acquired programmes that may have resulted from commercial arrangements, broadcasters should pay particular attention to the requirements of Sections One, Two and Ten of the Code.

Programme-related material

10.6 Programme-related material may be promoted in programmes only where it is editorially justified.

10.7 The broadcaster must retain responsibility for all programme-related material.

10.8 Programme-related material may be sponsored, and the sponsor may be credited when details of how to obtain the material is given. Any credit must be brief and secondary, and must be separate from any credit for the programme sponsor.

Meaning of "programme-related material":

These are products or services that are both directly derived from a specific programme and intended to allow listeners or viewers to benefit fully from, or to interact with, that programme.

Premium rate numbers

10.9 Premium rate numbers will normally be regarded as products or services, and must therefore not appear in programmes, except where:

- they form part of the editorial content of the programme; or

- they fall within the meaning of programme-related material (see above).

10.10 Any use of premium rate numbers must comply with the Code of Practice issued by PhonepayPlus.

Competitions

10.11 References to brands within competitions must be brief and secondary. (See Rule 1.30 in Section One: Protecting the Under-Eighteens and Rules 2.13 to 2.16 in Section Two: Harm and Offence.)

Use of advertisements in programmes

10.12 Advertising must be clearly separated from programmes. Advertisements must not appear in programme time, unless editorially justified.

Charity appeals

10.13 Charity appeals that are broadcast free of charge are allowed in programmes provided that the broadcaster has taken reasonable steps to satisfy itself that:

- the organisation concerned can produce satisfactory evidence of charitable

- status, or, in the case of an emergency appeal, that a responsible public fund has been set up to deal with it; and

- the organisation concerned is not prohibited from advertising on the relevant medium.

10.14 Where possible, the broadcast of charity appeals, either individually or taken together over time, should benefit a wide range of charities.

Appeals for funds for programmes or services

10.15 Broadcasters may broadcast appeals for donations to make programmes or fund their service. The audience must be told of the purpose of the donation and how much has been raised as a result of the appeal. All donations must be separately accounted for and used for the purpose for which they were donated.

Financial promotions and investment recommendations

10.16 When broadcasting financial promotions and investment recommendations broadcasters must comply with the relevant provisions in Appendix 4 to this Code.

Meaning of "financial promotion(s)":

A financial promotion is an invitation or inducement to engage in investment activity (in accordance with section 21(1) of the Financial Services and Markets Act 2000 (Restrictions on financial promotion).)

Meaning of "investment recommendation(s)":

An investment recommendation occurs when someone directly recommends a particular investment decision, for example, buying or selling a particular share or underwriting a particular share offer.

Virtual advertising

Television

10.17 The use of electronic imaging systems during broadcast coverage of an event must comply with the following requirements:

- broadcasters and viewers must be informed in advance of the presence of virtual images;

- virtual advertising may only replace existing on-site advertising—virtual advertising messages must not be more visible or conspicuous than the actual advertising at the venue;

- rules relating to prohibited advertisers also apply to virtual advertising; and the broadcaster may not trade in virtual advertising.

Meaning of "virtual advertising":

Virtual advertising normally (but not exclusively) takes place at events, for example, sporting events, and involves altering the broadcast signal to replace existing venue advertising with other advertising in the television picture (potentially targeted at a particular geographical audience).

Appendix G
THE NUJ CODE OF CONDUCT

The NUJ's Code of Conduct has set out the main principles of British and Irish journalism since 1936. It is part of the rules and all journalists joining the union must sign that they will strive to adhere to it.

Members of the National Union of Journalists are expected to abide by the following professional principles:

A journalist:

1. At all times upholds and defends the principle of media freedom, the right of freedom of expression and the right of the public to be informed

2. Strives to ensure that information disseminated is honestly conveyed, accurate and fair

3. Does her/his utmost to correct harmful inaccuracies

4. Differentiates between fact and opinion

5. Obtains material by honest, straightforward and open means, with the exception of investigations that are both overwhelmingly in the public interest and which involve evidence that cannot be obtained by straightforward means

6. Does nothing to intrude into anybody's private life, grief or distress unless justified by overriding consideration of the public interest

7. Protects the identity of sources who supply information in confidence and material gathered in the course of her/his work

8. Resists threats or any other inducements to influence, distort or suppress information

9. Takes no unfair personal advantage of information gained in the course of her/his duties before the information is public knowledge

10. Produces no material likely to lead to hatred or discrimination on the grounds of a person's age, gender, race, colour, creed, legal status, disability, marital status, or sexual orientation

11. Does not by way of statement, voice or appearance endorse by advertisement any commercial product or service save for the promotion of her/his own work or of the medium by which she/he is employed

12. Avoids plagiarism.

The NUJ believes a journalist has the right to refuse an assignment or be identified as the author of editorial that would break the letter or spirit of the code. The NUJ will fully support any journalist disciplined for asserting her/his right to act according to the code.

Appendix H
USEFUL ADDRESSES AND WEBSITES

ADVERTISING STANDARDS AUTHORITY
Mid City Place
71 High Holborn
London
WC1V 6QT

Tel: 020 7492 2222
Fax: 020 7242 8159
www.asa.org.uk

BAR COUNCIL
289–293 High Holborn
London
WC1V 7HZ

Tel: 020 7242 0082
Fax: 020 7831 9217
www.barcouncil.org.uk

BRITISH FILM COMMISSION
UK Film Council International
10 Little Portland Street
London
W1W 7JG

Tel: 020 7861 7860 224 4000
Fax: 020 7861 7864
www.britfilmcom.co.uk

CHARLES RUSSELL LLP
5 Fleet Place
London
EC4M 7RD

Tel: 020 7203 5000
www.cr-law.co.uk

LAW SOCIETY
113 Chancery Lane
London
WC2A 1PL

Tel: 020 7242 1222
www.lawsociety.org.uk

NATIONAL UNION OF JOURNALISTS
Headland House
308–312 Gray's Inn Road
WC1X 8DP

Tel: 0171 278 7916
www.nuj.org.uk

OFCOM
Riverside House
2a Southwark Bridge Road
London
SE1 9HA

Tel: 020 7981 3000
Fax: 020 7981 333
www.ofcom.org.uk

PRESS COMPLAINTS COMMISSION
Halton House
20/23 Holborn
London
EC1N 2JD

Tel: 020 7831 0022
Fax: 020 7831 0025
www.pcc.org.uk

PDP COMPLIANCE
16 Old Town
London
SW4 0JY

Tel: 0845 226 5723
Fax: 0870 137 7871
www.pdpcompliance.com

PRIVACY & DATA PROTECTION JOURNAL
16 Old Town
London
SW4 0JY

Tel: 0845 226 5723
Fax: 0870 137 7871
www.pdpjournal.com

INDEX

Absolute discharge
sentencing, 26–27
Absolute privilege
And see **Defamation**
generally, 52
judicial proceedings, 54–55
meaning, 277
parliamentary proceedings, 52–53
Abuse of process
data protection, and, 226–227
Accuracy
OFCOM Broadcasting Code, 247–248
Acquittals
meaning, 277
Acts of Parliament
generally, 2
meaning, 277
Adaptations
And see **Copyright**
restricted acts, 90
Advocates
meaning, 277
Affidavits
meaning, 277
Anonymity
data protection, and, 227–229
rape victims, 186
Antisocial behaviour orders
reporting restrictions, 184–185
Appeals
meaning, 277
Arrestable offences
meaning, 277–278
Artistic works
And see **Copyright**

Artistic works—*cont.*
artists' resale rights, 105–106
generally, 79
Assignments
copyright, 83–84
Attorney General
generally, 30
meaning, 278
Authorship
copyright, 82–83
Automated decisions
data protection, 211–212

Bail
meaning, 278
Balance of probabilities
meaning, 278
"Balancing exercise"
And see **Privacy**
false private information, 127
generally, 124
public domain information, 125–127
Barristers
generally, 27–28
BBC
meaning, 278
provision of television services, 238
"Beyond reasonable doubt"
meaning, 278
Bills
meaning, 278
Blasphemy
meaning, 278
Blocking orders
And see **Data protection**

Blocking orders—*cont.*
  generally, 213
Blogs
  And see **Internet**
  data protection, and, 229–230
  generally, 208
British Board of Film Classification
  meaning, 278
  obscenity, and
    cinema exhibition, 146–147
    DVD recordings, 147–149
    internet, 149
    videotape recordings,
      147–149
Broadcasters
  BBC, 238
  Broadcasting Code
    accuracy, 246–247
    background, 243
    crime, 246
    elections, 247
    fairness, 247–248
    generally, 243–244
    harmful material, 244–246
    impartiality, 246–247
    offensive material, 244–246
    privacy, 248–249
    protecting under 18s, 244
    referendums, 247
    religion, 246
    text, 345–375
    undue prominence of views and
      opinions, 246–247
  cable television, 241
  Channel 4, 239
  Channel 5, 239
  digital television, 241–242
  Five, 239
  introduction, 237–238
  ITV, 238–239
  legacy codes, 243
  legacy regulators, 241
  OFCOM
    Broadcasting Code, 244–250
    decisions, 251–277
    generally, 243–244
    introduction, 238–239
  provision of services, 239
  regulation
    introduction, 243
    OFCOM, 243–244
  reporting current affairs, 192–194
  satellite television, 241
Broadcasts
  And see **Copyright**
  generally, 80–81
  meaning, 279
"Bulletin boards"
  And see **Internet**
  generally, 207
Burden of proof
  meaning, 279

Byelaws
  generally, 3

Cable television
  provision of television services, 241
Chancery Division
  civil courts, and, 10
Channel 3 services
  provision of television services,
    238–239
Channel 4
  provision of television services, 239
Channel 5
  provision of television services, 239
Children
  OFCOM Broadcasting Code, 245
  reporting restrictions
    adult courts, 182–183
    generally, 181–182
Civil proceedings
  contract, 18–19
  introduction, 18
  tort, 19
Claimants
  meaning, 279
Class of persons
  defamation, 44–45
Codes of practice
  Editors' Code, 340–344
  PACE, 201–202
Committal proceedings
  reporting current affairs, 185–186
Common law
  meaning, 279
Community punishment orders
  sentencing, 26
Community rehabilitation orders
  sentencing, 26
Compensation
  data protection, 213
Computer programs
  See **Software**
Conditional discharge
  sentencing, 26–27
Confidential information
  And see **Privacy**
  generally, 109–111
Consent
  defamation, 66
Contempt of court
  active proceedings, 167
  circulation of publication, 164
  court hearing the case, 162
  defences
    discussion of public affairs, 170–171
    fair and accurate report of legal
      proceedings, 168
    innocent publication or distribution,
      168–170
    introduction, 168
  delay to trial, 164–164
  discussion of public affairs, 170–171

Contempt of court—*cont.*
  fair and accurate report of legal
    proceedings, 168
  generally, 158–160
  injunctions, 176–177
  innocent publication or distribution, 168–
    170
  intentional contempt, 172–174
  journalists' sources, 198–201
  meaning, 279
  "prejudice", 158
  publishing jury deliberations, 175–176
  reporting current affairs
    generally, 190–192
    journalists' sources, 198–201
  strict liability contempt
    active proceedings, 167
    defences, 168–171
    introduction, 161
    recent criticism, 171–172
    substantial risk of serious prejudice, 161–
      167
  substantial risk of serious prejudice
    circulation of publication, 164
    court hearing the case, 162
    delay to trial, 164–164
    examples, 166–167
    guiding principles, 164–166
    introduction, 161–162
    time delay to trial, 164–164
Contracts
  civil proceedings, 18–19
Copying
  And see **Copyright**
  restricted acts, 88
Copyright
  And see **Intellectual property**
  adapting, 90
  artistic works, 79
  assignments, 83–84
  authorship, 82–83
  broadcasts, 80–81
  communicating to public, 89
  computer programs
    database right, 234–236
    generally, 230–234
    permitted acts, 234
  copying, 88
  copyright works
    artistic works, 79
    broadcasts, 80–81
    dramatic works, 78–79
    films, 80
    introduction, 76–77
    literary works, 78
    musical works, 79
    sound recordings, 80
    typographical arrangements, 81–82
  creation, 77
  criticism or review, 90–93
  dealings
    assignments, 83–84

Copyright—*cont.*
  dealings—*cont.*
    introduction, 83
    transfers, 83–87
  derivative works
    broadcasts, 80–81
    films, 80
    introduction, 79–80
    sound recordings, 80
  dramatic works, 78–79
  duration
    generally, 82–83
    list, 86
  exclusive licences, 84
  fair dealing
    criticism or review, 90–93
    introduction, 90
    reporting current events, 93–95
    "sufficient acknowledgment", 92
  films, 80
  generally, 76
  home video use, 99
  incidental inclusion, 95–96
  infringement
    adapting, 90
    communicating to public, 89
    copying, 88
    introduction, 87–88
    issuing copies to public, 88–89
    lending, 89
    performing, 89
    playing, 89
    rental, 89
    showing, 89
  Internet, and
    database right, 234–236
    generally, 230–234
    permitted acts, 234
  introduction, 76
  issuing copies to public, 88–89
  lending, 89
  licences, 84–87
  literary works, 78
  meaning, 279
  musical works, 79
  ownership, 82–83
  performing, 89
  permitted acts
    fair dealing, 90–95
    incidental inclusion, 95–96
    introduction, 90
    other, 99
    public interest, 96–98
    reproducing speeches and interviews,
      98–99
  playing, 89
  primary infringement, 87–89
  private research or study, 99
  public interest, 96–98
  qualification, 82
  rental, 89
  reporting current events, 93–95

Copyright—*cont.*
reproducing speeches and interviews, 98–99
restricted acts
adapting, 90
communicating to public, 89
copying, 88
introduction, 87–88
issuing copies to public, 88–89
lending, 89
performing, 89
playing, 89
rental, 89
showing, 89
secondary infringement, 87–89
showing, 89
software
database right, 234–236
generally, 230–234
permitted acts, 234
sound recordings, 80
substantial part, 87
temporary copies, 99
time-shifting, 99
transfers
assignments, 83–84
licences, 84–87
transient copies, 99
typographical arrangements, 81–82
works, 77–82
County court
civil courts, and, 9–10
Court of Appeal
civil division, 11
criminal division, 15–16
Court proceedings
see **Proceedings**
Courts
civil courts
Chancery Division, 10
county court, 9–10
Court of Appeal, 11
Divisional Court, 10
Family Division, 10
High Court, 10–11
Queen's Bench Division, 10
structure, 8
Supreme Court, 12
criminal courts
Court of Appeal, 15–16
Crown Court, 15
introduction, 12
magistrates' court, 13–14
structure, 13
Supreme Court, 16
European courts
European Court of Human Rights, 17
European Court of Justice, 16–17
introduction, 16
generally, 7
Crime
OFCOM Broadcasting Code, 247

Criminal proceedings
absolute discharge, 26–27
community punishment orders, 26
community rehabilitation orders, 26
conditional discharge, 26
death penalty, 24–25
driving ban, 26
fine, 26
imprisonment, 25–26
indictable offences, 24
introduction, 20–22
mode of trial, 22–24
penalty points, 26
sentencing, 24–26
trials, 24
"Criticism or review"
copyright, 90–93
Crown Court
criminal courts, and, 15
Crown Prosecution Service
generally, 29

DA notices
generally, 196–197
Damages
defamation, 67–69
meaning, 279–280
privacy, 130
Data protection
abuse of process, 226–227
access rights, 210–211
automated decisions, 211–212
blocking, 212
blogs, 229–230
combating anonymity, 227–229
compensation, 213
'data'
generally, 209
meaning, 280
'data controller', 209
'data subject', 209
data subject's rights
access rights, 210–211
automated decisions, 211–212
blocking, 212
compensation, 213
definitions, 209–210
destruction, 212
direct marketing, 212
erasure, 212
introduction, 209
preventing processing, 212–213
rectification, 212
definitions, 209–210
destruction, 212
direct marketing, 212–213
erasure, 212
exception, 218–220
fair and lawful processing
criteria, 216
generally, 214–215
sensitive personal data, 216–217

Data protection—*cont.*
  generally, 208
  individual's rights
    access rights, 210–211
    automated decisions, 211–212
    blocking, 212
    compensation, 213
    definitions, 209–210
    destruction, 212
    direct marketing, 212
    erasure, 212
    introduction, 209
    preventing processing, 212–213
    rectification, 212
  introduction, 208–209
  journalism, literature and art, 218–220
  'personal data', 209
  preventing processing
    direct marketing, 212–213
    general, 212
  principles
    fair and lawful processing, 214–217
    introduction, 213–214
    technical and organisational measures,
      218
    transfer of personal data, 218
  'processing', 209–210
  rectification, 212
  'relevant filing system', 210
  sensitive personal data, 216–217
  technical and organisational measures, 218
  transfer of personal data, 218
Data subjects' rights
  access rights, 210–211
  automated decisions, 211–212
  blocking, 212
  compensation, 213
  definitions, 209–210
  destruction, 212
  direct marketing, 212–213
  erasure, 212
  introduction, 209
  preventing processing
    direct marketing, 212–213
    general, 212
  rectification, 212
Database right
  generally, 234–236
Death penalty
  sentencing, 24–25
Defamation
  absolute privilege
    generally, 52
    judicial proceedings, 54–55
    parliamentary proceedings, 52–53
  class of persons, 44–45
  classification, 35–36
  comparison with malicious falsehood, 73–
    74
  consent, 66
  damages, 67–69
  Defamation Act 1952, 287–290

Defamation—*cont.*
  Defamation Act 1996, 291–308
  defamatory words, 39–42
  defences
    absolute privilege, 52–55
    consent, 66
    fair comment, 49–52
    generally, 46
    innocent dissemination, 62–63
    justification, 47–49
    offer of amends, 63–66
    qualified privilege, 55–62
  definition, 33–34
  duty or interest, 57–62
  entities, 45
  fair comment
    generally, 49–50
    malice, 52
    opinion based on fact, 50–51
    public interest, 51–52
  forum shopping, 45–46
  generally, 31–33
  injunctions, 69–70
  innocent dissemination, 62–63
  innuendo, 42–43
  Internet, and
    international publication, 224–226
    internet service providers, 220–223
    introduction, 220
    online archives, 223–224
  judicial proceedings (absolute privilege)
    generally, 54
    reports, 54–55
  judicial proceedings (qualified privilege)
    common law privilege, 57–57
    generally, 55
    reports, 55
    statutory privilege, 56–57
  justification
    evidence, 48
    generally, 47–48
    post-publication evidence, 49
    malice, and, 49
  libel, 35–36
  malice
    fair comment, 51–52
    justification, 49
    qualified privilege, 62
  meaning, 280
  offer of amends, 63–66
  parliamentary proceedings
    generally, 52–53
    reports, 53
  publication, 36–39
  qualified privilege
    duty or interest, 57–62
    generally, 55
    malice, 62
    reports of judicial proceedings, 55–57
  reference to claimant, 43–44
  remedies
    damages, 67–69

Defamation—*cont.*
  remedies—*cont.*
    generally, 67
    injunctions, 69–70
    slander, 35–36
    statement in open court, 70
    trial by judge and jury, 34–35
Defence advisory notices
  See **DA notices**
Defences
  contempt of court
    discussion of public affairs,
      170–171
    fair and accurate report of legal
      proceedings, 168
    innocent publication or distribution,
      168–170
    introduction, 168
  defamation
    absolute privilege, 52–55
    consent, 66
    fair comment, 49–52
    generally, 46
    innocent dissemination, 62–63
    justification, 47–49
    offer of amends, 63–66
    qualified privilege, 55–62
  inciting racial hatred
    broadcast material, 156–157
    introduction, 156
    non-broadcast material, 156
Defendants
  meaning, 280
Delegated legislation
  See **Subordinate legislation**
Derivative works
  And see **Copyright**
  broadcasts, 80–81
  films, 80
  introduction, 79–80
  sound recordings, 80
Derogatory treatment
  see **Integrity right**
Destruction orders
  And see **Data protection**
  generally, 213
Digital television
  provision of television services, 241
Direct marketing
  data protection, 212–213
Directives
  generally, 6
Director of Public Prosecutions
  generally, 29
  meaning, 280
Disclosure
  privacy, 128–130
Discussion forums
  And see **Internet**
  generally, 207
Disqualification from driving
  sentencing, 26

Distribution right
  And see **Performers' rights**
  generally, 103
  meaning, 280–281
Divisional Court
  civil courts, and, 10
Domain names
  And see **Internet**
  generally, 205–206
Dramatic works
  And see **Copyright**
  generally, 78–79
Duty and interest
  defamation, 57–62

EC law
  Directives, 6
  generally, 4–6
  Regulations, 6
  Treaty provisions, 6
Elections
  OFCOM Broadcasting Code, 248
Electronic Commerce (EC Directive)
    Regulations 2002
  text, 332–341
Electronic mail
  And see **Internet**
  generally, 207
Email
  See **Electronic mail**
Endorsements
  sentencing, 26
Entities
  defamation, 45
Erasure orders
  And see **Data protection**
  generally, 213
EU legislative process
  generally, 6
European Commission on Human Rights
  meaning, 281
European Convention on Human
    Rights
  generally, 6–7
  meaning, 281
European Council
  generally, 5
European Court of Human Rights
  civil courts, and, 17
  generally, 4
  meaning, 281
European Court of Justice
  civil courts, and, 16–17
  generally, 6
European Parliament
  generally, 5–6
European law
  See **EC law**
European Union
  meaning, 281
European Commission on Human Rights
  meaning, 281

Ex parte injunctions
See **Without notice injunctions**
Exclusive licences
copyright, 84

Fair and accurate reports
contempt of court, 168
generally, 158–160
Fair and lawful processing
And see **Data protection**
criteria, 216
generally, 214–215
sensitive personal data, 216–217
Fair comment
And see **Defamation**
generally, 49–50
malice, 52
meaning, 281
opinion based on fact, 50–51
public interest, 51–52
Fair dealing
And see **Copyright**
criticism or review, 90–93
introduction, 90
reporting current events, 93–95
"sufficient acknowledgment", 92
Fairness
OFCOM Broadcasting Code, 248–249
False attribution right
moral rights, 102
Family Division
civil courts, and, 10
Films
And see **Copyright**
generally, 80
Fines
sentencing, 26
Five
See **Channel 5**
Forfeiture
inciting racial hatred, 155
Forum shopping
defamation, 45–46
Forums
See **Discussion forums**
Freedom of expression
generally, 30–31
privacy, 108–109

Harassment
generally, 131–132
journalists, from, 133
Harmful of offensive material
OFCOM Broadcasting Code, 245–247
High Court
civil courts, and, 10–11
House of Lords
See **Supreme Court**
Human rights
privacy, 108–109
reporting current affairs, 179
text of Act, 307–329

ICANN
And see **Internet**
generally, 205
Identified, right to be
See **Paternity right**
Impartiality
OFCOM Broadcasting Code, 247–248
Imprisonment
sentencing, 25–26
Incidental inclusion
copyright, 95–96
Inciting racial hatred
background, 153
defences
broadcast material, 156–157
introduction, 156
non-broadcast material, 156
forfeiture of material, 155
introduction, 153
meaning, 283
offences
broadcast material, 155–156
introduction, 154
non-broadcast material, 154–155
"racial hatred", 153–154
sentencing
broadcast material, 155–156
non-broadcast material, 154–155
Inciting religious hatred
background, 153
defences
broadcast material, 156–157
introduction, 156
non-broadcast material, 156
forfeiture of material, 155
introduction, 153
offences
broadcast material, 155–156
introduction, 154
non-broadcast material, 154–155
"religious hatred", 154
sentencing
broadcast material, 155–156
non-broadcast material, 154–155
Indecency
British Board of Film Classification
cinema exhibition, 146–147
DVD recordings, 147–149
internet, 149
videotape recordings, 147–149
broadcasts, and, 140
children, 150–151
cinema exhibition, 146–147
defences
aversion, 142
depraved activities, 142
innocent publication or possession, 141–142
introduction, 140
public good, 140–141
definition, 136–139
digital multi-channel television, 145–146

Indecency—*cont.*
  DVD recordings, 147–149
  generally, 135–136
  "harm and offence" test, 145
  internet, 149
  introduction, 135
  OFCOM, and
    child protection, 145
    cinema exhibition, 146–147
    digital multi-channel television, 145–146
    DVD recordings, 147–149
    generally, 144
    internet, 149
    videotape recordings, 147–149
  offences
    common law, 142–143
    statutory, 140
  "significant proportion", 138
  statutory obscenity, 136–139
  "taste or decency" test, 145
  terrestrial television, 144
  videotape recordings, 147–149
Indictable offences
  sentencing, 24
Indictments
  meaning, 281
Infringement
  And see **Copyright**
  adapting, 90
  communicating to public, 89
  copying, 88
  introduction, 87
  issuing copies to public, 88–89
  lending, 89
  performing, 89
  playing, 89
  rental, 89
  showing, 89
Injunctions
  contempt of court, 176–177
  defamation, 69–70
  meaning, 281–282
  privacy
    generally, 130–131
    interim, 96–111
    super, 131
Innocent dissemination
  defamation, 62–63
Innocent publication
  contempt of court, 168–170
Innuendos
  defamation, 42–43
  meaning, 282
Instant messaging
  generally, 207
Integrity right
  moral rights, 100–101
  performers' rights, 104
Intellectual property
  artists' resale rights, 105–106
  copyright
    And see **Copyright**

Intellectual property—*cont.*
  copyright—*cont.*
    authorship, 82–83
    creation, 77
    dealings, 83–87
    duration, 82–83
    infringement, 87–89
    introduction, 76–77
    ownership, 82–83
    permitted acts, 90–99
    transfers, 83–87
    works, 77–82
  database right, 234–236
  introduction, 76
  moral rights
    false attribution right, 102
    integrity right, 100–101
    introduction, 99
    paternity right, 100
    privacy right, 103
  performers' rights, 102–106
  rental rights
    generally, 106
    introduction, 103
  resale rights, 105–106
  software
    database right, 234–236
    generally, 230–234
    permitted acts, 234
Intention
  contempt of court, 172–174
"Inter alia"
  meaning, 282
Interim injunctions
  And see **Injunctions**
  meaning, 281
  privacy, 110–111
Internet
  ARPANET, and, 204
  blogs, 208
  copyright
    database right, 234–236
    generally, 230–234
    permitted acts, 234
  data protection
    And see **Data protection**
    data subject's rights, 209–213
    generally, 208
    introduction, 208–209
    principles,
      213–220
  database right, 234–236
  defamation
    And see **Defamation**
    abuse of process, 226–227
    blogs, 229–230
    combating anonymity, 227–229
    international publication, 224–226
    internet service providers, 220–223
    introduction, 220
    online archives, 223–224
  domain names, 205–206

Internet—*cont.*
  email, 206
  forums, 207
  generally, 204–206
  ICANN, 205
  instant messaging, 207
  internet service providers
    defamation, and, 220–223
    generally, 206
  internet voice calls, 207
  introduction, 204
  IP address, 205
  message boards, 207
  online archives, 223–224
  origins, 204–205
  passing off, 206
  pornography, 230–232
  search engines, 207
  Skype, 207
  social networking sites, 208
  structure, 204–208
  world wide web, 206–207
Internet service providers
  And see **Internet**
  defamation, and, 220–223
  generally, 206
Internet telephony
  generally, 207
IP addresses
  And see **Internet**
  generally, 205
ITV
  See **Channel 3 services**

"Jigsaw identification"
  reporting restrictions, 183–184
Journalism
  data protection, 218–220
Journalists' sources
  see **Sources of information**
Judges
  generally, 3–4
Judicial proceedings
  And see **Defamation**
  absolute privilege
    generally, 54
    reports, 54–55
  qualified privilege
    common law privilege, 57–57
    generally, 55
    reports, 55
    statutory privilege, 56–57
Judicial rev iew
  meaning, 282
Jury deliberations
  contempt of court, 175–176
Justification
  And see **Defamation**
  evidence, 48
  generally, 47–48
  meaning, 282
  post-publication evidence, 49

Lawyers
  Attorney General, 29
  barristers, 27–28
  Crown Prosecution Service, 29
  Director of Public Prosecutions, 29
  introduction, 27
  legal executives, 28
  Lord Chancellor, 28–29
  solicitors, 28
"Legacy codes"
  television services, 243
"Legacy regulators"
  television services, 241
Legal action
  see **Proceedings**
Legal aid
  meaning, 282
Legal executives
  generally, 28
Legal sources
  Acts of Parliament, 2
  byelaws, 3
  delegated legislation
    byelaws, 3
    introduction, 2
    Orders in Council, 2
    statutory instruments, 2–3
  Directives, 6
  EC law, 4–6
  European Convention on Human Rights,
    6–7
  European legislation
    Directives, 6
    generally, 4–6
    Regulations, 6
    Treaty provisions, 6
  European Union, 4–6
  introduction, 1
  judges, 3–4
  Orders in Council, 2
  Parliament
    Acts of Parliament, 2
    introduction, 1
    delegated legislation, 2–3
    judges, 3–4
    sovereignty, 3
  Parliamentary sovereignty, 3
  Regulations, 6
  statutory instruments, 2–3
  subordinated legislation
    byelaws, 3
    introduction, 2
    Orders in Council, 2
    statutory instruments, 2–3
  Treaty provisions, 6
"Lending"
  copyright, 89
Lending right
  And see **Intellectual property**
  infringement of copyright, 89
  introduction, 76
  meaning, 282

Lending right—*cont.*
performers' rights
generally, 106
introduction, 103
Libel
And see **Defamation**
generally, 35–36
meaning, 282
Licences
copyright, 84–87
Literary works
And see **Copyright**
generally, 78
Lord Chancellor
generally, 29

Magistrates' court
criminal courts, and, 13–14
Malice
defamation
fair comment, 52
justification, 49
qualified privilege, 62
malicious falsehood, 72–73
meaning, 282
Malicious falsehood
comparison with defamation, 73–74
definition, 71
introduction, 71
malice, 72–73
special damage, 73
untrue statement, 71–72
"Message boards"
And see **Internet**
generally, 207
Mitigation
meaning, 282
Mode of trial
sentencing, 22–24
Moral rights
false attribution right, 102
generally, 99
integrity right, 100–101
introduction, 76
meaning, 282
paternity right, 100
performers' rights, and, 104
privacy right, 102–103
Musical works
And see **Copyright**
generally, 79

News reporting
anonymity of rape victims, 186
contempt of court
generally, 190–192
journalists' sources, 198–201
copyright, and, 93–95
court proceedings
access to the courts, 179
committal proceedings, 185–186
contempt of court, 190–192

News reporting—*cont.*
court proceedings—*cont.*
early hearings, 188–189
generally, 179
human rights, and, 179
rape, 186–187
reporting restrictions, 180–185
serious fraud, 187–188
sexual offences, 186
television, and, 192–194
witnesses, 189–190
introduction, 178
journalists' sources
contempt of court, 198–201
introduction, 197–198
official secrets, and, 202
PACE, and, 201–202
terrorism, and, 202
official secrets
1911 Act, under, 194–195
1989 Act, under, 195–196
defence advisory notices, 196–197
introduction, 194
journalists' sources, and, 202
PACE, and, 201–202
Parliamentary proceedings, 194
reporting restrictions
anti-social behaviour orders, 184–185
children, 181–182
children in adult courts, 182–183
generally, 180–181
"jigsaw" identification, 183–184
young persons, 181–182
youth courts, 184
sources of information
contempt of court, 198–201
introduction, 197–198
official secrets, and, 202
PACE, and, 201–202
terrorism, and, 202
terrorism, and, 202

Obiter dicta
generally, 4
Obscenity
British Board of Film Classification
cinema exhibition, 146–147
DVD recordings, 147–149
internet, 149
videotape recordings, 147–149
broadcasts, and, 140
children, 150–151
cinema exhibition, 146–147
defences
aversion, 142
depraved activities, 142
innocent publication or possession, 141–142
introduction, 140
public good, 140–141
definition, 136–139
digital multi-channel television, 145–146

Obscenity—*cont.*
DVD recordings, 147–149
generally, 135–136
"harm and offence" test, 145
internet, 149
introduction, 135
meaning, 282
OFCOM, and
child protection, 145
cinema exhibition, 146–147
digital multi-channel television, 145–146
DVD recordings, 147–149
generally, 144
internet, 149
videotape recordings, 147–149
offences
common law, 142–143
statutory, 140
"significant proportion", 138
statutory obscenity, 136–139
"taste or decency" test, 145
terrestrial television, 144
videotape recordings, 147–149
OFCOM
Broadcasting Code
accuracy, 247–248
background, 244
crime, 247
elections, 248
fairness, 248–249
generally, 244–245
harmful material, 245–247
impartiality, 247–248
offensive material, 245–247
privacy, 249–250
protecting under 18s, 245
referendums, 248
religion, 247
text, 347–375
undue prominence of views and
opinions, 247–248
decisions, 251–277
generally, 243–244
indecency and obscenity, and
child protection, 145
cinema exhibition, 146–147
digital multi-channel television, 145–146
DVD recordings, 147–149
generally, 144
internet, 149
videotape recordings, 147–149
introduction, 238–239
meaning, 283
Offences
inciting racial hatred
broadcast material, 155–156
introduction, 154
non-broadcast material, 154–155
"Offensive language"
OFCOM Broadcasting Code, 245–247
Offer of amends
defamation, 63–66

Official secrets
1911 Act, under, 194–195
1989 Act, under, 195–196
defence advisory notices, 196–197
introduction, 194
journalists' sources, and, 202
meaning, 282
"Online archives"
defamation, 223–224
Orders in Council
generally, 3
Ownership
copyright, 82–83

PACE codes of practice
reporting current affairs, 201–202
Parliament
Acts of Parliament, 2
introduction, 1
delegated legislation, 2–3
judges, 3–4
meaning, 283
sovereignty, 3
Parliamentary proceedings
And see **Defamation**
generally, 52–53
reporting current affairs, 194
reports, 53
Parliamentary sovereignty
generally, 3
Passing off
Internet, and, 206
Paternity right
moral rights, 100
performers' rights, 104
Penalty points
see **Endorsements**
Performers' rights
generally, 102–106
introduction, 76
meaning, 283
Permitted acts
And see **Copyright**
fair dealing
criticism or review, 90–93
introduction, 90
reporting current events, 93–95
"sufficient acknowledgment", 92
incidental inclusion, 95–96
introduction, 90
other, 99
public interest, 96–98
reproducing speeches and interviews, 98–99
Photographs
privacy, 116–120
Plays
meaning, 283
Pornography
And see **Obscenity**
generally, 230–230
Precedent
generally, 4

Prejudice
contempt of court, 158
Press Complaints Commission
generally, 74–75
meaning, 283
Primary infringement
And see **Copyright**
generally, 87–89
Privacy
balancing exercise
false private information, 127
generally, 124
public domain information, 125–127
Campbell confidence, 111–114
confidential information, 109–111
damages, 130
disclosure in public interest, 128–130
'doorstepping', 133
false private information, 127
freedom of expression, 108–109
harassment
generally, 131–132
journalists, from, 133
human rights, 108–109
injunctions
generally, 130–131
interim, 96–111
super, 131
interim injunctions, 110–111
introduction, 107–108
misuse of private information
balancing exercise, 124–127
false private information, 127
generally, 111–114
photographs, 116–120
pre-existing relationship, 120–124
'private information', 114–124
public domain information, 125–127
triviality, 115–116
two-step test, 114–127
OFCOM Broadcasting Code, 249–250
photographs, 116–120
pre-existing relationship, 120–124
'private information'
generally, 114–115
photographs, 116–120
pre-existing relationship, 120–124
triviality, 115–116
proportionality test
false private information, 127
generally, 124
public domain information, 125–127
public domain information, 125–127
public interest, 128–130
remedies
damages, 130
injunctions, 130–131
super-injunctions, 131
right to respect for private and family life,
108–109
secret recipes, 114
stalkers, 131–132

Privacy—*cont.*
super-injunctions, 131
trade secrets, 109
trivial information, 115–116
unauthorised use, 127–128
Privacy right in commissioned photographs
moral rights, 102
Proceedings
access to the courts, 179
civil proceedings
contract, 18–19
introduction, 18
tort, 19
committal proceedings, 185–186
contempt of court, 190–192
criminal proceedings
absolute discharge, 26–27
community punishment order, 26
community rehabilitation order, 26
conditional discharge, 26
death penalty, 24–25
driving ban, 26
fine, 26
imprisonment, 25–26
indictable offences, 24
introduction, 20–22
mode of trial, 22–24
penalty points, 26
sentencing, 24–26
trials, 24
early hearings, 188–189
generally, 179
human rights, and, 179
introduction, 17–18
rape, 186–187
reporting restrictions
anti-social behaviour orders,
184–185
children, 181–182
children in adult courts, 182–183
generally, 180–181
"jigsaw" identification, 183–184
young persons, 181–182
youth courts, 184
serious fraud, 187–188
sexual offences, 186
television, and, 192–194
witnesses, 189–190
"Programme service"
meaning, 283
Proportionality
privacy
false private information, 127
generally, 124
public domain information, 125–127
Prosecution
meaning, 283
Public domain
privacy, 125–127
Public interest
copyright, 96–98
privacy, 128–130

Publication
defamation, 36–39

Qualified privilege
And see **Defamation**
duty or interest, 57–62
generally, 55
malice, 62
meaning, 283
reports of judicial proceedings, 55–57
Queen's Bench Division
civil courts, and, 10

Racial hatred
See **Inciting racial hatred**
Rape
reporting current affairs, 186–187
Ratio decidendi
generally, 5
Rectification orders
And see **Data protection**
generally, 212
Referendums
OFCOM Broadcasting Code, 248
Regulations
generally, 4
Religions
OFCOM Broadcasting Code, 247
Religious hatred
See **Inciting religious hatred**
Remedies
defamation
damages, 67–69
generally, 67
injunctions, 69–70
privacy
damages, 130
injunctions, 130–131
super-injunctions, 131
"Rental"
copyright, 89
Rental rights
And see **Intellectual property**
infringement of copyright, 89
introduction, 76
meaning, 283–284
performers' rights
generally, 106
introduction, 103
Reporting current affairs
See **News reporting**
Reporting restrictions
anti-social behaviour orders, 184–185
children, 181–182
children in adult courts, 182–183
generally, 180–181
"jigsaw" identification, 183–184
young persons, 181–182
youth courts, 184
"Reproducing speeches and interviews"
copyright, 98–99

Reproduction right
And see **Performers' rights**
generally, 103
meaning, 283
Reputation
defamation
absolute privilege, 52–55
class of persons, 44–45
classification, 35–36
comparison with malicious falsehood, 73–74
consent, 66
damages, 67–69
defamatory words, 39–42
defences, 46–67
definition, 33–34
entities, 45
fair comment, 49–52
forum shopping, 45–46
generally, 31–33
injunctions, 69–70
innocent dissemination, 62–63
innuendo, 42–43
justification, 47–49
libel, 35–36
malice, 62
offer of amends, 63–66
publication, 36–39
qualified privilege, 55–62
reference to claimant, 43–44
remedies, 67–70
slander, 35–36
statement in open court, 70
trial by judge and jury, 34–35
flowchart, 75
generally, 30–31
malicious falsehood
comparison with defamation, 73–74
definition, 71–72
introduction, 71
malice, 72–73
special damage, 73
untrue statement, 71–72
Press Complaints Commission, 74–75
Resale rights
generally, 105–106
"Research"
copyright, 99
Restricted copyright acts
And see **Copyright**
adapting, 89
communicating to public, 89
copying, 88
introduction, 87
issuing copies to public, 88–89
lending, 89
performing, 89
playing, 89
rental, 89
showing, 89
Right to respect for private and family life
privacy, 108–109

Satellite television
generally, 240
meaning, 284
Search engines
And see **Internet**
generally, 207
Secondary infringement
And see **Copyright**
generally, 87–89
Sentencing
criminal proceedings, 24–26
inciting racial hatred
broadcast material, 155–156
non-broadcast material, 154–155
Serious arrestable offences
meaning, 283
Serious fraud cases
reporting current affairs, 187–188
Sexual offences
reporting current affairs, 186
"Skype"
And see **Internet**
generally, 207
Slander
And see **Defamation**
generally, 35–36
meaning, 284
Social networking
And see **Internet**
generally, 208
Software
copyright
database right, 234–236
generally, 230–234
permitted acts, 234
Solicitors
generally, 3
Sound recordings
And see **Copyright**
generally, 80
Sources of information
contempt of court, 198–201
introduction, 197–198
official secrets, and, 202
PACE, and, 201–202
terrorism, and, 202
Sources of law
see **Legal sources**
Sovereignty
Parliament, and, 3
Special damage
malicious falsehood, 73
"Stalkers"
privacy, 131–132
Standard of proof
meaning, 284
Stare decisis
see **Precedent**
Statements in open court
defamation, 70
Statutory instruments
generally, 3

Strict liability
contempt of court
And see **Contempt of court**
active proceedings, 167
defences, 168–171
introduction, 161
recent criticism, 171–172
substantial risk of serious prejudice, 161–167
Subordinate legislation
byelaws, 3
'delegated legislation', 280
introduction, 2–3
Orders in Council, 3
statutory instruments, 3
Substantial part
copyright, 87
"Substantial risk of serious prejudice"
And see **Contempt of court**
circulation of publication, 164
court hearing the case, 162
delay to trial, 164–164
examples, 166–167
guiding principles, 164–166
introduction, 161–162
time delay to trial, 164–164
"Super injunctions"
privacy, 130–131
Supreme Court
civil division, 12
criminal division, 16

Technical and organisational measures
And see **Data protection**
generally, 218
Television
BBC, 238
Broadcasting Code
accuracy, 246–247
background, 243
crime, 246
elections, 247
fairness, 247–248
generally, 243–244
harmful material, 244–246
impartiality, 246–247
offensive material, 244–246
privacy, 248–249
protecting under 18s, 244
referendums, 247
religion, 246
text, 345–375
undue prominence of views and
opinions, 246–247
cable television, 241
Channel 4, 239
Channel 5, 239
digital television, 241
Five, 239
introduction, 237–238
ITV, 238–239
legacy codes, 243
legacy regulators, 241

Television—*cont.*
OFCOM
Broadcasting Code, 244–250
decisions, 251–277
generally, 243–244
introduction, 238–239
provision of services, 239
regulation
introduction, 243
OFCOM, 243–244
reporting current affairs, 192–194
satellite television, 241
Terrorism
reporting current affairs, 202
"Time-shifting"
copyright, 99
Tort
civil proceedings, 19
Trade secrets
privacy, 109
Transfer of personal data
And see **Data protection**
generally, 218
Transient copying
copyright, 99
Trials
criminal proceedings, 24
defamation, 34–35
"Trivial information"
privacy, 115–116

Typographical arrangements
And see **Copyright**
generally, 81–82

Undertakings
meaning, 284
Undue prominence
OFCOM Broadcasting Code, 247–248

"Video on demand"
meaning, 284

Websites
And see **Internet**
generally, 206–207
Without notice injunctions
meaning, 281
Witnesses
reporting current affairs, 189–190
World wide web
See **Websites**

Young offenders
meaning, 284
Young persons
reporting restrictions, 181–182
Youth courts
meaning, 284
reporting restrictions, 184